LANCASTER COUNTY, VIRGINIA

ABSTRACTS OF ORDER BOOK 8
(Part 1)
1728-May 1737

Richard S. Hutchinson

Colonial Roots
Millsboro, Delaware
2014

COLONIAL ROOTS
34491 Sunset Drive
Millsboro, Delaware 19966
1-800-576-8608

Visit our website at www.colonialroots.com to determine if we have researched your family during the colonial period. Search our surname index which includes our "Colonial Families" books and other family histories of Delaware, Maryland, New Jersey, Pennsylvania, and Virginia.

VISIT US AT OUR WEBSITE:
www.colonialroots.com

CONTENTS

Introduction

In this volume the author has abstracted the essentials of the information contained in the first half of Order Book 8 which covers the period 1729 through May 1737. The balance of Order Book 8 will be covered in Volume 2 of this title. A wide range of transactions are covered. Especially helpful to genealogists are the relationships revealed in these records. Often the names of wives, children and other relationships are shown.

Most of the book covers land transactions, bills of sale, and probate matters. Also recorded are bonds, agreements of indentured servants, and accounts of estates.

This book contains the names, sex, ages, relationships (if any) of hundreds of Negro slaves and the Indentured servants; including the names of the persons, who bought, sold, gifted, and bartered these unfortunate persons.

The original records can be found on microfilm at the Library of Virginia (Land Records, microfilm roll 4).

Other books of genealogical value pertaining to Lancaster County during the Colonial period:

Duvall, Lindsay O. *Lancaster County, Virginia, Court Orders and Deeds, 1656-1680. Virginia Colonial Abstracts, Series 2, Vol. 2.*

Hutchinson, Richard S. *Lancaster Virginia Deeds 1714-1728.*

Hutchinson, Richard S. *Lancaster County, Virginia Abstracts of Wills, Administrations, Deeds, Inventories, etc. 1726-1735.*

Lee, Ida J. *Abstracts of Lancaster County, Virginia, Wills. 1653-1800.*

Lee, Ida J. *Lancaster County, Virginia, Marriage Bonds 1652-1850.*

Lancaster County, Virginia, Will Book 28, Abstracts and Index of Wills Recorded 1796-1839.

Nottingham, Stratton. *The Marriage License bonds of Lancaster County, Virginia, From 1701 to 1848.*

Nottingham, Stratton, *Revolutionary Soldiers and Sailors from Lancaster County, Virginia: Muster Rolls and Pay Rolls of the Ninety-Second Regiment of Virginia Militia, Lancaster County, 1812.*

Waske, Tawny, *Lancaster County, Virginia Land Records 1770-1782*.

Waske, Tawny and Hutchinson, Richard S., *Lancaster County, Virginia Abstracts of Wills, Administrations, Deed, Inventories, etc. 1736-1742*.

Debbie Hooper
Millsboro, Delaware
2014

ABBREVIATIONS

a. – acre, acres
absd. – abovesaid
abt. – about
ackn. - acknowledge
adj. - adjoining
Admin. – administration,
  administrator, administratrix
afsd. – aforesaid
apprd. - appeared
atty. – attorney, attorneys
bef. – before
beg.- begins, beginning
betw. – between
bnd. – bound, bounds
bot. – bought
Clk. - clerk
Co. – county
Complt. - Complaintant
crk. – creek
d. – died, dead
dau. – daughter
daus.- daughters
dec'd. – deceased
Deft./deft. - Defendant

e. – east
Esqr. - Esquire
Exec./exec. – executor, executors
Execx. - executrix
excep. – except, excepting
[FNU] – First Name Unknown
form. – formerly
Gent. – gentleman
[LNU] - Last Name Unknown
n. – north
Pltf./pltf - Plaintiff
pt. - part
pt/o. – part of
Rec./recr'd. – record, recorded
ref - reference
Respndt. - Respondent
s. – south
sd. – said
tr. – tract, tracts
Twp. – township
w. – west
wch.- which
wits.- witness, witnesses
w/o. - without

Glossary

Acre: A common measure of area, 43,560 square feet. There are 640 acres in a square mile.

Administration/administrator/administratrix: Administratrix is the feminine of administrator. When a person dies intestate (without a will), the estate is administered by an appointed administrator. An intestancy is often called an administration. The administrator usually is the person who sells the deceased's land.

Ad Quod Domnum: The name of a writ formerly issuing from the English chancery, commanding the sheriff to make inquiry "to what damage" a specific act, if don, will tend.

Agreement: Type of instrument (document) often related to land and recorded in deed books.

Appurtenance: An intangible right associated with land, such as an easement or right-of-way.

Assigns: Anyone to whom the grantee might assign the property in the future.

Bond: An agreement to pay a penalty if a certain obligation is not filled.

Certificate: Similar to a warrant.

Chain: The Gunter chain was used to measure distances by a surveyor in early America. It was made of one hundred straight pieces of metal (about seven inches long), connected by three small loops. The length between the center loops, a link, was 7.92 inches. The chain was sixty-six feet long. One hundred links equals four rods, each of which is sixteen and a half feet long.

Consideration: The amount of money or other item of value that is exchanged for land. Consideration includes love and affection.

Convey: To transfer title or ownership from one person to another.

Corner: The geographical anchor between two lines in a metes-and-bounds survey. Usually, but not always, this is the point at which there is a change of direction in lines. The corner may mention adjoining (abutting) landowners, whose property may run along one or both lines or may simply touch at this corner.

Dedimus: (potestatem) Latin for "we have the power" whereby commission is given to one or more private persons for the expedition of some act normally performed by a judge. It is granted most commonly upon the suggestion that a party, who is to do something before a judge or in a court, is too weak to travel.

Deed of Gift: A deed in which the monetary or practical consideration is less than the value of the land and in which "love and affection" may be mentioned.

Deed of Trust: A deed in which the grantee does not have full legal ownership. In some times and places, it was used instead of a mortgage.

Do.: The abbreviation for "ditto."

Dock the entail/intail: Land is entailed if someone wills it to the oldest son to the oldest son etc. To dock this means to break the link of descendancy.

Dower or **Dower of Rights:** The lifetime interest that the law allowed a widow to retain in the real property of her deceased husband in order to maintain herself and her children.

Dower Release: The specific statement, usually recorded directly following a deed, that the wife has been examined "privily" (alone, without the husband in the room) and has agreed to the sale of the land, including her dower rights.

Enfeoffed: To invest with a feudal estate or fee. Deed by which a person was given land in exchange for a pledge of service.

Entail: The restrictions placed on the transfer of real property.

Esquire: A term denoting social status.

Fee Simple: The type of title or ownership in which the owner can do whatever he wants with the land and can dispose of it in any way he likes.

Feoffment: The grant of an estate held in fee.

Gentleman: A member of the gentry, a descendant from an aristocratic family whose income came from the rental of his land. Later in the colonial period this address was used generally out of respect.

Halfpenny: British coin worth one half penny.

Head: The place at which a body of water originates.

Heir at Law: Oldest living son to whom the land descended if there were not a will.

Hereditaments: Property that can be inherited.

Hogsheads: A very large barrel used to transport tobacco or liquids. A tobacco hogshead measured 48 inches long and 30 inches in diameter. Fully packed with tobacco, it weighed about 1000 pounds.

Indenture: Originally, an instrument (document) that is written twice (or more) on the same sheet of paper, and then the copies were cut apart with a curvy or jagged line (to prevent forgery). This was used when both parties continued to have an interest in the terms of the agreement. Eventually, the term came to apply to the instrument, even if it wasn't done with two copies and a jagged cut.

Interlined: Written between the lines. The scribe might add at the bottom of a deed what was added to indicate that place where "^" appears and information added above the line was not a later addition by someone else.

Intestate, intestacy: A person who dies without a valid will.

Lease: The transfer of possession but not ownership. Any agreement that gives rise to a relationship of landlord and tenant.

Lease and Release: The type of transaction used, especially in areas under proprietorships, to transfer estate or possession. It involved two transactions, executed one day after the other, between the same two parties, one of which is for a nominal sum, such as one dollar.

Line: The "sides" in a land description.

Link: 7.92 inches, 1/100 of a pole.

Livery and Seisin: See Seisin.

Meanders: The winding turns of a waterway. Used as a general term in land platting to describe a line that does not have both a distance and a direction. Down the meanders means with the direction of water flow; up the meanders means against the direction of water flow.

Messuage: A dwelling house. Sometimes indicates land with a dwelling house.

Metes-and-bounds: A description specifying the measures and boundaries of a parcel of land.

Moiety: One half of property or land.

Mortgage: When a person borrows money using land as a security.

Mouth: The place where a body of water empties into a body of water.

Moveables: All property not classed as heritable.

Pence: Plural of penny.

Penny: Equal to one hundredth of a pound.

Perch: 16.5 feet. Equivalent to a pole or rod.

Plantation: Property with land under cultivation or growing crops. It carries no connotation of size, wealth, or slaves. It didn't even have to have a house on it.

Plat: The drawing and accompanying text, usually prepared by a surveyor, showing the boundaries of a piece of property, commonly showing lines with direction and distance, corners with geographical features and adjoining property owners.

Pole: 16.5 feet. Equivalent to a perch or rod.

Pound: A basic unit of money in Great Britain equal to 100 pence.

Power of Attorney: The instrument (document) giving a person the right to act for another person, usually to transact specific business.

Quitrent: A fixed annual payment or rent, somewhat like a tax, that the landholder paid to the government or proprietor.

Relict: A widow or widower; the surviving spouse.

Remainder: the part of the estate that is left after a prior interest ends.

Rod: 16.5 feet. Equivalent to a perch or pole.

Seisin, seizin: A common-law term meaning possession or tenure of property. The transfer of tenure was called livery of seizin (delivery) and was done literally and physically, when the holder of the tenure stood on the land in the presence of neighbors and give the new holder a piece of dirt and a twig. "delivery of Turf & Twigg"

Shilling: English coinage valued at $1/20^{th}$ of a pound or twenty shillings in one pound.

Tenement: A dwelling house; also used to refer to real property irrespective of the presence of a house.

Testable, test: Capable of making or witnessing a will.

Turf and Twig: See Seisin.

Vizt: a contraction of videlicet, to wit; meaning that is to say.

Lancaster Co., VA

Abstracts of Order Book No. 8

1729-1743

Volume One

Pg 1. At Lancaster Co., VA, Court on Wednesday 12th Nov 1729 – Present – Justices - William Ball, Thomas Carter, George Heale, James Ball, William Ball, Junr.

Additional Inventory of Letitia Kelley, dec'd, was returned & Ordered to be recorded.

Agnes Robinson, wife of Giles Robinson, of Lancaster Co., VA, relinquished all of her Rights of Dower for two tracts of land in St. Mary's White Chappel Parish, Lancaster Co, VA, conveyed by her husband, unto Joseph Heale, being 50 a. and the other 100 & [?] acres with appurtenances.

Thomas Bruce[?], a bastard child of Margaret Bruce, of this Co., aged 7 years, the 12th December next at the prayer of the sd. mother is by the Court, bound to John Pinckard, Junr., till he attains the age of 21 years, the sd. John to teach him to read & write & the trade of Cooper and to find sufficient diet, lodging, apparel, and at the expiration of his servitude to pay him as is appointed for servants by Indenture or custom.

William Jones, who married the widow & Executrix, of John Lowry, late of this Co. dec'd, for making his account against the sd. testator's Estate and praying to have it allowed. Thomas Carter & Edwin Conway, Gent., are appointed to examine the acct. and to report their proceeding to the next Court.

2

The petition exhibited by William Reves against Henry Fleet, Junr., Sheriff of this County, for his Estate of Thomas Kirk, dec'd in [can't read] on a full hearing is rejected.

Tarr against Ball – John Tarr, Pltf., and James Ball, Deft., is continued till the next Court.

The Action between David Ball, Pltf., and George Heale, Deft. is continued till the next Court.

In the suit betw. Nathaniel Wildey, Pltf., and Arthur Howard, Deft., by petition Judgment is granted to the Pltf. on his Oath in Court.

The suit in Chancery betw. John Nutt & Sarah, his wife, and James Harris, & Sarah, his wife, audit of the Estate of Wm. Dymer, Deft., is dismissed.

In the action of debt between William Flowers, Pltf., and Alexander Turnbull, for 1,530 of tobacco due by obligation the opinion of the Court, being that the Deft., ought to give special bail in this case [can't read], the sd. Deft., confessed [can't read] custody of the Co. Sheriff. Ordered that he forthwith pay unto the sd. Pltf. his afsd. debt, with costs and remain in custody of the Sheriff, till his Judgment be fully satisfied.

In the action of trespass, assault and battery between John Stepto, Junr., and John Cristy[?], Deft., for £5 damage, the sd. Deft. being returned and not appearing, the sd. Pltf.is awarded against the sd. Deft. returnable to the next Court.

Giles Robinson appearing to answer the complaint of Joseph Carter, Sub. Sheriff of him for assaulting [can't read] Joseph in execution of his office. The parties were fully heard & also the testimony of Joseph Chinn and evidence in this defense, whereupon the sd. Giles before his offence fined five shillings … that he gave security in the penalty of £20 of like money for his good evidence for [can't read] for one year and pay all costs.

Giles Robinson & Joseph Heale, of St. Mary's White Chappel Parish, came into the Court and ackn. themselves severally indebted to the King of £20 to be upon the goods & chattels, lands and tenements to the use under the condition for the good behavior of the sd. Giles for one year from the date hereof.

Joseph Chinn an evidence for Joseph Carter, Sub-Sheriff of county having attend out a day as a witness for the sd. Joseph between him & Giles Robinson. It is Ordered that the sd. Joseph Carter pay the sd. Joseph Chinn for his attendance according to law & costs.

Pg 2. The Sheriff under Proclamation that the Court was about to lay the County William Ball, George Heale, Edwin Conway and they proceeded accordingly. Lancaster Co. – **Pounds of Tobacco:**

Robert Carter, Esqr., for keeping the Public Ferry one year -1,400

John Pyne for cleaning the Court House & other services – 300

John Tarpley, Junr., Gent., Attorney for the King in this co. for one year service, there having been three criminal trials, this Court allows levie - 1,200

William Hutchings & Fortunatus Sydnor for counting tobacco this year - 960

Abraham Currell & William Brent for the same - 1,270

George Brent and James Pollerd for the same - 525

William Stephens & Thomas Carter for the same - 515

Joseph Chinn & Thomas Young for the same - 715

David Ball & Thomas Chattin for the same - 830

John Rogers & John Stott, Junr., for the same - 770

George Payne & George Lite, Junr., for the same - 430

William Jones & James Brent for the same - 575

Clement Lattimer & William Haydon for the same – 620

Ditto a mistake in their due for the same last year – 55

The Hon., Court Clk., on his ano. – 160

Thomas Edwards, Clk., for his Court for one year's service – 1,000

Ditto for his attendance at three Criminal Trials – 600

Ditto for two record books – 1,135

4

Capt. Henry Fleet, Co. Sheriff, for one year's service – 1,000

Ditto on his account – 3,647

Dr. Thomas Thorton on his acct. – 250.

Nathaniel Wildy on his acct – 60

Jno. Sibly for guarding the prison eight nights – 80

Thomas Bryan for the same – 80

Job Wildy for guarding the prison twelve days & nights – 120

Hopkins Wildy for the same – 120

Total Tobacco – 18,917

Plus Cash & Salary – 3,404

<u>Total lbs. – 22,324</u>

The County Levy for the present year 1,729 amounting to 15 ¼ lbs. tobacco, It is Ordered that the Co. Sheriff collect so much of every Co. tithable & pay the same to the Co. Creditors, as it is bef. proposed.

Ferry - Ordered that Robert Carter, Esqr., do keep the Public Ferry over Corotomon River in the Co., the ensuing year and that he be paid for the same as usual.

Court House – Ordered that John Pyne [?] do find this Court with water & Candles & then the Court house for the ensuing year and that he be paid for the same as usual.

Ordered that the Court be adjourned till the second Wednesday in December next.

Pg 3. At a Court for Lancaster Co., Wednesday, the 10th day December 1729. Present: Gent., Justices - Henry Fleet, William Ball, John Selden, Thomas Carter, William Ball, Junr., Edwin Conway, James Ball, Nicholas Martin.

The last Will of Ann Chichester, dec'd, being proved by the Oaths of Elizabeth Davenport , late Elizabeth Heale & Catherine Quirk, witnesses thereto was admitted to record and Rawleigh Chinn, Exec., therein Open Court refusing to intermingle any part of the Estate, which was in the possession of the deceased at the time of the death belonging to the goods un-administered of William Fox, Gent., dec'd. It was objected that Richard Chichester had the Right to the Administration of the sd. Anne's Estate whereupon it was Ordered that the sd. Richard Chichester be summoned to the next Court to set forth his Right to the sd. Admin.

A bond from Richard Chichester, Esqr., & John Chichester, Gent., to William Payne, Gent., for 1,000 to be the act & deed of the sd. Richard & John, by the Oath of Rawleigh Chinn, witness – admitted to Record.

Petition of Charles Burges, Gent., and Frances, his wife, for Admin. of the goods & etc. of William Store[?], Gent., & Parish Gardiner, in behalf of Frances, his wife, came into Court & was told that his wife was of equal relation to the afsd. Frances Burges to the sd. dec'd, and had equal Right to the Administration and prayed that he & his wife might be joined with sd. petitioners in the law whereupon the opinion of the Court that the sd. Parish Gardiner & his wife ought to be joined to the Administration.

The Will of William Store[?] was presented in Court by Charles Burges & Francs, his wife, & Parish Gardiner, who made Oath and the Will was presented and proved & a certificate granted for obtaining Letters of Admin.

The last Will of William Mitchell, dec'd, with a Codicil annexed, was presented in Court by Margaret Mitchell, Execx., who made Oath and the Will was proved by Charles Burges, Wm. [LNU] and Martin Shearman, Junr., and to the Codicil, by the Oaths of Edwin Conway, Junr., John Mitchell & Elizabeth Chilton, was admitted to Probate.

Ordered that Margaret Mitchell, Execx., of the Will of William Mitchell, dec'd, to bring an Inventory of the testator's Estate to the next Court..

Alexander Turnbull charged in execution with a Judgment on 12 Nov last against William Flower for 1,530 lbs. tobacco and costs, brought and sd. Alexander subscribed & delivered under Oath, and it was Ordered that the sd. schedule remain with the Court Clk. and the Co. Sheriff was commanded that forthwith that [can't read] sd. Alexander.

Thomas Carter & Edwin Conway, Gent., reporting their settlement of the amount of William Jones, of the Estate of John Lowry re: the order the Court,

6

the sd. William made oath & thereupon the amount was allowed & Ordered to be recorded and in the opinion of the Court, the tobacco in the sd. amount to be set at 12 shillings @ 6 lbs. per hundred.

Henry Horne, who married the mother of Thomas Dare, late of this Co., came to Court and made Oath that he died without a Will, as far as he knows, and on a Petition to give his faithful Admin. of the sd. dec'd Estate & a certificate was granted for Letters of Admin.

Pg 4. James Brent, Richard Davis, Richard Flint, Alexander Flint, being sworn bef. Co. Justice, met & appraised the Estate of Thos. Dare, dec'd, in money & returned it to the Court, and Henry Stone, Admin., of sd. Estate.

John Tarr, Pltf., and James Ball, Deft., agreed to a Special verdict in their cause and is Ordered that the arguments be referred till the next Court.

In the action bet. David Ball, Pltf., and George Heale, Deft., by consent of the parties – Thomas Carter, Edwin Conway, & John Selden, Gent., are appointed to take the evidence of Elizabeth Higgins in this cause, and not being able to do so, it is Ordered that the cause be continued and the return of the sd. Elizabeth's deposition to the next Court.

Action of trespass, assault & battery betw. John Stepto, Junr., Pltf., and John Cristy, Deft., for £5 damage & Declaration is dismissed.

Action of debt betw. Samuel Maynard, Pltf., & William Ballendine, Deft., for £9.3.0, the Deft. being returned & not appearing attachment awarded to sd. Pltf., for his debt and costs against the Deft., returnable to next Court for Judgment.

On the attach. by Arthur Wright, against the Estate of Hugh Donahue for 600 lbs. tobacco. Alexander Matson, by his Attorney, moved that for as much as the sd. Arthur had failed to file a Petition setting forth his claim in this prosecution ought to abate, but was corrected, and the sd. Arthur made Oath that the sd. 600 lbs. of tobacco was justly due from the sd. Hugh by bill and that he had not received any satisfaction. Judgment was granted to the sd. Arthur for his debt and costs & it is Ordered that a horse shall not be sold & disposed of for towards of this Judgment in the same manner as goods taken in execution upon a writ. The attach. to continue to next Court.

Frances Angel be summoned to next Court to answer the petition of Charles Angel against her.

Thomas Marshall, orphan of John Marshall, late of the sd. Co., dec'd, Joseph Carter is appointed his Guardian thereto Joseph giving security for the same.

Ordered that the Court be adjourned till second Wednesday in January next.

At Lancaster Co. Court on 11 Feb1729. Present: William Ball, Thomas Carter, Charles Burges, George Heale, John Selden, Edwin Conway, Hugh Brent, James Ball, Nicholas Martin – Gent., Justices.

David Alexander Flint came to Court & ackn. his release to Charles Burges, Gent., for the continuing certain lands in St. Mary's White Chapel, Lancaster Co., which was admitted to record.

Charles Burges, Gent., came to Court & ackn. his lease to David Alexander Flint for & certain lands in St. Mary's White Chapel, Lancaster Co., was admitted to record.

The inventory of the Estate of William Mitchell, dec'd, was Returned and , Margaret Mitchell, Execx., making Oath and Ordered to be recorded.

Pg 5. A writing from Charles Burges, Gent., to Martha, the wife of David Alexander Flint concerning land lying in St. Mary's White Chapel Parish, in this Co., was ackn. in open Court by the sd. Charles, and admitted to record.

The appraisal of the Estate of Archibald Robinson, dec'd, was returned and William Heale, Admin., making Oath, re: the Inventory, and Ordered recorded.

Frances Gardiner, wife of Parish Gardiner presenting the Will of William Fox, Gent., dec'd, made oath and afsd. Parish last Dec. Court & obtained Letters of Admin, to administer the Estate's goods, with the Will annexed.

George Heale, Gent., is admitted to prosecute on behalf of his children, who are minors, against the Admin. of William Fox, Gent., dec'd, which is Ordered recorded.

The Appraisement of the un-administered goods of William Fox, Gent., dec'd. was Ordered returned & Charles Burges, Gent., one of the Admin. thereof with the Will annexed & made Oath re: the Inventory; recorded.

The Will of James Fouchee [?], dec'd, was presented to Court by John Fouchee [?], Exec., made Oath and the Will was proved by Edward Blakemore & David Smith, witnesses, and was admitted to record and Probate was granted.

8

Ordered that John Fouchee, Exec., Exec. of the Will of James Fouchee, dec'd, to bring Inventory of the Estate to next Court.

The Will of Elizabeth Pasquet, dec'd, was presented by William Pasquet, Exec., who made Oath and the Will was proved by Robert Edwards, & Edwin Conway and it was proved and recorded.

Ordered that William Pasquet, Exec. of the sd. Elizabeth Pasquet, to bring the Inventory of her Estate to the next Court.

The Petition of Margaret Mitchell against Thomas Williams praying that her daughter, Ann Mitchell, might not be admitted to prove her Guardian, in order to be married to the sd. Thomas, on hearing is rejected.

On the prayer of Ann Mitchell, orphan of William Mitchell, dec'd, William Bailey is appointed her Guardian, the sd. William given security for the same.

On the prayer of Chattin Chowning, orphan of George Chowning, dec'd, Thomas Chattin is appointed Guardian and the sd. gave security.

On the Attachment obtained by Robert Gibson against the Estate of John Nichols, which was on one feather bed, rug, blanket, pr. sheets, 2 pillows, the sd. Gibson made oath that 635 lbs. of tobacco was justly due to him from the sd. John, on balance of all amounts whereupon Judgment is granted him for the same& costs with attorney fee. It is Ordered that in case the goods afsd. shall not be repaid [?] then they be sold & disposed of towards the satisfaction of the Judgment, and the attachment shall be returned to next Court.

On the Attachment obtained by Robert Carter, Esqr., against the Estate of John Nichols, which attachment which was on 18 sides of tanned leather, one old bed, rug, blanket 7 bedstead, a horse, a mare colt abt. 2 years, 3 old chairs, five old chests, 21 old lasts, on the Oath of sd. Carter & the evidence of William Edwards & William Mc Dade [?] in this Judgment is granted to the Pltf., for 2,066 lbs. tobacco & costs. And, it is Ordered that in case the goods afsd. shall not be repaid [?] then they be sold & disposed of towards the satisfaction of the Judgment, and the attachment shall be returned to next Court.

James Stott came to Court and made oath that Bryan Stott, late of this Co., dec'd, departed this life without making a Will, and on petition of the afsd. James & giving security was granted for obtaining Letters of Admin. in due form.

Pg 6. Ordered that John Rogers, John Callahan, Thomas Chattin, & James White, or any three of them, to appraise the Estate of Bryan Stott, dec'd, in money and submit a report at next Court and James Stott, Admin. of the Estate to in ref. to the Inventory.

The action betw. David Ball, Pltf., and George Heale, Deft., continued to next Court.

In action of debt, Samuel Maynard, Pltf., and William Bertrand, Deft., for £9.1.3, due for principal charges of profit & damage on a bill of Exchange. The Deft. appeared and confessed Judgment, wherefore it was considered the that the sd. Deft. pay unto the Pltf. the debt with costs.

An attachment obtained by Arthur Wright, against the Estate of Hugh Donham is discontinued.

The suit betw. Charles Angell, Pltf., against Frances Angell, Deft., by petition is continued to next Court.

John Selden, William Ball, Junr., and Hugh Brent, Gent., are presented to the Hon. Governor, as persons fit & able to execute the Office of Co. Sheriff for the ensuing year.

The action of the case betw. William Stevenson, Pltf., and James Ball, Gent., late Co. Sheriff. Wherein on a Judgment on 18 Nov 1728 for he Deft. in this cause, the sd. Pltf., appealed, which Judgment as appears by an Order of the 27th Oct. last, was revoked and the record permitted to this Court to execute a writ of inquiry of damages. The sd. Deft. consented to a Judgment for 1,429 lbs. of tobacco. The contents of a Judgment heretofore recovered by the Pltf. against Patrick Mc Coy on whose case this suit was brought. Wherefore, it is considered that the sd. Pltf. recover against the sd. 1,409 lbs. tobacco and his costs with attorney fee.

James Hogan came to Court & ackn. his writing to Charles Burges, Gent., his master for service which was admitted to record.

Nicholas Cary in Court ackn. his writing to Charles Burges, Gent., his master for service, which was admitted to record.

Isbell Rend, a servant woman, belonging to john Morris, of sd. Co., having been lately delivered a bastard child. It is Ordered that for the loss & trouble re: her master, thereby she shall serve him for the same one whole year after her time by Indenture or former order of the Court is expired or pay him 1,000 lbs. tobacco.

In the action of debt between William Ranken, Pltf., and Edward Nicken [Nickens?], Deft., being called & not appearing Judgment is granted to the Pltf., against the Deft., and Joseph George, his security, shall appear to justly due to him at the next Court unless the sd. Deft. appears & answered the action.

The action of trespass between Margaret Mitchell, Pltf., and Thomas Williams, Defts., is dismissed.

The action upon the case betw. Henry Newby, Pltf., and Robert Walls, deft., is dismissed.

The attachment obtained by Thomas Edwards against the Estate of James Hathaway is continued till next Court.

The action of trespass betw. John Brooks, Pltf., and Robert Thompson, Deft., for £5 damages is dismissed.

The action of debt betw. William Jones, Pltf., and Margaret Burne, Deft., for 500 lbs. tobacco due by note the sd. Deft. confessed & Judgment is considered that she forthwith pay unto the Pltf. the debt, & costs and attorney fees.

The action of debt betw. Richard Longworth[?] and Thomas Lee, Deft., dismissed.

The attachment afsd. by Thomas Edwards against the Estate of Edward Johnson is continued till the next Court.

Pg 7. The ejection betw. John Tarr, Pltf., and James Ball, deft. is continued at the next Court.

The action of debt betw. Alexander Graves, Pltf., and William Chossell [?], Deft., is dismissed.

Charles Sulwan, servant, to Robert Carter, Esqr., stated that in March 1725 he agreed to serve his sd. master 2 years after his Indenture time should be expired in consideration that his master would keep him to the carpenter trade and this duration has notwithstanding, hired him to work in the crop of cover tobacco. That this Indenture time is now expired & and that he ought now to be set at liberty, The partied being fully heard and it appearing that the sd. Charles was put to work in the crop at his own instance request. It is the opinion of the Court that he is still bound by the afsd. agreement. But, it is Ordered for the residue of his time he be kept & employed at his trade afsd.

Ordered by the Court be adjourned till the 2nd Wednesday in March next.

At Court for Lancaster Co., on Wednesday, 11th March 1729 – Present: William Ball, Thomas Carter, Charles Burgess, George Heale, John Selden, Edwin Conway, James Ball, William Ball, Junr.; Gent., Justices.

On the Petition of Nicholas George setting forth that George Dogget has turned then ancient road leading from his [can't read] Corotoman Neck. It is Ordered that the sd. Dogget be summoned to Court to answer this matter and that Thomas Carter & Edwin Conway, Gent., are to view the sd. road and then report their opinion of the convenience or not thereof.

On the petition of Bersheba Hall setting forth that she had served Judith Conner, of this Co., widow, till she has attained the age of 18 years, and that she ought to be set free & the parties were fully heard, and the Court ruled that Bersheba is not legally bound and she was to be free.

David Alexander Fleet cane to Court and ackn. his deed to Thomas Fleet for 150 acres in St. Mary's White Chapel, in the sd. Co., which was recorded.

Martha, the wife of David Alexander Flint also came to Court & freely relinquished her right of Dower unto Thomas Flint and in the sd. lands with their appurtenances and was recorded.

Edward Nicken, and wife, Mary, came to Court & ackn. their deed to Elias Edmunds for 80 a., in Christ Church Parish, Lancaster Co., and the sd. Mary was privately examined, and the sd. Edward also ackn. the deed and his bond for performance of the covenants in the sd. deed, and was recorded.

The Will of Ann Chichester heretofore proved in Court was presented by Rawleigh Chinn, who made oath and Exec. in the Will, and upon his Motion he was granted probate of the Will.

James Brent, George Payne, and Daniel Stephens, and Joseph Stevens, or any three go bef. a Justice of Peace, and appraise the Estate of Ann Chichester, dec'd, in money and make a report and that the sd. Rawleigh Chinn appear to thr Next Court.

The Motion of Richard Chichester, Esqr., for the Admin. of the Estate of Ann Chichester, dec'd, is dismissed, the sd. Richard summoned to set forth his Right to the same, and he failed to appear.

James Ball came to Court and made Oath to the truth of his account against Mariolia Feganm and that [can't read] not received part of satisfaction for the balance therein mentioned, which is Ordered to be certified by the Court Clerk on the sd. amount.

Pg 8. Attachment obtained by Robert Gibson against the Estate of John Nichols is continued for the Sheriff's return to next Court.

Attachment obtained by Robert Carter, Esqr., against the Estate of John Nichols is continued to next Court.

The appraisement of the Estate of Thomas Dare, dec'd, was this day returned and Henry Stone [?], Admin., thereof making Oath according to this subscription on the Inventory, recorded.

The action betw. David Ball, Pltf., and George Heale, Deft., at the Deft.'s [can't read] and costs, continued to next Court.

The suit betw. Charles Angell, Pltf., and Frances Angell, Deft., is continued to next Court.

The Debt. betw. William Ranken, Pltf., and Edward Nickon, Deft., for 486 lbs. tobacco due by note, is dismissed.

Attachment obtained by Thomas Edwards against the Estate of Edward Johnson is continued till next Court.

Mary Snow, a servant woman, belonging to William Stamps, of this Co., having lately delivered a bastard child, it is Ordered that due to the loss & trouble occasioned, her sd. Master thereby that she serve her sd. master one whole year, after her time by Indenture custom or order of the Court is expired, or pay him 1,000 lbs. tobacco.

In action of a debt betw. Robert Carter, Esqr., & Thomas Cater, Church Wardens of Christ Church Parish, of sd. Co., Pltfs., and John Edwards & William Edwards, Defts., the sd. Defts. being called and not appearing, not any security returned. Judgment is granted to the sd. Pltf. against the Defts., and Henry Fleet, Junr., Gent., Co. Sheriff for what shall appear to be justly due to the sd. Pltfs. at next Court, unless the sd. Defts., then appear and answer the action.

The action of Debt betw. Thomas Edwards, Pltf., and John Mc Genius, Deft., is continued as it is till the next Court.

The action on the case betw. David Ball, Pltf., and George Heale, Deft., the sd. Deft. being called and not appearing, nor any security returned, Judgment is granted to the Pltf., against the Deft., and Henry Fleet, Junr., Gent., Co. Sheriff, what that appear justly due to him at the next Court unless the sd. Deft., do then appear and answer this action.

In the suit in Chancery betw. George Heale, Gent., for & in behalf of his daughters, Sarah Heale, Catherine Heale, & Ann Heale, Co-Pltfs., and Charles Burges, Gent., and Frances, his wife, & Parish Gardiner & Frances, his wife, Admin., with the Will annexed of the goods not administered by William Fleet, Gent., on the action of the sd. Defts. have given them to answer till next Court.

Honor Clark, a servant woman, belonging to Benjamin Brown of this Co., having lately delivered a bastard child. It is Ordered that in due of the loss & damage occasioned her sd. master thereby she serve her sd. master one whole year after her time by Indenture custom or former order of the Court is expired or pay him 1,000 lbs. tobacco.

Isabel Rend being brought to the bar & confessing she had been lately delivered of a bastard child and failing to give security or make payment of the fine for the offense it is Ordered that the prisoner on her bare back at the Public Whipping post twenty five lashes, and be well laid on, and then be discharged.

The Will of James Connor, dec'd, was presented in Court by Judith Connor, Execx., who made oath and being proved by the oaths of William Ranken, a witness, and it is admitted to the record. And, on the Motion of the Execx. and her performing usual certification, she was granted Probate.

Ordered that Ezekiel Gilbert, John Wren, William Brent, and Henry Lawson, or any three, after being first sworn before a Co Judge, are to appraise the Estate of James Connor, dec'd, in money and return same before next Co. Court, and Judith Connor, Execx., also appear at Court.

14

Pg 9. James Ball, Gent., late Sheriff of the Co., setting forth that by means of the refuge of a certain Patrick Mc Coy out of the Co. Goal at the suit of William Stevenson, the sd. William had recovered against him, the sd. the sd. James, 1,409 lbs. tobacco & costs. The Court stated that the tobacco afsd. & all costs & damages sustained in the recovery thereof be paid & reimbursed to the sd. James, by Henry William Ball, John Turbervile, Richard Ball, Thomas Carter, George Heale, Thomas Lee, Charles Burges, & Henry Fleet, Junr., Gent. Co. Magistrates of this Court at the time of the. sd. escape.

In pursuance to a clause in the Act of Regulating Ordinarys & restraint of Tipling houses, the Court doth set & rate:

Cider at 15 pence or 12 pounds of tobacco the gallon. Rum & Brandy (except Irish[?] Brandy) at 8 shillings or 76 lbs. of tobacco the gallon. Punch at 15 pence or 12 lbs. tobacco the Quart. Strong beer at 15 pence or 12 lbs. tobacco the bottle. Madera wine at one shilling, 10 pence half penny or 18 lbs. tobacco the quart. Dyet with small beer to drink at 11 pence, farthing or 9 lbs. tobacco the meal. Lodging at 7 pence, half penny or 6 lbs. tobacco the night. Stabloage & fodder for a horse at 6 pence or 5 lbs. of tobacco the night. Oats or Indian Corn at 6 pence or 5 lbs. tobacco the gallon. [?]

Order the Court for Lancaster Co. on Wednesday 2 April 1730 – Present: William Ball, Thomas Carter, Charles Burgess, Hugh Brent, Henry Fleet, John Selden, Edwin Conway, James Ball, William Ball, Junr.; Gent., Justices.

The Sheriff was Ordered to summon 24 Co. inhabitants, freeholders, to appear at the next Court, and that out of them a grand jury my be impaneled & sworn to make inquiry in the breach of the penal laws & to present the offenders.

Ordered that the several Co. Constables be summoned to the next Court to take the Oath for and due execution of their office & have the Oaths to the Government & the costs administered to them.

The Inventory of the Estate of Elizabeth Pasquet, dec'd, was returned and William Pasquet, her Exec., making or handling to his subscription thereon Ordered to be recorded.

The Inventory of the Estate of James Fouchee, dec'd, was returned and John Fouchee, Exec., making oath & Ordered recorded.

The depositions of William Edwards & Thomas Crowder concerning a Negro man named Mingo, belonging to Robert Carter, Esqr., who was killed by virtue of an Outlawry from his [can' read] was taken & sworn to in Court, and it is Ordered hat the same be certified & sd, depositions brought to the next Court of Claims by the Clerk of the [can't read] in order for a value to be set on the sd. Negro as the law provides.

Pg 10. A certificate from Bryan Blandell, Esqr., Mayor of London, concerning an affidavit of John Stansfield & Richard Hayworth was proved by the Oath of Nicholas Gallamore & John Nowhouse, witness thereto and together; the affidavit recorded.

Letter of Attorney from James Kenan, of Liverpool, merchant, to Capt. Hugh Breakhill was proved in open Court by Oath of Nicholas Gallamore & John Breakhill witness; recorded.

Deeds of Lease & Release from Col. Gawin Corbin to James Ball, Gent., for 740 a. of land in St. Mary's White Chappell, Lancaster Co., VA, were proved in Court to be the act of the afsd. Corbin by the Oaths of John Tarpley & Charles Burges, James Brent, and William Heale, recorded.

On the Petition of Mary Mc Boyd [can't read] to Daniel Carter setting forth that she is not legally bound to have the sd. Daniel, appeared and the Court having fully heard the arguments on both sides are of the opinion that the sd. Mary be free.

On the Petition of James Haines leave is given him to set draw bares or great gates for wheel carriages & small gates for passengers on the main road which leads to Mr. Dymer's plantation from Col. Carter's little mill.

On the Petition of James Ball, Gent., leave is given him to draw barrs or great gates for wheel marriages & small gates for passengers on the main road which leads thro his plantation from his mill to Moratico mill.

The Petition of Nicholas George against George Dogget concerning the road leading from the sd. Nicholas' to Corotomon Neck, neither party appearing; dismissed.

Attachment obtained by Robert Gibson, against the Estate of John Nichols is discontinued – 900 lbs. tobacco made of ye goods attached in October next – Henry Fleet [can't read].

Attachment obtained by Robert Carter, Esqr., against the Estate of John Nichols is continued to next Court.

Attachment of Detinue between David Ball, Pltf., and George Heale, Deft., is continued at the Deft.'s Motion & costs till next Court.

Petition of Charles Angell against Frances Angell praying of the sd. Frances may be obliged to give security for the Estate of the Orphans of Robt. Angell, dec'd, in her hands & neither party appearing; dismissed.

Attachment obtained by Thomas Edwards against the Estate of James Hathaway is continued till next Court.

Attachment obtained by Thomas Edwards against the Estate of Edward Johnson is continued Next Court.

In the action of debt betw. Robert Carter, Esqr., and Thomas Carter, Church Wardens of Christ Church, in this Co., Pltfs., and John Edwards & William Edwards, Defts., for £15 due by Bond dated 11 Oct 1728, & the sd. Defts. confessed Judgment for £7.10.0 or 1,500 lbs. tobacco to the sd. Pltfs., who accepted and the Defts. to pay the costs and attorney fees.

The action of debt betw. Thomas Edwards, Pltf., and John Mc Gennis, Deft., for 312 lbs. tobacco due on balance of an account the Deft. being dead; dismissed.

The action betw. David Ball, Pltf., and George Heale, Deft., is continued by Deft., with costs to next Court.

In the suit in Chancery betw. George Heale, Gent., for & in behalf of his daughters – Sarah Heale, Catherine Heale, and Ann Heale, Complt., and Charles Burges, Gent., & Francis, his wife, Defts., & Parish Gardiner & Frances, his wife, Admins., with the Will annexed of goods not administered of William Fox, Gent., dec'd. Further time is given to the sd. Defts. to answer, next Court.

The last Will of Henry Chelton, dec'd, was presented in Court by William Chelton, who made Oath, and being proved by the Oath of Henry Pasquet, a witness thereto, was admitted to Record, on the Motion of the sd. Wm. Chelton, who obtained Letters of Admin., with Will annexed.

Ordered that Thomas Purcell, George Brent, James Pollard, James Webb, & any three, being sworn bef. a Co. Magistrate, are to appraise the Estate of Henry

Chelton, dec'd, in money with report to the next Co. Court and that Wm. Chelton, Admin, appear with Will annexed.

Ordered the Court be adjourned till second Wed. in May. At Court for Lancaster Co., on Wednesday, 11th March 1729 – Present: William Ball, Thomas Carter, Charles Burgess, George Heale, Nicholas Martin, Edwin Conway, James Ball, William Ball, Junr.; Gent., Justices. The Act of an Assembly concerning Public Claims was read in Court.

Pg 11. Robert Carter, Esqr., making application to this Court to set a value on his Negro man slave named Mingo, lately killed by virtue of an Outlawry from this Co. This Court des value the sd. Slave to £26, which is Ordered to be certified to the Gen. Assembly.

William Mc Dade making oath that he had not received any satisfaction for his taking up a Negro woman belonging to James Webb, of this Co. It is Ordered that the Co. Clk. certify the same to the Gen. Assembly.

Thomas Bryan making oath that he had not received any satisfaction for his taking up a Negro slave belonging to Thomas Lee, Gent., of this Co. It is Ordered that the Co. Clk. certify the same to the Gen. Assembly.

Thomas Starte making oath that he had not received any satisfaction for his taking up a servant man belonging to William Kilber, late of this Co., dec'd. It is Ordered that the Co. Clk. certify the same to the Gen. Assembly.

Thomas Wren making oath that he had not received any satisfaction for his taking up a servant man belonging to Thomas Connelly. It is Ordered that the Co. Clk. certify the same to the Gen. Assembly.

William Wren making oath that he had not received any satisfaction for his taking up a servant man belonging to John Butterworth, of York Co. It is Ordered that the Co. Clk. certify the same to the Gen. Assembly.

Thomas Hunton making oath that he had not received any satisfaction for his taking up a Negro man belonging to John Shapleigh, Gent., of Northumberland Co. It is Ordered that the Co. Clk. certify the same to the Gen. Assembly.

James Hogan making oath that he had not received any satisfaction for his taking up a servant man belonging to John Woodbridge, Gent., late of Richmond Co. It is Ordered that the Co. Clk. certify the same to the Gen. Assembly.

18

Charles Burgess, Gent., making oath that he had not received any satisfaction for his taking up a servant man belonging to Mary Gibbs, late of Middlesex Co., dec'd. It is Ordered that the Co. Clk. certify the same to the Gen. Assembly.

Mr. Elias Edwards making oath that he had not received any satisfaction for his taking up a servant man belonging to Adam Cockburne, Esqr., late of Middlesex Co, VA, dec'd. It is Ordered that the Co. Clk. certify the same to the Gen. Assembly.

Thomas Flint making oath that he had not received any satisfaction for his taking up a servant man belonging to Thomas Smith. It is Ordered that the Co. Clk. certify the same to the Gen. Assembly.

John Flint making oath that he had not received any satisfaction for his taking up a servant belonging to Revd. Walter Jones, of Westmoreland Co. It is Ordered that the Co. Clk. certify the same to the Gen. Assembly

Petition of Rawleigh Chinn, Gent., directed to the General Assembly setting forth that by a mistake an order was entered up against him for of attendance of John Bailey, who was summoned in behalf of the King against the sd. Rawleigh in which suit & Judgment was in his favor. The sd. Rawleigh & ye sd. John, making Oath to truth of allegations in that [can't read]. It is Ordered that the Court Clk. by the same to the Gen. Assembly.

Pg 12. A petition directed to the Gen. Assembly for the removal of the Court house, of this County was presented at Court by Thomas Pinckard, James Ball, George Heale, William Haydon, Thomas Haydon, John Simons, Cline Stoplier, Kirk Thomas Hubbard[?], Richard Boatman, Thomas Hunton, George Brent, William Chelton, John Pinckard, Elias Edmunds, John Merrideth, John Yerby, Edward Sanders, Henry Boatman, William Heale, James Brent, Joseph Heale, William Baily, Francisco Frizell, Dennis Couree, John Webb, Isaac Cundiff, John Cundiff, Jonathan More, George Payne, Thomas Flint, William Ballendine, John Bailey, George Doggett, subscribers. Ordered that the Co. Clk. certify the same to the Gen. Assembly.

A proposition directed to the Gen. Assembly for selecting the crops to 4,000 plants of tobacco for every laboring tithable was [can't read] & subscribed in Court Ordered that the Court Clk. certify the same to the Gen. Assembly. grievance directed to the Gen. Assembly concerning the forfeited Estates & quit rents in the Northern Neck was presented & subscribed in Court & Ordered that the County Clk. certify the same to the Gen. Assembly.

At a Court for Lancaster Co on Wedn. the 13th May 1730. Present: William Ball, William Ball, Junr., James Ball, Thomas Carter, Charles Burgess, Nicholas Martin; Gent., Justices.

On the Motion of Charles Angell, one of the Exec. of the Will of Robert Angell, dec'd, setting forth that the Estate of the sd. dec'd, has continued in the hands of Frances Angel, the other Exec., of the Will, & that the sd. Frances doth embezzled & waste the same. Thomas Lee, Hugh Brent, Nicholas Martin, Gent., are appointed to examine the Estate & settle the account of the auditor of the sd. Estate & to make a report of their proceedings. And, it is Ordered that unless the sd. Frances do give in security for rendering to the younger children of the sd. decedent what of the sd. Estate shall become due to them when they come of age that this Court other ways dispose thereof at the next Court.

The appraisement of the Estate of Henry Chelton, dec'd, was returned and William Chelton, Admin., of the Will annexed, making oath thereto on the Inventory; Ordered record.

Ordered that James Flemon be summoned to the Court to answer the petition of Sarah Thompson against him.

Ordered that Robert Gibson be summoned to the Court to answer the petition of William Hattaway against him.

The Will of Eleanor Robert, dec'd, was prosecuted in Court by William Cone, who made oath and was proved by the oath of Charles Russell, a witness thereto, is admitted to record and on the Motion of William Cone was granted Letters of Admin. for the Estate of the sd. dec'd.

Robert Schofield came to Court and ackn. his deed to Elias Edmunds for 80 a. of land in Christ Church Parish in sd. Co., and is Ordered and his bond for performance of the covenants in the sd. deed; admitted to record.

The appraisement of the Estate of Ann Chichester, dec'd, was returned and Rawleigh Chinn, her Exec., making oath on the Inventory was recorded.

On the Motion of Henry Lawson leave is given him to set draw bars or great gates for wheel carriages & small gates for passengers on the main road, which leads through his plantation for the white stone to Major Fleet's. But by his own consent they are to remain as long than his tobacco shall be growing on his plantation.

Pg 13. James Mc Coudero [?], orphan of Dugal Mc Coudero, late of this Co., dec'd, aged 11 years the 25th March next, on the [can't read] of his master, is by this Court bound to Jane Heard, widow, till he attains the age of 21 years, The sd. Jane is to teach him to read & write & and the trade of a shoemaker, and provide sufficient diet, lodging and apparel, and at the expiration, to pay him as a servant re: Indenture or Custom.

Henry Horne & Edward Sanders, two of his Co. Constables having taken the Oaths & subscribed the test had the Oaths of Constable admin. to them.

William Sydnor appointed Constable in St. Mary's, White Chappel Parish, Lancaster Co., in place of John Pollard, Ordered that he summon the sd. William to next Court to be sworn.

George Dogget appointed Constable in Christ Church Parish, Lancaster Co., in place of Thomas Hubbard, Ordered that he summon the sd. George to next Court to be sworn.

Thomas Hunton appointed Constable in Christ Church Parish, Lancaster Co., in place of John Cox, having taken the Oaths & subscribed the test had the Oaths of Constable admin. to him.

Joseph Cotes & Elizabeth, his wife, came to Court and made oath the at George Robinson, late of this Co., died without a Will, and on the petition & giving security for their just Admin. of the decedent's Estate, is granted Letters of Admin.

Ordered that Thomas Chattin, George Payne, Thomas Flint & William Bailey, or any three being sworn bef. a Co. Justice to appraise the Estate of George Robinson, dec'd in money and make a report to the next Court for obtaining Letters of Admin. and that Joseph Cotes and Elizabeth, his wife, appear and make oath of the Inventory.

A Grand Jury for the Co. being impanelled by an Order of the last Court having appointed Henry Lawson, foreman, who was sworn & the rest to wit: Abraham Carroll, John Wale, Thomas Chelton, Anthony Garton, Walter James, Matthias James, Thomas Hunton, Thomas Yerby, John Merrideth, John Mott, Junr., Thomas Chelton, James Stott, Isaac White, John Rogers, John Callahan, John

Stott, Junr., Thomas Stott, Brian Pullen, Nathaniel Carpenter, William Roberson, Giles Roberson, Junr., George Brent, & William Hutchins, who having reviewed their charge withdrew and after some time returned unto Court and gave their Presentments & were discharged which Presentments were by the Court Ordered to be recorded and are as followeth: Lans. Is., May 13the, 1730.

We, the Grand Jury present:

Andrew Donalson & Mary , his wife of Christ Church Parish for not going to Church for one month past.

Thomas Edwards of the afsd. Parish for not keeping a good sufficient bridge over the waste of his Mill dam.

Bridget Spexton of St. Mary's Chappel for having a mulatto bastard child.

John Culley and is wife, Elizabeth, and Sarah Haines, and Matthew Bolton, and James Curtis, and John Morris, all of Christ Church Parish for not going to Church for one month past.

Ann Bam of St. Mary's White Chappel for having a bastard child.

Catherine Read of the afsd. place, for not going to Church in one monthly last past.

Signed: Henry Lawson, Foreman.

The Presentment of the Grand Jury against Thomas Edwards for not keeping a good sufficient bridge over the water of his Mill Dam is dismissed not lying within the present mounts.

Ordered that John Culley and is wife, Elizabeth, and Sarah Haines, and Matthew Bolton, and James Curtis, and John Morris, all of Christ Church Parish for not going to Church to be summoned to the next Court to answer the Presentment against them.

Ordered that Bridget Spexton, Ann Bam & Catherine Road, of St. Mary's Chappel to be summoned to the next Court to answer the Presentment against them.

Pg 14. On a present from Thomas Carter, Gent., one of the Co. Justices, against Robert Scofield on the information of John Tully setting forth that the sd. Robert is a person of a lewd life & conversation and a common disturber of the Peace, that he has several times forewarned the sd. Robert of his house yet nevertheless he found him on 12 April last in bed with his wife in his the sd. John's own house & the door shut and bolted. Its well the sd. Robert, as the afsd. John appeared and were fully heard. But, for much as there was no window whereby to charge ye sd. Robert in this matter. It is confirmed that this prosecution be dismissed.

In the attachment of Robert Carter, Esqr., against the Estate of John Nichols, the Sheriff having made a Return of which is in his hands towards satisfaction of the sd. Robert's Judgment in this to use the same was Ordered to be recorded being as follows. I have made the goods attached by the sd. Robert Carter, Esqr. belonging to Jno. Nichols' Estate 738 lbs. of tobacco to be pd. in October next Feb 10, 1729. Henry Fleet, Sheriff.

The action of detinue betw. David Ball, Pltf., and George Heale, Deft., is continued till the next Court on the Pltf.'s notion.

On the attachment obtained on Thomas Edwards against the Estate of James Hattaway for 360 lbs. of tobacco due by acc't the Pltf. having rec'd 334 lbs. of tobacco of Abel Baufle[?] on whom this attachment was [can't read] made oath the 26 lbs. of tobacco was justly due him whereupon Judgment was granted him for sd. 26 lbs. & costs and it is Ordered the attachment be discontinued.

The attachment obtained by Thomas Edwards against the Estate of Edward Johnson is continued till next Court.

In the action upon the case betw. David Ball, Pltf., and George Heale, deft., having this day put in a plea time is given for the Pltf. till next Court to consider it.

In the suit in Chancery betw. George Heale, Gent., for & in behalf his daughters, Sale Heale, Catherine Heale, & Ann Heale, Compl., and Charles Burges, Gent., and Frances, his wife, & Parish Gardiner & Frances, his wife, Admin., with the Will annexed of the goods un-administered of William Ker, Gent, deft., put in a demurrer, till next Court.

The action of trespass betw. Thomas Walls, Pltf., and James Mango, Deft., is continued till next Court.

In the suit by Petition betw. John Dozer, Pltf., and John Gill, Deft., for 322 lbs. of tobacco due by bill by the sd. Deft., appeared & offering nothing to the contrary, Judgment is granted to the sd. Pltf., for his debt & costs with attorney's fee.

On the Petition of Hester Frond in behalf of her daughter, Eliza. Branson against Sarah Wiley praying her sd. daughter night be Pltf. as in the sd. petition is set forth, the sd. Sarah coming into Court & confronting to the same. It is Ordered that the sd. Elizabeth be free according to the prayer of the sd. Petition.

William Ball, Junr., Gent., is appointed to take the list of Titihables in the upper precinct in St. Mary's, White Chappel Parish this year.

James Ball, Gent., is appointed to take the list of Titihables in Corotomon precinct in Christ Church, Wicocomoco Parish this year.

George Heale, Gent., is appointed to take the list of Titihables in the Moratico precinct in Christ Church, for this year.

Hugh Brent, Gent., is appointed to take the list of Titihables in the middle precinct in Christ Church Parish this year.

Henry Fleet, Gent., is appointed to take the list of Titihables in the lower precinct in Christ Church Parish this year.

Nicholas Martin, Gent., is appointed to take the list of Titihables between Corotomon River & the main road, which leads from the Church to Col. Carter's great Mill in Christ Church Parish for this year.

William Catlet appointed surveyor of the highways from this County Court House to Mr. Payne's in St. Mary's White Chappel Parish.

Pg 15. James Brent is appointed surveyor of the highways from Mr. Payne's to Mr. Burges' Mill in St. Mary'[s White Chappel Parish.

Henry Towles is appointed surveyor of the highways from Clehood's [?] Ferry to Mr. Payne' in St. Mary's White Chappel Parish.

John Bailey is appointed surveyor of the highways from the Church to Deep Bottom River in St. Mary's White Chappel Parish.

Thomas Wharton is appointed surveyor of the highways from Burges' Mill to Mr. Selden's Mill in St. Mary's Chappel Parish.

William Morris is appointed surveyor of the rolling rod which leads from the Church Road to Carpenter's Landing in St. Mary's Chappel Parish.

John Mott is appointed surveyor of the highways from Brian Stott's to the road that leads from Col. Ball's Mill to Mr. Burges's Mill in St. Mary's Chappel Parish.

Thomas Chattin is appointed surveyor of the highways from Bartle Woods to the cross-roads near Dr. Thorton's in St. Mary's Chappel Parish.

Therriat Taylor is appointed surveyor of the highways from the main road to Giles Robinson's to the main road which leads to Selden's Mill & from that main road to Cundiff's old field and also of the rolling road in the sd. Precinct in St. Mary's Chappel Parish.

William Bertrand is appointed surveyor of the highways from Deep Bottom River to Morattico Mill in St. Mary's Chappel Parish.

Richard Curtis is appointed surveyor of the highways from Mr. Selden's Mill to Col. Carter's Great Mill and all the main roads betw. those two branches of Corotomon River in Christ Church Parish.

George Flower is appointed surveyor of the highways from Col. Carter's Great Mill to his Little Mill and to the Co. Clk's Office in Christ Church Parish.

William Stepto is appointed Surveyor of the highways from the cross-roads to the Church in Christ Church Parish.

William Martin is appointed Surveyor of the highways from the white stone to Col. Carter's Little Mill and of all the main roads in Nantoperizon Neck in Christ Church Parish.

William Brent is appointed Surveyor of the highways from the Church to Maj. Fleet's in Christ Church Parish.

John Yerby is appointed Surveyor of the highways from Col. Carter's Quarter to the Mill Road and from the sd. road to the Church in Christ Church Parish.

Ordered that the Court be adjourned till the 2nd Wednesday in June next.   At a Court for Lancaster Co. on Wedn. 10 June 1730. Present: Present: William Ball, Thomas Carter, Charles Carter ,James Ball, William Ball, Junr., Henry Fleet, Hugh Brent, Nicholas Martin, John Selden; Gent., Justices

The appraisement of the Estate of Eleanor Roberts, dec'd, was returned and William Cone, Admin., with Will annexed made Oath according to the Inventory; recorded.

Pg 16. Lawrence Thompson, a servant man, belonging to Robert Carter, Esqr., came voluntarily to Court and agreed to serve his Master one year after his hire by Indenture is expired in consideration of his sd. Master's having purchase him from Capt. Thomas Woodward.

Samuel Hambleton, a servant man, belonging to Thomas Webster of this CO., came to Court & voluntarily agreed to serve his Master one year & 28 days after his hire by Indenture is expired in consideration of which his Master agrees to keep him in the tailor's trade.

The consideration of the Court entered by Giles Robinson, against Joseph Cotes, & Elizabeth, his wife, or either of them obtaining Letters of Admin. on the goods, rights and credits of George Robinson, dec'd, is referred to next Court on the sd. Joseph's Motion & costs.

William Alexander, orphan of William Alexander, dec'd, aged 9 years the 14th[?] day of October next on the prayer of his sd. mother is by the Court bound unto Roger Winter, of Northumberland Co., till he attains the age of 21 years, and the sd. Winter is to teach him to read & write and the trade of a carpenter, and to find & allow him sufficient food, lodging & apparel, and at the expiration to pay him as is appointed from servants by Indenture or custom.

The differences betw. Charles Angell, Pltf., & Frances Angell, Exec., of the last Will of Robert Angell, dec'd, concerning the sd. decedent's Estate is dismissed being neither party appeared.

The appraisement of the Estate of James Connor, dec'd, was returned and Judith Connor, his Execx., making oath hereto according to her subscription of the Inventory; Ordered recorded.

John Bailey on the prayer of William Sydnor, being appointed a Constable in St, Mary's White Chappel Parish, is the room of him, the sd. William, the sd. John appeared and the sd. George Doggett, who was at the last Court appointed Constable of Christ Church Parish, and the Oaths of their office were Administered.

Elizabeth Preston, a bastard child, aged 11 years in May last by the Court bound to Judith Connor, widow, till she attains the age of 18 years to sd. Judith to teach her to read, sew, knit, spin & to find & allow her sufficient food & lodging, apparel and at the end of her servitude to pay her as is appointed for servants by Indenture or custom.

The suit by Petition betw. Sarah Thompson, Pltf., and James Flemon, Deft., praying that John Thompson, her son, might be set at liberty from the sd. Deft., is dismissed; the sd. Pltf. not appearing.

John Thompson, orphan of William Thompson, late of this Co., dec'd, of his own free will & consent is by the Court bound to James Flower till be attains the age of 21 years. The sd. James is to teach him to read & write and the trade of shoemaker and to find sufficient & good food, apparel and at the end of his servitude to pay him as is appointed for servants by indenture or custom.

The Will of Nathaniel Wildy[Wildey], dec'd was presented by Hopkins Wildy, one of Execs., made Oath, and being proved by the oaths of John Payne & George Lite, Junr., was admitted to record and on Motion of the sd. Exec., it was granted probate.

Ordered that George Lite, George Lite, Junr., and Walter Armes & Richard Flint, or any three sworn bef. a Co. Magistrate to appraise the Estate of the sd. Nathaniel Wildy, dec'd, in money and return the report bef. the next Court and Hopkins Wildy, Exec., appear and make oath re: the inventory.

The suit by the Petition of William Hattaway, Platf., and Robert Gibson, Deft., on Motion of sd. Deft., is continued till next Court.

On the Presentment of the Grand Jury against Andrew Donalson & Mary, his wife, of Christ Church Parish, for not going to Church in one month. The consideration of the sd. Andrew's offense is referred, till the next Court but the Judgment is granted against the sd. Andrew for 5 shillings or 50 lbs. tobacco for the St. Mary's offense and that he pay the same to the Church Wardens at their next levy for the use of the poor.

Pg 17. On the Presentment of the Grand Jury against John Tully & Elizabeth, his wife, of Christ Church Parish, and for not going to Church one month, and being called and not appearing Judgment is granted to the Church Wardens against them for 10 shillings or 100 lbs. tobacco, for the use of the poor.

Presentment of the Grand Jury against Sarah Haines, of Christ Church Parish, continued to next Court.

Presentment of the Grand Jury against Matthew Bolton, of Christ Church Parish for not going to Church one month, and being called and not appearing Judgment is granted to the Church Wardens against them for 5 shillings or 50 lbs. tobacco, for the use of the poor.

Presentment of the Grand Jury against James Curtis, of Christ Church Parish for not going to Church one month, and being called and not appearing Judgment is granted to the Church Wardens against them for 5 shillings or 50 lbs. tobacco, for the use of the poor.

Presentment of the Grand Jury against John Morris, of Christ Church Parish for not going to Church one month, and being called and not appearing Judgment is granted to the Church Wardens against them for 5 shillings or 50 lbs. tobacco, for the use of the poor.

Presentment of the Grand Jury against Bridget Spexton, of St. Mary's, White Chappel Parish, a Motion of special Imparlance is granted her till next Court.

Presentment of the Grand Jury against Ann Bam, of St. Mary's, White Chappel Parish, not appearing, it is Ordered she be taken into custody till she gives security for her appearance at next Court.

Presentment of the Grand Jury against Katherine Read, of St. Mary's, White Chappel Parish, for not going to Church one month and on hearing from her; dismissed.

Motion on continuance betw. David Ball, Pltf., and George Heale, Deft., is continued till next Court on Pltf.'s Motion & costs.

Attachment obtained by Thomas Edwards against the Estate of Edward Johnson is continued till next Court.

Motion in case betw. David Ball, Pltf., and George Heale, Deft., is continued till next Court on Pltf.'s Motion and costs.

The action of trespass betw. Thomas Wells, Pltf., and James Mungo, Deft., for £5 damages is dismissed, but the sd. Deft., is to pay the costs.

In action of trespass & assault & battery betw, John Veldon, Pltf., and James Chelton & Shaw Dailey, Defts., for £5 damages & James Chelton not being arrested nor appearance, on the Motion of the sd. Pltf., an ats. Copias is awarded him against the sd. James returnable at next Court and on Motion of the sd. Dayley, this cause is continued till next Court.

In the Motion upon the case betw. John Buckles, Pltf., and Henry Boatman, Deft., for 335 lbs. tobacco due by account, the sd. Deft. pleaded and the Pltf. joined issue with issue being by the sd. parties referred to the Court for trial, the Pltf. & Deft., were fully heard and it is considered that the sd. Pltf. recover against the sd. Deft., 35 lbs. tobacco, costs & attorney fees.

Ordered that the Court be adjourned till the 2nd Wednesday in July next.   At a Court for Lancaster Co. on Wedn. 8 July 1730. Present: William Ball, Thomas Carter, George Heale, Charles Carter, James Ball, William Ball, Junr., Henry Fleet, Hugh Brent, Nicholas Martin, John Selden; Gent., Justices.

Pg 18. Letter of Attorney from Mrs. Martha Corbin to Mr. Charles Burges & Thomas Edwards was proved in Court by the oaths of William Fleet & John Green to be the act & deed of the sd. Martha and admitted to record.

Thomas Edwards, Att., of Mrs. Martha Corbin freely gave her Right of Dower in 740 a. of land in St. Mary's White Chappel Parish & appurtenances sold by her husband, Col. Gawin Corbin, to James Ball, gent., to which is on the Motion of the sd. James, was admitted to record.

Petition of John Cornelius against the Estate of Capt. Adam Graves, dec'd, in the hands of Capt. John Graves for £27.10.0 set forth in the sd. Petition and a hearing of the parties is projected.

Petition of Charles Chelton & Elizabeth, his wife, , late widow of Richard Doggett, against George Doggett, Exec., of the Will of Richard Doggett, is continued to next Court.

Petition of Job Wildy [Wildey?] against Hopkins Wildy. Exec., of Nathaniel Wildy, dec'd, for £5.10.3 due from the Estate by amount the parties being fully heard, and the sd. Job making Oath to his account, Judgment is granted him on the same for 40 shillings & 5 pence & costs of the Estate of the afsd. Nathaniel in the hands if his sd, Exec.

The appraisement of the Estate of Nathaniel Wildy, dec'd, was returned and Hopkins Wildy, his Exec., making Oath thereto according to his subscription on the Inventory; Ordered recorded.

Ordered that John Stepto, Junr., be summoned to next Court to answer the complaint of Catherine Cusly [?] against him.

Margaret Mohon, Orphan of Timothy Mohon, dec'd, by this Court is bound to Brian Phillips, till she attains the age or 18 years, the sd. Brian is to teach her to read, knit, & spin and to find & allow her sufficient diet, lodging, & apparel & at the expiration of her forthwith to pay her as is appointed for servants by Indenture & Custom.

The Suite in Chancery betw. George Heale, Gent., for & in behalf of his daughters, Sarah Heale, Catherine Heale & Ann Heale, Complts., & Charles Burges, Gent., and Frances, his wife, Admin., with the Will annexed of the goods & un-administered of William Fox, Gent., dec'd, Defts., in continued till next Court.

The consideration of the Caveat entered by Giles Robinson, against Joseph Cotes & Elizabeth, his wife, or either of their obtaining Letters of Admin., of the goods, rights & credits of George Robinson, dec'd, is continued till next Court on the sd. Gile's Motion & costs.

The suit by Petition betw. William Hattaway, Pltf., and Robert Gibson, Deft., for the sd. Pltf.'s part of the Estate of Francis Hattaway, dec'd, in the hands of the Defts., as in the sd. petition is set forth, is dismissed.

On the Presentment of the Grand Jury against Andrew Donalson & Mary, they having heard & considered the sd. Andrew's excuse, Judgment is granted to the Church Wardens of the afsd. Parish for 5 shillings or 50 lbs. of tobacco for the sd. offence, and to be used for the poor, with costs & attorney fees.

The Presentment against Sarah Haines of Christ Church Parish for not going to Church one month and on hearing Sarah's excuse, dismissed.

Presentment against Bridget Spexton, of St. Mary's White Chappel Parish, is continued to next Court.

30

The Presentment against Ann Bam, of St, Mary's White Chappel Parish for having a bastard child, the sd. Ann being removed out of this Co.; dismissed.

The action of detinue betw. David Ball, Pltf., and George Heale, Deft., is continued till next Court on Defts. Motion & costs.

In the action of trespass & assault & battery betw. John Velden, Pltf., and James Chelton & Shaw [?] Dayley, Defts., for £5 damages, the Deft. Chelton not being yet arrested nor appearing at his call, on the Motion of the Pltf., a Capias is awarded him against the sd. Chelton, returnable to next Court.

Pg 19. Attachment obtained by Thomas Edwards against the estate of Edward Johnson, which was served on one feather bed & furniture, 4 chairs, a chest, 8 pieces of earthen ware, a iron pot & pot hooks, tub, 9 pieces of meat, 2 sows, 3 pigs, a pail, piggon, sifter, a barrel & half of corn, bushel of wheat, the sd. Thomas made Oath that 1,430 lbs. of tobacco was justly due to him from the sd. Edward by obligation under his hand & seal. And, it is Ordered that unless the goods afsd. shall be replevied as Law directs, that they be sold & disposed of for & towards satisfaction of this Judgment. And, the attachment be continued till next Court.

Ordered that the Court be adjourned till the 2nd Wednesday in August next. At a Court for Lancaster Co. on Mon. 20 July 1730, for examination of Thomas Turner & Mary, his wife. Present: William Ball, Thomas Carter, George Heale, Edwin Conway, William Ball, Junr., Henry Fleet, Hugh Brent, Nicholas Martin, John Selden; Gent., Justices.

Thomas Turner & his wife, Mary, charged with the felonious taking of sundry good of George Davenport of Richmond Co., VA. Ignatious Shereman & James May of Middlesex Co, VA, and a horse belonging to James Ball, Gent., of this Co., who being brought to the bar in Court subscribed their confession. Thomas Turner confessed that the goods hereafter mentioned by his wife, belonged to the afsd. Davenport were brought to him on the night of the 2nd day of this instant in the woods near Rose's old field and that she told him she got them from the afsd. Davenport. On the night of the 2nd day of June last, he did brake open the dwelling house of the afsd. Ignatious Shereman in Middlesex Co. afsd, and took from the house a cap and a bag which were found upon him. Also, a moodier[?] in gold, which he passed away to Patrick Dunn, of Westmoreland Co., VA, and several other things which he hid in the woods near the sd. Sherman's house & has since discovered to the sd. Shereman. That on the 5th

day of June afsd., he stole from the house of the afsd., Ann Maya, in Middlesex
Co. afsd., a Virginia cloth vest, a pr. of leather breeches, a pr. of shoes & a pr.
of garters, which were found upon him and some other goods which he hid in
the woods near the sd. Maya's house & has since discovered. And that on the
9th of this instant a little bef. day, he did take the horse afsd. out of the sd. James
Ball's pasture, which horse was found upon him.

Mary Turner for herself confessed that she took the side saddle & saddle cloth,
15 yrds. of clammy[?], table cloth, a mortar & pestle, meal sifter, pr. of shears,
dram glass & fork, produced in Court, by the afsd. George Davenport, out of
the sd. George's house on the night of the 2nd day this instant. The doors of the
sd. house being open and that her husband was not in the house but waited at a
tobacco house upon the plantation to assist her in carrying the sd. goods away.
That on the night of the 5th of July afsd., she did take out of the house of Ann
Maya in Middlesex Co., VA, afsd., a woman's gown, which was found upon
her, also several other things which she left behind her and that she opened the
door of the sd. house by the latch & went in at the window of one of the inner
rooms of the sd. house to get these things. And, that she was waiting under the
fours of Capt. James Ball's pasture the night her husband took the afsd. horse,
but did not help to catch him. Signed: Mary Turner, made here mark.

Pg. 20. Whereupon, the sd. George Davenport, Ignatious Shereman, James
Maya, and James Ball, & Henry Still & James Ball & James Steward, the
witnesses against the sd. prisoners were sworn & examined & their depositions
taken in Court testimony with the afsd. confession. It was the opinion of the
Court that the sd. Thomas Turner & Mary, his wife ought to be tried for the afsd.
facts at the General Court, and is Ordered that they return to the Co. Goal and be
thence removed to the public Goal in Williamsburg, as the law directs.

George Davenport, of North Farnham Parish, Richmond Co., Va., planter,
Ignatious Shereman, & James Maya, of Christ Church Parish in Middlesex Co.,
planters, James Ball, Gent. & Henry Still & James Steward of St. Mary's, White
Chappel Parish, came to Court & ackn. themselves indebted to the Court, in the
sum of £20 to be levied upon their several goods & chattels, lands and
tenements under condition that they severally make their personal appearances
at the next General Court on the 4th day at the trial of Thomas Turner & Mary,
his wife, then & there to give their evidence in behalf of the Court against the sd.
Thomas Turner & Mary Turner, his wife.

At Court for Lancaster Co. on Wednesday, 12 Aug 1730. Present: William Ball, Thomas Carter, George Heale, James Ball, Charles Burges, William Ball, Junr., Nicholas Martin; Gent., Justices.

The additional Inventory of the Estate of Elizabeth Pasquet, dec'd, was returned and Ordered to be recorded.

James Mumford came into Court and voluntarily ackn. his writing to John Wale for services which was admitted to record.

Upon the Complaint of Catherine Cristy, a servant girl, belonging to John Stepto, Junr., against her sd. master for beating & abusing her & refused to give her learning or to provide for her by law. The sd. parties were heard and it was considered that the sd. Catherine return to her sd. master's services and that he was to treat her better and forthwith teach her & provide for her and it was Ordered that he pay the Court costs.

The Petition by Charles Chelton & Elizabeth, his wife, late widow of Richard Dogget, dec'd, against George Dogget, Exec. of the Will of the afsd. Richard Dogget for the dower of lands for sd. Elizabeth & for her part of the rest of the Estate; but neither party appeared; dismissed.

In Chancery, betw. George Heale, Gent., for & in behalf of his daughters, Sarah Heale, Catherine Heale & Ann Heale, Complt., and Charles Burges, Gent., & Frances, his wife, and Parish Gardiner & Frances, his wife, Admin. of the Will annexed to the goods un-administered of William Fox, Gent., dec'd. On Motion of the sd. Complt., to amend his bill, but he is to pay and time, till next Court.

Entered by Giles Robinson & Joseph Cates & Elizabeth, his wife, or either of their containing Letters of Admin, of the goods & credits of George Robinson, dec'd. The sd. Joseph & Elizabeth renounced their right to same and the sd. Giles has leave to prove the non-cupative Will of the dec'd & to take out Letters of Admin., if he sees fit.

The Presentment of Bridget Spexton, of St. Mary's White Chappel Parish is continued till the next Court due to Tarpley being absent.

The Detinue betw. David Ball, Pltf., and George Heale, Gent., Deft., is continued to next Court

Pg. 21. The attachment obtained by Thomas Edwards against. the Estate of David Johnson is continued to next Court.

In the action of trespass, assault & battery, betw. John Velden, Pltf., and James Chelton & Shaw Bailey, Defts. The sd. James Chelton being arrested offered to appear by his attorney and to give special bail to the Court against him in this cause. But confessing, he was a minor under the age of 21 years, it was the opinion of the Court that he ought not to appear, except by his Guardian, which he refusing to do & no bail bond being returned. Judgment was granted to the sd. Pltf., against the sd. James Chelton. And, Henry Fleet, Junr., Gent., Co . Sheriff for what shall appear to be justly due to the sd. Pltf. at the next Court until the sd. James shall then appear as afsd. & answer this and on the Motion of the deft., Shaw Bailey, a Special imparlance is granted him till next Court.

In the suit in Chancery betw. William Chelton, Stephen Chelton, Thomas Purcell, & Elizabeth, his wife, & George Chelton, son of Benony Chelton, by the afsd. Benony Chelton, his next friend, William Chelton, son of the afsd. William Chelton, by his sd. father & next friend & George Purcell & Judith Purcell, son & daughter of the sd. Thomas Purcell & Elizabeth, his wife, by their sd. father & next friend, Complts., and Charles Smith, Clk., & Elizabeth, his wife, Exec. of the last Will of George Chelton, dec'd, Defts., is given to the Defts., till next Court.

Conditional Judgment this day granted to John Velden against James Chelton, Junr., & Henry Fleet, Junr., Gent., Co. Sheriff , for £5 on the Motion of the sd. Henry an attachment is awarded him against the Estate of the sd. James for the sd. money & costs returnable to the next Court for Judgment.

Ordered by the Court be adjourned till the 2nd Wednesday in Sept. next. At a Court for Lancaster Co. on Wednesday, the 14th of Oct, 1730. Present: William Ball, Thomas Carter, George Heale, Edwin Conway, Hugh Brent, Nicholas Martin, Henry Fleet; Gent., Justices.

Ordered that the Co. Sheriff summon at least 24 Freeholders of this Co., inhabitants, to appear at next Court that out of them a grand jury may be then Impaneled & sworn to make an inquiry into the Breach of the Penal Laws and to present the offenders.

William Ball, Junr., Gent., producing a Commission to be Co. Sheriff took the Oaths and subscribed the test and had the Oath of Co. High Sheriff administered to him.

34

A Bond from William Ball, Junr., William Ball, and James Ball, Gent., to the King for £1,000 in Court ackn. by William Ball, Junr., William Ball, and James Ball, Gent.; Ordered to record.

Present: James Ball, Gent.

On hearing the Complt. of Jane Hall in behalf of her bastard child, Caleb Hall, against Andrew Donaldson. It is opinion of the Court that the Judgment by which the sd. Caleb is bound is void. But, in consideration of sd. Andrew has taken care of him ever since he was born. It is Ordered that the sd. Caleb be now bound to the sd. Andrew till he arrives at 21 years of age.

Caleb Hall, a bastard child, is by the Court bound to Andrew Donalson till he attains the age of 21 years. The sd. Andrew is to teach him to read & write & to find and allow him sufficient & cleanly diet, lodging and apparel, and at the expiration of his [can't read] to pay him as appointed for servants by Indenture or Custom.

Pg 22. On the Motion of Andrew Donalson, he is admitted to take the examination of witnesses concerning the age of Caleb Hall, a bastard Child bef. a Justice of Peace, giving notice thereof to Jane Hall, mother of the sd. Caleb as returning his proceeding herein to next Court.

Letter of Attorney from Robert Thompson to Samuel Hallurin was proved in open Court, the Oaths of Job Wildy & Charles Cox, witnesses hereto and admitted to record.

Thomas Kirk, orphan of Thomas Kirk of this Co., dec'd, aged 9 years, the 1st of this Instant, on a prayer of his mother, is by the Court bound to Elias Loury till he attain the age of 21 years. The sd. Elias is to teach him to read & write & the trade of carpenter, and to find & allow him sufficient diet, lodging & apparel and at the expiration to pay him as is appointed for servants by Indenture or custom.

On the attachment obtained by George Payne against the Estate of Thomas Webster for 2,700 lbs. of tobacco, which attachment was served on a servant man named Samuel Hambleton, the sd. George made oath to his debt whereupon Judgment is granted him for the same & costs, and it is Ordered that unless the servant afsd. shall be repleved , that to he be sold & disposed of towards satisfaction of his Judgment in the same manner, as goods taken in execution by a writ of fiere facias. And, that the attachment be continued till next Court.

The Sheriff having made proclamation that the Court was about to lay the Co. Levy, they proceeded accordingly. Lancaster Co. – Paid in Tobacco.

Robert Carter, Esqr., for keeping the Public Levy one year – 1,400 lbs.; John Payne for cleaning the Court House & other services – 800 lbs. ; John Tarpley, Junr., Gent, Co. Attorney – 1,000 lbs.; Thomas Edwards, Clk. of the Court for one year service – 1,000 lbs.; Thomas Edwards doe his attendance & on one criminal trial – 200 lbs.; Maj. Henry Fleet for Coroner's Inquests & the Constable's fee – 316 lbs.; Col. William Ball for Coroner's Inquests 266 lbs.; Henry Stonum[?] Constable for summoning the juries – 100 lbs.; Henry Stonum[?] – for viewing tobacco in his Precinct – 220 lbs.; Henry Stonum[?] – for levies over-charged last year – 37 lbs.; George Dogget, Constable, for viewing tobacco in his Precinct – 188 lbs.; Thomas Hunton for the same – 220; Edward Sanders for the same – 96 lbs.; John Bailey for the same – 186 lbs; George Yerby for the same – 299 lbs.; Thomas Flint for the same – 279; Thomas Flint for levies over charges last year – 37 lbs.; Capt. Wm. Ball, Co. Sheriff for one year service – 1,000 lbs.; Capt. Henry Fleet, late Co. Sheriff on his attendance – 900 lbs.; a balance due to the sd. late Sheriff out last yrs. levy – 67 lbs.; Joseph Carter for 5 levies over charged last year – 76 lbs.; Cash & Salary at 18 percent – 1,563 lbs.; To the Public Levy – 15,235 lbs. Total – 25,485 lbs. tobacco. Credit – 1,488 tithables re: tobacco – 25,296 lbs. & a balance due the Sheriff next year – 189 lbs. Total – 25,485 lbs.

Pg. 23. The Co. Levy for the present year – 1,730 lbs. amounting to 71 lbs. of tobacco per poll. It is Ordered that the Co. Sheriff collect so much of every tithable person in the Co. and pay the same to the Creditors in this Co., and Co. Levy as the same in proportioned.

Ordered that Robert Carter, Esqr., do keep the Public Ferry over Corrotomon River in this Co. the ensuing year and that he be paid for the same as usual.

Ordered that John Pyne do find this Court with water & candles & clean the Court House for the ensuing year and that he be paid for the same as usual.

William Ball, Junr., Gent., Co. Sheriff acquainting this Court that this Co. Prison was insufficient & not in the repair directed by Law. Ordered that a substantial plank floor be forthwith laid in the Prison & iron bars put cross the chimney thereof as the Law directs and that James Ball & Charles Burges, Gent., do agree workmen to do the same and also to mend the Court House windows & repair the doors so as they will open & shut and that the Charge thereof be paid in the next County Levy.

Ordered by the Court be adjourned till the 2nd Wednesday in Nov. next. At a Court for Lancaster Co. on Wednesday, the 11th of Nov., 1730. Present: William Ball, Thomas Carter, James Ball, Edwin Conway, Hugh Brent, Charles Carter; Gent., Justices.

The last Will of Daniel Feagin, dec'd, was presented in Court by Lazarus Sutton, Exec., who made Oath thereto and being Proved by the Oath of Aaron Taylor, William Taylor, witnesses, it is admitted to record and a Motion it was Probated.

Ordered that Moses Taylor, Benjamin Taylor, Charles Craven and James Taylor or any three of them being sworn before a Co. Justice, and to meet & appraise the Estate of Daniel Feagin, dec'd in money & make a Return of their proceedings & Lazarus Sutton, Exec., to appear with the Will & make Oath to the Inventory at the next Court.

On Petition of Henry Lawson for leave to turn the Main Road thru his plantation from Christ Church to Maj. Fleet's . Thomas Lee, Nicholas Martin & William Martin, Gent., are appointed to view the place where the sd. Lawson wants thru the sd. road & report their opinion of the convenience or inconvenience thereof at the next Court.

Ordered that Mary Rogers, widow, be summoned to the next Court to answer the Petition of Gilbert Crosoell[?] & Ellen, his wife, against her.

William Cottrill, a servant man belonging to Joseph Ball, Esqr., came into Court & voluntarily agreed to serve his sd. Master or assigns four years from the 9th day Sept. last, being something more than his Indentured time in consideration of the sd. Ball's ending purchased him from his former Master.

Pg 24. In the suit between George Payne, Pltf., and Thomas Webster, Deft., by attachment, the Sheriff made a return of what is in his hands towards satisfaction of the Judgment granted to the sd. Pltf. in his cause, the same was Ordered to be recorded as follows: I have made of the [can't read] attached by George Payne belonging to the Estate of Thomas Webster 1,250 lbs. tobacco. And the sd. Pltf., failing further to prosecute the sd. attachment is discontinued.

A grand jury for the body of this Co., being this day impaneled and appointed George Payne, foreman, who was sworn and then the rest, to wit: Tobias Horton, Matthew Machan, William Chelton, Giles Robinson, Henry Newby, Richard Mullis, Peter Rivere, Junr., George Dogget, John Buckley, Thos. Young, George Flower, Peter Bailey, George Light, Christopher Kirk, John

Hendley, William Catlet, James Webb, Thos. Hubbard, George Brent, John Mott, Junr., Joseph Stephens & Wm. Dogget, after having their charge, withdrew & after some time, returned and gave their Presentments and were discharged. The Presentments were Ordered to be recorded, being as follows: Lancaster – Nov 11, 1730. We, the grand jury make our Presentments as follows: Ann Bamer of White Chappel Parish for having a bastard child within 5 months last past. William Gready & Rachel, his wife, of Wiccocomoco Parish for not going to Church in one month last past. Richard Jackson of Christ Church Parish for filling drink w/o license when 6 months past. Sarah Haines of Christ Church Parish for not going to Church in one month last past. Elizabeth Currell, of Christ Church Parish past for not going to the sd. Parish Church in two months last past. Elizabeth Taylor of White Chappel Parish for closing the highway by falling a tree across it within 6 months past.

Ordered that the Deputy Attorney for the Co. forthwith prepare a Presentment against Richard Jackson of this Co. for retailing liquor w/o license.

Ordered that Ann Bamer & Elizabeth Taylor of St. Mary's White Chappell Parish & William Grady and Rachel, his wife, of Wiccocomoco Parish & Sarah Haines & Elizabeth Currell, Christ Church Parish to be summoned to the next Court to answer the Presentment.

In the suit betw. Thomas Edwards, Pltf., and Edward Johnson, Deft., by attachment& the Sheriff making return it in the hands towards satisfaction of the Judgment granted to the sd. Pltf., it is Ordered to be recorded being as follows: I have made of the goods attached of the Estate of Edward Johnson 908 lbs. tobacco, which is ready to be paid to the within Thomas Edwards per Hen. Fleet, Junr., and the Pltf. failing further to prosecute the sd. attachment discontinued.

Motion of debt betw. Benjamin Neale, Pltf., and Lawrence Bleed, Deft.; dismissed.

Motion of debt betw. Benjamin Neale, Pltf., and Lawrence Bleed, Deft.; dismissed.

Motion upon the case betw. William Ballendine, Pltf., and William Jarvis, Deft; dismissed.

Motion upon the case betw. Thomas Scott, Pltf., and Henry Lawson, Deft; dismissed.

38

Motion upon the case betw. Phillip Fisher, Pltf., and William Chelton, son of William Chilton, Deft., for £50 damages; dismissed.

Motion upon the case betw. Thomas Edwards, Pltf., and William Morgan, Deft., for 478 lbs. tobacco due by the amount the Deft. confessed Judgment whereupon it is considered that he forthwith pay unto the sd. Pltf., the sd. 428 lbs. tobacco, with costs.

In Chancery betw. George Heale, Gent., for & in behalf of his daughters, Sarah Heale, Catherine Heale & Ann Heale, Complts., against Charles Burges, Gent., & Frances, his wife, and Parish Gardiner & Frances, his wife, Admin., with the Will annexed the goods un-administered of William Fox, Gent., dec'd, Defts., the sd. defendants this day put in a [can't read] to sd. Complts. bill which being joined the same is referred till the next Court.

Pg 25. Allison Price[?], orphan of Richard Price, late of this Co., dec'd, aged 12 years the 26th of March last, on her prayer by the Court bound to Nicholas Tarkelson, till she attains the age of 18 years, the sd. Nicholas is to teach her to read & sew, knit & spin, and to find & allow her sufficient [can't read] diet, lodging & apparel & at her expiration of her servitude to pay her as is appointed for servants by Indenture or custom.

Presentment against Bridget Spexton, of St, Mary's White Chappel Parish is continued to next Court.

The case betw. Charles Cox, Pltf., and Hopkins Wildy, Deft., is dismissed.

In the Detinue betw. David Ball, Pltf., and George Heale, Deft., the Co. Sheriff being of kin to the patches by which the array was challenged. Ordered that Henry Fleet, Gent., a Co. Coroner summoned a jury to appear at the next Court by the issue joined in this cause and that the same be continued.

On the case betw. David Ball, Pltf., and George Heale, Deft., the sd. Pltf. this day put in a demurred to the sd. Deft's pleasure and this cause which was joined & referred till the next Court for argument.

In the suit in Chancery betw. William Chelton & Stephen Chelton, Thomas Purcel & Elizabeth, his wife, George Chelton, son of Benoni Chelton, by the afsd. Benoni his next friend, William Chelton, son of the afsd. William Chelton by his sd. father & next friend, and George Purcell & Judith Purcell for the daughter of the sd. Thomas Purcell & Elizabeth, his wife, by their father & next friend, Complts., and Charles Smith, Clk., & Elizabeth, his wife, Exec. of the Will of George Chelton, dec'd, Defts., on the Motion of the sd. Complts. leave is given them to amend their Bill in this cause and time is given the sd. Defts. till next Court.

The Motion of James Chelton, John Tarpley, Junr., Gent., is admitted his Guardian to defend a suit continued against him by Jno. Velden.

In the action of trespass & assault & battery betw. John Velden, Pltf., and James Chelton, Shaw Dayley, Defts., the sd. Deft. pleaded and the Pltfs. joined issue whereupon it is Ordered that the trial of the sd. offense be referred till next Court.

On the Motion of Andrew Donalson, the evidence taken bef. a Justice concerning Caleb Hall's age is admitted to record.

Robert Tobin, a servant, belonging to Philip Fisher of this Co., came into Court & voluntarily agreed to serve his Master 2 years after his Indenture time is expired in consideration that his sd. Master is not to employ him in tending tobacco by water in boats or [can't read].

The Attachment obtained by James Ball, Gent., against the Estate of Thomas Webster, which attachment came too late to ye Sheriff's hands to execute.

William Dogget being appointed a Constable in Christ Church Parish, in this Co., in the room of George Dogget, the sd. William took the Oath to the Government and subscribed the cost and the Oath of a Constable administered to him.

Ordered that the Sheriff & the respective Co. Constables for which he take such sufficient horse as they shall see fit & go in search of thee Negro slaves belonging to French Mason of Stafford Co., VA, who lie lurking & doing mischief to the inhabitants of the Co. & in case they shall apprehend the sd. slaves, they secure them till further proceeding be had against them.

Ordered by the Court be adjourned till the 2nd Wednesday in December. next. At a Court for Lancaster Co. on Wednesday, the 9th of Dec, 1730. Present: William Ball, Thomas Carter, George Heale, Edwin Conway, Charles Burges, John Selden, Nicholas Martin, Henry Fleet; Gent., Justices.

Pg. 26. The appraisement of the Estate of Daniel Feagins. dec'd, was returned and Lazarus Sutton, his Exec., making Oath thereto according to his subscription on the Inventory; Ordered recorded.

Mary Mc Coy, orphan of Hugh Mc Coy, dec'd, is by the Court bound to John Callahan & Mary, his wife, till she attains the age of 18 years, her sd. Master & [can't read] to teach her to read, sew, knit, and spin, & to find & allow her sufficient & dyet, lodging, & apparel and at the expiration of her servitude to pay her as is appointed for servants by Indenture or customs and it is agreed by the sd. John Callahan & Mary, his wife, that in case of their death before the sd. Mary Mc Coy shall have served her full time as afsd.; that she be free.

In the action of Detinue betw. David Ball, Pltf., and George Heale, Deft., the Deft. having heretofore pleaded and the Pltf. joined the issue in this case Joseph Carter, Henry Towles, Thomas Young, Richard Flint, Robert Newman, Benjamin George, Junr., William Chelton, Henry Lawson, Robert Biscoe, Daniel Stephens, Bryan Pullen, Francisco Frizell, were impaneled and sworn to try the issue, who brining in a Special Verdict on the Motion of the sd. Pltf, it is admitted to record and it is Ordered that the arguments be referred till the next Court.

The presentment of Ann Bamer of St. Mary's Chappel Parish in sd. Co., for having a bastard child, the sd. subject appeared, confessed but refused to pay the fine, whereupon it was Ordered that she receive on her bare back at the public whipping post 25 lashes, well laid on and be then discharged.

The Grand Jury against Elizabeth Taylor of St. Mary's White Chappel Parish in sd. Co., interfering of the highway by felling a tree across it and on hearing her defense was dismissed.

The Grand Jury against William Grady & Rachel, his wife, of Wiccocomoco Parish, sd. Co., for not going to Church one month, and the William & Rachel not appearing, Judgment is granted to the Church Wardens for 10 shillings or 100 lbs. tobacco, and the sd. William is Ordered to pay for the use of the poor in the afsd. Parish, with costs & attorney's fee.

The Grand Jury against Sarah Haines, of Christ Church Parish, of sd. Co., for not going to Church one month, and not appearing, Judgment is granted to the Church Wardens for 5 shillings or 50 lbs. tobacco, and her husband, James, is Ordered to pay for the use of the poor in the afsd. Parish, costs & attorney's fee.

The Grand Jury against Elizabeth Currell, of Christ Church Parish, of sd. Co., for not going to Church two months, and not appearing, Judgment is granted to the Church Wardens for 10 shillings or 100 lbs. tobacco, and her husband, Abraham, is Ordered to pay for the use of the poor in the afsd. Parish, with costs & attorney's fee.

The Grand Jury against Bridget Spexton, of St. Mary's White Chappel Parish is referred till next Court for consideration of her pleas this day put in and it is agreed that the testimony of Ann Spexton taken bef. Thomas Carter, Edwin Conway & John Selden, Gent., returned to next Court.

Upon the case betw. David Ball, Pltf., and George Heale, Deft., is continued till next Court. In suit in Chancery betw. George Heale, Gent., for & in behalf his daus. Sarah Heale, Catherine Heale & Ann Heale, Complt., and Charles Burges, Gent., Frances, his wife, & Parish Gardiner & Frances, his wife, Admins., and the Will annexed, of the unadministered of William Fox, Gent., dec'd, Defts., is continued till next Court.

In the suit in Chancery betw. William Chelton & Stephen Chelton, Thomas Purcell & Elizabeth, his wife, George Chelton, son of Benony Chelton by the afsd. Benony Chelton, his next friend, William Chelton, son of the sd. William Chelton, by his sd. father, & next friend, and George Purcell & Judith Purcell, son & dau. of the sd. Thomas Purcell & Elizabeth, his wife, by their sd. father & next friend, Complts., and Charles Smith, Clk., & Elizabeth, his wife, Execs. of the last Will of George Chelton, dec'd, the Deft, Charles this day put in & made oath to his answer in this case and time was given to the sd. Complt. to consider it. But, for so much as sd. Deft. Eliza did not appear on sd. Motion of the sd. Complt., an attachment is awarded thou against the body of the sd. Elizabeth for her personal appearance to answer at next Court.

Pg 27. The action of trespass, assault & battery betw. John Velden, Pltf., and James Chelton & Steve Dayley, Defts. is continued.

In the action upon the case betw. Thomas Poolen[Pullen?], Pltf., and William Robinson, Deft., for £6.13.7, the sd. Deft., being returned but not appearing on the Motion of the Pltf., a Capias is awarded him against the sd. Deft., returnable to the next Court.

The action upon the case betw. Vallentine Bell, Pltf., and William Cone for 538 lbs. of tobacco due by amount is dismissed.

42

In the Motion upon the case betw. Vallentine Bell, Pltf., and Robert Scofield on the Motion of the sd. Deft., an imparlance is granted him till next Court.

Catherine Quirk having attended 2 days as a witness for George Heale against him by David Ball. It is Ordered that sd. George pay her for attendance & costs, etc.

Elizabeth Higgins making oath that she attended 11 days as a witness for David Ball in suit against George Heale. It is Ordered that sd. Ball pay her for attendance & costs, etc.

Mary Frizzell making oath that she attended 4 days as a witness for David Ball in suit against George Heale. It is Ordered that sd. Ball pay her for attendance & costs, etc.

In the suit betw. Gilbert Croswell & Ellen, his wife, Pltfs., and Mary Rogers, Widow, Deft., by petition for a servant's freedom. The parties were heard & the Plts., are to recover against the Deft., 15 bushels of Indian corn & 40 shillings for goods & costs & attorney's fees.

Thomas Lee, Nicholas Martin and Wm. Martin, Gent., having returned their report on the view of the road moved for & by Henry Lawson. It is Ordered that the consideration of the sd. Report be referred to the next Court.

Ordered by the Court be adjourned till the 2nd Wednesday in January. next. At a Court for Lancaster Co. on Wednesday, the 12th of January 1730. Present: William Ball, James Ball, Charles Burges, John Selden, Nicholas Martin; Gent., Justices.

Ellis Howard, a servant belonging to James Stott of this Co., came to Court and voluntarily agreed to [can't read] his sd. Master from the payment for her freedom dues in consideration of his having purchased her from her former Master at her [can't read].

The petition of William Clatton against John Wilcox concerning Mariam Wilcox, her Estate is [can't read].

The action of Detinue betw. David Ball, Pltf., and George Heale, Deft., is continued till next Court with costs.

The Grand Jury against Bridget Spexton of St. Mary's White Chappel Parish is continued till next Court. It is Ordered that the testimony of the sd. Ann Spexton be then returned in this cause according to the last Court order.

The action on the case betw. David Ball, Pltf, and George Heale, Deft., is continued till the next Court at the Pltf.'s Motion & costs.

In the suit in Chancery betw. William Chelton & Stephen Chelton, Thomas Purcell & Elizabeth, his wife, George Chelton, son of Benony Chelton by the afsd. Benony Chelton, his next friend, William Chelton, son of the sd. William Chelton, by his sd. father, & next friend, and George Purcell & Judith Purcell, son & dau. of the sd. Thomas Purcell & Elizabeth, his wife, by their sd. father & next friend, Complts., and Charles Smith, Clk., & Elizabeth, his wife, Exec. of the last Will of George Chelton, dec'd, the Deft, is continued till next Court at the Depts.' Motion & costs.

Pg. 28. The action of trespass, assault & battery betw. John Velden, Pltf., and James Chelton & Mary Dailey, Deft.'s, is continued to next Court at the Deft.'s Motion & costs.

In the case betw. Thomas Poole, Pltf., and William Robinson, Deft., for £6.13.7, & not appearing on the Motion of the Pltf., Capias is awarded against the Deft. returnable to next Court.

Action on the case betw. Vallenhue [Vallentine]Bell, Pltf., & Robert Schofield, Deft., continued.

Suit in Chancery betw. George Heale, Gent., for & in behalf of his daughters Sarah Heale, Catherine Heale & Ann Heale, Complt., and Charles Burges, Gent., Frances, his wife, & Parish Gardiner & Frances, his wife, Admins., and the Will annexed, of the un-administered of William Fox, Gent., dec'd, Defts., is continued till next Court.

Petition of Henry Lawson for leave to turn the main road leading thru his plantation from Christ Church to Maj. Fleet's is dismissed the sd. Petition failing to prosecute the same.

William Martin, greatest creditor of Alexander Edgar late of the Co., dec'd, stated in Court that the sd. Edgar died with no Will, as far as he knows or believes, and on petition and security for his just & full Admin. of the Estate of

44

the sd. dec'd & certificate is granted.

Ordered that Thomas Thornton, William Stepto, Christopher Kirk & Thomas Pinckard, or any three after being first sworn to appraise the Estate of Alexander Edgar, dec'd in money and make a report to the next Court and William Martin, Admin. of the Estate made oath to the Inventory.

Motion of Henry Lawson leave is given him to set bars and great gates for wheel carriages and small gates for passengers on the main road that leads to his plantation from Christ Church to Maj. Fleet's.

Ordered by the Court be adjourned till the 2nd Wednesday in February next. At a Court for Lancaster Co. on Wednesday, the 10th of Feb 1730. Present: William Ball, James Ball, Edwin Conway, Charles Burges, John Selden, Nicholas Martin; Gent., Justices.

The appraisement of the Estate of Alexander Edgar, dec'd was returned and William Martin, Admin. made oath re: the Inventory; recorded.

The last Will of Frances Edwards, dec'd, was presented in Court by William Edwards, Exec., who made oath, proved by oaths of Henry Carter, Charles Chelton, & John Carter, witnesses, was admitted and on Motion of Exec., probate was approved.

Henry Carter, Thomas Yerby, William Stephens & George Brent, or any three, first sworn, met & appraised the Estate of Frances Edwards, dec'd in money and made report with William Edwards, Exec., appeared and made oath of the inventory.

Pg 29. In action of Detinue betw. David Ball, Pltf., and George Heale, Deft., the special verdict found in his cause at this Co. Court on 9 Dec last in these words, "We find that before so or the Pltf. had the Negro in the Declaration mentioned in his possession, the Pltf.'s wife asked the Deft. to give her the sd. Negro. The Deft. told her that he would not but said that he did not know but that he might buy her another, and that afterwards and bef. the sd. Pltf. had the sd. Negro in possession, the Pltf. asked the Deft. to give him the sd. Negro, but the Deft. told him he would not give her to him but lend her to him, and that afterwards the sd. Pltf. had the sd. Negro in his possession and so continued during the life of the sd. Pltf.'s wife, and that about 3 weeks bef. the sd. Pltf.'s wife's death, the Deft. sd. that wench (being the same in the declaration mentioned) will ruin my Negro fellow, and being asked what wench, replied the Negro wench I gave my daughter, Ellen, wife to sd Pltf. We find that after the death of the sd. Pltf.'s wife, the Deft. tool the sd. Negro woman & put her under his overseer where she died. We find by the evidence of Elizabeth Higgins that when the Deft., brought house, the sd. Negro woman he told the Pltf.'s wife to furnish her with clothes telling her she would have the most good of her and that she the sd. Elizabeth Higgens always reputed the sd. Negro woman belonged to the sd. Pltf.'s wife till she died, and that the sd. Pltf.'s wife gave charge to & overseer to be kind to the sd. Negro woman for that she was her Negro. We, find that the sd. Deft. offered the Pltf. that if he would swear he doth gave him or his wife the afsd. Negro woman, he would let him have her or the value of her without going to Law. If upon the whole, the Court shall be of opinion that the Law is with the Plft., then we find for the Pltf. damage £30 Sterling, if not, we find for the Deft." Signed: Joseph Carter, Foreman. And, was this day fully argued and the parties being deliberately heard on the matter of Law arising thereupon, the Court are of the opinion that the Law is with the Pltf. whereupon the Deft. offered to move in arrest of the Judgment to be given in the cause. But forasmuch as the Court were [can't read] to advise in this matter, the cause is continued, till next Court, and, it is Ordered that the sd. Deft. be then ready with his pleas in Arrest & his arguments thereon in case the Court shall determine to admit it.

John Wilcox came into Court & acknowledged his deed to Rawleigh Chinn, Gent., for & concerning 70 a. of land in St. Mary's White Chappel Parish, in this Co., together with the livery & Seizen, endorsed, his performance bond of the Covenants expressed; recorded.

Rawleigh Chinn, Gent., came into Court & Ackn. his deed to Martin Shearman & Ann, his wife, concerning 70 a. of land in St. Mary's White Chappel Parish, in this Co., recorded.

In Chancery betw. George Heale, Gent., for & in behalf of his daughters Sarah Heale, Catherine Heale & Ann Heale, Complt., and Charles Burges, Gent., Frances, his wife, & Parish Gardiner & Frances, his wife, Admins., and the Will annexed, of the un-administered of William Fox, Gent., dec'd, Defts. Wherein, the sd. Complt. by his bill sets forth that William Fox, Gent., dec'd, by his Will, dated 22 Mar 1717, did devise all such remaining part of his Estate, after the death of his wife, to whom he decided to use during her life, in the words – "It is my will that after the decease of my wife all my Estate shall be & remain unto my nephew, David Fox [except all the plate which I am possessed of and not herein bef. particularly bequeathed the sd. which sd. plate I hereby give & bequeath unto my wife Ann Fox and her heirs for ever] and the heirs of the

46

body lawfully begotten But if its shall so happen that my sd. nephew shall not
be alive nor have any such heirs as afsd. at the time of the decease of my wife,
that then is such case I give my sd. Estate after the death of my wife unto
Frances Fox & Frances Spelman & all the daughters of Capt. George Heale that
shall be alive at the time of my wife's decease and to their heirs to be equally
divided betw. them. And, the sd. testator of his Will … and appoint his sd. wife,
Ann Fox, Execx., and one William Payne, Gent., dec'd, Exec. And, further that
the afsd. William Payne departed life some years since and that the afsd. Ann
departed this life some time in the month of November last, and that David Fox
in the sd. Will died an infant in some short time after the testator during the life
of the afsd. Ann. And ye Orator further showeth that since the death of the
afsd. Ann and Charles Burges, Gent., who intermarried with the afsd. Frances
Fox, and one Parish Gardiner that intermarried the afsd. Frances Spelman have
obtained Letters of Admin with the Will annexed of the Estate of William Fox
and by virtue thereof have taken all or the greatest part of unto their possession
& further showeth that he had one daughter, named Sarah, which is young &
unmarried and one other daughter named Elizabeth, which is lately married to
our William Davenporte, of Richmond Co., VA, who were both at the time of
the making the Will of William Fox, dec'd, and who are mentioned in the sd.
Will and two other daughters named Catherine & Anne, who were born since
the death of the afsd. Testator, which daughters of ye Orator cousins have an
equal Right to the afsd. Frances Burges & Frances Gardiner to the remaining
part of the afsd. testator's Estate. But, by the afsd. Admins. or some of them
have reported and given out ye Orator's daughter's have nor any of them ought
to have by any construction of the Will of the afsd. Testator any part of the sd.
Testator's Estate and that they will keep & convert the same to their own use
which sd. sayings and actings of the sd. Admins. Your Orator conceives to be
contrary to equity and good conscience.

Pg 30. In tender consideration whereof and for usual as ye Orator can have no
relief in the premises unless by the assistance of this Court in equity where cases
of this nature are properly retainable to the end. Therefore, the sd. Admin. may
be compelled on their several oaths to set forth & discover whether the sd.
William Fox did not make such Will as afsd. and thereby devisors bequeath to
ye sd. Orator afsd. daughters a part of his Estate as afsd. and thereby devises &
bequeath to sd. Orator's afsd. daughters a part of his Estate as afsd., and what
the same accounted to or certified in and also full particular & direct answer to
all & singular the premises herein contained as if particularly here again
interrogated and that they, the sd. Admins. may be directed & compelled to pay

& deliver to ye Orator, the Estate due to his daughters Sarah, Catherine, & Ann, by the Will of the sd. William Fox for their use and also his coats hereby occasioned. May it please ye workings to grant unto ye Orator his most gracious Writ of Subpoena.

And, ye Orator as in duly bound shall ever pray & the sd. Defts at a Court held for this Co., on 11th Nov last past out in demurrer. The several demurrer of Charles Burges, Gent, one of the Defts. to the Bill of Complaint bill to be true in such manner & form as the same are therein set forth & alleged saith there is no matter or thing in the sd. Bill of Complaint contained good & sufficient in Law whereby to call this Deft., in [can't read] to this Court for the same but that there is good cause of demurrer there unto for that it appears by the Complt.'s own showing in the sd. Bill that the scope & end thereof is to have a discovery of the residuary Estate of William Fox in the Bill mentioned and to recover part thereof in behalf of his three younger daughters, Sarah born at the time of making the Will of the sd. William Fox and Catherine & Ann born since the sd. William's death by virtue of a clause in the sd. Will whereby the sd. William devised the residue of his Estate to his nephew, David Fox & the heirs of his body after his decease of his wife, to whom he devised the use thereof during her life, and in case his sd. nephew should not be alive nor have any such heirs as afsd. at the time of his wife's death then to Frances Fox, the Defts. wife & Frances Spelman & all the daughters of the sd. Complts. that should be alive at the time of his wife's death to be equally divided between them to which sd. matters & all other things in the sd. Bill contained, this Deft. does demur and for cause of demurrer showeth that it appears by the Complts. non showing that the property of the sd. residuary Estate was absolutely vested in the sd. David Fox and the remainder limited upon the contingency of his dying in the lifetime of the Testator's wife or without fine was void and if it were otherwise, the daughters of the Compt., who were in [can't read] at the time of making the Will & not the after born daughters could only take any thing by the sd. Will. And, the Complts. hath not set forth how many daughters he had living at the time of the death of the Testator's wife, who were born when the sd. Will was made. And these daughters are not parties to the sd. ill. And, also for that the sd. Bill runs in the sd. George Heale's own name and not in the names of his children. And, for that, the Complts. hath not set forth sufficient matter of equity to entitle him to any relief.

This Deft. therefore for all the sd. causes & for several other defects & manifest imperfections of the sd. Bill of Complaint doth demur. In law the bill abides the

48

Judgment of this Court whether he shall be enforced to make any other or further action thereunto and pray to be hence Dismissed with his reasonable costs in his behalf most wrongfully sustained. The Court joins the Demurrer afsd. Signed: Jos. Ball, Defts. Ge. Eskridge, Compltf. The Parties afsd. this day appeared to argue the matter of law arising herein and being fully [can't read] on both sides & makes deliberation had on the premises. It is the opinion of the Court that the Law is with the Defendants. And, it is decreed & Ordered that this suit be dismissed and that the sd. Complt. pay unto the sd. Deft. their costs hereby sustained together in one attorney's fee, from which decree the sd.

Appeal - Complts. prayed an appeal to the 9th of next General Court, which is granted him Thomas Edwards becoming his security to prosecute the same with effect.

Pg 31. George Heale, of St. Mary's White Chappel Parish, Gent., and Thomas Edwards, of Christ Church Parish, Lancaster Co., VA, came into Court and jointly & morally ackn. themselves indebted to Charles Burges, Gent., & Parish Gardiner in the sum of £20 to be levied upon their goods & chattels, lands and tenements under condition that the afsd. George Heale shall effectually prosecute an appeal this day granted from Judgment of this Court by his suit in Chancery against the Admins. of William Fox, Gent., dec'd, to the 9th day of the next General Court.

Ordered by the Court be adjourned till the 2nd Wednesday in March next. At a Court for Lancaster Co. on Wednesday, the 14th of April 1731[?]. Present: Thomas Carter, William Ball, James Ball, George Heale, Edwin Conway, Charles Burges, John Selden; Gent., Justices.

Dennis Couree came into Court & made oath that Dennis Couree, late of this Co., dec'd, died without making a Will, as far as he knows, and on his Petition and security obtained Letters of Admin. of the sd. decedent's Estate.

Joseph Heale, William Heale, George Payne & John Everet, or any three being first sworn were to appraise the afsd. Estate of Dennis Couree, in money and make a report of the Inventory & to appear at the next Co. Court.

Mary Brush, relict of Abel Brush, late of this Co., dec'd, and died without a Will, as far as she knows, and she made a Motion & gave security for obtaining Letters of Admin. for his Estate.

James Hains, George Yerby, John Wale and Tobias Horton, or any three, after being first sworn, met to appraise the Estate of Abel Bruch, dec'd, in money and to make a report and then appear at next Court re: the inventory.

The Indenture betw. Charles Ewell, orphan of Charles Ewell, late of this Co., dec'd, and Charles Burges, Merchant, whereby the sd. Ewell, binds himself as an apprentice of the sd. Charles Burges, till he attains 21 years of age in Court, which is approved by the Court.

Benjamin Brown came to Court and ackn. his deed to George Payne for & concerning 50 a. of land in Saint Mary's, White Chappel Parish, in Lancaster Co., which was recorded. And, Ann, the wife of Benjamin Brown also came to Court and freely ackn. her right of Dower in sd. 50 a. of land to sd. George Payne, which was recorded.

A Letter of Attorney from Edward Hayworth to Charles Burges, Merchant, was proved in open Court by the oath of Edward Loram[?] with John Broadkill[?], witness, and was recorded.

Pg 32. The appraisement of Frances Edwards, dec'd was returned and William Edwards, her Exec., making oath re: the Inventory; Ordered proved.

On the Petition of John Brooks & Frances, his wife, against Mary Brush, Admin. of the Estate of Abel Brush, dec'd, setting forth that the sd, Frances is entitled to 2/3rds of the Real & half the personal Estate of the afsd. Estate. The sd. Petitioner agreeing that the Ad minx. shall have the use of the housing belonging to the sd. dec'd & if fenced ground which includes the same for this year by consent of the sd. parties Hugh Brent, Nicholas Martin, & William Martin, Gent., are appointed to divide the real estate and to set apart her Dower thereof, as the law directs, and it is Ordered that the sd. Hugh Brent, Nicholas Martin, & William Martin, first set apart sufficient of the sd. personal estate to satisfy the debts of the dec'd, which is to be left in the hands of the Adminx., divide the remainder of the personal estate betw. the sd. parties and make a report of their whole proceedings in the premises of the next Court.

On the Petition of John Johnson against Hopkins Wildy, Exec., of the Will of Nathaniel Wildy, dec'd, for £2 due to the petitioner from the sd. Nathaniel in his life by account on hearing the parties & oath of ye petitioner to the afsd. audit, Judgment is granted him for a pair of spoon molds in the sd. amount mentioned and 30 shillings & costs of the Estate of the sd. testator in the hands of the sd. Exec.

Indenture betw. Benjamin Kelley, orphan of Charles Kelley, late of this Co., dec'd and Thomas George, carpenter, whereby the sd. Benjamin binds himself an apprentice to the sd. Thomas for 6 years was in open Court voluntarily ackn. by the sd. Benjamin to be his act & deed and approved of by the Court and admitted to record.

The action upon the case betw. Thomas Poole, Pltf., and William Robinson, Deft., for £6.13.7 due by note & amount being agreed; dismissed.

The suit betw. Ruth Sydnor, Pltf., and James Haynes, Defts., by petition for 200 lbs. tobacco due by account to the Thos. Austin and assigned to ye Pltf., on hearing the parties; dismissed.

Fortunatus Sydnor came to Court and made oath that Thomas Austin, late of this Co., dec'd, departed life w/o making a Will to his belief, and on Motion and giving security for his just Admin. of the sd. dec'd Estate and he is granted to obtain Letters of Admin., in due form.

Ordered that William Stepto, William Hutchins, Thomas Purcell, & William Edwards or three of them first sworn, meet and appraise in money and make a report on the Estate of Thomas Austin, dec'd, to the next Court and Fortunatus Sydnor's Admin. of the Inventory.

The action of debt betw. Robert Bisco, Pltf., and William Martin, Admin., of Alexander Edgar, dec'd., Deft., is continued till next Court at the Pltf.'s Motion & costs.

The action of Debt betw. Robert Biscoe, Pltf., and Frances Angell, Deft., is continued to next Court.

The action upon the case betw. Robert Biscoe, Pltf., and John Morris, Deft., is dismissed.

In the action upon the case betw. Thomas Edwards, Pltf., and Frances Angell, Deft., the sd. Deft. being called and not appearing, a conditional Judgment is granted him against the sd. Deft., and Charles Angell, her security, for what shall appear to be justly due to the sd. Pltf., at next Court unless the sd. Deft., shall then appear & answer the sd. action.

The action upon the case betw. William Stepto, Pltf., and William Martin, Admin. of Alexander Edgar, dec'd, Deft., is continued to next Court on the Pltf.'s Motion & costs.

In the action upon the case betw. Thomas Edwards, Pltf., and William Martin, Admin. of Alexander Edgar, dec'd, Deft., on hearing the parties and the oath of the sd. Pltf., to [can't read] in this cause, Judgment is granted to the Pltf. for £1.8.2 & costs of the Estate of the sd. Intestate in his hands of the sd. Deft.'s, Exec.

Pg 33. The Motion of William Martin, Admin. of the Estate of Alexander Edgar, dec'd, praying the Court will direct what allowance he shall make out of the Estate, which is appraised in money, for tobacco debts against the same and the Court's opinion was to discount after the rate of 10 shillings per hundred.

The action in the case betw. William Chelton, Pltf., and John Wilcox, Deft., for £10 due by account but no one appearing, dismissed.

The attachment obtained by William Forte against the Estate of Lawrence Blade for 40 lbs. tobacco, a plow, shear & cutter for value of 100 lbs. tobacco, being agreed and discontinued.

In action betw. Thomas Edwards, Pltf., & William Galloway, Deft., for 482 lbs. tobacco due by account & Judgment was granted for Pltf. and Deft for his debt and costs.

In action betw. Thomas Edwards, Pltf., & Robert Scofield, Deft., for 30 shillings cash & 236 lbs. tobacco due by account by consent of the parties, Thomas Carter, Gent., is appointed to settle the accounts and report to the next Court.

In action betw. Thomas Gaskins, Pltf., and Neil Johnston, Deft., for 2,000 lbs. tobacco damage but neither party appearing; dismissed.

In action of debt betw. Edward Nicken, Pltf., and Arthur Howard, Deft., is continued till next Court.

Action of trespass & assault & battery betw. Richard Haines & Million, his wife, Plts., and Thomas Kelley, Deft., for £10damages but neither party appearing; dismissed.

The attachment obtained by William Grady against the Estate of Thomas Wells is continued to next Court.

The suit in Chancery betw. John Edwards, Complt., and William Edwards, Exec. of the Will of Frances Edwards, dec'd, Deft., continued next Court.

Ordered that the Co. Sheriff summon at least 24 freeholders to appear at the next Court for a Grand Jury may be impanelled & sworn and make inquiry into recent offenders of the law.

In pursuance to a clause in the Act of Regulating Ordinarys & restraint of Tipling houses, the Court doth set & rate:

Cider at 15 pence or 12 pounds of tobacco the gallon. Rum & Brandy (except French Brandy) at 8 shillings or 76 lbs. of tobacco the gallon. Punch at 15 pence or 12 lbs. tobacco the Quart. Strong beer at 15 pence or 12 lbs. tobacco the bottle. Madera wine at one shilling, 10 pence half penny or 18 lbs. tobacco the quart. Dyet with small beer to drink at 11 pence, farthing or 9 lbs. tobacco the meal. Lodging at 7 pence, half penny or 6 lbs. tobacco the night. Stabloage & fodder for a horse at 6 pence or 5 lbs. of tobacco the night. Oats or Indian Corn at 6 pence or 5 lbs. tobacco the gallon.

Ordered by the Court be adjourned till the 2nd Wednesday in May next.

Pg 34. At a Court for Lancaster Co. on Wednesday, the 12th of May 1731. Present: William Ball, James Ball, Thomas Carter, George Heale, Edwin Conway, Henry Fleet, John Selden, Hugh Brent, Nicholas Martin; Gent., Justices.

The Will of Timothy Hinton, dec'd, was presented in Court by Henry Fleet, Gent., Exec., was proved by oaths of Johannah George, & Frances Kelley, witnesses, and was admitted to record and obtained probate. And, Ordered that Henry Fleet, Junr., Gent., Exec. of the Will to bring an Inventory of the Estate to next Court.

The Will of John Reves, dec'd, was presented I Court by James Reves, Exec., and being proved by oaths of James Mouro, Hester Johnson, witnesses, and obtained probate.

Ordered that Henry Towles, Joseph Carter, William Chelton and Joseph Stephens, or any three being first sworn meet & appraise the Estate of John Reves, dec'd, in money, make a report, and appear with the inventory at next Court.

Robert Young came into Court & ackn. his deeds of lease & release & bond to James Ball, Gent., for 50 a. in St, Mary's White Chappel Parish, in sd. Co., which were recorded.

A Letter of Attorney from John Tayloe, Gent., to Thomas Edwards was proved in open Court by oath of John Pally, a witness, & was recorded.

Col. John Tayloe's deeds of Lease & Release to William Tayloe, Gent., for 1,038 a. of land in Christ Church Parish in sd. Co., were first proved by oath of John Pally, a witness, and afterwards ackn. by Thomas Edwards, attorney of the sd. John Tayloe, admitted to record.

The appraisement of the Estate of Dennis Couree, dec'd, was returned and Dennis Couree, Admin., made oath and the inventory was recorded.

The appraisement of the Estate of Abel Brush, dec'd, was returned and Mary Brush, Adminx., made oath and the inventory was recorded.

Archibald Cammell [Campbell?], a servant man belonging to Mrs. Judith Payne, of this Co., came to Court and agreed to serve her one year after his time by Indenture custom or order of Court is expired in consideration of her leaving purchased from Mr. George Payne and keeping him to the shoemaker's trade.

The Will of Sarah Howell, dec'd, was presented in Court by John Gibson & Ezekiel Gilbert, who made oath and being proved by the oaths of John Howell & Thomas Howell, witnesses, admitted to record, and on Motion were granted Letters of Admin on the Estate with Will annexed.

Ordered that Thomas Lee, Henry Lawson, William Martin, William Brent, or any three being first sworn meet & appraise the Estate of Sarah Howell, dec'd, in money, make a report, and appear with the Will annexed & inventory at next Court.

Pg 35. Additional Inventory of the Estate of William Dymer, dec'd, returned by James Haines, one of the auditor's, Ordered recorded.

John Mohon, servant to James Haines, of this Co., came to Court and agreed to serve his master 5 years from this date, in consideration that his sd. master is to read & write and the trade of a shop joiner and turner and to find& allow him sufficient diet, lodging and apparel and at the expiration of his term to pay & allow him as is appointed for servants by Indenture or custom.

John Brown, orphan of John Brown, late of this Co., dec'd, aged 16 years the 15th inst., came to Court & voluntarily agreed to serve Thomas Kelley, of this Co., 4 years next ensuing in consideration of which agreement, the sd. Thomas

Kelley obliges himself to teach him to write & the trade of shoemaker, and to find & allow him sufficient diet, lodging and apparel during his sd. term.

David P[can't read] making oath that he had not received any satisfaction for taking up a runaway Negro woman belonging to Mr. Thomas Lee, of this Co. It is Ordered that the Clerk certify the same to the next General Assembly.

Mr. Elias Edwards making oath that he had not received any satisfaction for taking up a runaway Negro man belonging to Mr. Thomas Gaskins, of Northumberland Co. It is Ordered that the Clerk certify the same to the next General Assembly.

A Grand Jury was impaneled for this Co. and appointed William Stephens, foreman, and the rest were William Shelton, Nicholas Tarkelson, James Haines, Henry Boatman, Thomas Yerby, Benjamin George, Junr., Thomas Hayden, William George, John Merridith, James Gibson, Thomas Shelton, Francis Hattaway, John Steptoe, Ezekiel Gilbert, George Light, Walter Armes, James Reves, William Catlett and Thomas Young, and after being sworn returned with their Presentments in Lancaster Co., 12 May 1731.

The Presentments as follows: James Flemen, of Christ Church Parish, for not going to Church in one month, Elizabeth Waugh, of Wiccocmoco Parish, for not going to Church in one month, Anthony Coleson of Christ Church Parish, for not going to Church in one month, Eaton Reves & wife, Priscilla, of Christ Church Parish, for not going to Church in one month, Thomas Chetwood, of Christ Church Parish, for not going to Church in one month, for not going to Church in one month, Thomas Pearsifull & his wife, Elisha, of Christ Church Parish, Mr. Thomas Edwards, of Christ Church Parish, for not keeping a lawfull bridge over the waste of his mill dam, Elizabeth Edwards, of Wiccocmoco Parish, for not going to Church in one month, Elizabeth Poor, of Christ Church Parish, for not going to Church in one month, Simon Showcraft, of Christ Church Parish, for not going to Church in one month.

The Presentment of the Grand Jury against Thomas Edwards for not keeping a lawful bridge over the waste of his mill dam; dismissed.

Ordered that James Flemen, Anthony Coleson, Eaton Reves & wife, Priscilla, Thomas Pearsifull & his wife, Elisha, Elizabeth Poor, Simon Showcraft, all of Christ Church Parish; Thomas Chetwood, of St. Mary's White Chappel Parish; Elizabeth Waugh & Elizabeth Edwards, of Wiccocmoco Parish were summoned to next Court to answer the Presentment against them.

Presentment against Bridget Spexton, of St. Mary's White Chappel Parish, in this Co., has given her till next Court to consider the demurrer put in to her plea in the cause and it is Ordered that the Ann Spexton be returned according to a former order.

Pg 36. In the suit in Chancery betw. William Chelton & Stephen Chelton, Thomas Purcell & Elizabeth, his wife, George Chelton, son of Benony Chelton by the afsd. Benony Chelton, his next friend William Chelton, son of the afsd. William Chelton by his sd. father & next friend & George Purcell & Judith Purcell, son & daughter of sd. Thomas Purcell & Elizabeth, his wife, by their sd. father & next friend, Complts., and Charles Smith, Clerk & Elizabeth, his wife, Execx., of the Will of George Chelton, dec'd, Defts. The sd. Complts. this day put in their joinder as demurrer & reply to the Defts. answer & demurrer in this suite and on the Motion of the sd. Defts. time is given them to consider the same till the next Court.

In the Action upon the case betw. Ballentine Bell, Pltf., and Robert Scofield, Deft., the sd. Deft. pleaded and the Pltf. joined the issue   & it is Ordered that the trial of the sd. issue be referred till next Court.

In the suit betw. John Brooks & Frances, his wife, Pltf., and Mary Brush, Admin. of the Estate of Abel Brush, dec'd, Deft., by petition for the sd. Frances, for her share of the afsd. Estate of the sd. per the report of Hugh Brent, Nicholas Martin & William Markum. This cause was this day returned and Ordered to be recorded whereupon it is considered the sd. suit be defunct and that the sd. Plts. & Deft., pay the costs betw. them.

In the action upon the case betw. David Ball, Pltf., and George Heale, Deft., the sd.. Pltf. demurrer to the Defts. plea in abatement in the cause was argued & adjudged good whereupon the sd. Deft. put in another plea which on the Motion of the sd. Pltf. time is given him to consider till next Court.

In the action of trespass & assault & battery betw. John Velden, Pltf., and James Chelton, Shaw Dailey, Defts., for £5 current damages as in the Declaration is set forth the sd. Defts. having pleaded & the Pltfs. joined the issue in this cause Joseph Carter, William Hutchins, Elias Edmunds, Joseph Chinn, Thomas George, Ezekiel Gilbert, Clement Lattimore, William Edwards, Robert Edmunds, John Yerby, Thomas Purcell & Robert Biscoe were impanelled & sworn to try the sd. issue who bringing their verdict in these words – "Lancaster Co., we of the Jury do find for the Defts." Signed: Joseph Carter, Foreman.   The verdict on the Motion of the Defts. is recorded and it is considered that this

56

action be dismissed and that the sd. Defts. recover their cost against the Pltfs. together with one attorney's fee.

The action d Detinue betw. David Ball, Pltf., and George Heale, Deft., is continued till next Court.

 In the action on the case betw. Thomas Edwards, Pltf., and Robert Scofield, Deft., a report of Thomas Carter, Gent., in this cause was this day returned & admitted to record. Whereupon Judgment is granted to the sd. Pltf. against the sd. Deft., for 30 shillings cash & 229 lbs. tobacco by the report afsd. to be due & costs.

James Mc Carroll making oath he was a witness for John Velden in the suite against James Chelton & Shaw Dayley for 5 days and it was Ordered Velden pay sd. Mc Carroll for his attendance and his costs.

Richard Jackson of Christ Church Parish be summoned to next Court to answer the information of John Tarpley, Junr., Gent., the King's attorney, on behalf of the King against him.

William Ball, Thomas Carter, Nicholas Martin & Thomas Edwards, Gent. took the oath passed by the last Session in Assembly for amending the staple of tobacco & to be taken by Commissioners & Jury men to the Gov's Commission for that purpose.

John Selden, Gent., was appointed to take the list of tithables in the upper precinct in St Mary's White Chappel Parish in this Co. for the next year.

Pg 37. James Ball, Gent., is appointed to take the list of tithables in Moraticco Precinct in St. Mary's White Chappel Parish in this Co. this year.

Charles Burges, Gent., is appointed to take the list of tithables from Mr. Payne's to the Church in St. Mary's White Chappel Parish in this Co. this year.

William Ball, Gent., is appointed to take the list of tithables in the Lower Precinct in St. Mary's White Chappel Parish in this Co. this year.

Edwin Conway, Gent., is appointed to take the list of tithables in the Upper part of Corotomon Precinct in Wiccocomoco Parish in this Co. this year.

Hugh Brent, Gent., is appointed to take the list of tithables in the Middle Precinct in Christ Church Parish in this Co. this year.

Nicholas Martin, Gent., is appointed to take the list of tithables between Corotomon River and the main road which leads from the Church to Col Carter's great mill in Christ Church Parish in this Co. this year.

Henry Fleet, Gent., is appointed to take the list of tithables in the Lower Precinct in Christ Church Parish in this Co. this year.

William Catlet is appointed surveyor of the highways from the Court House to Mr. Payne's in St. Mary's White Chappel Parish in this Co. this year.

James Brent is appointed surveyor of the highways from the Court House from to Mr. Burges's Mill in St. Mary's White Chappel Parish in this Co. this year.

Henry Towles is appointed surveyor of the highways from Chetwood's Ferry to the main road near Mr. Payne's in St. Mary's White Chappel Parish in this Co. this year.

William Bailey Towles is appointed surveyor of the highways from the Church to Deep Bottom Run to St. Mary's White Chappel Parish in this Co. this year.

William Bertrand is appointed surveyor of the highways from Deep Bottom Run to Morattico Mill in St. Mary's White Chappel Parish in this Co. this year.

Thomas Wharton is appointed surveyor of the highways from Mr. Burges's Mill to Mr. Selden's Mill in St. Mary's White Chappel Parish in this Co. this year.

William Norris is appointed surveyor of the Rolling Road which leads from Church Road to Carpenter's Landing in St. Mary's White Chappel Parish in this Co. this year.

John Mott is appointed surveyor of the highways from Brian Stott's to the road leading from Col. Ball's Mill to Mr. Burges's Mill in St. Mary's White Chappel Parish in this Co. this year.

Thomas Chattin is appointed surveyor of the highways from Bartle Woods to the cross roads near Doctor Thornton's in St. Mary's White Chappel Parish in this Co. this year.

Theriatt Taylor is appointed surveyor of the highways from the main road by Gile's Robinson's to the main road which leads to Mr. Selden's mill and from that main road to Cundiff's old field and also of the rolling road in St. Mary's White Chappel Parish in this Co. this year.

58

Richard Curtis is appointed surveyor of the highways from Mr. Selden's Mill to Col. Carter's great mill and of all the main roads betw. these two branches of Corotomon River in Christ Church Parish in this Co. for this year.

William Stepto is appointed surveyor of the highways from Col. Carter's great mill to the cross roads in Christ Church Parish in this Co. for this year and it is Ordered that he take to his assistance the male laboring tithables belonging to Thomas Pinckard's, Ruth Sydnor's, George Yerby's, Mary Brush's, & John Kilgore's families besides those in ye sd. precinct.

George Flower is appointed surveyor of the highway from the cross roads to the Clerk's Office of this Court in Christ Church Parish in this Co. for the year.

Pg 38. William Edward's is appointed surveyor of the highways from Col. Carter's little mill to the main road which leads from the Clerk's Office of this Court in Christ Church Parish in this Co. for the year and it is Ordered that he keep the sd. road in repair which the male laboring tithables belonging to Coll. Robert Carter in this precinct.

Charles Jones is appointed surveyor of the highway from the cross roads to the Church in Christ Church Parish in the Co. this year and it is Ordered that he keep the sd. road in repair which the male laboring tithables belonging to Col. Robert Carter in this precinct.

William Martin is appointed surveyor of the highway from the White Stone to Col. Carter's Little Mill & of all the main roads in [can't read] neck in Christ Church parish in this Co. for this year.

William Brent is appointed surveyor of the highway from the Church to Maj. Fleet's in Christ Church Parish in this Co. for this year.

John Yerby's appointed surveyor of the highway from Col. Carter's Quarter to the mill road and from the sd. road to the Church in Christ Church Parish in this Co. for this year.

Ordered that the Court be adjourned till the 2nd Wednesday in June next. At a Court for Lancaster Co. on Wednesday, the 9th day of June 1731. Present: William Ball, Thomas Carter, Edwin Conway, Henry Fleet, John Selden; Gent., Justices.

On the prayer of John Davis, of Wiccomoco Parish in this CO., setting forth that he was very ancient & past his labor. It is Ordered that he be excused from paying any Co. or Country levies for the future.

On the prayer of Gabriel Thatcher of Christ Church Parish, in this CO., setting forth that his son, William Thatcher is a distempered & unhealthy person & not able to labor. It is Ordered that the sd. Gabriel excused from paying any Co. or Country levies for his afsd. son during the time he shall be unable to work.

By virtue of a Commission of the Peace & a [can't read] relating thereto both dated 6 May past and directed to Henry Fleet, William Ball, Thomas Carter, Richard Chichester, George Heale, Edwin Conway, James Brent, Charles Burges, Charles Carter, John Selden, Henry Fleet, Junr., William Ball, Junr., Robert Mitchell, Henry Carter, Hugh Brent, Nicholas Martin & Henry Lawson, Gent., John Selden & Henry Fleet, Junr., administered the Oaths to the Government to Henry Fleet & William Ball, who subscribed the test & took the oath appointed by a late act of Assembly of this Colony, to be taken by Justices of the Peace and administered the sd. Oaths & Test unto the sd. John Selden & Henry Fleet, Junr., and also to Thomas Carter, George Heale, Charles Burges, Charles Carter, Hugh Brent and Nicholas Martin.   Present: Henry Fleet, William Ball, John Selden, Thomas Carter, Henry Fleet, Junr., George Heale, Hugh Brent, Charles Burges, Charles Carter, and Nicholas Martin.

Edwin Conway & James Ball, Gent., refused to [can't read] of the Commission of the Peace at this time.

Ordered that the Co. Sheriff acquaint Richard Chichester, Robert Mitchell, Henry Carter & Henry Lawson, Gent., that they be at the next Court to be sworn to the Commission of Peace for this Co.

Charles Burges. Gent., took the Oath by an act passed the last session of assembly for amending the staple of tobacco & to be taken by commission [can't read] to the Governor's Commission for that purpose.

Pg 39. The Inventory of the Estate of Timothy Staiton[?], dec'd was returned and Henry Fleet, Junr., Gent., Exec., making oath thereto and his subscription, Ordered recorded.

The appraisal of the Estate of Sarah Howell, dec'd, was returned and john Gibson & Ezekiel Gilbert, Admin., making Oath according to their subscription on the inventory, Ordered recorded.

The appraisement of the Estate of Thomas Austin, dec'd, was returned and Fortunatus Sydnor, Admin., making Oath and subscription, Ordered recorded.

James Stott came into Court & ackn. his deed to Luke Stott for & concerning50 a. lying in St. Mary's White Chappel Parish, in this Co., was admitted to record.

In the ejection betw. John Tar, Pltf., and Thomas Gar, Deft., for lands & [can't read] in Christ Church Parish, in this Co. demised to the sd. Pltf., by Robert Scofield for [can't read] in the declaration set forth the sd. Robert made oath that he had delivered a copy of it to William Brent, the tenant in possession whom he claims (being legally served with a copy of the order) do appear at the next Court and make him or themselves, Defts., in this suite, contest, lease entry and ouster and agree to insist only on the title at the trial Judgment be them entered up for the Pltf. by default.

The Presentment against James Fleming, of Christ Church Parish is continued till next Court on James' Motion & costs.

On the Presentment against Elizabeth Waugh, of Wiccocomoco Parish in this Co. for not going to Church one month. She was summoned and not appearing, Judgment was granted to the Church Wardens against her for 5 shillings or 50 lbs. tobacco and it is Ordered that she pay the same to the Church Wardens for use of the poor in the sd. Parish.

On the Presentment against Anthony Coleson, of Christ Church Parish in this Co. for not going to Church one month. She was summoned and not appearing, Judgment was granted to the Church Wardens against her for 5 shillings or 50 lbs. tobacco and it is Ordered that she pay the same to the Church Wardens for use of the poor in the sd. Parish.

On the Presentment against Eaton Reves & Priscilla, his wife of Christ Church Parish for not going to Church one month. They were summoned and not appearing, Judgment was granted to the Church Wardens against her for 10 shillings or 100 lbs. tobacco and it is Ordered that she pay the same to the Church Wardens for use of the poor in the sd. Parish.

On the Presentment against Thomas Chetwood, of St. Mary's White Chappel Parish, for not going to Church one month. They were summoned and not appearing, Judgment was granted to the Church Wardens against her for 5 shillings or 50 lbs. tobacco and it is Ordered that she pay the same to the Church Wardens for use of the poor in the sd. Parish.

On the Presentment against Thomas Percifull & Lika, his wife, of Christ Church Parish for not going to Church one month was dismissed.

On the Presentment against Elizabeth Edwards, of Wiccocomoco Parish, for not going to Church one month was dismissed.

On the Presentment against Elizabeth Peore[?], of Christ Church Parish, for not going to Church one month was dismissed.

The Action of debt betw. Robert Bisco, Plts., and William Martin, Admin. of Alexander Edgar, dec'd, is continued to next Court on the Pltf.'s Motion & costs.

Pg 40. In the case betw. Thomas Edwards, Pltf., and Frances Angell, Deft., 642 lbs. tobacco & £4.2.0, due by account the Deft. being called and the conditional Judgment granted to the Pltf., and Charles Angell, her security is confirmed. Ordered the sd. Deft. and her security forthwith pay unto the afsd. Pltf. 298 lbs. tobacco & costs.

The action of Debt betw. Robert Biscoe, Pltf., and Frances Angell, Deft., is continued till next Court.

In the case betw. William Stepto, Pltf., and William Martin, Admin. f Alexander Edgar, Deft., for £3.6.6 due to the Pltf from the decedent's account. The Pltf. in this cause, Judgment is granted him for £3.4.0 & costs of the sd. Estate & attorney's cost.

The action of debt betw. Edward Nicken, Pltf., and Arthur Howard, Deft., for £5.6.3 and 300 lbs. tobacco due by account, neither party appearing; dismissed.

The attachment obtained by William Grady against the Estate of Thomas Wells for 300 lbs. tobacco, the sd. William not appearing; dismissed

In Chancery betw. John Edwards, Complt., & William Edwards, Exec. of the Will of Frances Edwards, dec'd, Deft., on the defense's Motion therein given him till next Court to answer.

The action of debt betw. William Eustace, Pltf., and Shaw Daylie, Deft., is dismissed.

On the Presentment against Bridget Spexton, of St. Mary's White Chappel Parish in the Co., on the prayer of the sd. Bridget, she is admitted to amend her plea in this cause and time is given to Mr. Tarpley, King's attorney, to consider the same & it is Ordered that if testimony of the sd. Ann be taken in this cause bef. a single Justice & returned to the next Court.

The suit in Chancery betw. William Chelton & Stephen Chelton, Thomas Purcell & Elizabeth, his wife, George Chelton, son of Benony Chelton by the afsd. Benony Chelton, his next friend William Chelton, son of the afsd. William Chelton by his father & next friend & George Purcell & Judith, son & dau. of the sd. Thomas Purcell & Elizabeth, his wife by their sd. father & next friend, Complts., and Charles Smith, Clerk & Elizabeth, his wife, Exec., of the Will of George Chelton, dec'd, Defts., is continued till the next Court, & the Defts. Motion & costs.

The action betw. Vallentine Bell, Pltf., and Robert Scofield, Deft., is continued till next Court on the Pltf.'s Motion & costs.

On the case betw. David Ball, Pltf. and George Heale, Deft., the sd. Pltf. put in replication which the sd. Deft., joined and is Ordered that the trial hereon be referred; till next Court.

On the case betw. David Ball, Pltf. and George Heale, Deft., the Court determining the Defts. might plead in arrest of the Judgment to be given in this cause, the sd. plea was lodged and on the Motion of the sd. Pltf., given him to consider the same, till the next Court.

In the suit betw. John Tarpley, Junr., , Attorney for the King, Pltf., and Richard Jackson, Deft., a special Imparlance is granted to the sd. Deft.; till next Court.

In the action betw. Thomas Pinckard, Pltf., and Maurice Jones, Gent., Deft., an Imparlance is granted to the sd. Deft., till next Court.

In the action of assault & battery betw. Murrough Nicken, Pltf., and Robert Scofield, Deft., the sd. Deft. pleaded and the sd. Pltf. joined issue and it was Ordered that the trial of the sd. issue be referred till next Court.

Ordered that the Vestry of Christ Church Parish in the sd. Co. divide their Parish into so many precincts as to them shall issue most convenient for processing every particular person's land in the sd. Parish and appoint particular fines betw. the last day of September and the last day of March next, when such processing shall be made in every precinct. And, also appoint at least intelligent, honest freeholders in every precinct to see such processioning performed and to take &

return to the sd. vestry an amount of the every person's land. They shall procession and of the persons present at the same and of what lands in their precincts they shall fail to procession and of the particular reasons of such failure.

Pg 41. Ordered the Vestry of St. Mary's, White Chappel Parish in this Co., divide their Parish into so many districts as to there shall be most convenient for processing particular person's land in their sd. Parish. And, appoint particular lines between the last day of September and the last day of March next when such processioning shall be made. And, also appoint at least two intelligent, honest, freeholders of every precinct to see such processioning performed & to take & return to the sd. Vestry an amount of every person's land. They shall procession and of the person's present at the same and of what lands in their precincts they shall fail procession and of the particular reasons of such failure.

Ordered that the Court be adjourned till the 2nd Wednesday in July next. At a Court for Lancaster Co. on Wednesday, the 14th day of June 1731. Present: Henry Fleet, William Ball, Thomas Carter, Henry Fleet, Junr., Nicolas Martin; Gent., Justices.

Appraisement of the Estate of John Reves, dec'd, was returned and James Reves, his Exec. making oath re: his Inventory; Ordered recorded.

The suite betw. William Catlet & Sarah, his wife, Pltfs., and James Reves, Exec. of the Will of John Reves, dec'd, Deft., by petition on the Motion of the sd. Deft.; continued till next Court.

Fillis, a Negro girl belonging to William Roach of this Co. is by the Court judged to be 10 years of age.

By virtue of a late Commission of the Peace for this Co. and the dedimus relating to Edwin Conway & Henry Carter, Gent., took the Oaths of government subscriber the test, and had the Oaths appointed by a late act of the Assembly of this Colony to be taken by Justices of the Peace administered to them. Present: Edwin Conway & Henry Carter, Gent. Richard Chichester & Robert Mitchell, Gent., refused to be sworn Commission according as they are lately appointed at this [can't read]. Present: George Heale, Charles Burges & John Selden; Gent.

The Commission appointed to settle the rents on the several warehouses in this Co. certifying to this Court that no person had with them undertaken to build the warehouses directed at Geeles Davis' land on Corotomon River. It is Ordered that Henry Fleet, Junr., Joseph Carter & David Ball agree with workmen to build the sd. houses – two 40 foot houses - 20 foot wide, 10 foot pitch, light wood thorough nailed (double raftered if built with 5 foot boards. And, substantial work together with a good wharf at the landing adjoining thereto as the Law directs. And, that they take Bond of the undertaking for the performance of the sd. work. And, it further Ordered that the consideration by them agreed for shall be levied for the sd. undertaking at the laying o the next levy for this Co.

Joseph Grey, Thomas Hancock and Harry Augustison, servant men, belonging to Charles Burge, Gent., confessing they had runaway from their sd. Master's service 13 days and their sd. Master making appear he had expended 1,010 lbs. of tobacco in regaining them. It is Ordered that the sd. three serve their sd. Master 26 days each for their afsd. 13 days absence, and each 2 years & one calendar month for the charges afsd. expended in regaining them after their time by Indenture customs or for sd. order of Court that be expired.

Samuel Brown, a servant man, belonging to Charles Burge, Gent., confessing he had runaway from his sd. Master's service 26 days and his Master making appear he had expended 200 lbs. tobacco in regaining him. It is Ordered that the sd. Samuel serve his sd. Master 52 days for his sd. 26 days absence and three calendar months for the charges afsd. expended regaining him after his time by Indenture custom & former order of Court expired.

Pg 42. Joseph Grey, Thomas Hancock & Henry Augustison, servant men, of Charles Burges, while they were away have also confessed that they took a boat from John Baily, of this Co., which was lost. It was Ordered that they, the sd. Joseph, Thomas, & Henry that after they become free from their Master, that they pay John Bailey 667 lbs. tobacco back or serve the sd. John Bailey 10 calendar months for their afsd. offence.

The ejection offense betw. John Tar, Pltf., and Thomas Gar, Deft., is continued on Pltf.'s Motion till next Court.

The Grand Jury against James Flemon, of Christ Church Parish, in the Co., for not going to his Parish Church in one month; dismissed.

In the action of debt betw. Robert Bisco, Pltf., & William Martin, Admin. of Alexander Edgar, dec'd, Deft., for 1,105 lbs. of tobacco due to the Pltf. from the sd. decedent in his life time by account the sd. Pltf. making oath to his sd. amount Judgment is granted him for his afsd. debt and costs of the Estate of the sd. intestate in the hands of the sd. Deft.

In the action of debt betw. Robert Bisco, Pltf., & Frances Angell, Deft., the sd. Deft. being call and not appearing on the Motion of the sd. Pltf, a Conditional Judgment is granted him against the sd. Deft., and Charles Angell, security, for what shall appear to be justly due to the sd. Pltf. at the next Court unless the Deft. shall then appear and answer the sd. action.

The suit in Chancery betw. John Edwards, Complt., and William Edwards, Exec. of the Will of Frances Edwards, dec'd, on the sd. Deft.'s Motion is continued till next Court.

The Presentment against Bridget Spexton, of St. Mary's White Chappel Parish, in sd. Co., in continued and Ordered that the testimony of sd. Spexton be taken before a Justice in this cause & returned to next Court.

In the suit in Chancery betw. William Chelton, Stephen Chelton, Thomas Purcell, & Elizabeth, his wife, & George Chelton, son of Benony Chelton, by the afsd. Benony Chelton, his next friend, William Chelton, son of the afsd. William Chelton, by his sd. father & next friend & George Purcell & Judith Purcell, son & daughter of the sd. Thomas Purcell & Elizabeth, his wife, by their sd. father & next friend, Complts., and Charles Smith, Clk., & Elizabeth, his wife, Exec. of the last Will of George Chelton, dec'd, Defts., is given to the Defts., till next Court on Defts. Motion & costs.

The action of detinue betw. David Ball, Pltf., and George Heale, Deft., is continued till next Court on the Pltf.'s Motion & costs.

The suit betw. John Tarpley, Junr., Gent., Attorney for the King, Pltf., and Richard Jackson, Deft., by information is continued, till the next Court.

The action upon the case betw. Thomas Pinckard, Gent., Pltf. and Maurice Jones, Gent., Deft., the sd. Deft. pleaded and the Pltf. joined issue and it is Ordered that the trial on the issue be referred till the next Court.

The action upon the case betw. Vallentine Bell, Pltf., and Robert Scofield, Defts., is continued till next Court.

The action of trespass & assault & Battery betw. Murrough Nicken, Pltf., and Robert Scofiled, Deft., is continued till next Court on the Deft.'s Motion & costs.

Ordered that the Court be adjourned till the 2nd Wednesday in August next. At a Court for Lancaster Co. on Wednesday, on the 8th day of September 1731.

66

Present: William Ball, Thomas Carter, George Heale, Henry Fleet, Junr., Edwin Conway, Henry Carter, Charles Burges, Charles Carter, Nicolas Martin; Gent., Justices.

Robert Carter, Esqr., came into Court & ackn. his deed of gift to his son, Charles Carter, Esqr., for & reserving 200 a. of land in Christy Church Parish, of this Co., admitted to record.

Pg 43. Richard Flint came into Court & ackn. his deed of surrender to Thomas Edwards for & rent owing100 a. of land lying in St Mary's White Chappel Parish; admitted to record.

Liddy, a Negro girl belonging to the Rev. John Bell, Clk., is adjudged to be 10 years old.

Jane, a Negro girl belonging to William Norris is adjudged to be 10 years old.

John Cooper, a servant of Angus Alexander came into Court & voluntarily ackn. his consent to serve his master a half a year after his time by Indenture custom or order of the Court is expired in consideration of his master leaving at his special request purchased him from his former master.

The Will of Mary Rogers, dec'd, was presented in Court by Brian Pullen, Exec., who made oath thereto and being proved by oaths of John Stott, Junr., and Brian Stott, witnesses; admitted to probate & recorded.

Joseph Chinn, Nathaniel Carpenter, Henry Stonenum & John Mott or any three, being first sworn bef. a Judge, to meet & appraise & inventory the Estate of Mary Rogers, dec'd, in money & make a report with the Exec. at the next Co. Court.

Miriam Wilcox, dau. of John Wilcox, of this Co., dec'd, Pltf., and William Clutton, Deft., by Petition is continued till next Court.

The attachment obtained by John Burkley, against the Estate of Samuel Smith for 300 lbs. tobacco due by bill was served on James Pollard, Thomas Pollard, & Isaac White, Pltfs., making oath to his Judgment is granted him thereon for 290 lbs. tobacco & costs against the estate of the Deft., in the hands of the sd. Thomas Pollard and the remainder in the hands of the sd. Isaac White, att. exec.

The suit betw. William Catlet and Sarah, his wife. Pltfs., and James Reves, Exec. of the Will John Reves, dec'd, Deft., by petition is continued till next Court on the Pltfs. Motion & costs.

The ejection firme betw. John Tar, Pltf., and Thomas Gar, Deft., is continued till next Court.

In the Action of Debt. betw. Robert Bisco, Pltf., and Frances Angell, Deft., for 2,390 lbs. of tobacco due by obligation & amount, the sd. Deft. being called and not appearing, the conditional Judgment granted to the Plft., in his cause against, the Defts., and Charles Angell her security is confirmed, and it is Ordered that the Defts., and her security forthwith pay unto the sd. Pltf., the afsd. 2,390 lbs. tobacco & costs.

The suit in Chancery betw. John Edwards, Complt., and William Edwards, Exec. of the Will of Frances Edwards dec'd, Deft., is continued till next Court.

The Presentment of the Grand Jury against Bridget Spexton, of St. Mary's White Chappel Parish in the Co.; is continued till next Court.

In the suit in Chancery betw. William Chelton, Stephen Chelton, Thomas Purcell, & Elizabeth, his wife, & George Chelton, son of Benony Chelton, by the afsd. Benony Chelton, his next friend, William Chelton, son of the afsd. William Chelton, by his sd. father & next friend & George Purcell & Judith Purcell, son & daughter of the sd. Thomas Purcell & Elizabeth, his wife, by their sd. father & next friend, Complts., and Charles Smith, Clk., & Elizabeth, his wife, Exec. of the last Will of George Chelton, dec'd, Defts., is given to the Defts., till next Court on Defts. Motion & costs.

The action upon the case between Valentine Bell, Pltf., and Robert Scofield, Deft., is continued till next Court on the Pltf.'s Motion & costs.

The action of Detinue betw. David Ball, Pltf., and George Heale, Deft., is continued till next Court on the Pltf.'s Motion & costs.

The action betw. John Tarpley, Junr., Gent., attorney of the King, Pltf., and Richard Jackson, Deft., by information is continued, till the next Court.

The action betw. Thomas Pinckard, Gent., Pltf., and Maurice Jones, Deft., is continued, till the next Court.

68

Pg 44. Action of trespass, assault & battery betw. Murrough Nicken, Pltf., and Robert Scofield, Deft., is continued till next Court.

The Commission appointed to set the rents on the several store houses in this Co. testifying that no person had with them undertaken to build the warehouses directed at Deep Creek on the land of William Sydnor. Protest was made for person to [can't read] and undertake the same. Whereupon, James Ball, Gent., in Court undertook to build the sd. houses according to the dimensions in the certificate afsd. set forth together with a good wharf at the landing adjoining thereto for the consideration of 12,430 lbs. tobacco to be paid him at the laying of the next Levy for this Co. One of the sd. houses & wharf to be built before the 11th day of November & the other before the 25th day of December next for the performance of which undertaking the sd. James gave Bond & Security accordingly.

Henry Stonum[?], a Constable in St. Mary's White Chappel Parish in this Co., returning to the Court that Thomas Charles Chattin declaring William Stamps and James Gaylor had turned out & tented tobacco seconds in his Precinct. Ordered that Thomas Chattin & William & James[?] be summoned to Court to show any cause they have wherefore [can't read] be removed against them for their sd. offense.

In the debt betw. Robert Carter, Esqr., and Thomas Carter, Church Wardens of Christ Church Parish, Pltf., and Francis Murrough, Deft., for 500 lbs. of tobacco & cask or 50 shillings to the Deft., being returned and not appearing on the Motion of the sd. Pltfs. capias is against the Defts. returnable to the next Court.

Ordered that the Court be adjourned till the 2nd Wednesday in October next. At a Court for Lancaster Co. on Wednesday, on the 13th day of October 1731. Present: William Ball, Thomas Carter, George Heale, Edwin Conway, Hugh Brent; Gent., Justices.

Mary Harwood came to Court & ackn. her deed of gift to her grandchildren George & William Currel for & concerning two Negroes which was admitted to record.

Charles Feagin, a servant man, belonging to John Davis came into Court and voluntarily agreed to serve his Master 6 weeks after his time by Indenture custom or former order of Court is expired and to release his freedom dues for a valuable consideration already received which was Ordered to be recorded.

the appraisement of the Estate of Mary Rogers, dec'd, was returned and (Bryan Pullen her Exec. making oath according to his subscription of the Inventory) Ordered to be recorded.

John Bailey, a Constable in St Mary's White Chappel Parish, in this Co., informing the Court that Robert Wells, Richard Wooden, John Grinsteed[?], Thomas Cotes, James Stott, Benj. George had severally been guilty of breach of the Law, made against tending of slips or seconds in his Precinct. It is Ordered that John Tarpley, Gent., the King's attorney appointed to present to the Court to bring suit against the sd. offenders for the forfeiture by them by the breath of the sd. acts.

Thomas Flint, a Constable in St Mary's White Chappel Parish, in this Co., informing the Court that William Delany had been guilty of breach of the Law, made against tending of slips or seconds in his Precinct. It is Ordered that John Tarpley, Gent., the King's attorney appointed to present to the Court to bring suit against the sd. Wm. for the forfeiture by him by the breath of the sd. acts.

William Dogget, a Constable in St Mary's White Chappel Parish, in this Co., informing the Court that John Hubbard had been guilty of breach of the Law, made against tending of slips or seconds in his Precinct. It is Ordered that John Tarpley, Gent., the King's attorney appointed to present to the Court to bring suit against the sd. John for the forfeiture by him by the breath of the sd. acts.

Pg 45. In a suit betw. Miriam Wilcox, dau. of John Wilcox, late of this Co., dec'd, by John Callahan, her next friend, Pltf., and William Clutton, Deft., by petition for the sd. Pltf., her share of her sd. father's Estate in the Deft.'s hands, the sd. Pltf. having by the [can't read] of the Court amended her petition, the sd. Deft. confessed Judgment for £8.10.0. Wherefore, it is considered that the sd. Deft. forthwith pay unto the sd. Pltf. the sd. money & Court costs.

In the suit betw. William Catlet & Sarah, his wife, Pltfs., and James Reves, Exec., of the Will of John Reves, dec'd, by petition for the sd. Sarah, her part of the Estates of Wm. Clark & Arthur Clark, her grandfather & father, as in the sd. petition is set forth by consent of the parties, Robert Mitchell, Henry Carter, & Joseph Carter, Gent., are appointed to settle all amounts in difference relating to this suit and to make a report herein to the next Court.

In the ejection betw. John Tar, Pltf., and Thomas Gar, Deft., William Brent by George Eskridge, his attorney, appeared and on his prayer was admitted Deft. in the room of the sd. Thomas Gar and confessed lease entry & ouster pleaded the general issue & agreed to [can't read] on the title at the trial, whereupon the sd. Pltf. joined the sd. issue and it is Ordered that the trial thereof be referred to next Court.

The suit in Chancery betw. John Edwards, Complt., and William Edwards, Exec. of the Will of Frances Edwards, dec'd, Deft., is continued for an answer, till the next Court.

In the Presentment of the grand jury against Bridget Spexton of St. Mary's, White Chappel Parish in this CO., a replication was this day put in to the sd. Bridget's pleas & time is given her to consider it till next Court.

In the suit in Chancery betw. William Chelton, Stephen Chelton, Thomas Purcell, & Elizabeth, his wife, & George Chelton, son of Benony Chelton, by the afsd. Benony Chelton, his next friend, William Chelton, son of the afsd. William Chelton, by his sd. father & next friend & George Purcell & Judith Purcell, son & daughter of the sd. Thomas Purcell & Elizabeth, his wife, by their sd. father & next friend, Complts., and Charles Smith, Clk., & Elizabeth, his wife, Exec. of the last Will of George Chelton, dec'd, Defts., is given to the Defts., till next Court on Defts. Motion & costs.

In the case of Valentine Bell, Pltf., and Robert Scofield, Deft., for 307 lbs. tobacco due by amount the parties agrees to refer the trial of the issue joined in this cause and being heard, it is considered the suit be defunct, and that the Pltf. pay unto the Deft., his costs with one attorney's fee.

The case betw. David Ball, Pltf., and George Heale, Deft., is continued to next Court.

The suit between John Tarpley, Junr., Gent., the King's attorney, Pltf. and Richard Jackson, Deft., by Information is continued till next Court on the Deft.'s Motion & costs.

The action upon the case of Thomas Pinckard, Gent., Pltf., and Maurice jones, Deft., is continued till next Court.

The action of trespass & assault & battery betw. Murrough Nicken, Pltf., and Robert Scofield, Deft., for £10 damages in the declaration, a jury impaneled & on the issue joined in the cause brought in their verdict – "We of the Jury find for the Pltf. £6". Signed: Willm. Brent, Foreman. Verdict on the Pltf. Motion is recorded and it is considered that the sd. Pltf. recover against the Deft., the damages afsd. by the jurors afsd. & costs together with one attorney's fees

In the Debt betw. Robert Carter, Esqr., and Thomas Carter, Church Wardens of Christ Church Parish, Pltf., and Frances Murrough, Deft., on the Motion of the sd. Deft., an Imparlance is granted her till the next Court.

The action of debt betw. Thomas Purcell, Pltf., and Joseph George, Deft., for 13 barrels of Indian Corn & one from the Pltf. by a note under his hand, dated 22 Feb last payable to Tobias Purcell by the sd. Tobias assigned to the Pltf. is dismissed.

On the petition of Epaphroditus Lawson & debt for Epaphroditus Lawson, Gent., dec'd, praying to be possessed in the Estate of his sd. father, he being of age which entitles him to same according to the Will of his father, which Estate is in the hands of Hugh Brent, Gent., & William Martin, Execs. of his father's Will, as in the petition is set forth. It is Ordered that the sd. Execs. deliver unto the sd. petition of the Estate in their hands and that the sd. petition and William Stepto's security into bond of the Court for the payment of the legacies of the sd. deceased's Will continued at the Clerk's office and appear at the next Court & ackn. the sd. Bond.

Pg 46. Ordered the Co. Sheriff summon at least 24 freeholders of the inhabitants of this Co. to appear at the next Court and that out of these a Grand Jury may be the impanelled & sworn to make inquiry into the breach of the penal laws and to present the offenders.

Elizabeth Yerby, wife of George Yerby, having attended 4 days as a witness for Murrough Nicken in her suit against Robert Scofield & is Ordered that the sd. Murrough pay the sd. George for the sd. attendance & costs.

John Kilgore attended 4 days as a witness for Murrough Nicken in her suit against Robert Scofield. & is Ordered that the sd. Murrough pay the sd. John for the sd. attendance & costs.

William Cone having attended one day for Vallentine Bell in his suit against Robert Scofield. It is Ordered the sd. Vallentine pay the sd. William for the attendance & costs.

Henry Stone[?], Constable in St. Mary's White Chappel Parish in this Co., having informed this Court that Thomas Charles, Chattin Chowning, William

Stamps & James Tayler[?] had severally been guilty of the breach of laws of this Colony made against the tending of Slips or Seconds. It is Ordered that John Tarpley, Gent., the King's attorney, to Present for [can't read] in this Co., bring prosecution against the sd. offender for the forfeitures by them incurred by the breach of the sd. acts

Ordered that the Court be adjourned till the 2nd Wednesday in November next. At a Court for Lancaster Co. on Wednesday, on the 10th day of November next. Present: Henry Fleet, William Ball, Thomas Carter, Edwin Conway, Hugh Brent, Charles Burges, Henry Carter; Gent., Justices.

Creawford, a Negro boy, belonging to Robert Mitchell, Gent., is adjudged to be 11 years old.

An additional Inventory of the Estate of Daniel Feagin, dec'd was returned & recorded.

A Grand Jury for this County being impaneled and having appointed James Haines, Foreman, the sd. James was sworn & then the rest, to wit: John Buckles, John Callahan, Bryan Pullen, William Dogget, Henry Horne, William Fort, Thomas Yerby, Stephen Tomlin, Peter Rivere, Junr., James Gailer, Richard Davis, Junr., John Cundiff, John Angell, John Brooks, William Scofield, Thomas Chilton, Robert Necosum, James Straton, David Alexander Flint & Joseph Stepthens[?], who having revised their charge withdrew and after some time returned into Court gave in their Presentments & were discharged, which Presentments were Ordered to be recorded being as follows: "November 10, 1731, we of the Grand Jury do make our Presentments as follows:

Mary Lewis for having a mulatto bastard in White Chappel Parish within six months last past. Francis Leun, of Christ Church Parish, for not coming to Church the last month past. Ellinor Southern for having a bastard child in White Chappel Parish which six months last past. Job Carter for swearing one oath in Christ Church Parish within 6 months last month past. Frances Angell, of Christ Church Parish for not coming to Church for the last month past. Robert Angell of Christ Church Parish for not coming to Church for the last month past. James Munger & wife of Christ Church Parish for not coming to Church for the last month past. Catherine Johnson of White Chappel Parish for not coming to Church for the last month past. Ann Wood of White Chappel Parish for not coming to Church for the last month past. John Cornelius of White Chappel Parish for not coming to Church for the last month past. Robert Scofield & wife, of Christ Church Parish for not coming to Church for the last month past.

James Lary of White Chappel Parish for not coming to Church for the last month past. Thomas Chetwood of White Chappel Parish for not coming to Church for the last month past.

Pg 47. Ordered that Mary Lewis, Catherine Johnson, Ann Wood, John Cornelius, James Lary & Thomas Chetwood, of St. Mary's White Chappel Parish be summoned to the next Court to answer the Presentment.

Ordered that Frances Leun[?], Job Carter, Frances Angell, Robert Angell, James Munger & his wife & Robert Scofield & wife, of Christ Church Parish be summoned to the next Court to Court to answer the Presentment.

Job Wildy came to Court & ackn. his deed to Charles Burges, Gent., concerning 2 lots situated in Queens town in this Co., & Ordered recorded.

Ordered John Cornelius be summoned to the next Court to answer the petition of Cornelius Sary[?] against him.

The Sheriff having made proclamation that the Court was about to Lay the County levy they proceeded accordingly: To Robert Carter, Esqr., for keeping the Public Ferry one year – 1,400 lbs. tobacco; John Payne for cleaning the Court House & other services – 800 lbs. tobacco; John Tarpley, Junr., Gent., King's Co. Attorney – 1,000 lbs. tobacco; Thomas Edwards, Court Clerk, for one year service – 1,000 lbs.; Capt. William Ball, Co. Sheriff, for one year's service – 1,000 lbs. tobacco for one year's service; Thomas Hunton, Constable, for viewing tobacco in this precinct – 228 lbs. tobacco & also for his last year's levy overpaid – 17 lbs. tobacco; Thomas Flint, Constable for viewing tobacco in his precinct – 243 lbs. tobacco; John Bailey for the same – 239 lbs. & for summoning a jury for a Coroner's Inquest – 50 lbs. tobacco; Edward Sanders, Constable for viewing tobacco in his precinct -62 lbs. tobacco; William Dogget for the same – 196 lbs. tobacco; Henry Howe for the same – 240 lbs. tobacco; George Yerby for the same – 300 lbs. tobacco & for 1 levy overpaid in 1728 & 1729 – 32 lbs. tobacco; Col. William Ball for a Coroner's Inquest – 133 lbs. tobacco; Mr. Secretary Carter for a Commission of the Poore – 160 lbs. tobacco; James Carter for repairing the Prison – 2,000 lbs. tobacco; Mr. Charles Burges for glazing the Court House windows – 476 lbs. tobacco; Capt. James Ball for the Store Houses & Wharf at Deep Creek – 12,440 lbs. tobacco; Capt. William Ball for the Store Houses & Wharf at Geeles Davis' – 12,440 lbs. tobacco; John Davis for the acre of land at Davis's – 500 lbs. tobacco; Wm. Sydnor for the use of the heir of the acre of land at Deep Creek – 250 lbs. tobacco; the Co. Sheriff

74

for a balance due to him in the last levy – 67 lbs. tobacco & 4 percent for Salary – 1,419 lbs. tobacco & 10 percent for convenience – 3,546 lbs. tobacco.

The fraction to be amounted for next year – [can't read]. The County's proportion for Criminals – 296 lbs. tobacco. 1,501 Tithables – 37, 525 lbs. tobacco.

Pg 48. The County Levy for this present year 1,731 amounting to 25 lbs. tobacco poll. It is Ordered that the Co. Sheriff collect so much of every tithable person in this Co. and pay the same to the Co. Creditors, as it is before proportioned.

Order the Robert Carter, Esqr., do keep the public ferry over Corotomon River for the ensuing year & that he be paid for the same as usual.

Order that John Pyne do find this Court with water & candles & clean the Court House the ensuing year and that he be paid the same as usual.

On the prayer of William Jones, of St. Mary's White Chappel Parish, in this Co., setting forth that his son-in-law, Arthur Lawry is unable to labor. It is Ordered that he be excused from paying any Country or County levies for the sd. Arthur hereafter.

The Presentment of the grand jury against Ellinor Southern, of St. Mary's White Chappel Parish, in this Co., for having a bastard child, and she appeared & confessed the fact but refused to pay or give sufficient ration for the payment of the fine inflicted whereupon it is Ordered that she receive on her bare back at the whipping post 25 lashes, well laid on and the discharged.

In the trespass betw. James Bell, Gent, Pltf., and Thomas Mason, Deft., , the sd. parties set forth that Thomas Lee, George Turbervile & George Eskridge, Gent., to whom the several matters relating to the cause, was by the sd. Robert Mitchell, Junr., & John Pollard hereto referred refused to determine the same. Whereon, the sd. Platf. & Deft. agreed to submit the determination & final award of Richard Lee & William Eustace, of Northumberland Co., Gent., and Thomas Pinckard of this Co., Gent. But, on the Motion of the sd. Deft.,, this course is continued till next Court for the sd. john Pollard & Robert Mitchell, Junr., their consent to this reference.

Ordered that the Court be adjourned till tomorrow 10 o'clock. At a Court for Lancaster Co. continued on Thursday, on the 11th day of November 1731.

Present: Henry Fleet, William Ball, Thomas Carter, Edwin Conway, George Heale, Hugh Brent, Charles Burges, Henry Carter; Gent., Justices.

Whaley, a Negro boy, belonging to Robert Carter, Esqr., is adjudged to be 11 years old.

James, a Negro boy, belonging to Robert Carter, Esqr., is adjudged to be 12 years old.

George, a Negro boy, belonging to Robert Carter, Esqr., is adjudged to be 13 years old.

Betty, a Negro girl, belonging to Robert Carter, Esqr., is adjudged to be 10 years old.

The suite betw. William Catlet & Sarah, his wife, Pltfs., and James Reves, Exec. of the Will of John Reves, dec'd, Deft., by the order of the last Court for an audit in his cause being not performed, it is Ordered that the same be performed and a return thereof made next Court.

Thomas Carter is appointed to clear a road 15 feet wide from the Neck Road to Davis's Warehouses in Christ Church Parish, and it is Ordered that the male laboring tithables adjacent to the sd. road assist him in the clearing of same.

The ejection firma betw. John Tar, Pltf. and William Brent, Deft., is continued till next Court.

The suit in Chancery betw. John Edwards, Complt., and William Edwards, Exec. of the last Will of Frances Edwards, dec'd, Deft., for the sd. Complt., his part of the sd. decedent's Estate, by her to him, ye sd. Complt., given & bequeathed as in the Bill is set forth, is dismissed.

In the Presentment against Bridget Spexton, of St. Mary's White Chappel, in this Co., the sd. Bridget this day joined the issue [can't read] in the replication lodged in this issue at the last Court, it is Ordered that the trial of the sd. issue be & referred till the next Court.

Pg 49. In the suit in Chancery betw. William Chelton, Stephen Chelton, Thomas Purcell, & Elizabeth, his wife, & George Chelton, son of Benony Chelton, by the afsd. Benony Chelton, his next friend, William Chelton, son of the afsd. William Chelton, by his sd. father & next friend & George Purcell & Judith Purcell, son & daughter of the sd. Thomas Purcell & Elizabeth, his wife, by their sd. father & next friend, Complts., and Charles Smith, Clk., & Elizabeth, his wife, Execx. of the last Will of George Chelton, dec'd, Defts., demurrer to the Complt.'s bill in this cause was this day argued and over-ruled, audit is Ordered that the further proceedings of the sd. parties in this suit be continued till next Court.

Elizabeth Wilde, wife of Job Wilde, came into Court & relinquished all her Right to Dower in the 2 lots of land in Queen's Town sold by her husband to Charles Burges, Gent., unto him the sd. Charles, the sd. Elizabeth being first privately examined which was admitted to record.

In action of betw. David Ball, Pltf., and George Heale, Deft., for £40 damages by means of the Deft. detaining one Negro woman called Pegg belonging to the Pltf., as in the declaration sets forth at Co. Court held 10 Feb last, the special verdict found in this cause was argued and the opinion of the Court being that the Law was to the Pltf. The Deft. put in his plea in arrest of the Judgment to be given in this cause in these words "And the sd. George by joseph Ball, his Council as a friend to the Court humbly showeth to the Justices that the sd. Justices to Judgment against the sd. George ought not to proved but that the sd. Judgment ought to be stayed & arrested because there are divers manifest errors appearing in the record of the sd. suit & process thereof and first in this – That the original writing this suit is not conformable to the register of original writs nor is otherwise warranted by the law of the land. 2nd in this that the Deft. declares in trover for a Negro whereas by the Law of the land trover lies not of a Negro. 3rd in this That the writ warrants not the declaration 4th In this that us issue was ever referred by either Pltf. or Deft. to the Country to be tried by them. 5th in this That there are diverse discontinuances in the proofs of the sd. suit. Signed – Jos. Ball.

And, this day to wit, the 11th Nov 1731, the parties as well Pltf. as Deft. by their attorneys appeared to argue the sd. plea and were fully heard & understood whereupon it is the opinion of the Court that the reasons afsd. are insufficient to arrest the Judgment afsd. And, it is considered that the Pltf. recover against the sd. Deft. £30 the damages afsd. by the Jury in this cause assessed and costs with one attorney's fee. From which Judgment, the sd. Defts. an appeal to the 9th of the next General Court it is granted him Thomas Edwards becoming his security to prosecute the same with effect.

George Heale of St. Mary's White Chappel Parish, Gent., and Thomas Edwards, of Christ Church Parish came into Court and jointly ackn. themselves indebted to Davis Ball, of the St. Mary's White Chappel Parish, Gent., for £50 to be levied upon their goods & chattels, lands & tenement under the condition that the sd. George shall appear on the 9th day of the next Court and then & there prosecution appeal his day granted him from a Judgment against him at the suit of the sd. David Ball for £30 & costs and if cast in the appeal shall pay & satisfy to the sd. David per the law.

The action of the case betw. David Ball, Pltf., and George Heale, Deft., Thomas Pinckard, Francis Velden, James Reves, Thomas Carter, Thomas Purcell, Fortunatis Sydnor, William Chelton, Joseph Stephens, Christopher Kirk, Robert Biscoe, Joseph Carter & Henry Horne were impanelled to try the issue & bringing a special verdict, it is admitted to record and it is Ordered that the arguments thereon be referred till next Court.

In the action betw. Thomas Pinckard, Gent., Pltf., and Maurice Jones, Gent., Deft., for £10damages as in the declaration is set forth by consent of the parties the amounts in difference upon his suit is referred to determination of Edwin Conway, Gent., & Thomas Edwards, who are hereby empowered to examine the witness's cause. And, it is Ordered that their award be the Judgment of the Court and to be referred to the next Court.

Robert Wells, Richard Wooden, John Grinsteed, Thomas Cates, James Stott, Benjamin George, William Delaney, John Hubbard, Thomas Charles, Chattin Chowning, William Stamps, & James Gaylor, be summoned to the next Court to answer the information of John Tarpley, Junr., Gent., the King's attorney, against them.

Pg 50. In the suit betw. John Tarpley, Junr., King's attorney, Pltf., and Richard Jackson, Deft., by information the Deft. pleaded and the Pltf. joined issue and it was Ordered that the trial of ye issue be referred till next Court.

The debt betw. Robert Carter, Esqr., and Thomas Carter, Church Wardens of Christ Church Parish, Pltf., and Frances Murrough, Deft., is continued to next Court.

The suit betw. Epaphroditis Lawson, eldest son of Epaphroditis Lawson, Gent., dec'd, Pltf., and Hugh Brent, Gent., and William Martin, Execs., of the Will of Epaphroditis Lawson, Gent., dec'd,, by petition is continued till next Court.

The debt betw. Charles Holmes, Pltf., and Joseph Robison, Deft., for 800 lbs. tobacco due by bill is dismissed.

The debt betw. George Heale & John Heals, Gent., Church Wardens, of St. Mary's White Chappel Parish, Pltf., and Ellinor Southern, Deft., for 500 lbs. tobacco or 50 shillings as set in the declaration is dismissed.

Peter James Bailey making oath that he had attended 5 days as an evidence for George Heale in an action upon the case brought by David Ball, against him. it is Ordered that the sd. Heale pay the sd. Bailey for his attendance & costs.

Thomas Williams making oath that he had attended 5 days as an evidence for George Heale in an action upon the case brought by David Ball, against him. it is Ordered that the sd. Heale pay the sd. Bailey for his attendance & costs.

Ordered that the Court be adjourned till tomorrow 10 o'clock. At a Court for Lancaster Co. continued on Wednesday, in 8th day of December 1731. Present: Henry Fleet, Junr., William Ball, Thomas Carter, Edwin Conway, Charles Burges, Charles Carter, Henry Carter; Gent., Justices.

Epaphroditis Lawson, eldest son of Epaphroditis Lawson, Gent., dec'd, and William Stepto came to Court & ackn. their Bond to the Court for £600 and was recorded and the further petition preferred by the sd. Epaphroditis against Hugh Brent, Gent. and William Martin, Execs., of the Will of the sd. Epaphroditis Lawson, dec'd, is dismissed.

Rawleigh Chinn, Gent., came into Court & ackn. his deed to be his son, Joseph Chinn for & concerning196 a. of land in St. Mary's White Chappel Parish, which was admitted to record.

The certificate of George Brent and James Webb, two freeholders, appointed to procession the lands of William Chelton in Christ Church Parish presented in Court by Thomas Carter, Gent, one of the Church Wardens, in these words: November 22, 1732, William Chelton refused to have his land processioned his reason is the lines that is now he thinks was made by William King, dec'd. Signed: George Brent, James Webb.

Order that the Sheriff summon a jury, who are liable to no just exception for affinity consanquinity or interest to meet on the land of William Chelton some time betw. this & next Court, which jury being hereby Ordered the assistance of Co. William Ball, Co. Surveyor, to lay out & procession the land of the sd. William Chelton, and it is also Ordered that the return of the survey & proceedings be made to next Court.

Pg 51. Thomas Carter, Gent., acquainting this Court that the Public Ware Houses erected at Davis's on Corotomon River in this Co. were not well & substantially built as to preserve the tobacco which are to be brought to the same. It is Ordered that Henry Flett, Junr., Gent., Joseph Carter & William Brent meet & view the sd. warehouses & report their opinion of the sufficiency or the insufficiency of them to the at next Court. And, it is Ordered that Capt. William Ball, who undertook the building of the sd. houses have notice of the time of their sd. meeting.

On the petition of John Pyne here admitted to keep an Ordinary at the County Court House, Joseph Carter becoming his security

In the action of trespass betw. James Ball, Gent. Pltf., and Thomas Mason, Deft., for £50 damages by the Deft. breaking the case of the sd. Pltf., in St. Mary's White Chappel Parish, taking & carrying away the timber as in the declaration is set forth, the sd. Pltf. Robert Mitchell, Junr., and John Pollard, the parties concerned in this suit came into Court and consented to stand to & abide, perform, fulfill & keep the award final & determination of Richard Lee, of Northumberland Co., Gent., not touching this or any other dispute now betw. them or either of them relating to lands in controversy audit. It is Ordered that this cause be continued for a return of the sd. award to next Court.

On the attachment obtained by George Dogget against the Estate of Patrick Connelly for 500 lbs. tobacco which attachment served on one coat, 3 blankets, 20 yards. of Virginia Cloth, pr. of breeches, one sheet, pillow, 6 lbs. cotton, 2 lbs. spun cotton, 1 lb. spun yarn, 7 spoons, lathing hammer, 3 pecks of wheat, box full of old lumber, & some corn[?]. The sd. George made oath to his debt whereupon Judgment is granted him for the same & costs. It is Ordered that unless the goods[?] afsd. shall be replevied as the Law directs that they be sold and disposed of towards satisfaction of this Judgment in the same manner as goods taken in execution by a writ and that this attachment be continued till the next Court.

Petition of John Howell & Thomas Howell or place of Thomas Howell, dec'd, late of this Co. Henry Fleet, Junr., Gent., is appointed the Guardian and Thomas Edwards becoming the sd. security of the sd. Guardianship.

Mary Lewis, a servant woman, belonging to William Stamps confessing she had lately been delivered of a mulatto bastard in the time of her service to her sd. master. It is Ordered that in recompence of the loss & trouble occasioned her sd. master herby she serve her master one whole year after her time by Indenture reference or former order of Court that be expired or pay her master 1,000 lbs. tobacco.

Motion of Bushrode Dogget, orphan of Richard Dogget, late of this Co., dec'd. William Mitchell is appointed Guardian. Matthew Mathan[?] is security of the sd. William's security for the Guardianship.

Mathias James having taken the oath of the Government & subscribed the test and the oath of Constable for Fleet's Bay Precinct in Christ Church Parish was administered to him.

Thomas Hunton is appointed surveyor of the highways from Col. Carter's little mill to the main road, which leads from the clerk's Court Office in Christ Church Parish, in this Co., for this year and is Ordered that he keep the sd. road in repair [can't read] belonging to Col. Carter in this precinct.

Isaac Currell is appointed Surveyor of the highways from the Church to Maj. Fleet's in Christ Church Parish in this Co. for this year.

The Presentment against Job Cater of Christ Church Parish, of this Co. for swearing one oath, the sd. Job being summoned and appearing Judgment is granted to the Church Wardens of the afsd. Parish against him for 5 shillings or 50 lbs. tobacco for the offense and it is Ordered that the sd. Job pay the same to them for the use of the poor & costs.

The Presentment against Robert Scofield & his wife, of Christ Church Parish, of this Co. for not going to church in one month and the sd. Robert having has a note left to his sd. wife & neither of them appearing Judgment granted to the Church Wardens of the afsd. Parish against Robert for 10 shillings or 100 lbs. tobacco for the afsd. offense and it is Ordered that he make payment and costs.

The Court for summoning Mary Lewis, Catherine Johnson, Ann Wood, John Cornelius & Thomas Chetwood, of St. Mary's White Chappel Parish in this Co, to answer the Presentment against them for not being presented [?], is revised and it is Ordered that the afsd. be severally summoned to answer the sd. Presentment at the next Court.

The last Court for summoning Frances Senn[?], Frances Angell, Robert Angell & James Munger & his wife, of Christ Church Parish, in this Co., to answer the Presentment against them bot being presented a renewed audit Ordered that the afsd. [can't read] be summoned to answer the sd. Presentment at the next Court.

Pg 52. The Presentment against James Lary, of St. Mary's White Chappel Parish, this Co., for not going to Church in one month is dismissed.

The Presentment against Bridget Spexton, of St, Mary's White Chappel Parish, this Co., on the prayer of the sd. Bridget, it is Ordered that the testimony of her be taken in this cause before a single Justice and returned to the next Court.

The Order of the last Court for summoning John Cornelius to answer the petition of Cornelius Lary not being performed, is renewed and it is Ordered that the sd. John be summoned to answer the sd. petition at the next Court.

In the suit between William Catlet & Sarah, his wife, Pltfs., and James Reves, Exec. of the Will of John Reves, dec'd, Deft., by petition a report of the auditor appointed in this cause was returned and admitted to record and Judgment is granted to the Deft., for £2.0.9, the sum by the auditor's afsd. found to be due & costs of the Estate of the sd. dec'd, John Reves, in the hands of the sd. Deft., if so much thereof he has, otherwise the sd. costs are to be voided of the proper Estate of the sd. Deft.

In the suit in Chancery betw. William Chelton, Stephen Chelton, Thomas Purcell, & Elizabeth, his wife, & George Chelton, son of Benony Chelton, by the afsd. Benony Chelton, his next friend, William Chelton, son of the afsd. William Chelton, by his sd. father & next friend & George Purcell & Judith Purcell, son & daughter of the sd. Thomas Purcell & Elizabeth, his wife, by their sd. father & next friend, Complts., and Charles Smith, Clk., & Elizabeth, his wife, Execx. of the last Will of George Chelton, dec'd, Defts., is continued till next Court.

The action betw. David Ball, Pltf. and George Heale, Deft., is continued till next Court.

The action betw. Thomas Pinckard, Gent., Pltf. and Maurice Jones, Gent., Deft., is continued doe a return of the award of Edwin Conway, Gent., & Thomas Edwards, arbitrators appointed in this cause till next Court.

The suit betw. John Tarpley, Junr., Gent. attorney of the King, Pltf., and Richard Jackson, Deft., is continued till next Court.

The suit betw. John Tarpley, Junr., Gent. attorney of the King, Pltf., and Robert Wells, Deft., by information is continued till next Court.

The suit betw. John Tarpley, Junr., Gent. attorney of the King, Pltf., and John Hubbard, Deft., by information is continued till next Court.

The last Court for summoning Richard Wooden, John Grinsteed[?], Thomas Cotes, James Stott, Benj. George, William Delaney, Thomas Charles, Chattin Chowning, William Stamps & James Gaylor severally to answer the Information of John Tarpley, Junr., Gent., the King's attorney against them not being preformed is renewed and it is Ordered that they be summoned to answer the sd. Information at the next Court.

The debt betw. Robert Carter, Esqr. and Thomas Carter, Church Wardens, of Christ Church Parish, Pltfs., and Frances Murrough, Defts., the sd. Defts. pleaded and the Pltfs. joined whereupon the trial of the sd. issue was referred till next Court.

Action of trespass, assault & battery betw. Joseph Hagan[?], Pltf., and William Delaney, Deft., is dismissed.

The action of debt, betw. Dennis Ryan, Pltf., and Will Ballendine, Defts., for £3.7.6 due by account, the Deft. failing to appear on the Motion of the sd. Deft., a non-suit is awarded him and it is Ordered that the sd. Pltf. forthwith pay unto the sd. Deft., 5 shillings for the same together with one attorney's fee & costs.

In the action of trespass & assault & battery betw. Dennis Ryan, Pltf., and William Ballentine, Defts., for £10 damages in the declaration is set forth the sd. Pltf. failing to appear on the Motion of the sd. Deft. awarded him audit is Ordered that the sd. Pltf. forthwith pay unto the sd. Deft., 5 shillings for the same together with one attorney's fee & costs.

Action of debt betw. William Richardson, Pltf. and William Abby, Deft., for 360 lbs. tobacco due by bill is dismissed.

In the debt betw. Matthew Zuill, merchant, Pltf., and Thomas Bridgford, Deft., for 1,000 lbs. tobacco, the Deft. being returned [can't make out?] & not appearing on the Motion of the sd. Pltf. a copias is awarded him against the sd. Deft., returned to next Court.

In the Debt between Thomas Edwards, Pltf., and Thomas Bridgford, Deft., for £2.18.2 & 529 lbs. tobacco, the Deft. being returned non-[can't read] & not appearing on the Motion of the sd. Pltf. at cupias is awarded him against the sd. Deft. returnable to the next Court.

Pg 53. Ordered that the Court be adjourned till 2nd Wednesday in January next. At a Court for Lancaster Co. continued on Wednesday, in 9th day of January next. Present: William Ball, Thomas Carter, Edwin Conway, Charles Burges, Nicholas Martin; Gent., Justices.

Edwin Conway, Charles Burges & John Selden, Gent., this Court presented to the Hon. Gov. as persons fit & able to execute the office of Co. Sheriff for the ensuing year.

Edwin Conway, Gent, a Co. Justice, James Ellis charged by Josian Hunter of Wiccocomoco Parish, in this Co., single woman, that he had carnal knowledge of her body at several times. And that the sd. Josian Hunter is now with child by the sd. James Ellis, which when born will be a bastard, He the sd. James Ellis appeared and together with Lewis Crane, of the afsd. Parish, jointly & severally ackn. themselves indebted to our King, now his heirs & successors in the sum of £20 to be levied upon the goods & chattels, lands & tenements under the condition that he, the sd. James Ellis, shall from henceforth save, keep, [can't read] and indemnified the Church Wardens of the sd. Wiccocomoco Parish from all manner of charge, trouble, & incumberanc3e which to the sd. Church Wardens or the Parish may or happen for or by means of the birth & maintenance of the child. And, also that the sd. James Ellis shall & will during one year ensuing keep the Majesty's peace be of good behavior toward the sd. the sd. Josian Hunter & all other his Majesty's other people, and further that he, the sd. James Ellis, shall pay the costs hereby occasioned.

The Will of Ruth Fouchee, dec'd, was presented in Court by William Bertrand, Exec., therein named, who made Oath thereto and being proved by the Oath of Henry Newby, a witness, is admitted for and on the Motion of the sd. Exec., the certificate was made for obtaining Probate.

William Bertrand, Exec., of the Will of Ruth Fouchee, dec'd, to bring an Inventory of the sd. Ruth's Estate to the next Court.

William Mitchell Ordered to exhibit an amount of all the Estate of Bushrode Doggett to whom he hath lately been appointed Guardian, which he received in his hands or the sd, Bushrode shall be entitled to at the next Court.

Ordered Henry Fleet, Junr., Gent, Guardian of John Howell & Thomas Howell exhibit an amount of all the Estate of the sd. Orphans which he hath received into his hand or the sd. Orphans shall be entitled to at the next Court and then appear and make Oath thereto.

84

The attachment obtained by James Ball, Gent., against the Estate of john Brown for 595 lbs. tobacco is dismissed.

The attachment obtained by Charles Burges, Gent., against the Estate of Thomas Sanders for 325 lbs. of tobacco, which attachment was found on some tobacco lying at Robert Pritchard's, which tobacco was attached by virtue of another attachment granted against the sd. Sander's Estate of the sd. Robert Pritchard. The Court being of the opinion that the sd. Burgesses attachment ought to be first satisfied notwithstanding the other service the sd. Burgess made Oath to the half of the debt, whereupon Judgment is granted for the same & costs. Audit is Ordered that the afsd. Robert Pritchard be summoned to the next Court to make oath what of the Estate of the sd. Thomas Sanders was in his hands at the time when the attachment was served.

The attachment obtained by Robert Pritchard against the Estate of Thomas Sanders for 950 lbs. tobacco, which attachment was served on all the tobacco that was in the hands of the sd. Robert Pritchard belonging to the Thomas Sanders, is continued till next Court

In pursuance to the Order of the last December Court for viewing the public Warehouses at Geeles Davis's in this Co., a report of Henry Fleet, Junr., Gent., & Joseph Carter was this day returned which is admitted to record. And, it is Ordered that William Stephens, Thomas Carter, Carpenter, and James Carter meet at the sd. warehouses & examine whether the workmanship thereon is performed according to the Condition of the Bond given for the sd. undertaking and what other or further work ought to be done towards the full performance of the sd. Bond and report their opinion herein to the next Court.

Pg 54. John Bailey is appointed to clear a road from the main road betw. Joseph Chinn's & John Stott's to the Wharf belonging to the warehouses at Deep Creek in St. Mary's White Chappel Parish, in this Co. And, it is Ordered that the male laboring tithables adjacent to the sd. road assist him in clearing the same.

Ordered that the Court be adjourned till 2nd Wednesday in March next. At a Court for Lancaster Co. continued on Wednesday, in 8th day of March 1731. Present: William Ball, Thomas Carter, Edwin Conway, John Selden, Nicholas Martin, Henry Fleet, Junr., Henry Carter; Gent., Justices.

William Angell, orphan of Robert Angell, late of this Co., dec'd, aged 12 years in April next, on the prayer of Frances Angell, his mother, & Charles Angell, Exec., of the Will of Robert Angell, dec'd, is by the Court bound to William

Martin & Elizabeth, his wife, till he attains 21 years of age, his sd. master & wife are to teach him to read & write and the trade of a Clapboard Carpenter and to find & allow him sufficient diet & lodging & apparel & at the expiration of his servitude to pay him as is appointed for servants by Indenture or custom.

Susanna Cope, orphan of William Cope, aged six years the first of August next on the prayer of Ann Cope, her mother, is by the Court bound to John Wren & Hannah, his wife, till she attains her age of 18 years, her sd. master & wife are to teach her to read, sew, knit & spin and to find & allow her sufficient dirt, lodging and apparel & at the expiration of his servitude to pay him as is appointed for servants by Indenture or custom.

On the prayer of John Howell, Thomas Howell, Orphans of Thomas Howell, dec'd, by Henry Fleet, Junr., Gent., their Guardian and Ezekiel Gilbert & John Gibson, Admins., of the Estate of Sarah Howell, dec'd, who was Execx. of the Will of the sd. deceased Thomas. Thomas Carter, Gent., and Thomas Edwards are appointed to settle an account of the Estate of the afsd. Orphans, which the Estate of the sd. Execx. and to make a report of their proceedings to the next Court.

A report of William Stephens, Thomas Carter, Carpenter, and James Carter on their view of the Public Warehouses at Gele's Davis' in this Co. was returned and admitted to record, whereupon it is Ordered that the further proceedings in the matter be dismissed and that William Ball, Junr., Gent., who undertook the building the sd. warehouses pay the costs hereby occasioned.

John Mullis with the consent of his father, Richard Mullis, of this Co., came into Court and consented and voluntarily agreed to force John Curlet the full term of 5 years from this day the sd. John Curlet to teach him the trade of a Carpenter & Joyner and to find and allow him sufficient diet, lodging and apparel and at the expiration of his servitude to pay him as is appointed for servants by Indenture or Custom.

The action of trespass betw. James Ball, Gent, Pltf., and Thomas Mason, Deft., is continued till next Court.

In the suit betw. George Dogget, Pltf., and Patricia Connelly, Deft., by attachment, the Sheriff having returned that he had caused the debt & costs to be delivered to the sd. Pltf. It is Ordered that the attachment be revoked.

86

The Presentment against Mary [can't read] of St. Mary's White Chappel Parish, for having a mulatto bastard, is dismissed.

The Presentment against Frances [can't read] of Christ Church Parish for not going to Church one month, is dismissed.

The Presentment against Robert Angell, of Christ Church Parish, for not going to Church for a month, he was summoned and not appearing, Judgment was granted to the Church Wardens for 5 shillings or 50 lbs. of tobacco for the fine inflicted for the sd. offense. An Audit is Ordered that the sd. Robert pay the same to the Church Wardens for the use of the poor in the sd. Parish and costs.

The Presentment against James Munger, & his wife of Christ Church Parish, for not going to Church in one month, is dismissed.

The Presentment against Catherine Johnson, of St. Mary's White Chappel Parish in this Co. for not going to Church for one month is dismissed.

Pg 55. The Presentment against Frances Angell, of Christ Church Parish, for not going to Church in one month she was summoned & not appearing Judgment was granted to the Church Wardens against her for 5 shillings or 50 lbs. of tobacco for the use of the poor of the sd. Parish, and to pay the costs.

The Presentment against Ann Wood, of St. Mary's White Chappel Parish, for not going to Church in one month she was summoned & not appearing Judgment was granted to the Church Wardens against her for 5 shillings or 50 lbs. of tobacco for the use of the poor of the sd. Parish, and to pay the costs.

The Presentment against John Cornelius, of St. Mary's White Chappel Parish, for not going to Church in one month is dismissed.

The Presentment against Thomas Chetwood, of St. Mary's White Chappel Parish, for not going to Church in one month she was summoned & not appearing Judgment was granted to the Church Wardens against her for 5 shillings or 50 lbs. of tobacco for the use of the poor of the sd. Parish, and to pay the costs.

The Presentment against Bridget Spexton, of St. Mary's White Chappel Parish, for having a mulatto bastard child, is dismissed.

The suit betw. Cornelius Sary[?], Pltf., & John Cornelius, Deft., by petition is continued till next Court.

The Ejection betw. John Tar, Pltf., and William Brent, Deft., is continued till next Court.

Ordered that Richard Wooding, William Delaney, John Chinn, James Stott, William Tyler be summoned to the next Court to answer the Presentment of Joseph Ball & Joseph Heale, Church Wardens of St. Mary's White Chappel Parish, in this Co., against them.

In the suit in Chancery betw. William Chelton, Stephen Chelton, Thomas Purcell, & Elizabeth, his wife, & George Chelton, son of Benony Chelton, by the afsd. Benony Chelton, his next friend, William Chelton, son of the afsd. William Chelton, by his sd. father & next friend & George Purcell & Judith Purcell, son & daughter of the sd. Thomas Purcell & Elizabeth, his wife, by their sd. father & next friend, Complts., and Charles Smith, Clk., & Elizabeth, his wife, Exec. of the last Will of George Chelton, dec'd, Defts., wherein the sd. Complts. in their Bill pray that the sd. Defts. may be compelled to give security for the delivery of the several legacies in the sd. Will bequeathed to them after the death of the Deft., Elizabeth or immediately surrender & deliver the same. The parties were this day heard on the Bill answer and replication in this cause and matters deliberations being had on the whole premises, it is Ordered that this suit be dismissed and that the sd. Complts. pay unto the sd. Defts., their costs in this behalf expended and one attorney's fee.

Action betw. David Ball, Pltf., and George Heale, Deft., is continued till next Court.

Action betw. Thomas Pinckard, Gent., Pltf., and Maurice Jones, Gent., Deft., for £10 due by the report of the auditors appointed. Judgment is granted the sd. Pltf., against. the sd. Deft. for 9 shillings, the damages by the auditors in this cause and costs together with one attorney's fee.

William Townsend having attended one day as a witness in the suit of Thomas Pinckard, and it was Ordered Townsend to pay to recover his travelling 20 miles, going & returning and costs.

Thomas Pinn[?] having attended 3 days & one day before the auditors as a witness in the suit of Thomas Pinckard, and it was Ordered to pay to recover his travelling 60 miles, going & returning and costs.

Thomas Pinn[?] having attended one day before the auditors as a witness in the suit of Thomas Pinckard, and it was Ordered to pay for his attendance and to recover his travelling 60 miles, going & returning and costs.

William Pinckard having attended 2 days as a witness for William Chelton and others in their case and it was Ordered that the Pltfs. pay for his attendance at their case.

Pg 56. In the performance to a Cause in the act for Regulating Ordinary's & Restraint of Tipling Houses. The Court doth Set & Rate: Cider at 15 pence or 12 lbs. of tobacco the gallon; Rum & Brandy (except French Brandy) at 8 shillings or 76 lbs. tobacco the gallon; Punch at 15 pence or 12 lbs. tobacco the Quart; Strong beer at 15 pence or 12 lbs. tobacco the bottle; Madera wine at one shilling, 10 pence half penny or 18 lbs. tobacco the quart. Dyet with small beer to drink at 11 pence, farthing or 9 lbs. tobacco the meal. Lodging at 7 pence, half penny or 6 lbs. tobacco the night. Stabloage & fodder for a horse at 6 pence or 5 lbs. of tobacco the night. Oats or Indian Corn at 6 pence or 5 lbs. tobacco the gallon.

Ordered that the Court be adjourned till 2nd Wednesday in April next. At a Court for Lancaster Co. continued on Thursday, in 4th day of May 1732. Present: Henry Fleet, Thomas Carter, George Heale, Edwin Conway, Charles Burges, John Selden, Henry Fleet, Junr., Henry Carter, Hugh Brent, Nicholas Martin; Gent., Justices.

The Act of Assembly concerning Public claims was read in Court.

William Richardson making oath to his certificate for taking up a Negro slave belonging to Col. Charles Grymes, of Richmond Co., that no satisfaction had been received for the same. It is Ordered that the Court Clk. certify the sd. proof to the Assembly.

George Dogget making oath to his certificate for taking up a Negro slave belonging to Samuel Hopkins, of Richmond Co., that no satisfaction had been received for the same. It is Ordered that the Court Clk. certify the sd. proof to the Assembly.

William Hutchins making oath to his certificate for taking up a making oath to his certificate for taking up a servant woman named Honora Clark belonging to Elizabeth Brown of Northumberland Co. & that no satisfaction had been received for the same. It is Ordered that the Court Clk. certify the sd. proof to the Assembly.

Christopher Kirk making oath to his certificate for taking up a making oath to his certificate for taking up a servant man named Charles McGuire belonging to John Chelton, of Northumberland Co. & that no satisfaction had been received for the same. It is Ordered that the Court Clk. certify the sd. proof to the Assembly.

Thomas Fleet making oath to his certificate for taking up a making oath to his certificate for taking up a servant woman named Mary Cotes servant to Francis Loakhouse[?], of Prince William Co., & that no satisfaction had been received for the same. It is Ordered that the Court Clk. certify the sd. proof to the Assembly.

An account subscribed by William Ball, Junr., one of the Inspectors of Deep Creek Warehouses in this Co., of the tobacco loft in the sd. houses when they were burnt down, was presented & [can't read word] to by the sd. William and proof Ordered to be certified to the Assembly.

A certificate under the hands of William Downman, William Glascock, and William Ball, Junr., Inspectors, of Deep Creek Warehouses in this Co. concerning tobacco belonging to William Ballendine, Judith Payne, John Bailey, & David Smith left in the sd. houses when they were burnt was presented in Court by the sd. William Ball and Ordered to be transmitted to the Assembly

An account subscribed by William Ball, Junr., against the Colony of Virginia for £8.0.4 was presented and sworn to by the sd. William and [word missed] Ordered to be certified to the Assembly.

An amount subscribed by Dale Carter, sub. Co. Sheriff against the Colony of Virginia for 200 lbs. tobacco was presented & sworn to by the sd. Dale and Ordered to be certified to the Assembly.

John Cox, Junr. making oath to his certificate for taking up a Negro belonging to Matthew Mathan[?] of this Co., and that no satisfaction has been received for the same. Ordered that the Court Clk. certify this proof to the Assembly.

A petition directed to the Mr. Speaker & the rest of the House of Burgesses praying a repeal of the Act made at the last Assembly for improving the staple of tobacco and for preventing fraud in his Majesty's customs & proposing that a

Law be made for restraining the crops of tobacco for the future was subscribed in Court by the several subscribers thereto and Ordered to be certified to the Assembly.

Pg 57.   At a Court for Lancaster Co. on Wednesday the 10th day of May 1732. Present: Henry Fleet, William Ball, Thomas Carter, Edwin Conway, Charles Burges, John Selden, Henry Fleet, Junr., Henry Carter, Nicholas Martin; Gent., Justices.

Thomas Chetwood be summoned to the next Court to answer the Petition of Peter Hardin against him.

The suit betw. John Tarpley, Junr., Gent., King's attorney, Pltf., and Richard Jackson, Deft, by Information for 200 lbs. tobacco due by means of the Defts., having retailed liquors contrary to Law as in the sd. Information set forth. is dismissed.

John Selden, Gent, is appointed to take the list of Tithables in the Upper Precinct of St. Mary's White Chappel Parish, in this Co, for this year.

George Heale, Gent., is appointed to take the list of Tithables in the Middle Precinct of St. Mary's White Chappel Parish, in this Co, for this year.

William Ball, Gent., is appointed to take the list of Tithables in the Lower Precinct in St. Mary's White Chappel Parish, in this Co, for this year.

Thomas Carter is appointed to take the list of Tithables in the lower part of Corotomon Precinct of Christ Church Parish, in this Co, for this year.

Henry Carter, Gent., is appointed to take the list of Tithables in the upper part of Corotomon Precinct of Christ Church Parish, in this Co, for this year.

Hugh Brent, Gent., is appointed to take the list of Tithables in the Middle Precinct of Christ Church Parish, in this Co, for this year.

Nicholas Martin, Gent., is appointed to take the list of Tithables between Corotomon River and the main road which leads from the Church to Col. Carter's great mill in Christ Church Parish, in this Co, for this year.

Henry Fleet, Gent., is appointed to take the list of Tithables in the Lower Precincts in Christ Church Parish, in this Co, for this year.

In the suit betw. John Tarply, Junr., Gent. King's attorney, Pltf., and Robert Wells, Deft., by Information Judgment is granted to the sd. Pltf., by Nihil Dicit.

In the suit betw. John Tarply, Junr., Gent. King's attorney, Pltf., and Robert Wooden, Deft., by Information, the Deft. pleaded and the Pltf. joined issue whereupon it is Ordered that the trial of the sd. issue be referred to the next Court.

In the suit betw. John Tarply, Junr., Gent. King's attorney, Pltf., and John Grinstead, Deft., by Information, the Deft. pleaded and the Pltf. joined issue whereupon it is Ordered that the trial of the sd. issue be referred to the next Court.

In the suit betw. John Tarply, Junr., Gent. King's attorney, Pltf., and Thomas Cotes, Deft., by Information, the Deft. pleaded and the Pltf. joined issue whereupon it is Ordered that the trial of the sd. issue be referred to the next Court.

In the suit betw. John Tarply, Junr., Gent. King's attorney, Pltf., and James Stott, Deft., by Information, the Deft. pleaded and the Pltf. joined issue whereupon it is Ordered that the trial of the sd. issue be referred to the next Court.

In the suit betw. John Tarply, Junr., Gent. King's attorney, Pltf., and William Delaney, Deft., by Information, the Deft. pleaded and the Pltf. joined issue whereupon it is Ordered that the trial of the sd. issue be referred to the next Court.

In the suit betw. John Tarply, Junr., Gent. King's attorney, Pltf., and Benjamin George, Deft., by Information, for 6,000 lbs. tobacco arising due by means of the Deft. leaving tended tobacco seconds contrary to Law as in the sd. Information set forth, is dismissed.

In the suit betw. John Tarply, Junr., Gent. King's attorney, Pltf., and John Hubbard, Deft., by Information, Judgment is granted to the sd. Pltf., by Nihil Dicit.

In the suit betw. John Tarply, Junr., Gent. King's attorney, Pltf., Thomas Carter, Deft., pleaded and the Pltf. joined issue whereupon it is Ordered that the trial of the sd. issue be referred to the next Court.

In the suit betw. John Tarply, Junr., Gent. King's attorney, Pltf., and Chattin Chowning, Deft., by Information, the Deft. pleaded and the Pltf. joined issue

92

whereupon it is Ordered that the trial of the sd. issue be referred to the next Court.

In the suit betw. John Tarply, Junr., Gent. King's attorney, Pltf., and William Stamp, Deft., is continued till next Court on Deft's Motion & costs.

In the suit betw. John Tarply, Junr., Gent. King's attorney, Pltf., and James Gaylor, Deft., is continued till next Court on Deft's Motion & costs.

Ordered that William Read & William Sydnor be summoned to the next Court to answer the Presentment of Joseph Ball & Joseph Heale, Church Wardens, of St. Mary's White Chappel Parish, in this Co. against them.

The Presentment of Joseph Ball & Joseph Heale, Church Wardens, of St. Mary's White Chappel Parish, in this Co. against John Carter for going out of the sd. Parish Church in time of Devine Service, is dismissed.

Pg 58. In the action of Debt betw. Robert Carter, Esqr., and Thomas Carter, Church Wardens of Christ Church Parish, Pltf.s and Frances Murrough, Deft., for 500 lbs. of tobacco & cask or 5 shillings damage as in the declaration, a jury was impaneled & sworn to try the issue & joined in the same who bringing in their verdict in these words " We find for the Pltfs. 500 lbs. tobacco or five shillings damages. Signed- James Carter, Foreman. The sd. verdict was recorded and the sd. Defts. lodged a plea in arrest of the Judgment to be given in this cause whereupon it is Ordered that the arguments on the sd. plea be referred to the next Court.

In the action of debt betw. Robert Carter, Esqr., Pltf., and Sarah Gregory, Deft., Judgment is granted to the sd. Pltf. against the sd. Deft. for £24 and costs. But this Judgment is to be discharged by the payment of £12 together with lawful interest for the same from the 5th day of June 1728 and the costs.

In the action in the case betw. Thomas Edwards, Pltf., and Sarah Gregory, Deft., for 982 lbs. tobacco due by and Judgment is granted to the Pltf. for the afsd. debt and it is Ordered that the sd. Deft., forthwith pay the same & costs.

The action of trespass & assault & battery betw. Joseph Hogan, Pltf., and William Delaney, Deft., for £5 damages as in the declaration, is dismissed.

In the action of Detinue betw. Sarah Flower, Pltf., and Robert Scofield, Deft., for £10, the sd. Deft. being returned & not appearing on the Motion of the Pltf. is awarded against the sd. Deft., returnable to next Court.

Henry Fleet, Junr., Gent., exhibited and made oath to his account of the estate of John & Thomas Howell, Orphans under his Guardianship, was admitted to record.

In the action betw. Charles Burges, Gent., Pltf. and Thomas Sanders, Deft., by attachment Robert Pritchard in whose hands this attachment was served having been summoned to appear & declare what of the Estate of the sd. Deft. was in his hands, the sd. attachment was served upon him and failing to appear. It is Ordered that the sd. Robert be taken into custody, he to give [can't read] by his appearance to declare afsd. at the next Court.

The action of Debt betw. William Townsin, Pltf., and William Stepto, Deft., for 1,600 lbs. tobacco or £8 due by obligation is dismissed.

The action upon the case betw. Joseph Chinn, Pltf., and Henry Taylor, Deft., for 1,000 lbs. tobacco due by account is dismissed.

The action upon the case betw. Thomas Gwyn, Pltf., and Thomas Scott, Deft., for 430 lbs. of tobacco by costs Judgment to the Pltf. against the Deft. for the sd. debt & costs.

On the difference depending betw. John Howell & Thomas Howell, orphans of Thomas Howell, dec'd, against John Gibson & Ezekiel Gilbart [Gilbert?], Admins., of the Estate of Sarah Howell, dec'd, with the Will annexed, a report of the auditors appointed in this cause was returned and admitted to record and it is Ordered that the further proceedings in this matter be dismissed.

The suit betw. Robt. Pritchard, Pltf., and Thomas Sanders, Deft., by attachment for 950 lbs. tobacco & neither party appearing, is dismissed.

The suit betw. Joseph Sary[?], Pltf., and John Cornelius, Deft., by petition for the Pltf. freedom dues & was in the petition is set forth that the sd. Pltf. being dead, is dismissed.

The ejection betw. John Tar, Pltf., and William[?] Brent, Deft., is continued till next Court on Deft's Motion & costs.

The Presentment of Joseph Ball & Joseph Heale, Church Warden's of St. Mary's White Chappel Parish, in this Co against James Stott for going out of the Parish Church in time of Divine Service, the sd. James being summoned and not appearing, Judgment is granted against him for 5 shillings or 50 lbs. tobacco, the

94

fine fulfilled by Law for the sd. offence and it is Ordered that he pay the same to the sd. Church Wardens for the use of the poor in the sd. Parish with all costs.

The Presentment of Joseph Ball & Joseph Heale, Church Warden's of St. Mary's White Chappel Parish, in this Co against William Tyler for going out of the Parish Church in time of Divine Service, is dismissed.

The case betw. David Ball, Pltf., and George Heale, Deft., is continued till next Court.

Pg 59. In the action of trespass betw. James Ball, Gent., Pltf., and Thomas Mason, Deft., for £50 damages by reason of the Deft. breaking and entering the close of the sd. Pltf. in St. Mary's White Chappel Parish, in this Co., & taking & carrying away the timber thereon growing & digging up the soil thereof as in the declaration is set forth, the sd. Pltfs. Robert Mitchell, Junr., & John Pollard, the parties concerned in the suit came into Court and consented to stand to & abide, perform, fulfill and keep the award final end and determination of the Honorable John Grymes, of Middlesex Co., Esqr., touching this or any other dispute betw. them or other of the three relating to the land in controversy and further that the death of either of the parties before named shall not abate this action. And, it is Ordered that this cause be continued till next Court.

Suit in Chancery betw. William [?]erato & Margaret, his wife, Complts., and William Bertrand, Exec. of the Will of Ruth Fouchee, Deft., time is given for sd. Deft., to answer or demur till next Court.

In the action of trespass betw. William Martin, Admin. of all the goods, chattels, rights & credits that were Alexander Edgar's, late of the Parish of Christ Church, in this Co., dec'd, & at the time of his death, Pltfs. and William Stepto, Defts., a special imparlance is granted the Defts., till next Court.

Thomas Marshall, orphan of Thomas Marshall, late of this Co., dec'd, aged 5 years the 10th day of February last, is by the Court bound to Thomas Gwynn, till he attains the age of 21 years, the sd. Gwynn is teach him to read & write and the trade of a Shoemaker, and to find and allow him sufficient diet, lodging & apparel and at the expiration of his servitude to pay him as appointed as servants by Indenture or custom.

Petition of Moses Carter, Orphan of Peter Carter, late of this Co., dec'd, Henry Towles is appointed his Guardian Robert Mitchell, Gent., becoming the St, Mary's security for the sd. Guardianship.

Ordered that Henry Towles, Guardian of Moses Carter exhibits an amount of all the Estate of the sd. Orphan, which hath received into his hands or the sd. Orphan shall be entitled to at the next Court, and then appear & make oath thereto.

In the suit betw. Sarah Dogget by John Mott, Junr., her next friend, Pltf., and Richard Boatman, Deft., petition for 300 lbs of tobacco due for one year's service. On hearing the parties, it is conditioned that the sd. Pltfs., recover against the sd. Deft. the sd. 300 lbs. tobacco & costs.

Upon the case betw. James Haines, Pltf., and Robert Mitchell, Gent., Deft., for £7.3.10 due by amount is dismissed.

The action of Debt betw. William King, Pltf., and John Gill, Deft., a special imparlance is granted to the sd. Deft., in custody of the Co. Sheriff, till next Court.

In the action betw. Thomas Pollard, Pltf., and Joseph Carter, Deft., the sd. Deft. being called & not appearing nor any security returned, Judgment is granted to the Pltf. against the Deft. and William Ball, Junr., Gent., Co. Sheriff for what shall appear to be justly due to the sd. Pltf. at the next Court unless the sd. Deft. appears & answers this action.

On the Presentment of Joseph Ball & Joseph Heale, Church Wardens, of St. Mary's, White Chappel Parish, in this Co., against William Delaney for going out of the sd. Parish Church in time of Divine Service. The sd. William being summoned and not appearing, Judgment is granted against him for 5 shillings or 50 lbs. tobacco, the fine for the offense to be paid to the sd. Church Wardens for the use of the poor of the sd. Parish., plus costs.

In the action of Debt betw. Henry Fleet, William Ball, Thomas Carter, George Heale, Edwin Conway, Charles Burges, Charles Carter, Junr., John Selden, Henry Fleet, Junr., Henry Carter, Hugh Brent & Nicholas Martin, Gent., Justice of the Co., Pltfs., and Robert Gibson, Deft., a special imparlance is granted to the sd. Deft. till next Court.

The suit betw. Thomas Thorton, Pltf. and John Buckley, Deft., by Petition for 325 lbs. tobacco due by note is dismissed.

The action of Debt betw. Robert Carter, Esqr., and Thomas Carter, Gent., Church Wardens, of Christ Church Parish, in this Co., Pltf., and Ellinor Clark,

Deft., for 500 lbs. of tobacco & cask or 50 shillings damages as is declaration as set forth, the sd. Ellinor being a runaway is dismissed.

In the action of debt betw. Matthew Zuillinorold[?], Pltf., and Thomas Bridgford, Deft., for 1,000 lbs. tobacco & the Deft. not appearing on the action of the Pltf., an attachment awarded against the Estate of the sd. Deft. for the sd. tobacco & costs returnable to the next Court for Judgment.

Pg 60. In the action of Debt betw. Thomas Edward, Pltf., and Thomas Bridgford, Deft., for £2.18.2 and 579 lbs. tobacco. The sd. Defts. not appearing on the Motion of the sd. Pltfs., an attachment is awarded him against the Estate of the sd. Defts. for the sd. money & tobacco and costs returnable to the next Court for Judgment.

On the Motion of John Selden, Gent., he is admitted to set draw bar or gates for wheel carriages & dual gates for passengers on the main road which leads thru his plantation over his mill in this Co.

 By virtue of a precept from Edwin Conway, Gent., a Co. Justice of the Peace, Margaret Galbreath appeared to answer a charge for several misbehaviors by her against Capt. Thomas Carter whereupon the parties were fully heard and it is considered that the sd. Margaret be discharged.

Ordered that the Court be adjourned till 2nd Wednesday in June next. At a Court for Lancaster Co. continued on Wednesday, in 14th day of June 1732. Present: Henry Fleet, Junr., Thomas Carter, George Heale, Henry Fleet, Junr., Hugh Brent; Gent., Justices.

On the prayer of Absolom Mohon, Orphan of Patrick Mohon, late of this Co., dec'd, John Angell is appointed his Guardian, john Wale becoming the sd. John Angell's security for the sd. Guardianship.

 On the Motion of John Angell, Guardian of Absolom Mohon, Orphan of Patrick Mohon, late of this Co., dec'd. It is Ordered that John Brook & Frances, his wife, Adminx. of the Estate of the sd. dec'd Patrick deliver up unto the sd. John Angell, the Estate of the sd. Orphan in their hands.

Ordered that John Angell, Guardian, of Absolom Mohon, exhibit an account of All the Estate of the sd. Orphan, which he has recorded into the hands or the sd. Orphan shall be exhibited at the next Court & then appear and make Oath.

Ordered that John Brooks be summoned to the next Court to signify his consent to the binding to Wm. Mohon & Patrick Moho, Orphans under his care.

The suit betw, Peter Hardin, Pltf., and Thomas Chetwood, Deft., by petition for "freedom dues", the parties being heard. It is considered that the sd. Peter recover against the sd. Deft., 10 bushels of Indian Corn, 30 shillings or the value thereof in goods & one well [can't read] or [can't read] of the value of 20 shillings at the least and costs.

In the suit betw. John Tarpley, Junr., the King's attorney, Pltf., and Robert Wells, Deft., by information that the sd. Deft. pleaded and the Pltf. joined issue whereupon it is Ordered that the trial of the issue be referred to next Court.

In the suit betw. John Tarpley, Junr., Gent., the King's Attorney, Pltf., and Richard Wooden, Deft., by Information for the 1,000 lbs. tobacco accruing due my means of the Deft., having tended tobacco seconds contrary to Law & William Stepto, Henry Knight, Martin Shearman, George Payne & James Cammell, William Sydnor, George Light, Henry Towles, [?] Wale, William Edwards, George Light, Junr., & Benjamin George, Junr., were impaneled & sworn to try the issue joined in this cause & bringing in there verdict in these words " We the Jury do find the Deft. guilty and that he had one tithable person and one other person above the age of 7 years then residing on his plantation. William Stepto, Foreman. The sd. verdict was admitted to record and the Deft. moving in arrest of the Judgment to be given in this cause the arguments on the sd. plea in arrest are referred till the next Court.

Pg 61. The suit between John Tarpley, Junr., Gent., the King's Attorney, Pltf., and James Stott, Deft., information the sd. Deft., pleaded & the Pltf. joined issue whereupon it is Ordered that the trial of the issue be referred till next Court.

 The suit between John Tarpley, Junr., Gent., the King's Attorney, Pltf., and John Hubbard, Deft., Information the sd. Deft., pleaded & the Pltf. joined issue whereupon it is Ordered that the trial of the issue be referred till next Court.

The suit between John Tarpley, Junr., Gent., the King's Attorney, Pltf., and William Stamps, Deft., Information the sd. Deft., pleaded & the Pltf. joined issue whereupon it is Ordered that the trial of the issue be referred till next Court.

The suit between John Tarpley, Junr., Gent., the King's Attorney, Pltf., and James Gayle, Deft., Information the sd. Deft., pleaded & the Pltf. joined issue whereupon it is Ordered that the trial of the issue be referred till next Court.

The Presentment of Joseph Ball & Joseph Heale, Church Warden's of St. Mary's White Chappel Parish, in this Co against William Read for going out of the Parish Church in time of Divine Service, Judgment granted against sd. William for 5 shillings or 50 lbs. tobacco to the Church Wardens for the use of the poor of the sd. Parish & costs.

In the action of debt betw. Robert Carter, Esqr., & Thomas Carter, Church Warden's of Christ Church Parish, Pltfs., and Frances Murrough, Deft. and the Pltf. justified that the sd. Deft. should be obliges to come to a hearing on her plea in arrest of the Judgment to be given in this cause. But, the Court were divided in opinion on the sd. Motion.

In the action of trespass betw. William Martin, Admin., of all singular the goods, chattels, rights, credits that were Alexander Edgars. late of Christ Church Parish, in this Co., dec'd, at the time of his death, Pltf., and William Stepto, Deft., the sd. Defts. pleaded and the Pltf. joined issue whereupon it is Ordered that the trial of the sd. issue be referred till next Court.

The action of detinue betw. Sarah Flower, Pltf. and Robert Scofield, Deft., for £10 damages as in the declaration is set forth is dismissed.

In the suit betw. Charles Burges, Gent., Pltf., and Thomas Sanders, Deft., by attachment Robert Pritchard on whom this attachment was served, appeared and had time granted him, till next Court to declare what of the sd. Deft.'s Estate was in his hands when the attachment was served upon him and it is Ordered that the sd. attachment be, till the next Court.

The action of trespass betw. James Ball, Gent., Pltf., and Thomas Mason, Deft., is continued till next Court.

The action betw. David Ball, Pltf., and George Heale, Deft., is continued till next Court.

The ejection issue betw. John Tarr, Pltf., and William Brent, Deft., is continued till next Court.

In the suit in Chancery betw. William Everate & Margaret, his wife, Complt., and William Bertrand, Exec. of the Will of Ruth Fouchee, dec'd, Deft., the sd.

Deft. lodged and made an oath to his answer and on the Motion of the sd. Complt. time is given them to consider the said answer, till the next Court.

In the action of Debt betw. William King, Pltf., and John Gill, Deft., the sd. Deft. lodged his plea and on the Motion of the sd. Pltf. time is given him to consider the plea till next Court.

In the action betw. Thomas Pollard, Pltf., and Joseph Carter, Deft., on the Motion of the sd. Deft., oyer is granted him of the account mentioned in the Pltf. Declaration, till next Court

In the action of debt betw. Matthew Quillmouth, Pltf., and Thomas Bridgford, Deft., for 1,000 lbs. tobacco due by account is dismissed.

In the action of Debt betw. Thomas Edwards, Pltf., and Thomas Bridgford, Deft., the attachment granted to the sd. Pltf. in the cause against the Estate of the Deft., is continued till next Court.

The suit between John Tarpley, Junr., Gent., the King's Attorney, Pltf., and Thomas Chetwood, Deft., by the petition for 50 shillings due by the obligation. Judgment is granted to the sd. Pltf for his afsd. debt and costs. But, the Deft. is to have what descent he makes appear upon oath before Col. William Ball betw. this & next Court.

In the action of debt betw. Clement Lattimer, Pltf., and Henry Bentley, Deft., for 500 lbs. tobacco damage in the declaration set forth, the Sheriff having failed to execute the writ in this cause. It is Ordered that a new writ issue returnable to the next Court.

In the action of debt betw. Henry Fleet, William Ball, Thomas Carter, George Heale, Edwin Conway, Charles Burges, Charles Carter, John Selden, Henry Fleet, Junr., Henry Carter, Hugh Brent, and Nicholas Martin, Gent. Justices of the Co., Pltfs., and Robert Gibson, Deft., Robert Tompson by his attorney declared himself to be the party injured and at whose costs & charges in the law this suit is presented whereupon at the prayer of the sd. Deft., further time is given him to plead, till next Court

Pg 62. George Ball is appointed surveyor of the highway from Wm. Payne's to this Court House in St Mary's White Chappel Parish, for this year and Coll. Wm. Ball is desired to direct the road there Queen's Street to the sd. Court House.

James Brent is appointed surveyor of the highway from Mr. Payne's to Mr. Burges mill in St Mary's White Chappel Parish, in this Co., for one year.

Henry Towles is appointed surveyor of the highway from the Church to Deep Bottom remained of the rolling road which leads from Mr. Joseph [can't read] Plantation to Deep Creek warehouse's in St. Mary's White Chappel Parish for this year.

William Bertrand is appointed surveyor of the highway from Deep Bottom run to Morarttico's Mill in St. Mary's White Chappel Parish, in this Co., for this year.

Thomas Wharton is appointed surveyor of the highway from Mr. Burges's mill to Mr. Selden's mill in St. Mary's White Chappel Parish, in this Co., for this year.

William Norris is appointed surveyor of the rolling road which leads from the Church road to Carpenter's Landing in St. Mary's White Chappel Parish, in this Co., for this year.

James Mott is appointed surveyor of the highways from Bryan Stott's to the road that leads from Col. Ball's Mill to Mr. Burges's mill in St. Mary's White Chappel Parish, in this Co., for this year.

Thomas Chattin is appointed surveyor of the highways from Barth Woods to the cross roads near Doctor Thorton's in St. Mary's White Chappel Parish, in this Co., for this year.

Therriat Taylor is appointed surveyor of the highways from the main road by Giles Robinson's to the main road which leads to Mr. Selden's mill & from the main road to Cundiff's old field and also of the rolling road in the sd. precinct in St. Mary's White Chappel Parish for the year.

Richard Curtis is appointed surveyor of the highways from Mr. Selden's mill to Col Carter's great mill and of all the main roads between those two branches of Corotomon river in Christ Church Parish in this Co. for the year.

William Stepto is appointed surveyor of the highways from Col. Carter's great Mill to the cross roads in Christ Church Parish in this Co. for this year. But, it is Ordered that he take to his assistance the male laboring tithables belonging to Thomas Pinckard, Ruth Sydnor, George Yerby, William Scofield & Frances

Angels' family besides these in the sd. precinct.

George Flower is appointed surveyor of the highways from the cross roads to the Office of the Court Clerk in Christ Church Parish in this Co. for this year.

Thomas Hunton is appointed surveyor of the highways from Col. Carter's great Mill to the main road which leads from the Clerk's office in Christ Church Parish in this Co. for the year. And, it is Ordered that he keep the road in repair which the male laboring tithables belonging to Col. Robert Carter in the sd. Precinct.

Charles Jones is appointed surveyor of the highways from the cross roads to the Christ Church Parish in this Co. for this year. And, it is Ordered that he keep the road in repair which the male laboring tithables belonging to Col. Robert Carter in the sd. Precinct.

William Martin is appointed surveyor of the highways from white stone to Col. Carter's Little Mill to the main roads in Nantepoiqon [?] Neck in Christ Church Parish in this Co. for this year.

Henry Fleet, Junr. is appointed surveyor of the highways from the Church to Major Fleet's in Christ Church Parish, in this Co., for this year.

John Yerby is appointed surveyor of the highways from Col. Carter's Quarter to the mill road and from the sd. road to the Church in Christ Church Parish, in this Co., for this year.

On the prayer of Tomazine Bond, widow, of Christ Church Parish in this Co. setting forth that her Negro woman Nan is sickly and unable to work. It is Ordered that she be excused from paying and Country or County levies for the sd. Negro woman while she remains at the present.

Ordered that William Mitchel be summoned to the next Court to make oath to the amount of the Estate of Bushrode Dogget in this Co.

The Order from Henry Towles to exhibit an amount of the Estate of Moses Carter in continued till next Court.

Thomas Carter, Gent., one of the Execs. of Peter Carter, dec'd, exhibiting his account against Moses [?] Carter, one of the Orphans of the sd. Peter by consent of the sd. Thomas & Henry Towles, guardian of the sd. Moses. William Ball

102

and James Ball, Gent., are appointed to examine & settle the sd. account and all matters & things relating thereto and it is Ordered that a report of their proceedings.

Pg 63. Ordered that the Court be adjourned till 2nd Wednesday in July next. At a Court for Lancaster Co. continued on Wednesday, in 12th day of July 1732. Present: William Ball, Thomas Carter, George Heale, Edwin Conway, John Selden, Henry Carter, Hugh Brent, Nicholas Martin; Gent., Justices.

William Shelton & Frances, his wife, & Rebecca Mazey came into Court and ackn. their deeds of lease and release to Thomas Hubbard re: 50 acres of land in Christ Church Parish, in this Co., to be their act and deed (the sd. Frances & Rebecca being first privately examined) which on the Motion of the sd. Hubbard were admitted to record.

John Nash came into Court ackn. his bond to Thomas Hubbard for 3,000 lbs. of tobacco & cask consignment which on the Motion of the sd. Thomas was admitted to record.

William Mohon, orphan of Patrick Mohon, late of this Co., dec'd, aged 13 years the third day of March last on the prayer of John Brooks & Frances, his wife, mother of the sd. orphan is by the Court bound to John Wale, till he is 21 years. His master is to teach him to read & write and the trade of a carpenter and to allow him sufficient diet, lodging and apparel and at the expiration of his servitude to pay him as is appointed for servants by Indenture or custom.

Patrick Mohon, orphan of Patrick Mohon late of this Co., dec'd, aged 11 years the ninth of June last on the prayer of John Brooks & Frances, his wife, mother of the sd. Orphan is by the Court bound to John Wale till he is 21 years of age. His sd. Master is to teach him to read & write and the trade of a weaver and to allow him sufficient diet, lodging and apparel and at the expiration of his servitude to pay him as is appointed for servants by Indenture or custom.

The Order of the last Court for summoning John Brooks to signify his consent to the binding William Mohon & Patrick Mohon is dismissed.

John Wale is appointed Guardian of William Mohon & Patrick Mohon, orphans of Patrick Mohon, late of this Co., dec'd. John Angell being his security for the sd. Guardianship.

On the Motion of John Wale, Guardian of William & Patrick Mohon, orphans of Patrick Mohon, dec'd. It is Ordered that he be forthwith possessed of the Estates belonging to the sd. Orphans.

John Wale, Guardian of William & Patrick Mohon, orphans of Patrick Mohon, dec'd, exhibited and made Oath to his account of the Estate of the sd. Orphans, which was Ordered to be recorded.

John Angell, Guardian of Absolom Mohon, orphan of Patrick Mohon, dec'd, exhibited & made oath to his account of the Estate of the sd. Orphans, which was Ordered to be recorded.

Robert Carter, Esqr., presented in Court four amounts currant and two letters & made oath that he recorded the sd. amounts & letters from John Hyde & CO., merchants in London, which are admitted to record and on the Motion of the sd. Robert, it is Ordered that the Court Clerk endorse a Certificate of the sd. Oath on the sd. amount & letters.

Dick, a Negro boy belonging to William Oliver is by the Court adjudged to be 13 years of age.

The action of debt betw. Robert Carter, Esqr., and Thomas Carter, Church Wardens of Christ Church Parish, Pltfs., and Frances Murrough, Deft., is continued till next Court.

Pg 64. The action of trespass on the case betw. William Martin, Admin. of all & singular the goods, chattels, rights & credits that were Alexander Edgars, late of the Parish of Christ Church in this Co., dec'd at the time of his death, Pltf., and William Stepto, Deft., is continued till next Court.

The Will of William Heale, dec'd, was presented in Court by John Heale, one of the Execs., who made oath thereto and being proved by the oath of Edwin Conway a Witness thereto, is admitted to record and on the Motion of the sd. Exec., and his performing , he obtained a certificate of Probate in due form.

Ordered that George Payne, Thomas Chattin, Thomas Flint, & Robert Mitchell or any three of them, being first sworn by a Justice of Peace, are to appraise the Estate of William Heale, in money and report same to the next Court, and John Heale, Exc. of the Will of the sd. Wm. Heale, dec'd, do make oath of the Inventory.

In a suit betw. Charles Burges, Gent., Pltf., and Thomas Sanders, Deft., by attachment Robert Pritchard failing to appear & declare what of the Estate of the sd. Deft., was in his hands when this attachment was served upon him according to the order of the last Court. it is Ordered that the sd. Robert be taken into custody till he gives security for his appearance to the order of the last Court and that his attachment be till then continued.

The action of trespass betw. James Ball, Gent., Pltf., and Thomas Mason, Deft., is continued till next Court. The ejection betw. John Tarr and William Brent, Deft., is continued to next Court.

The action upon David Ball, Pltf., and George Heale, Deft., is continued to next Court.

The suit in Chancery betw. William Everate & Margaret, his wife, Complts. and William Bertrand, Exec. of the Will of Ruth Fouchee, dec'd, Deft., is continued to next Court on the Complts. Motion & costs.

The action of William King. Pltf., and John Gill, Deft., is continued to next Court.

The action betw. Thomas Pollard, Pltf., and Joseph Carter, Deft., is continued to next Court.

The action of debt. betw. Thomas Edwards, Pltf., and Thomas Bridgford, Deft., the attachment granted to the sd. Pltf. in this cause against the Estate of the sd. Deft., is continued to next Court.

In the action of debt betw. Clement Lattimore, Pltf., and Henry Bentley, Deft., for 500 lbs. tobacco damages in the declaration is set forth & is dismissed.

The action of debt betw. Henry Fleet, William Ball, Thomas Carter, George Heale, Edwin Conway, Charles Burges, Charles Carter, John Selden, Henry Fleet, Junr., Henry Carter, Hugh Brent & Nicholas Martin, Gent., Justices of the Co., Pltfs., and Robert Gibson, Deft., is continued till next Court on the Pltf.'s Motion & costs.

The order for William Mitchell to exhibit an amount of the Estate of Bushrode Dogget is continued till the next Court.

The order for Henry Towles to exhibit an amount of the Estate of Moses Carter is continued till the next Court.

The difference betw. Moses Carter, one of the orphans of Peter Carter, dec'd, by Henry Towles, his Guardian, and Thomas Carter, Gent., one of the Execs. of the sd. dec'd, is continued till next Court on the sd. Execs. Motion & costs.

In the action betw. Robert Carter, Esqr., & Thomas Carter, Gent., Church Wardens of Christ Church Parish in this Co., Pltfs. and Ann Powell, Deft., for 500 lbs. tobacco & cask or 50 shillings by means of sd. Deft. having committed fornication & had a bastard child as in the declaration as set forth the sd. Deft. appeared & confessed the fact but failed to pay or to give sufficient for the payment of the afsd. fine, whereupon it is Ordered that she receive on her bare back at the public whipping post 25 lashes, well laid on and be then discharged.

In the action betw. Thomas Edwards, Pltf. and Thomas Kelley, Deft., for 30 shillings and 517 lbs. tobacco as in the declaration is set forth Judgment grant to the sd. Pltf. for his afsd. debt and it is Ordered that the sd. Deft. for herewith pay the same and costs.

Pg 65. The action upon the case betw. John Read, Pltf., and Joseph George, Deft., for 39 shillings due by account, is dismissed.

The action upon the case betw. Henry Knight Pltf., and Richard Jackson, Deft., for the 185 lbs. of tobacco due by account is dismissed, the sd. Pltf. not appearing.

The action upon the case betw. Jonathan Lyell, Pltf., and John Kilgore, Deft., is continued till next Court at the Deft's Motion & costs.

The action of debt betw. James Ellis, Pltf., and Andrew Donnaldson & John Gibson, Defts., for 600 lbs. tobacco as in the declaration is set forth, is dismissed.

The suit betw. James Chelton & Shaw Dailey, Pltfs. and John Chelton, Deft., by firie facias, till next Court at the Defts. Motion.

The suit betw. Robert Scofield, Pltf., and Thomas Harris, Deft., by petition is dismissed.

Ordered that the Court be adjourned till 2nd Wednesday in August next. At a Court for Lancaster Co. continued on Wednesday, in 9th day of August 1732. Present: Thomas Carter, George Heale, Edwin Conway, John Selden, Henry Fleet, Junr., Charles Burges, Henry Carter, Hugh Brent, Nicholas Martin.

Edwin Conway, Gent., acquainting this Court that four liters of tobacco marked XO No. 62, No. 63, No. 64 and WL No. 1, had been in the Public rolling house near the head of the Western branch of the Corrotomon River in this Co. for the space of 2 years & one month and that no person had hither to tendered him any record for the storage of the sd. tobacco. It is order that the Sheriff of this Co. take the sd. tobacco into his hands and make sale thereof for money by way of outcry and that the money which shall arise by the sd. sale (after the fees due to the sd. Clerk & Sheriff on the occasion and to the sd. Edwin Conway for his storage of the sd. tobacco) remain & continue in the hands of the sd. Edwin Conway for the use of the person or persons who shall appear to be the owners of the sd. tobacco. And it is further Ordered that a return of the proceedings in the premises be made to the next Court.

On the Motion of John Carter, Esqr., one of the Exec. of the Hon. Robert Carter, Esqr., dec'd, for amounts of sale of tobacco and one amount currant from Mr. James Bradley of London, Merchant, to the sd. dec'd, were admitted to record.

Peter, a Negro boy belonging to Henry Knight is by the Court adjudged to be 14 years of age.

Samuel Angell, orphan of Robert Angell, late of this Co., dec'd, aged 9 years the thirtieth day of December last on the prayer of Frances Angell, his mother, & Charles Angell, Exec., of the Will of the sd. deceased is by this Court bound to William Martin till he attains the age of 21 years, his sd. master is to teach him to read and to write and the trade of a Clapboard Carpenter and to find & allow him sufficient diet , lodging, & apparel and at the expiration of his servitude to pay him as is appointed for servants by indenture or custom.

On the Motion of Bushrode Dogget, Orphan of Richard Dogget, late of this Co., dec'd, George Dogget is appointed his Guardian, with William Oliver becoming his security for the sd. Guardianship.

On the Motion of George Dogget, Guardian of Bushrode Dogget, Orphan of Richard Dogget, dec'd, it is Ordered that he be forthwith possessed of the Estate belonging to the sd. Orphan.

Ordered that George Dogget, Guardian of Bushrode Dogget exhibit an account of all the Estate of the sd. Orphan, which he hath received into his hands or the sd. Orphan shall be entitled to, at the next Court and then appear & make oath to the sd. account.

The order of the last Court for William Mitchell, Guardian of Bushrode Dogget, to exhibit an account of the sd. Bushrode's Estate is dismissed.

Pg 66. Nicohal Feagan, a servant man belonging to Thomas Edwards, confessing he had runaway from his sd. Master's service 12 days and his master making appear he had expended 725 lbs. of tobacco in regaining him. It is Ordered that the sd. Nicholas serve his sd. master eleven calendar months & 24 days for the same after his time by indenture custom or former order of Court is expired.

Edward Kayley[?], a servant man belonging to George Kirk confessing he had runaway from his master's service 12 days and his sd. master making appear he had expended 705 lbs. tobacco in regaining him. It is Ordered that the sd. Edward serve his sd. master eleven calendar months & 24 days for the same after his time by indenture custom or former order of Court is expired.

James Donnellane, a servant man belonging to Christopher Kirk confessing he had runaway from his master's service 14 days and his sd. master making appear he had expended 705 lbs. tobacco in regaining him. It is Ordered that the sd. James serve his sd. master eleven calendar months & 28 days for the same after his time by indenture custom or former order of Court is expired.

James Donnellane, a servant man belonging to Christopher Kirk came into Court and voluntarily agreed to serve his Master 2 months after his time by Indenture custom or former order of Court is expired in consideration of a leather vest Breeches which he spoiled while he was runaway from his master's service. But, his sd. master agrees to acquit the sd. James of the 2 months service is case he honestly serves this Indenture time & what is this day adjudged against him for running away.

James Pursell, a servant to William Hutchins, of this Co., came into Court and voluntarily agreed to discharge his sd. Master from the payment of the freedom dues he is by law entitled to. In consideration of which his sd. master doth acquit him from all further service.

The Inventory of the Estate of Ruth Fouchee, dec'd, was returned and (Wm. Bertrand, her Exec., making oath thereto according to his subscription on the same) Ordered to be recorded.

In the suit betw. John Tarpley, Junr., King's attorney, Pltf., and John Grinsteed, Deft., by Information for 6,000 lbs. tobacco accruing due by means of the Deft,

108

having tended seconds & slip for tobacco as in the sd. Information is set forth
William Stepto, John Stepto, Ezekiel Gilbert, Robert Gibson, Henry Knight,
William Mitchell, George Dogget, Thomas Yerby, Robert Edmunds, William
Edwards, Christopher Kirk, and Peter Revere, Junr., were impanelled & sworn
to try the issue joined in this cause and bringing in their verdict in these words –
"We of the Jury find the Deft. guilty and that he then had one tithable person."
Signed: William Stepto, Foreman. The sd. verdict was admitted to record and
the sd. Deft. on his prayer has time given him to move in arrest of the Judgment
to be given in this cause at the next Court.

In the action of Debt betw. Robert Carter, Esqr. and Thomas Carter, Church
Wardens, of Christ Church Parish, Pltfs., and Frances Murrough, Deft., the sd.
Deft this day lodged a plea of abatement to which the Pltf. demurred being
joined by the sd. Deft.. It is Ordered that the argument thereon be referred till
next Court.

The action of trespass betw. William Martin, Admin., of the goods and chattels,
Rights and credits that were Alexander Edgar's, late of Christ Church Parish, in
this Co, Pltf., and William Stepto, Deft. By consent of both parties, the matter
of this cause is referred to the determination of Thomas Carter, Gent., & Thomas
Edwards, and it is agreed that their award in the premise or that be endorsed up
as the Judgment of the Court and it is Ordered that a return of the sd, award be
made to the next Court.

In the Ejection betw. John Tarr, Pltf., and Thomas Gar, Defts., for lands &
tenements in St. Mary's White Chappel Parish, in this Co., demised to the Pltf.
by William Mayers [?], planter, for the term as in the declaration is set forth,
Dale Carter Sub- Sheriff, of this Co., made oath that the contents of his return on
the back of the declaration in this cause was true which is in these words – " A
copy of the [can't read] declaration & endorsement deliver to the [can't read]
Charles Fleming – Dale Carter, Sub-Sheriff." Whereupon, the sd. Carter was
called but failed to appear. It is therefore Ordered that unless the sd. Parties or
those under whom [can't read] / being legally forced which a copy of this Order/
do appear at the next Court & make [can't read] Deft or Defts in this suit,
contest Lease entry & Ouster, and agree to insist only on the title at the trial,
Judgment be then entered.

Pg 67. The suit betw. Charles Burges, Gent., Pltf., and Thomas Sanders, Deft.,
by attachment is continued till next Court.

The action of trespass betw. James Ball, Gent., Pltf., and Thomas Mason, Deft., is continued till the next Court.

In the Ejection betw. John Tarr, Pltf., and William Brent, Deft., the parties as well Pltf.. & Deft., by their attorneys appeared and agreed too & presented a Special verdict in this cause, which is admitted to record. Whereupon, the Deft. urged he ought not to be compelled to a trial in this matter for that heretofore he had a hearing in this Court, which the same Pltf., on the same cause of action which was ruled in his favor, but for as much at the Court are of opinion that the parties afsd. ought to proceed to a trial in this cause. It is Ordered that the arguments of the matters of Law arising upon the afsd. Special Verdict be referred till the next Court.

The action betw. David Ball, Pltf., and George Heale, Deft., is continued till next Court.

In the suit in Chancery betw. William Everate & Margaret, his wife, Complts., and William Bertrand, Exec. of the Will of Ruth Fouchee, Dec'd, Deft., the sd. Complts., put in a replication which on the Motion of the sd. Deft., he has time to consider, till next Court.

Dick, a Negro boy belonging to Charles Burges, Gent., is by the Court adjudged to be 12 years old.

Absolom Payne, a servant, belonging to Charles Burges, Gent., came into Court & voluntarily agreed to serve his sd. master till the Christmas after his time by Indenture & custom or order of the Court shall be expired in consideration that his sd. master for the remainder of his service keep him to ye trade of a shoemaker.

In the action of debt betw. William King, Pltf., and John Gill, Deft., on the Motion of the sd. Deft., time is given him to consider the replication this day lodged in this cause by the sd. Pltf., till next Court.

In the action betw. Thomas Pollard, Pltf., and Joseph Carter, Deft., on the Motion of the sd. Pltf. time is given him to consider the Deft's plea this day put in, till next Court.

In the action of debt betw. Thomas Edwards, Pltf., and Thomas Bridgford, Deft., the attachment granted to the sd. Pltf. in this cause against the Estate of the sd. Deft. is continued, till the next Court.

In the action of debt betw. Henry Fleet, William Ball, Thomas Carter, George Heale, Edwin Conway, Charles Burges, Charles Carter, John Selden, Henry Fleet, Junr., Henry Carter, Hugh Brent, & Nicholas Martin, Gent., Co. Justices, Pltfs., and Robert Gibson, Deft., is continued till next Court.

The order of Henry Towles to exhibit an amount of the Estate of Moses Carter, is continued till the next Court.

In the action of debt betw. Jonathan Lyell, Pltf., and John Kilgore, Deft., for 800 lbs. tobacco in one account due by note, is dismissed.

In the suit betw., James Chelton and Shaw Dayley, Pltfs., and John Velden, Deft., by feiri facias for execution on a Judgment of this Court obtained by the sd. Pltfs., against the sd. Deft., the 12th May 1731, for 215 lbs. tobacco, the sd. Deft being dead, is dismissed.

In the action of trespass & assault & battery betw. Anthony Dunlevy, Pltf., and Robert Scofield, Deft., for John Kilgore, Deft., £20 damage, the sd. Deft. being returned non-[can't read] & not appearing on the Motion of the sd. Pltf., an Als. Capias is awarded against the sd. Deft. returnable to next Court and it is Ordered that the Co. Sheriff take such force as he shall think proper for the better apprehending the sd. Deft.

The suit betw. Henry Knight, Pltf., and Richard Jackson, Deft., by petition is continued till next Court.

The action betw. George Kirk, Pltf., and Michael Conner, Deft., is dismissed.

The action of trespass betw. William Ranken, Pltf., and William Hutchins, Deft., an Imparlance is granted to the sd. Deft., till next Court.

The action betw. John Read, Pltf., and Joseph George, Deft., for 39 shillings due by account, is dismissed.

The suit betw. William Goodridge, Pltf., and Thomas Chetwood, Deft., by petition for 350 lbs. tobacco or £.15.0 due by an obligation, is dismissed.

Pg 68. The action betw. Thomas Edwards, Pltf., and Thomas Harris, Deft., for 530[?] lbs. tobacco or £1.3.5 & half penny due by account, the sd. Pltf. making oath that 440 lbs. tobacco and £1.3.5 & half penny was justly due to him on balance of the afsd. amount, Judgment is granted him for the same and it is

Ordered that the sd. Deft. forthwith pay unto the sd. Pltf. the 440 lbs. tobacco and £1.3.5 & half penny, and costs.

In the difference betw. Moses Carter, one of the Orphans of Peter Carter, dec'd, by Henry Towles, his Guardian, and Thomas Carter, Gent., one of the Execs. of the sd. deceased. A report of auditors returned in this cause was admitted to record and on hearing the parties, it is considered that the sd. Moses recover against the sd. Exec., £24.9.5 & 3 farthings & 33 lbs. tobacco & costs of the Estate of the sd. Testator in his hands and by consent, Robert Mitchell, Gent., George Payne, William Chelton & James Brent or any three of them are appointed to set apart & appraise the Estate of the sd. deceased to the value of the money & tobacco before mentioned.

Ordered that the Court be adjourned till 2nd Wednesday in September next. At a Court for Lancaster Co. continued on Wednesday, in 13th day of September 1732. Present: Henry Fleet, William Ball, Thomas Carter, George Heale, Edwin Conway, Charles Burges, Nicholas Martin; Gent., Justices.

The Will of Onesiphorus Harvey, dec'd, was presented in Court by William Harvey, Exec., therein named, who made oath thereto and being proved by the paths of John Selden & William Chelton, Witnesses. thereto admitted to record. And, on the Motion of the sd. Exec., a certificate was granted to him for obtaining Probate.

Ordered that Francisco Firzzel, John Everet, Thomas Chattin & Theriat Taylor or any three of them sworn bef. a Co. Justice, to meet and appraise the Estate of Onesiphorus Harvey, dec'd, in money and make a report of same to the next Court attended by the Exec. to appear and make Oath to the Inventory.

A return of the sale of four liteds[?] of tobacco in Edwin Conway's rolling house according to the order of the last Court, was this day made & Ordered to be recorded.

John Selden, Gent., producing a Commission to be Co. Sheriff took the oaths and subscribed the test and had the oath of Co. High Sheriff administered to him.

A Bond from John Selden, Edwin Conway & Thomas Edwards, Gent., to the King for £1,000 in open Court ackn. by the sd. John Edwin & Thomas to be their acting deed and Ordered to be recorded.

Dale Carter, of the Commission of the Peace, William Ball, Junr.,. Gent., having taken the oaths of Under Sheriff of this Co., administered to him.

By virtue of the Commission of the Peace, William Ball, Junr., Gent., having taken the oaths of the government and subscribed the Test. And, the oaths appointed by a late act of Assembly of this Colony, to be administered to a Justice of Peace; administered to him. Present: William Ball, Junr., Gent.

Pg 69. William Sanders, a servant, belonging to David Alexander Flint, came into Court, and voluntarily agreed to serve his sd. Master five years from the fifth day of this instant in consideration of his having at his instance purchased him from his former Master and acquitted him from all service hitherto due for his running way.

George Yerby, one of the Constables for Christ Church Parish, in this Co., made Information that he found four tobacco seconds on the Plantation of John Merrideth & six tobacco seconds on the plantation of John Wale in his precinct. And, it appearing to this Court that the sd. seconds were not turned[?] out with any view of profit or in contempt of the acts for preventing the same and that they were defrayed in the presence of the Constable. It is considered that no prosecution issue against the sd. John Merrideth & Jno. Wale for this breach of the sd. Acts.

Matthias James, one of the Constables for Christ Church Parish, in this Co., making return that he found six tobacco seconds found on the plantation of Anthony Garton in his precinct, and it appearing to this Court, the seconds were not turned out with any view of profit or in contempt of the acts for preventing the same and that they were defrayed in the presence of the Constable. It is considered that no prosecution issue against the sd. Anthony for this breach of the sd. Acts.

George Dogget, Guardian of Bushrode Dogget, Orphan of Richard Dogget, dec'd, exhibit and made oath to his account of the sd. Orphan's Estate, which was Ordered to be recorded.

In the suit betw. John Tarpley, Junr., King's attorney, Pltf., and Thomas Cotes, Deft., by Information for 6,000 lbs. tobacco accruing due by means of the Deft, having tended seconds as in the sd. Information is set forth, the Deft insisted on a trial of the issue joined in this cause. And the Pltf., moved it might be referred urging that his witness did not appear. But, the sd. Pltf. being overruled, he refused to prosecute whereupon it is considered that this suit is dismissed.

In the suit betw. John Tarpley, Junr., King's attorney, Pltf., and William Delany, Deft., by Information for 6,000 lbs. tobacco accruing due by means of the Deft, having tended tobacco seconds as in the sd. Information is set forth is dismissed, the Pltf. failing to prosecute.

In the suit betw. John Tarpley, Junr., King's attorney, Pltf., and Thomas Charles, Deft., by Information for 6,000 lbs. tobacco accruing due by means of the Deft, having tended tobacco seconds as in the sd. Information is set forth is dismissed, the Pltf. failing to prosecute.

In the suit betw. John Tarpley, Junr., King's attorney, Pltf., and Chattin Chowning, Deft., by Information for 6,000 lbs. tobacco accruing due by means of the Deft, having tended tobacco seconds as in the sd. Information is set forth is dismissed, the Pltf. failing to prosecute.

In the suit betw. John Tarpley, Junr., King's attorney, Pltf., and Robert Wells, Deft., by Information for 6,000 lbs. tobacco accruing due by means of the Deft, having tended tobacco seconds as in the sd. Information is set forth is dismissed, the Pltf. failing to prosecute.

In the suit betw. John Tarpley, Junr., King's attorney, Pltf., and James Stott, Deft., by Information for 6,000 lbs. tobacco accruing due by means of the Deft, having tended tobacco seconds as in the sd. Information is set forth is dismissed, the Pltf. failing to prosecute.

In the suit betw. John Tarpley, Junr., King's attorney, Pltf., and John Hubbard, Deft., by Information for 6,000 lbs. tobacco accruing due by means of the Deft, having tended tobacco seconds as in the sd. Information Robert Gibson, George Dogget, Emanuel Walker, William Hutchins, Francis Timberlake, George Yerby, William Goodridge, Matthias James, Ezekiel Gilbert, George Light, William Martin & Thomas Harwood were impanelled & sworn to try the issue joined in this cause and bringing in their verdict in the words "We the Jury do find the defendants not guilty". Signed: Robt. Gibson, Foreman. The sd. verdict was admitted to record and it is considered that this suit be dismissed.

In the suit betw. John Tarpley, Junr., King's attorney, Pltf., and William Stamps, Deft., by Information for 6,000 lbs. tobacco accruing due by means of the Deft,

114

having tended tobacco seconds as in the sd. Information is set forth is dismissed, the Pltf. failing to prosecute.

In the suit betw. John Tarpley, Junr., King's attorney, Pltf., and James Gaylor, Deft., by Information for 6,000 lbs. tobacco accruing due by means of the Deft, having tended tobacco seconds as in the sd. Information is set forth is dismissed, the Pltf. failing to prosecute.

Pg 70. In the suit betw. John Tarpley, Junr., King's attorney, Pltf., and Richard Wooden, Deft., by Information for 6,000 lbs. tobacco accruing due by means of he Deft, having tended tobacco seconds as in the sd. Information is set forth is dismissed, the Pltf. failing to prosecute.

In the suit betw. John Tarpley, Junr., King's attorney, Pltf., and John Grimsteed, Deft., by Information for 6,000 lbs. tobacco accruing due by means of the Deft, having tended tobacco seconds as in the sd. Information is set forth is dismissed, the Pltf. failing to prosecute.

In the action of debt betw. Robert Carter, Esqr., and Thomas Carter, Church Wardens, of Christ Church Parish, Pltf., & Frances Murrough, Deft., the parties were heard on the plea in abatement in this cause which was overruled & afterwards on the arguments on the plea in arrest of the Judgment to be given in this suit, the Court took time to advise till next Court.

The action of trespass betw. William Martin, Admin., of the goods and chattels, Rights and credits that were Alexander Edgar's, late of Christ Church Parish, in this Co, Pltf., and William Stepto, Deft, for one silver watch of the value of £10, as in the declaration set forth a return of the determination of Thomas Carter, Gent., and Thomas Edwards to whom the matter of this cause was referred being this day made is admitted to record. And, it is considered that the sd. Deft. forthwith deliver unto the sd. Pltf., the silver watch afsd. and pay the costs of this suit together one attorney's fee.

In the Ejection betw. John Tarr, Pltf., and Thomas Gar, Defts., on the prayer of Charles Ewell, Charles Burges, Gent., is appointed Guardian for the defense of this cause. Whereupon, the sd. Charles Ewell by his sd. Guardian is admitted, Deft., in the room of the sd. Thomas Gar, and confessed lease entry & ouster pleaded the general issue and agree to insist only on the title at the trial which issue being joined by the Pltf., it is Ordered that the trial be referred till the next Court.

In the suit betw. Charles Burges, Gent., Pltf., against Thomas Sanders, Deft., by the attachment, Robert Pritchard made oath that he had no more than 45 lbs. of tobacco belonging to the Estate of the Deft in his hands at the time when this attachment was served upon him. Whereupon, Judgment is granted to the sd. Pltf. for the same and it is Ordered that this attachment be discontinued.

The action of trespass betw. James Ball, Gent., Pltf., and Thomas Mason, Deft., is continued till next Court at the Deft. Motion and costs.

The ejection betw. John Tar, Pltf., and William Brent, Deft., is continued till next Court at the Defts. Motion & costs.

The action upon the case betw. David Ball, Pltf. and George Heale, Deft., is continued till next Court.

The suit in Chancery betw. William Everate & Margaret, his wife, Complts., and William Bertrand, Exec. of the Will of Ruth Foushee, Dec'd, Defts, is continued till next Court.

In the action of debt betw. William King[?], Pltf., and John Gill, Deft., the sd. Deft., in a demurrer to the Pltf. replication in this cause which demurrer being joined by the sd. Pltf., it is Ordered that the arguments thereon be referred till next Court.

The action upon the case betw. Thomas Pollard, Pltf., and Joseph Carter, Deft, the sd. Pltf. put a replication & demurrer to the Defts. plea in this cause to which on the sd. Deft's Motion, he has time to consider till the next Court.

In the Debt between Thomas Edwards, Pltf., and Thomas Bridgford, Deft., for £2.18.2 & 589 lbs. tobacco due by account is dismissed.

The action betw. Henry Fleet, William Ball, Thomas Carter, George Heale, Edwin Conway, Charles Burges, Charles Carter, John Selden, Henry Fleet, Junr., Henry Carter, Hugh Brent, and Nicholas Martin, Gent., Co. Justices, Pltfs. & Robert Gibson, Defts, time is given to the sd. Pltfs. to consider the Deft.'s plea this day put in, till next Court.

Pg 71. In the action of trespass & assault & battery betw. Anthony Dunlavy, Pltf., and Robert Scofield, Deft., the Deft pleaded and the Pltf. joined issue and it is Ordered that the trial thereof be referred till the next Court.

In the action of trespass & assault & battery betw. William Ranken, Pltf., and William Hutchings, Deft., the Deft pleaded and the Pltf. joined issue and it is Ordered that the trial thereof be referred till the next Court.

The suit betw. Henry Knight, Pltf., and Richard Jackson, Deft. by petition for 285 lbs. tobacco due by account is dismissed.

The suit betw. Francis Timberlake, Pltf., and Robert Scofield, Deft. by petition for 440 lbs. tobacco due by account is dismissed.

The action of Debt betw. Thomas Webster, Pltf., and James Barton, Deft., for 1,400 lbs. tobacco due by obligation & account is dismissed.

Ordered that Richard Davis, Junr., and Thomas Young be summoned to the next Court to answer the Presentment of Joseph Ball & Joseph Heale, Church Warden of St. Mary's White Chappel Parish in this Co., against them.

Solomon Morthon [?] making oath to his account for attendance on Davis's Warehouses in this Co., that it was justly due & that he had not received any satisfaction for the same. It is Ordered that the Court Clerk certify the sd. proof on the account.

John Pynes making oath to the truth of his account for attendance on the warehouses in Queen's Town in this Co., that he had not received any satisfaction for the same. It is Ordered that the Court Clerk certify the sd. proof on the account.

Hopkins Wilder making oath to the truth of his account for attendance on the warehouses in Queen's Town in this Co., and that he had not received any satisfaction for the same. It is Ordered that the Court Clerk certify the sd. proof on the account.

Ordered that the Court be adjourned till 2nd Wednesday in October next. At a Court for Lancaster Co. continued on Wednesday, in 23rd day of October 1732 for the examination of Robert Ker, Francis Clemens and James Stuart, late of Norfolk Co., on suspicion of Felony. Present: Henry Fleet, William Ball, Thomas Carter, Edwin Conway, Henry Fleet, Junr., William Ball, Junr., Hugh Brent, Nicholas Martin; Gent., Justices.

Robert Ker, Francis Clemons, and James Stuart charged with the felonious taking an anchor & cable from on board a Schooner belonging to the Estate of Robert Carter, Esqr., dec'd, in the night of the eighth day instant. And, having certain dealings with several of the servants and a slave known by the name of Mulatto Billy belonging to the sd. Estate. And, endeavoring & encouraging the escape of the sd. Servants & slave from the sd. Estate and divers felonious acts to be committed for compassing the same, being brought to bear. The sd. Robert Ker confessed he had the anchor & cable afsd. with two other small anchors and the several other things mentioned to be delivered to him in the depositions of the witness against him and that he purchased them from the servants and the above mentioned slave belonging to the sd. estate. But, denied the other matters laid to his charge.

And, Francis Clemons confessed he assisted in taking out of the Schooner & bringing into the sd. Ker's shallop the anchor & cable afsd., as also a pot & a blanket as mentioned in the afsd. Depositions. But, that it was by the sd. Ker's orders. And, Barnabus Birch Andrews, Edwards Thomas Strongharm & John Banks, the witnesses against the sd. Prisoners were sworn & examined and a paper containing directions for sundry things mentioned in the sd. Andrew Edward's deposition was read. And, the sd. Robert Ker, Francis Clemons & James Stuart fully heard on the whole premises & whereupon, it is the opinion of the Court that the sd. Robert Ker and Francis Clemons ought to be tried for their afsd. facts before the General Court and for as much as nothing material appears against the sd. James Stuart it is considered that he be forth with discharged and go home hence without day. And, Command is given to the Sheriff of this Co. that he take the sd. Robert Ker and Francis Clemons to the Goal of this Co. and that they be thence removed to the public Goal at Williamsburgh as the Law directs.

Pg 72. James Stuart, late of Norfolk Co. and Barnabas Birch, Thomas Strougharm, & John Banks, of this Co., came into Court and ackn. themselves severally indebted to the King in the sum of £20 to be levied upon their several goods & chattels, lands & tenements under condition that they severally make their personal appearance at the trial of Robert Ker & Francis Clemons at the next Court of Oyer & Terminer, to be held for this Colony at the Capital in the city of Williamsburgh on the 2nd Tuesday in December next then & there to testify and the truth to say in behalf of the King against the sd. Robert Ker & Francis Clemons

Ordered that the Court be adjourned till 8th Wednesday in November . At a Court for Lancaster Co. continued on Wednesday, in 23rd day of October 1732.Present: Henry Fleet, William Ball, Thomas Carter, Edwin Conway, Henry Fleet, Junr., William Ball, Junr., Hugh Brent, Nicholas Martin; Gent., Justices.

Benjamin Shearman, Orphan of Martin Shearman, dec'd, aged 8 years in last August, is by the Court bound to Martin Shearman, of this Co., till he attains the age of 21 years, and his sd. master is to teach him to read and to write and the trade of Cooper and to find & allow him sufficient diet, lodging, & apparel and at the expiration of his servitude to pay him as is appointed for servants by indenture or custom.

William Rogers, Orphan of William Rogers, dec'd, aged 14 years in January last on the prayer of George Rogers, Exec., of the sd. dec'd, is by the Court bound unto Edward Rogers, of this Co., till he attains the age of 21 years, his sd. master is to teach him to read and to write and the trade of a Millwright and to find & allow him sufficient diet, lodging, & apparel and at the expiration of his servitude to pay him as is appointed for servants by indenture or custom.

Thomas Cox came to Court and ackn. his deed thereon endorsed to George Tubervile, Gent., for & concerning 64 acres of land in Christ Church Parish in this Co., which on the Motion of the sd. George was admitted to record.

A memorandum of Elizabeth Oliver endorsed on Thomas Cox's deed to George Turbervile, Gent., was proved by the oath of Thomas Cox, one of the witnesses thereto, and was admitted to record.

The appraisement of the Estate of Onesiphorus Harvey, dec'd, was returned and William Harvey, Exec., making Oath according to his subscription on the Inventory, Ordered to record.

John Coffy, a servant, belonging to Margaret Hineage, came to Court and voluntarily agreed to acquit his sd. note from further demand concerning his freedom in consideration of her promise to deliver him his share of the tobacco made on her plantation this year and to set him at Liberty.

Robert Watts in open Court ackn. his deed to William Ball, Gent, for & concerning 46 a. of land in St. Mary's White Chappel Parish, in this Co., thereon endorsed which on the Motion was admitted to record.

In the suit betw. Elizabeth Jones, Pltf., and Samuel Brumley, Defts., by the petition , the sd. Pltf. making oath to the truth of her allegations set forth in her petition was admitted to prosecute as a pauper, and the sd. Deft. appearing by consent of both parties, Robert Mitchell, Gent., is appointed to settle an account of the admin. of the estate of Henry jones, dec'd, and to make a report thereof to the next Court.

A Letter of Attorney from James Galor and Ann, his wife to John Selden was proved in open Court by Thomas Edwards & John Heale, witnesses, thereto and admitted to record.

Pg 73. A deed from James Gaylor & Ann, his wife to William Ball, Junr., Gent., for 47.5 a. of land lying in St. Mary's White Chappel Parish, in this Co., thereon endorsed & p[roved by the oaths of George Ball & Jonathan Pratt, witnesses thereto and ackn. by John Selden, Gent., attorney, of James & Ann, to be their act & deed and admitted to record.

The appraisement of the Estate of William Heale, dec'd, was returned and (John Heal, Exec., making Oath thereto according to his subscription on the Inventory) Ordered to be recorded.

The Sheriff having made proclamation that the Court was about to Lay the Lancaster County Levy, they proceeded accordingly:

To the Honorable Robert Carter, Esqr., for his keeping the Public Ferry one year – 1,400 lbs. tobacco.

John Payne for cleaning the Court House & other services – 800 lbs. tobacco.

John Tarpley, Junr., attorney for the King in this Co. – 1,000 lbs. tobacco.

John Selden, Co. Sheriff for one year service – 1,000 lbs. tobacco.

The sd. Sheriff on his Account – 1,507 lbs. tobacco.

Thomas Edwards, Court Clerk for one year service – 1,000 lbs., tobacco.

The sd. Clerk for his attendance at the Court for examination of criminals – 203 lbs. tobacco.

Edwin Conway for his attendance as a Burges at the last session of Assembly & for coming & going – 6,747 lbs. tobacco.

Charles Burges for his attendance as a Burges at the last session of Assembly & for coming & going –5,435 lbs. tobacco.

Matthias James, Constable for viewing tobacco Succors in his Precinct- 220 lbs. tobacco.

Thomas Flint Constable for viewing tobacco Succors in his Precinct - 310 lbs. tobacco.

John Bailey Constable for viewing tobacco Succors in his Precinct – 230 lbs. tobacco.

Edward Sanders Constable for viewing tobacco Succors in his Precinct –60 lbs. tobacco.

William Dogget Constable for viewing tobacco Succors in his Precinct – 190 lbs. tobacco.

Henry Horne Constable for viewing tobacco Succors in his Precinct – 226 lbs. tobacco

George Yerby Constable for viewing tobacco Succors in his Precinct - 300 lbs. tobacco.

The Secretary Carter for filing & recording the Inquisitions on the views of dead bodies since [can't read] – 450 lbs. tobacco.

Ezekiel Gilbart [Gilbert?] for one levy overcharged last year – 25 lbs. tobacco.

Thomas Young for one levy overcharged in 1730 – 17 lbs. tobacco.

William Dogget for one levy overcharged last year – 25 lbs. tobacco.

Majr. Henry Fleet for one Coroner's Inquest – 133 lbs. tobacco.

Matthias James, Constable, for summoning the Jury for the same – 50 lbs. tobacco.

The Public Levy – 13,509 lbs. tobacco.

The 14% for salary & convenience on 23,663 - 3,313 lbs. tobacco.

A fraction to be accounted for by the Sheriff in the next Levy – 367 lbs. tobacco.

Total – 39,168 lbs.

By The County's proportion in the Public Levy – 11,825 plus 1,478 tithables at 18 ½ = 27, 343 – Total 39, 168 plus the fraction to be accounted for as per last year's levy – 41. TOTAL – 39, 239.

The County & County Levy for the present year 1, 732 amounting as the whole for 18 ½ lbs. of tobacco per pol, it is Ordered that the Sheriff of this Co., collect much of every tithable person in this Co. discounting 10 % for the convenience Inspection notes and pay the same to the Country & County creditors, as the last directs.

Pg 74. Ordered that the Honorable John Cater, Esqr., do keep the Public Ferry over Corotomon River the ensuing year and that he be paid for the same as usual.

Ordered that John Payne do find this Court with water & candles and clean the Court House the ensuing year& that he be paid for the same as usual.

Ordered that the Court be adjourned till 2nd Wednesday in December next. At a Court for Lancaster Co. continued on Wednesday, in 14th day of March1732. Present: William Ball, Thomas Carter, Edwin Conway, William Ball, Junr., Henry Carter, Nicholas Martin; Gent., Justices.

Robert Mitchell, Gent., came to Court and mad Oath that the balance of £6.6.8 was justly due to him on his account against William Jarvis and it is Ordered that the Court Clerk certify the same on the sd. account.

The Will of William [Morris?]Norris, Dec'd, and also a memorandum relating thereto were presented in Court by Susannah Norris, Execx., named in the Will, who made oath thereto and the sd. Will being proved by the oaths of Thomas Thornton & Reuben Young and the sd. memorandum by the oath of Charles Sansford witnesses thereto were admitted to record and on the Motion of the sd. Execx., she obtained probate in due form.

Ordered that Susannah Norris, Execx, of the Will of William [Morris?] Norris, dec'd, being an Inventory of the sd. Estate to the next Court and appear and make oath.

Thomas Flint came into Court and made oath that Phillis Bell, late of the Co., dec'd, departed this life without making any Will, to his knowledge, and on his petition and giving security for his Administration of the sd. deceased's Estate and certificate was granted to him for Administration, in due form.

Ordered that James Pollard, Thomas Hubbard, James Webb and George Brent, or any three of them first being sworn before a Justice of Peace, and to meet and

122

appraise the Estate of Phillis Bell, dec'd, in money and make a report of same at Court and Thomas Flint, Admin., also appear and make Oath re: the Inventory.

The Will of Charles Burges, Gent., dec'd, was presented to the Court by James Ball, Edwin Conway, Gent, two of the Execs., therein named, who made oath and being proved by the oaths of Thomas Thornton, John Mitchell, and Joseph Ball, witnesses, was admitted to record and on the Motion of the sd. Execs., they were granted probate thereof in due form.

Ordered that James Ball & Edwin Conway, Gent., Exec. of the Will of Charles Burges, Gent, dec'd, bring an Inventory of the sd. Estate to the next Court and then appear & make Oath thereto.

The Will of David Ball, dec'd, was presented in Court by James Ball, Gent., one of the Execs., herein named and also a testimonial of the sd. James Ball's relating to a clause in the sd. Will under the sd. David's signing both, which the sd. James made oath to and the Will being proved by the oaths of Jesse Ball & George Ball, witnesses thereto, the sd. Will and the Clause under the testator's signing, and that the sd. testimonial were admitted to record and on Motion were admitted to probate in due form.

Ordered that James Ball, Gent., Exec., of the last Will of David Ball, dec'd, bring an Inventory of the sd. Estate to the next Court and then appear and make oath thereto.

The Will of Benony Chelton, dec'd, was presented in Court by Ann Chelton, Execx., therein named, who made other thereto and being proved by the oaths of William Miller, George Connelly & Elizabeth Connelly, witnesses thereto, and on the Motion of the sd. Execx., was admitted to probate in due form.

Pg 75. Ordered that Nicholas George, Elmore George, Benjamin George, and Richard Curtis, or any three of them, being first sworn before a Co. Judge, , are to meet and appraise the Estate of Benony Chelton, dec'd in money and make a return of their proceedings and that Ann Chelton, Execx., of the Will of the dec'd, to appear and make oath to the Inventory at the next Co. Court.

The last Will of John Mott, dec'd, and also a memorandum relating thereto was presented in Court by John Mott, Katherine Mayhane, Ats[?] Mott, Joseph Mott & Randolph Mott, Execs., named in the sd. Will, who made oath and the sd. Will was proved by the oaths of George Warrick & Robert by grave. and the sd. memorandum by the oath of Randolph Mott, witness thereto were admitted to record. And, on the Motion of he sd. Execs., they were admitted to obtaining probate in due form.

The Will of Francisco Frizell, dec'd, was presented in Court by Mary Frizell, Elizabeth Frizell, Execs., therein named, who made oath thereto & being proved by the oaths of John Curlete and James Hardin, witnesses, and on the Motion of the sd. Execx, a certificate was granted for obtaining probate.

Ordered that Mary & Elizabeth Frizell, Execs., of the Will of Francisco Frizzell, dec'd, to bring an inventory of the estate to the next Court and then appear and make oath thereto.

The last Will of Margaret Miller, dec'd, was presented in Court by Henry Miller, Exec., therein named who made oath and being proved by the oaths of Robert Edmunds & Edwin Conway, witnesses, and is admitted to record and on a Motion of he sd. Exec., ne was granted certificate for obtaining Probate.

Ordered that Henry Miller, Exec., of the Will of Margaret Miller, dec'd, that he bring an Inventory of the sd. decedent's Estate to the next Court and then appear and make oath.

On the Motion of George Chelton, Orphan of Benony Chelton, dec'd, Andrew Chelton is appointed Guardian, William Rankon becoming his security for the guardianship. And, it is Ordered that the sd. Andrew be forthwith possessed with the Estate of the sd. [blank] and exhibit & make oath to an account thereof to the next Court.

William Tayloe, Gent., came into Court and ackn. his deed to Robert Boatman for & concerning 200 a. of land in Christ Church Parish in this Co., and his bond for performance and ackn. of the covenants in the sd. deed, which were admitted to record.

Johanna Tayloe, of the afsd. Wm. Tayloe, came also into Court & freely & voluntarily relinquished all her Right of Dower in the sd. 200 a. of land & premises by the sd. deed conveyed unto the sd. Robert Boatman, was admitted to record.

Petition of William Edwards praying leave to turn the road thru his plantation to Robinson's Landing on the western branch of Corotomon River in this Co, is reported.

124

Petition of Edward Sanders praying the Court advise in relation to certain Martin Lee is rejected.

The action of Debt betw. Robert Carter, Esqr., and Thomas Carter, Church Wardens, of Christ Church Parish, and Francis Murrough, Deft., is continued till next Court at the sd. Pltfs. Motion & costs.

The ejection betw. John Tarr, Pltf., and Charles Ewell, Deft., in continued till next Court at the Pltf.'s Motion & costs.

The action of trespass betw. James Ball, Pltf., and Thomas Mason, Deft., is continued till next Court.

The ejection between John Tarr, Pltf., and William Brent, Deft., is continued till next Court at the Pltf.'s Motion & costs.

The action upon the case betw. David Ball, Pltf., and George Heale, Deft., £5 damages, as in the declaration is set forth, is dismissed, being the Pltf. is dead.

Pg 76. The suit in Chancery betw. William Everate & Margaret, his wife, Complts., and William Bertrand, Exec. of the Will of Ruth Fouchee, dec'd, Deft, in continued till nest Court on the sd. Complts. Motion and costs.

The action betw. William King, Pltf., and John Gill, Deft., in continued till next Court at the Plts. Motion and costs.

The action on the case betw. Thomas Pollard, Pltf., and Joseph Carter, Deft., in continued till next Court at the Deft's. Motion and costs.

The Presentment of Joseph Ball & John Heale, Church Wardens of St Mary's White Chappel Parish, in this Co., against Richard Davis, Junr, for not going to the sd. Church at Devine Services, dismissed.

The Presentment of Joseph Ball & John Heale, Church Wardens of St Mary's White Chappel Parish, in this Co., against Thomas Young, for Judgment granted against him for 5 shillings or 50 lbs. tobacco, the fine inflicted by law, which he is Ordered to pay to the Church Wardens for the use of the poor of the sd. Parish, with costs.

The action of debt betw. Henry Fleet, William Ball, Thomas Carter, George Heale, Edwin Conway, Charles Burges, Charles Carter, John Selden, Henry Fleet, Junr., Henry Carter, Hugh Brent, Nicolas Martin , Gent., Co. Justices.

Pltfs., and Robert Gibson, Deft., is continued to next Court on the Pltfs. Motion & costs.

The action of trespass & assault & Battery betw. Anthony Dunlevy, Pltf., & Robert Scofield, Deft., for £20 damages, is dismissed.

The action of trespass betw. William Ranken, Pltf., & William Hutchins, Deft., is continued till next Court at ye Pltfs. Motion and costs.

In the action of debt betw. Matthew Zuill, Gent, Pltf., and Isaac Cundiff, Deft., for 1,802 lbs. tobacco by account, is dismissed.

In the action of debt betw. Francis Waddy & Leonard Hereson, Gent., Church Wardens of Wicocomoco , Pltf., and Jesan Hunter, Deft., for 500 lbs. tobacco & cask or 50 shillings damage, is dismissed.

In the action of debt betw. Francis Waddy & Leonard Hereson, Gent., Church Wardens of Wicocomoco , Pltf., and Neil Johnson & Hannah, his wife, Defts., for 500 lbs. tobacco & cash or 50 shillings damage, is dismissed.

The suit betw. William Grady, Pltf., and Thomas Weles, Deft., by petition in continued till next Court at the Pltf.'s Motion & costs.

In the suit betw. William Goodridge, Pltf., and Thomas Chetwood, Deft., for 350 lbs. tobacco or £1.15.0 & cask due by note, the hand of the sd. Deft. payable to Wm. Clutton & assigned to the sd. Pltf., the parties being fully heard. It is Ordered that the Deft. forth with pay unto the sd. Pltf. the afsd. tobacco or cash and costs with one attorney's fees – Mar. ye 19th against the Deft's body.

The action betw. Dominick Newgent, Pltf. & Peter Darby, Deft., for 1,200 lbs. tobacco due by account is dismissed.

The suit betw. Robert Bisco, Pltf. and Thomas Harris, Deft., by attachment against the estate of the sd. Deft., is dismissed.

The suit betw. Robert Gibson, Pltf. and Thomas Harris, Deft., by attachment against the estate of the sd. Deft., is continued till next Court.

The suit betw. Ezekiel Gilbert, Pltf. and Thomas Harris, Deft., by attachment against the estate of the sd. Deft., is continued till next Court.

In the suit betw. Funion Flower, Pltf., and James Clerk, Deft., for 300 lbs. tobacco due by bill, the sd. Deft. not appearing and the sd. Pltf. making oath to his debt. It is considered that the sd. Deft. forthwith pay unto the sd. Pltf., the afsd. tobacco and costs – Mar. ye 19th 1732 against the Deft's body.

The suit betw. Philip Smith, Gent., Pltf., and Thomas Scott, Deft., for £4.10.5 due by account is dismissed.

Pg 77. The action of debt betw. Matthew Zuill, Gent., Pltf., and William Garret, Deft, for 1,367 lbs. tobacco due by account is dismissed.

The action of debt betw. Matthew Zuill, Gent., Pltf., and Matthew Garret, Deft, by petition for 378 lbs. tobacco due by account is dismissed.

In the suit betw. Elizabeth Jones, Pltf., and Samuel Brumbley, Deft., by petition for the estate of Henry Jones, dec'd, a report of Robert Mitchell, Gent., to whom this matter was referred being this day returned is Ordered to be recorded. And, it is considered that the sd. Deft. forthwith pay unto the sd. Pltf. £3.14.8, the money afsd. by the report afsd. found to be due to her and costs.

The action of trespass & assault & battery betw. Robert Jordan & Elizabeth Frizell, Deft., is continued till next Court at the Pltf.'s Motion & costs.

The suit in Chancery betw. Richard Harrison, & Ann, his wife, Complts., and John Fendley, surviving Exec. of the Will of Nicholas Read, dec'd, for the sd. Ann, her Dower, of all the slaves belonging to the Estate of the sd. testator as in the Bill is set forth, is dismissed.

The suit in Chancery betw. James Kirk, Complt., and Christopher Kirk, Deft., for a true account of the Estate of James Kirk, dec'd, as in the Bill is set forth, is dismissed.

The suit betw. Patrick Kavanaugh, Pltf., and Richard Mc Graw, Deft., for £2 due by the sd. Deft's. note to Christopher Collins assigned to the sd. Pltf, is dismissed.

The suit betw. Hopkins Wildey, Pltf., and Arthur Howard, Deft., by petition for 579 lbs. tobacco due by a Judgment of this Court obtained by the sd. Pltf., as Exec. of the Will of Nathaniel Wildey, dec'd, against the sd. Deft., is dismissed.

The suit betw. Robert Gibson, Pltf., and Swan Jones, Admin., of the estate of Richard Boyle, dec'd, Deft., by petition for 450 lbs. tobacco due by account, is dismissed.

In the suit betw. Robert Gibson, Pltf., and Swan Jones, Deft., by petition for £2.10.0 due by account. It is considered that the sd. Deft., pay unto the sd. Pltf., the afsd. amount and costs. But, the sd. money is to be discharged is case the sd. Deft., shall deliver to James Carter, Gent., of Stafford Co., for the Pltf.'s use the Dictionary mentioned in the sd. Pltf.s account in this cause bef. the 15th day of May next.

In the action upon the case betw. Dominick Nugent, Pltf., and Peter Darby, Deft., for 1,162 lbs. of tobacco due by account, the sd. Pltf. failing to appear on the Motion of the sd. Deft. a non-suit is awarded him and it is Ordered that the sd. Pltf. pay unto the Deft. 5 shillings for the same and costs together with one attorney's fee.

In the suit betw. Patrick Kavanaught, Pltf., and Richard Mc Grave[?], Deft., by petition for £2 due by the Deft. note to Christopher Collins assigned to the Pltf., the sd. Deft. not appearing, and the sd. Pltf. making oath to the truth of his debt. It is considered that the sd. Deft. forthwith pay unto the sd. Pltf the afsd. money & costs - – Mar. ye 19th against the Deft's body.

The suit betw. Hopkins Wildey, Pltf., and Frances Velden, Deft., by petition for £1.7.3 and 100 lbs. of tobacco due by account is dismissed, the Deft. being dead.

In the suit betw. Robert Mitchell, Junr., Pltf., and William Phillips, Deft., by petition for 400 lbs. tobacco due by obligation. The sd. Deft. confessed the debt wherefore it is considered that he forthwith pay the same to the sd. Pltf. & costs.

In the suit betw. Thomas Webster, Pltf., and Christopher Stevens, Deft., by petition for 620 lbs. tobacco due by account, the parties were fully heard and it is considered that the sd. Deft. forthwith pay unto the sd. Pltf. 557 lbs. tobacco & costs.

In the suit betw. Hopkins Wildey, Exec. of the Will of Nathaniel Wildey, dec'd, Pltf. and Arthur Howard, Deft., by petition of r 250 lbs. tobacco due by a Judgment of this Court, the sd. Deft. not appearing and the sd. Pltf. making oath to the truth of his debt. It is considered that the sd. Deft. forthwith pay unto the sd. Pltf.'s debt and costs.

The action upon the case betw. Michael Ryan, Pltf., and Edward Sanders, Deft., on the Motion of the sd. Deft., is continued, till next Court.

On the Motion of William Ball, Junr., Gent., he is admitted draw barrs or great gates for wheel carriages & [can't read] gates for passengers on the main road, which leads from Queens Town thru his plantation in this Court.

Ordered that the Court be dismissed till the 2nd Wednesday in April next.

Pg 78. At a Court for Lancaster Co. continued on Wednesday, in 11th day of April 1732. Present: William Ball, Thomas Carter, Edwin Conway, William Ball, Junr., Hugh Brent, Nicholas Martin; Gent., Justices.

Ordered that the Co. Sheriff summon at lease 24 freeholders of the Co, to appear at next Court, that out of them a Grand Jury may be them impanelled and sworn to make enquiry into the breach of the penal laws and to present the offenders.

Ordered James Fleming be summoned to the next Court to answer the complaint of John Thompson, his servant, and that the sd. servant he now remains under Mr. Brent's care.

The appraisement of the estate of Benony Chelton, dec'd was returned and Ann Chelton , his Execx., making oath according to her subscription on the Inventory, Ordered recorded.

The Inventory of the Estate of Charles Burges, Gent, dec'd, was returned and James Ball & Edwin Conway, Gent., his Execs., making oath according to their subscription, Ordered recorded.

The Inventory of David Ball, dec'd, was returned and James Ball, Gent., Exec., making oath according to his subscription on the same, Ordered recorded.

The Inventory of Margaret Miller, dec'd, was returned and Henry Miller., Exec., making oath according to his subscription on the same, Ordered recorded.

The Inventory of William Morris, dec'd, was returned and Susannah Norris, Exec., making oath according to his subscription on the same, Ordered recorded.

The appraisement of the Estate of Phillis Bell, dec'd, was returned sand Thomas Flint, Admin. of the Estate, making oath according to his subscription on the same, Ordered recorded.

Thomas Davis, Orphan of John Davis, dec'd, aged 5 years the 4th day of December next on the prayer of the sd. mother is by the Court, bound to William Heale., till he attains the age of 21 years, the sd. William to teach him to read & write & the trade of Cooper and his Master to find sufficient diet, lodging, apparel, and at the expiration of his servitude to pay him as is appointed for servants by Indenture or custom.

Thomas Flint exhibiting his account against the Estate of Phillis Bell, dec'd, on a full hearing, it is considered that he discount £5 for the same out of the appraisement of the sd. deceased's estate.

Henry Kelly, Orphan of Charles Kelley, Junr., dec'd, aged 14 years the last day of November next on the prayer of the sd. mother is by the Court, bound to John Hendley, of this Co., till he attains the age of 21 years, the sd. William to teach him to read & write & the trade of Weaver and his Master to find sufficient diet, lodging, apparel, and at the expiration of his servitude to pay him as is appointed for servants by Indenture or custom.

The action of debt betw. Robert Carter, Esqr. & Thomas Carter Church Wardens, of Christ Church Parish, Pltfs., and Frances Murrough, Deft., is continued till next Court on the Pltf.'s Motion and costs.

The ejection betw. John Tarr, Pltf., and Charles Ewell, Deft., is continued till next Court.

The action of trespass betw. James Ball, Gent., Pltf., and Thomas Mason, Deft., is continued till next Court.

The ejection betw. John Tarr, Pltf., and William Brent, Deft., is continued till next Court at the Pltf.'s Motion & costs.

In the suit in Chancery betw. Wm. Everate & Margaret, his wife, Complts., and William Berk, Execs., of the Will of Ruth Fouchee, Deft., is continued till the next Court at the Complt.'s Motion & costs

Pg 79. The action upon the case betw. Thomas Pollard, Pltf., & Joseph Carter, Deft/. is continued till the next Court at the Deft.'s Motion & costs.

The action of Debt betw. William King, Pltf., and John Gill, Deft. is continued till next Court at the Pltf.'s Motion and costs.

The action of debt betw. Henry Fleet, William Ball, Thomas Carter, George Heale, Edwin Conway, Charles Burges, Charles Carter, John Selden, Henry Fleet, Junr., Henry Carter, Hugh Brent, Nicolas Martin , Gent., Co. Justices. Pltfs., and Robert Gibson, Deft., is continued to next Court on the Pltfs. Motion & costs.

The action of trespass betw. William Rankin, Pltf. and William Hutchings, Deft., is continued till next Court at the Pltf.'s Motion & costs.

In the suit betw. William Grady, Pltf., and Thomas Wells, Deft., by petition for 350 lbs. tobacco due by account on hearing the parties & the oath of the Deft. in this cause Judgment is granted to the sd. Pltf., against the sd. Deft. for 318 lbs. tobacco, and costs.

Thomas Chetwood being brought into Court by virtue of an execution obtained against his body by William Goodridge on a Judgment of King CO. Court in March last for 350 lbs. tobacco or £1.15.0 cash, as also 269 lbs. of tobacco or 119 lbs. of tobacco & 15 shillings. The sd. Chetwood rendered unto the sd. Goodridge 1 lb. & 1 shilling & six pence of his afsd. debt and costs and Thomas Edwards becoming his security that he shall render unto the sd. Wm. Goodridge the remainder of his sd. debt & cash at the next Court, the sd. Chetwood was discharged.

In the suit betw. Robert Gibson, Pltf., and Thomas Harris, Deft., by attachment against the Estate of the sd. Deft. for 410 lbs tobacco due by and on the oath of the sd. Pltf. Judgment is granted him against the sd. Deft. for 270 lbs. tobacco & costs. And, it is Ordered that the sd. attachment be continued till next Court.

The suit betw. Ezekiel Gilbert, Pltf., and Thomas Harris, Deft., by attachment against the Estate of the sd. Deft., is continued

The action of trespass & assault & battery betw. Robert Jordan, Pltf., and Elizabeth Frizell, Deft., is continued till next Court.

The action of the case betw. Michael Ryan, Pltf., and Edward Sanders, Deft., is continued till next Court at the Deft's Motion & costs.

The action of the case betw. Thomas Bridgford, Pltf., and Thomas Pinckard, Gent, Deft., the sd. Deft pleaded & the Pltf. joined issue whereupon it is Ordered that the trial of the sd. issue be referred and William Oliver and Robert West are appointed to view the work mentioned in the sd. Pltf.'s account in this cause & report their opinion of the value thereof to the next Court.

In the suit betw. Henry Knight and William Scofield, Deft., for 300 lbs. tobacco due by bill, the sd. Deft. not appearing and the sd. Pltf. making oath to the truth of the debt. It is considered that the sd. Deft. forthwith pay unto the sd. Pltf. his afsd. debt & costs.

In the suit betw. Thomas Edwards, Pltf., and Thomas Flint, Admin. of the Estate of Phillis Bell, dec'd, by petition for 516 lbs. tobacco due to the Pltf. from the sd. decedent in her lifetime hence by account, the sd. Pltf. making oath to the truth of his debt, Judgment is granted him for the same & costs of the sd. decedent's Estate in the hands of the sd. Deft.

The suit betw. Thomas Thornton, Pltf., and Ralph Rutherford, Deft., by petition for 700 lbs. tobacco due by account is dismissed, neither party appearing.

The suit betw. William [can't read], Pltf. and Thomas Bridgford, Deft., by petition for 600 lbs. tobacco due by obligation, is dismissed.

The action upon the case betw. James Ball, Gent., Pltf., and Philip [can't read], Deft., is dismissed.

Pg 80. In the suit betw. Richard Chapman, Pltf., and James Haines, Deft., for 740 lbs. tobacco, due by account on hearing the parties, Judgment is granted to the sd, Pltf., for 470 [?] lbs. tobacco.

Ezekiel Gilbert is appointed guardian to Sarah Howell, Maudlin Howell & Deborah Howell, Orphans of Thomas Howell, dec'd, William Stepto & Thomas Edwards becoming his security for the sd. Guardianship. And, it is Ordered that the sd. Ezekiel be forthwith possessed of the Estate of the sd. Orphans and exhibit & make oath to an amount thereof at the next Court.

Ordered that the Court be adjourned till the 2nd Wednesday in May next. At a Court for Lancaster Co. continued on Wednesday, in 9th day of May 1733. Present: William Ball, Thomas Carter, Edwin Conway, Henry Fleet, William Ball, Junr., Henry Carter, Hugh Brent; Gent., Justices.

The Will of Henry Fleet, Gent, dec'd, was presented in Court by Abraham Currell, William Hobson, & Judith his wife, Elizabeth, the wife of Abraham & the sd. Judith, being the Execs. named in the Will. Whereupon, the sd. Abraham Currell & William Hobson & Judith, his wife, made oath and it being proved by the oath of Edwin Conway, Gent., a witness thereto , it is admitted to record and on the Motion of the afsd. Abraham & William & Judith, his wife, a certificate for Probate was obtained.

Ordered that Abraham Currell, William Hobson, & Judith his wife, Execs. of the Will of Henry Fleet, Gent., dec'd, bring an Inventory of the sd. Testator's Estate to the next Court and then appear & make oath thereto.

The Will of Phebe Reves, dec'd, was presented in Court by James Reves, Exec., therein named, who made oath thereto and being proved by the oaths of Joseph Carter & James Menro, witnesses thereto, is admitted to record and on the Motion of the sd. Exec., a certificate of Probate was issued.

Ordered that James Reves, Exec., of the Will of Phebe Reves, dec'd, bring an Inventory of the sd. Testatrix's Estate to the next Court and then appear & make oath thereto.

The Will of Thomas Purcell, dec'd, was presented in Court by Elizabeth Purcell & George Brent, Execs., therein named, who made oath thereto and being proved by the oaths of John Fendla & Alexander Poor, witnesses thereto, is admitted to record and on the Motion of the sd. Exec., a certificate of Probate was issued.

Ordered that John Fendla, Christopher Kirk, William Hutchings, and Clement Lattimore, or any three of them being sworn by a Co. Judge, are to meet and appraise the Estate of Thomas Purcell, dec'd, in money and make a report & with Elizabeth Purcell & George Brent, Execs., appear at the next Court re: the Inventory.

Thomas Barster [?] of Wicocomoco Parish, in this Co., setting forth that he is very ancient and unable to get his living, he is excused from payment of Country & County levies for the future.

James Kirk came to Court and ackn. a deed to John Fendla for 80 a. of land in Christ Church Parish, in this Co., , which was admitted to record.

The Will of William Heale, dec'd, was further proved by the oaths of Thomas Pritchard and Isaac Cundiff, witnesses thereto, which proof is Ordered to be certified on the sd. Will.

The Will of David Ball, dec'd was presented in Court by George Ball, one of the Execs. named in the Will, who made oath thereto and being proved, is admitted to record and on the Motion of the sd. Exec., a certificate of Probate was issued.

Pg 81. George Ball, Gent., one of the Exec. of the Will of David Ball, dec'd, made oath to the Inventory of the Estate, with his subscription, is Ordered certified to Probate.

Joseph Burne came into Court, made oath that Elinor Beck, late of this Co, dec'd, died without a Will, as far as he knows, and on his Motion and giving security for just Admin. of the Estate, a certificate of Admin. was given.

Ordered that William Sydnor, William Bertrand, John Pollard & Edward Blackmore, or any three, being sworn bef. a Co. Judge, do meet and appraise the sd. Estate in money and return a report and Joseph Burne, Admin., attend at the next Court.

A Grand Jury of this Co., being impaneled according to an Order of the Court , having appointed William Brent, foreman, and the rest were George Brent, Benjamin George, Junr., John Simmons, William George, Nathaniel Carpenter, William Goodridge, John Meredith, Charles Chelton, Robert Newsom, Anthony Garton, John Angell, George Yerby, Thomas Hubbard, Edward Sanders, James Reves, Richard Davis, Junr., John Yerby, John Fendla, Peter Rivere, Junr., Ezekiel Gilbert, John Gibson & Isaac Cundiff, were sworn, and then withdrew and after some time returned to Court to give their Presentments, which were Ordered to be recorded – "Lancaster – We of the grand jury make our Presentments as followeth . We present Henry Lawson for turning the main road that leads down to Maj. Fleet's in the Parish of Christ Church upon the 20th of April last by the Information of Capt. Henry Fleet, and William Stepto.

James Currell for not going to Church two months past Christ Church Parish, Charles Russell & his wife, for not going to Church one month past Christ Church Parish, Leroy Crane & his wife for not going to Church one month past Wiccocomoco Parish. Signed: William Brent, Foreman.

Order that Henry Lawson, James Currell, Charles Russell & his wife, of Christ Church Parish, and Leroy Crane & his wife of Wiccocomoco Parish, in this Co., be summoned to next Court to answer the Presentment.

Ordered that John Bailey be summoned to next Court to answer the petition of William Maconel against him.

An additional Inventory of the Estate of Benony Chelton, dec'd, was returned by his Execx., and Ordered recorded.

Andrew Chelton exhibited and made oath to his account of the Estate of George Chelton, an orphan under his Guardianship which was Ordered to be recorded.

On the prayer of John Young of St. Mary's White Chappel Parish in this Co., setting forth that he is very ancient & unable to get his living, he is excused from Country & county levies for the future.

On the complaint of John Thompson, a servant boy, belonging to James Fleming, against his sd. Master, the sd. James being summoned but not appearing. It is considered that the sd. Thompson be discharge from the sd. James' service.   And, Wm. Rand of Gloucester Co., joiner, undertaking the care of the sd. John Thompson and to teach him the trade of a Clapboard Carpenter by the consent of the sd. John Thompson, he is bound to the sd. William Rand till he attains the age of 21 years and to find sufficient diet, lodging, apparel, and at the expiration of his servitude to pay him as is appointed for servants by Indenture or custom. And, it is Ordered that James Fleming pay the costs hereby occasioned.

In the action of debt betw. Robert Carter, Esqr., and Thomas Carter, Church Wardens of Christ Church Parish, Pltfs., and Frances Murrough, Deft., for 500 lbs. tobacco and cask or 50 shillings, the fine by law against the sd. Deft. for having a bastard child is put forth. The Court having now fully advised on the argument on the Deft.'s plea is arrest of the Judgment to be given in this cause. The plea is overrated and it is considered that the sd. Pltf. recover against the sd. Deft., the afsd. tobacco & cask or money to the use of the afsd. Parish together with one attorney's fee and costs. But in case the sd. Deft shall surrender her body at the next Court to be held for this Co. & there receive the corporal punishment inflicted by Law for her afsd. offense this Judgment is to be discharged otherwise execution is to issue for the same as usual.

In the ejection betw. John Tarr, Pltf., and Charles Ewell, Deft., for one messuage & 500 acres of land, with all appurtenances, lying in Christ Church Parish, in this Co., demised to the sd. Pltf., by Wm. Mayers, as in the Declaration set forth the sd. Pltf. failing to prosecute, it is considered that this suit be dismissed and that the sd. Pltf. forthwith pay unto the sd. Deft., his costs in his behalf expended together with one attorney's fee.

Pg 82. The action of trespass betw. James Ball, Gent., and Thomas Mason, Deft., is continued till next Court.

The ejection betw. John Tarr and William Brent , Deft., is continued till next Court.

In the suit in Chancery, betw. William Everate & Margaret, his wife, Complts., and William Bertrand, Exec., of the Will of Ruth Foushee, dec'd, on the Motion of the sd. Complts. time is given to consider the Defts. rejoinder this day till next Court.

In the action upon the case betw. Thomas Pollard, Pltf., and John Gill, Deft., is continued till the next Court.

In the action on the case betw. Thomas Pollard, Pltf., and Joseph Carter, Deft., for 400 lbs. tobacco due by account, Joseph Chinn, Edward Sanders, Elias Lowry, Thomas Hubbard, George Brent, Henry Towles, Thomas Wharton, George Yerby, Ezekiel Gilbert, John Gibson, William Goodridge and John Callahan were impaneled & sworn to try the issue joined in this cause and bringing in their verdict in these words – "We of the Jury find for the Pltf. 200 lbs. tobacco & costs." Signed: Jos. Chinn, Foreman. The sd. verdict on the Pltf. Motion is recorded and it is considered that the sd. Pltf., recover against the Deft. 200 lbs. tobacco & the damages afsd. by the Jury afsd. and costs together with one attorney's fee.

In the action of Debt betw. Henry Fleet, William Ball, Thomas Carter, George Heale, Edwin Conway, Charles Burges, Charles Carter, John Selden, Henry Fleet, Junr., Henry Carter, Hugh Brent and Nicholas Martin, Gent., Co. Justices, Pltfs., and Robert Gibson, Deft., on the Motion of the sd. Deft., time is given him to the Pltf. replication this day put in till next Court.

In the suit betw. Robert Gibson, Pltf., and Thomas Harris, Deft., by attachment the sd. Pltf. filing to appear the attachment is discontinued.

In the action of trespass & assault & battery betw. Robert Jordan, Pltf., and Elizabeth Frizell, Deft., the sd. Defts. pleaded and the Pltf. joined issue whereupon the trial of the sd. issue is referred till next Court.

In the action on the case betw. Michael Ryan, Pltf., and Edward Sanders, Deft., on the Motion of the sd. Deft. at special imparlance is granted him in this cause, till next Court.

In the action on the case betw. Thomas Bridgford, Pltf., and Thomas Pinckard, Gent., Deft., is continued for a [?] trial, till next Court.

In the action on the case betw. John Mitchell, Doctor of Physick, Pltf., and Thomas Wharton, planter, Deft., the sd. Deft. being called and not appearing on the Motion of the sd. Pltf., Judgment granted against the sd. Deft., and John Selden, Gent., Co., Sheriff for what shall appear to be justly due to the sd. Pltf. at next Court unless the sd. Deft. shall then appear & answer to the sd. action.

In the action on the case betw. John brown, of the King George Co., Pltf., and Richard Davis, Junr., Deft., by petition, the sd. Def. pleaded & the Pltf. joined issue whereupon it is Ordered that the trial of the sd. issue be referred till next Court.

In the action on the case betw. Thomas Bridgford, Pltf., and William Eustace, Deft., for 1,200 lbs. tobacco due by account, the parties were heard and the Defts. evidence in this cause sworn & examined whereupon it is considered that the action be dismissed and that the sd. Pltf. pay unto the sd. Deft., his costs in this behalf expended.

In suit betw. Daniel Hornsby, Pltf., and Giles Robinson, Deft., by petition is continued for the Deft. to make debt till next Court.

In the suit betw. Robert Mitchell, Gent, Pltf., and Hopkins Wildy, Deft., for 942 lbs. tobacco due by bill, the sd. Deft. confessed Judgment wherefore it is considered that the Deft. further the payments to the sd. Pltf., his afsd. debt and costs.

In the suit betw/ Ezekiel Gilbert, Pltf., and Thomas Harris, Deft., by attachment for 1,500 lbs. tobacco and 20 shillings, due by account on the oath of the sd. Pltf., Judgment is granted him against the sd. Deft., for 394 lbs. of tobacco and £1.5.4 & half penny & costs and it is Ordered that the sd. attachment be continued till next Court.

Ezekiel Gilbert exhibited and made oath to his account of the Estate belonging to Sarah Howell, Maudlin Howell, and Deborah Howell, Orphans of Thomas Howell, dec'd, under his Guardianship which was afsd. to be recorded.

Pg 83. In the action of the case betw. William Rankin, Pltf., and William Hutchings, Deft., for £11 damages in the Declaration set forth, William Ballendine , Joseph Carter, Henry Horne, Thomas Pollard, Peter Reviere, Junr.,

Thomas Carter, Junr., Wm. Stamps, John Simonds, Nathaniel Carpenter, William George, Richard Davis, Junr., and John Fendla, were impaneled & sworn to try the issue joined in this cause and bringing in their verdict in these words – "We the Jury find for the Deft." Signed: Wm. Ballendine. The sd. verdict on the Deft.'s Motion is recorded. And, it is considered that this Action be dismissed and that the sd. Pltf. forthwith pay unto the sd. Deft., his costs in this behalf expended together with one attorney's fee.

Ordered that the return of the division of the Estate of John Mott, dec'd, be made to the next Court.

William Ball, Gent., is appointed to take the list of Tithables in the Lower Precinct in St. Mary's White Chappel Parish in this Co. for this year.

George Heale, Gent., is appointed to take the list of Tithables in the Middle Precinct in St. Mary's White Chappel Parish in this Co. for this year.

William Ball, Junr., Gent. is appointed to take the list of Tithables in the Upper Precinct in St. Mary's White Chappel Parish in this Co. for this year.

Thomas Carter., Gent., is appointed to take the list of Tithables in the lower part of Corotomon Precinct in Christ Church Parish in this Co. for this year.

Edwin Conway, Gent., is appointed to take the list of Tithables in the Upper part of Corotomon Precinct in Christ Church Parish & Wiccocomoco Parish in this Co. for this year.

Hugh Brent, Gent., is appointed to take the list of Tithables in the Middle Precinct of Corotomon Precinct in Christ Church Parish, in this Co. for this year.

Nicholas Martin, Gent., is appointed to take the list of Tithables between Corotomon River and the main road which leads from the Church to Col. Carter's Great Mill in Christ Church Parish, in this Co. for this year.

Henry Fleet, Gent., is appointed to take the list of Tithables in the Lower Precinct of Christ Church Parish, in this Co. for this year.

Mr. George Ball, is appointed as surveyor of the highways from Mr. Payne's to the Court House in St. Mary's White Chappel Parish in this Co. for this year.

James Brent St. Mary's White Chappel Parish in this Co. for this year to Mr. Burges' Mill in St. Mary's White Chappel Parish in this Co. for this year.

Henry Towles is appointed as surveyor of the highways from Chetwood's Ferry to the main road near Mr. Payne's in St. Mary's White Chappel Parish in this Co. for this year.

John Bailey is appointed as surveyor of the highways from the Church to Deep Bottom Run and of the rolling road which leads from Mr. Joseph Chinn's to Deep Creek Warehouses in St. Mary's White Chappel Parish in this Co. for this year.

William Bertrand is appointed as surveyor of the highways from Deep Bottom Run to Morattico Mill in St. Mary's White Chappel Parish in this Co. for this year.

Thomas Wharton is appointed as surveyor of the highways from Mr. Burges's Mill to Mr. Selden's Mill in St. Mary's White Chappel Parish in this Co. for this year.

John Mott is appointed as surveyor of the highways from Bryan Stott's to the road that leads from Col. Ball's Mill to Mr. Burges' Mill in St. Mary's White Chappel Parish in this Co. for this year.

Thomas Chattin is appointed as surveyor of the highways from Bartle's Woods to the cross roads near Doct. Thorton's in St. Mary's White Chappel Parish in this Co. for this year.

Thomas Taylor is appointed as surveyor of the highways from the main road by Giles Robinson to the main Road which leads to Mr. Selden's Mill and from that main road to Cundiff's old field and also of the rolling road in the sd. Precinct in St Mary's White Chappel Parish in this Co. for this year.

Richard Mullis is appointed as surveyor of the highways from Mr. Selden's Mill to Col. Carter's Great Mill and of all the main roads between these two branches of roads Corotomon River in Christ Church & Wiccocomoco Parish in this Co. for this year.

William Stepto is appointed as surveyor of the highways from Col. Carter's Great Mill to the cross roads in Christ Church Parish in this County for this year. And, it is Ordered that he take his assistance, the male laboring tithables belonging to Thomas Pinckard, Ruth Sydnors, George Yerbys, William Scofields & Robert Scofields Family's besides these in the sd. Precinct.

George Flower is appointed as surveyor of the highways from the cross roads to the Clerk's Office of this Court in Christ Church Parish, in this Co. for this year.

Thomas Falkner is appointed as surveyor of the highways from Mr. Charles Carter's Mill to the main road, which leads from the Clerk's Office in Christ Church Parish, in this Co. for this year and he is to keep the sd. road in repair, with the male laboring Tithables belonging to the sd. Carter in this Precinct.

Pg 84. Charles Jones is appointed as surveyor of the highways from the Church to the cross roads in Christ Church Parish, in this Co., for this year and he is to keep the road in repair which the male laboring tithables belonging to Co. john Carter in the sd. precinct.

William Martin is appointed as surveyor of the highways from the White Stone to Charles Carter's mill and of all the main roads in Nantopouron[?] Neck in Christ Church Parish, in this Co., for this year.

Henry Fleet, Gent., is appointed as surveyor of the highways from the Church to Mr. Fleet's in Christ Church Parish in this Co. for this year.

John Yerby, is appointed as surveyor of the highways from the Col. Carter's Quarter to the mill road and from the sd road to the Church in Christ Church Parish in this Co. for this year.

Elias Loury is appointed Guardian of Thomas Kirk, Orphan of Thomas Kirk, dec'd. John Simmonds becoming his security for the Guardianship, and it is Ordered that the sd. Elias be forthwith possessed with the Estate of the sd. Orphan and exhibit an amount thereof at the next Court on oath.

John Mason having attended 5 days as witness for William Hutchins in a suit brought by William Ranken, against the sd. Hutchins. It is Ordered that the sd. Hutchins pay the sd. John Mason for his attendance & costs.

John Coleman having attended 5 days as witness for William Ranken in a suit brought by him against sd. William Hutchins. It is Ordered that the William Rankin pay the sd. John Coleman for his attendance & costs.

John Tully having attended 5 days as witness for William Ranken in a suit brought by him against sd. William Hutchins. It is Ordered that the William Rankin pay the sd. John Tully for his attendance & costs.

William Hammond having attended 4 days as witness for William Ranken in a suit brought by him against sd. William Hutchins. It is Ordered that the William Rankin pay the sd. William Hammond for his attendance & costs.

Thomas Hart having attended 5 days as witness for William Ranken in a suit brought by him against sd. William Hutchins. It is Ordered that the William Rankin pay the sd. Thomas Hart for his attendance & costs.

Frances, wife of John Mc Gregger having attended 5 days as witness for William Hutchins in a suit brought by William Ranken. It is Ordered that the William Hutchins pay the sd. John Mc Gregger for his attendance & costs.

John Tarpley, Junr., Gent., producing his Commission empowering him to plead as an attorney in the Co. Courts, took the oaths to the government subscribed the test, and had the oath appointed to be taken by attorneys practicing in the Co. Courts admitted to him.

Ordered that the Court be adjourned till the 2nd Wednesday in June next. At a Court for Lancaster Co. continued on Wednesday, in 13th day of June 1733. Present: William Ball, Thomas Carter, George Heale, Edwin Conway, Henry Fleet, William Ball, Junr., Nicholas Martin; Gent., Justices

Sarah, a Negro girl, belonging to John Carter, Esqr., by the Court adjudged to be 10 years old.

Sally, a Negro girl, belonging to John Carter, Esqr., by the Court adjudged to be 13 years old.

Punch, a Negro boy, belonging to John Carter, Esqr., by the Court adjudged to be 11 years old.

Tom[?],a Negro boy, belonging to John Carter, Esqr., by the Court adjudged to be 12 years old.

Jemmy[?],a Negro boy, belonging to John Carter, Esqr., by the Court adjudged to be 13 years old.

Jack, a Negro boy, belonging to John Carter, Esqr., by the Court adjudged to be 13 years old.

Robin, a Negro boy, belonging to John Carter, Esqr., by the Court adjudged to be 13 years old.

Loudon, a Negro boy, belonging to John Carter, Esqr., by the Court adjudged to be 13 years old.

Doll, a Negro girl, belonging to John Carter, Esqr., by the Court adjudged to be 11 years old.

Judy, a Negro girl, belonging to John Carter, Esqr., by the Court adjudged to be 14 years old.

Pg 85. The appraisement of the Estate of Thomas Purcell, dec'd, was returned and Elizabeth Purcell & George Brent, his Exec., making oath according to their subscription on the same, Ordered recorded.

The Inventory of the estate of Phebe Reve's, dec'd, was retuned by James Reves, her Exec., who made oath thereto to his subscription on the Inventory, and is Ordered recorded.

On the Petition of John Davis, Peter James Bailey, William Mitchell & John Mitchell, setting forth that Capt. George Heale has stopped the old & ancient path to their houses and set but one gate for the whole neck, which makes new paths & cart roads through their lands very much to their prejudice and praying that the sd. Heale may be compelled to put gates where they formerly stood. Thomas Chattin, George Payne & Thomas Flint are appointed to view the roads in the petition mentioned and report the convenience & inconvenience thereof to the next Court.

Elias Loury exhibited & made oath to his account of the Estate belonging to Thomas Kirk, orphan of Thomas Kirk, dec'd, under his Guardianship, which is Ordered to be recorded.

The difference betw. Daniel Mc Key and Charles Chelton afsd. to this Court by a report from Henry Carter, Gent., Co. Justice, is dismissed neither party appearing.

Lucy Holmes, daughter of John Holmes, of Christ Church Parish, in this Co., 8year old the 10th of November next is by her sd. father, bound in open Court to William Watts, of this Co., till she attains 18 years. The sd. Watts obliges himself to give the sd. Lucy, one year schooling and to teach her to sew, knit and spin, and to find sufficient diet, lodging, apparel, and at the expiration of his servitude to pay him as is appointed for servants by Indenture or custom.

142

William Goodridge is appointed surveyor of the rolling road which leads from the Church road to Carpenter's Landing in St. Mary's White Chappel Parish, in this Co., for one year.

Jane Bell, a mulatto woman, servant to John Hubbard of this Co., came to Court and voluntarily agreed to continue in her sd. Master's service till Christmas next, and from that time to serve Majr. Charles Lee (by the assignment of William Hutchins, who has bought the sd. Jane from the said John Hubbard) the remainder of her Indenture time and one year thereafter in consideration of her then living with her husband, which is sd. Lee's Slave.

In the suit betw. James Ball, Gent., Pltf., and Benjamin Neale, Deft., by attachment against the Estate of the sd. Deft., for 2,080 lbs. tobacco & costs. And, the sd. attachment being returned re: 6 flag chairs, one pot, sifter, frying pan, and in the hands of Capt. George Heale & Martha, his wife, of the Deft. Ordered that the sd. George & Martha, be summoned to the next Court to declare what of the Estate of the sd. Deft., was in their hands when this attachment was served on them and that in case the goods afsd. shall not be replevied as the Law directs that they be sold & disposed of toward satisfaction of this Judgment in the same manner a goods taken in Execution upon a writ of fiere facias and on hearing the sd. Pltf., and the sd. George . It is the opinion of the Court that the corn & meat in the Deft's possession at the time of his running away was his proper Estate and is liable to this attachment. And, it is Ordered that this attachment be continued till next Court.

William Stepto making oath to the truth of his account against Phillis Bell, dec'd, and that there was due to him thereon a balance of 86 lbs. tobacco, by consent of Thomas Flint, Admin. of the sd. Estate, Judgment is granted to the afsd. William for the sd. balance and costs of the Estate of the sd. dec'd, in the hands of her sd. Admin.

The appraisement of the Estate of Ellinor Beck, dec'd, was returned and Joseph Burne[?] therefore ackn. thereof making oath according to his subscription on the Inventory, Ordered recorded.

In the suit in Chancery betw. William Ball, and infant by William Ball, Junr., Gent., his father, and next friend, Complt. and James Ball, Gent., Exec. of the Will of David Ball, dec'd, Defts., the sd. Complt. having failed to Lodge his bill in this suit is dismissed and it is considered that the sd. Complt. pay unto the sd. Deft., his costs in this behalf expended together with one attorney's fee.

In the suit betw. William Stepto, Pltf., and William Wallas, Deft., by petition for 242 lbs. tobacco due by the Deft.'s obligation payable to James Mc[?], dated 29 July last & assigned to the sd. Pltf., the sd. Deft. not appearing on the oath of the sd. Pltf. to the truth of his claim, Judgment is granted him against the sd. Deft., for the sd. 242 lbs. of tobacco.

Pg 86. In the suit betw. William Stepto and Benjamin Taylor, Deft., by petition for 376 lbs. tobacco, due by obligation payable to James Mc Cae[?], dated 8 Aug. and assigned to the sd. Pltf. , the sd. Deft not appearing and the sd. Pltf. making oath to the truth of his debt., Judgment is granted him for the sd. 376 lbs. tobacco against the sd. Deft. and costs.

In the action betw, Robert Carter, Junr., Esqr., and Thomas Carter, Church Wardens, Christ Church Parish, Pltf., and Frances Murrough, Deft., betw. the sd. Deft., this day surrendered her body & received the corporal punishment inflicted by Law, for the offense charged against her in this action whereupon it is Ordered that she be discharged from Judgment against her in this cause and from all costs & charges relating thereto.

In the action of trespass & assault& battery betw. James Robinson, Pltf., and Joseph Bolton, Deft., for £20 damages as in the Declaration is set forth, is dismissed, neither party appearing.

On the Presentment against Henry Lawson for turning the main road that leads down to Maj. Fleet's, in the Parish of Christ Church, in this Co. The sd. Henry was heard whereupon it is considered that he be fined 10 shillings, for his afsd. offense against the King, which is hereby Ordered to pay together with costs. And, it is Ordered that he forthwith put gates 5 foot wide and bar 10 foot wide where they usually stood on the road and constantly keep a strong bridge over ditch which runs across the sd. road of width sufficient for coaches & carts.

On the Presentment of the grand jury against James McCarroll, of Christ Church Parish in the Co. for not going to Church in two months is dismissed.

On the Presentment of the grand jury against Charles Russell & Margaret, his wife, of Christ Church Parish in the Co. for not going to Church in one month is dismissed.

On the Presentment of the grand jury against Lewis Crane & his wife, of Wiccocomoco Parish, in the Co., for not going to Church in one month, the sd. Lewis being summoned & not appearing, Judgment is granted against him for

100 lbs. tobacco or 10 shillings, and it is Ordered that the sd. Lewis pay the same to the Church Wardens for the use of the poor of the sd. Parish & costs.

In the suit betw. Wm. Mc Connel, Pltf., and Wm. Bailey, Deft., by Petition on hearing both parties, it is Ordered that the sd. Deft., put the Pltf. to school the 10th of Nov next, and continue him there, till he shall be able to read & write according to the order, by which the sd. Pltf., was bound to the sd. Deft. And, that he forthwith proceed to teach him a trade, which by the sd. order, the sd. Deft. undertook the sd. Pltf. should be taught.

The action of trespass betw. James Ball, Gent., Pltf., and Thomas Mason, Deft., is continued till next Court.

The ejection betw. John Tarr, Pltf., and William Brent, Deft., is continued till next Court on the Deft.'s Motion & costs.

In the suit in Chancery betw. William Everate & Margaret, his wife, Complts., and William Bertrand, Exec., of the Will of Rught Fouchee, dec'd, Deft., is continued till next Court and by consent of the parties, this cause is [can't read], then to be tried.

The action of debt betw. Henry Fleet, Wm. Ball, Thomas Carter George Heale, Edwin Conway, Charles Burges, Charles Carter, John Selden, Henry Fleet, Junr., Henry Carter, Hugh Brent and Nicholas Martin, Gent., Co. Justices, Pltfs., and Robert Gibson, Deft., is continued till next Court.

In the suit betw., John Brown, of the Co. of King George, Pltf., and Richard Davis, Junr., Deft., by petition for 5 large well-dressed deer skins, of the value of 500 lbs. tobacco on hearing the parties and the oath of the sd. Deft., in his cause it is considered that the suit be dismissed and it is Ordered that the sd. Pltf. pay unto the sd. Deft., his costs in this behalf expended.

In the action of trespass & assault & battery betw. Robert Jordan, Pltf., and Elizabeth Frizell, Deft., for £20 damages, as in the declaration, is set forth William Brant, George Brent, Thomas Hubbard, William Hutchings, William Edmunds, Martin Shearman, John Stepto, Wm. Bertrand, James Currell, George Payne, Joseph Stephen and George Yerby were impaneled & sworn to try the issue joined in this cause and bringing in their verdict in these words – "We of the Jury do find for the Defendant." William Brent, Foreman. The verdict on the Motion is recorded and it is considered that this action be dismissed and that the sd. Pltf. pay unto the sd. Deft., her costs I this behalf, expended together with one attorney's fee.

Pg 87. In the action upon the case betw. Michael Ryan, Pltf., and Edward Sanders, Deft., the sd. Deft. put in a demurrer which was joined by the sd. Deft., whereupon it is Ordered that the argument thereof be referred till next Court.

In the action of debt betw. John Mitchell, Doctor of Physick, Pltf., and Thomas Wharton, planter, Deft., an Imparlance is granted to the sd. Defts., till the next Court.

The suit betw. Daniel Horneby, Pltf., and Giles Robinson, Deft., by Petition for 951 and ¾ lbs. of tobacco, due by account is dismissed.

In the suit betw. Ezekiel Gilbert, Pltf., and Thomas Harris, Deft., by attachment against the Estate of the sd. Deft., Thomas Thornton made oath that he had nothing of the Estate of the sd. Deft., in his hands at the time when this attachment was served upon him & by Consent of the sd. Deft., his attachment is continued.

Ordered that the return of the Division of the Estate of John Mott, dec'd, be made at next Court.

In the action of debt betw. William King, Pltf., and John Gill, Deft., for 400 lbs. tobacco due by obligation the parties were heard on the demurrer in this cause and the opinion of the Court being that the Law is with the Deft, it is considered that this action be dismissed and that the sd. Pltf. pay unto the sd. Deft., his costs in his behalf expended with one attorney's fee.

Grace Muchan, the wife of Matthew Mahan having attended one day as a witness for Robert Jordan in his suit against Elizabeth Frizell. It is Ordered that the sd. Robert pay the sd. Matthew for the attendance & costs.

The case betw. George Warrick, Pltf., and Thomas Pinckard, Gent., Deft., being called & not appearing on the Motion of the sd. Pltf., Judgment is granted him against the sd. Deft. and John Selden, Gent., Co. Sheriff for what shall appear to be justly due the Pltf. at the next Court unless the Deft. doth then appear & answer.

The case of debt betw. Wm. Stepto assigned of James Mc [?], Pltf., and Thomas Lee, Gent., Deft., the sd. Deft failing to appear, Judgment to the Pltf. against the sd. Deft. for what shall appear to be justly due to him at the next Court sd. Deft.,

146

and John Selden, Gent., Co. Sheriff, unless the sd. Deft. shall then appear & answer.

The case of debt betw. Henry Fleet, Gent., Pltf., and Thomas Lee, Gent., Deft., the sd. Deft failing to appear, Judgment to the Pltf. against the sd. Deft. for what shall appear to be justly due to him at the next Court sd. Deft., and John Selden, Gent., Co. Sheriff, unless the sd. Deft. shall then appear & answer.

The suit betw. Thomas Scott, Pltf., and Thomas Lawson, Deft., by petition for 530 lbs. tobacco due by account is dismissed.

The suit betw. Thomas Lawson, Pltf., and Epaphroditus Lawson, Deft., neither party appearing is dismissed.

The suit betw. Epaphroditus Lawson, Pltf., and Andrew Donalson, Deft., for 896 lbs. tobacco due by bill, is dismissed.

The suit betw. Epaphroditus Lawson, Pltf., and William Scofield, Deft., by petition for 224 lbs. tobacco due by bill, the sd. Deft. not appearing and the sd. Pltf. making oath to the truth of his claim, Judgment grant him against the sd. Deft., for the sd. 224 lbs. tobacco & costs.

The suit betw. Francis Timberlake, Pltf., and James Clark, Deft., by petition for 421 lbs. tobacco by account, the sd. Deft. not appearing and the Pltf. making oath to the truth of his claim, Judgment grant him against the sd. Deft., for the sd. 421 lbs. tobacco & costs.

In the suit in Chancery betw. William Ball, infant by William Ball, Junr., Gent., his father & next friend, Complt., and James Ball & George Ball, Gent., Execs. of the Will of David Ball, dec'd, Defts., the sd. William Ball, Junr., is admitted to prosecute this suit as Guardian of the sd. Complt. and time is given to the sd. Defts. to put in their answer till the next Court.

The suit betw. Miriam Wilcox, Pltf., and William Goodridge, Deft., by petition for £8.10.0 & 83 lbs. tobacco, the parties were heard and it is considered that the sd. Pltf. recover against the sd. Deft. seven shillings and one penny & costs.

Pg 88. The suit betw. Thomas Bridgford, Pltf. and Thomas Pinckard, Gent., Deft., is continued till next Court.

Ordered that August Alexander be summoned to the next Court to answer the Petition of John Cotes against him.

In the difference betw. Chattin Chowning & Anne, his wife, one of the daughters of John Taylor, dec'd, and Wm. Sydnor & Katherine, his wife, Execx. of the Will of the sd. dec'd, by consent it is referred to Robert Mitchell, Gent., to settle & make up the account of the Admin. of the sd. John Taylor's Estate and to deliver to the sd. Chattin, his wife's part thereof, and it is Ordered that a report of the proceedings in the premises be made to the next Court.

James Beck, Orphan of Bryan Beck, late of the is Co., dec'd, aged 13 year the 20th September next, is by the Court bound to Joseph Burne till he attains the age of 21 years his sd. master is to teach him to read & write & learn the trade of carpenter & Joyner, and to find sufficient diet, lodging, apparel, and at the expiration of his servitude to pay him as is appointed for servants by Indenture or custom.

Ordered that Col. Wm. Ball employ some person to repair this Court House doors and that the charge thereof be paid in the next levy.

Ordered that the Court be adjourned till the 2nd Wednesday in July next. At a Court for Lancaster Co. continued on Wednesday, in 11th day of July 1733. Present: William Ball, George Heale, Edwin Conway, Henry Fleet, William Ball, Junr., Henry Carter, Hugh Brent, Nicholas Martin; Gent., Justices

Cepio, a Negro boy belonging to Henry Fleet, Junr., is adjudged to be 11 years old.

Phill, a Negro boy belonging to Henry Fleet, Junr., is adjudged to be 11 years old.

Primus[?],a Negro boy belonging to Elias Edmonds., is adjudged to be 12 years old.

Charles, a Negro boy belonging to Henry Towles, is adjudged to be 11 years old.

Mingo, a Negro boy belonging to George Payne, is adjudged to be 9 years old.

Buiez[?],a Negro girl belonging to George Payne, is adjudged to be 13 years old.

William Sanders, a servant man belonging to David Alexander Flint, of this Co., came to Court voluntarily and greed to serve his master one year after his time by Indenture Custom or former Order of the Court shall be expired in consideration of the time his master has lost in his running away & the charges he has been at in regaining him.

Benjamin Dogget, Orphan of Wm. Dogget, dec'd, aged 16 years the 24th of June last is by the Court bound to Wm. Rawson[?], Junr., till her attains the age of 21 years, his sd. master is to teach him to read & write & learn the trade of carpenter, and to find sufficient diet, lodging, apparel, and at the expiration of his servitude to pay him as is appointed for servants by Indenture or custom.

The Inventory of the Estate of Henry Fleet, Gent., was returned and Abraham Currell, one of the Exec., making oath according to his subscription thereon Ordered to be recorded.

The difference betw. Joseph Carter & Robert Galbreth concerning a horse left out of the sd. Joseph's pasture referred to this Court by William Ball, one of the Justices of Peace for this Co., the parties were heard whereupon it is the opinion of the Court that for as nothing material appears against the sd. Robert in this protestation be dismissed and it is considered that the sd. Robert go hence without day.

The suit betw. James Mc Carroll, Pltf., and James Ball & George Ball, Gent, Exec. of the will of David Ball, dec'd, Deft., for 228 lbs. tobacco due by account, is dismissed.

Pg 89. The Inventory of Francisco Frizzel's Estate was returned and his Execs thereon named making oath according to their subscription thereon, Ordered to be recorded.

In the suit betw. John Davis, Peter James Bailey, William Mitchell & John Mitchell, Pltfs., and Capt. George Heale, Deft., by petition a report of the viewers appointed in this trespass returned and admitted to record and it is considered that the ancient paths to the sd. Pltf.'s houses be laid open & gates set thereon according to the prayer of the petition betw. this & the next Court and that the sd. Defts. pay unto the sd. Pltf.'s their costs hereby caution how which Judgment the sd. Defts. praying an appeal, the consideration of this Motion is referred for a fuller Court.

In the action of Thomas Bridgford, Pltf., and Thomas Pinckard, Gent., Deft., for £40 due by account Henry Towles, George Payne, Thomas Carter, Abraham Currell, Thomas Yerby, Joseph Chinn, Ezekiel Gilbert, William Hutchins, Robert Mitchell, Junr., Thomas Hubbard, William Brent, & Elias Edmunds were impaneled & sworn to try the issue joined in this cause and bringing in their verdict in these words – "We the jury do find for the Pltf. in balance £3.2.8 ½ ." Signed: Henry Towles, foreman.   The sd. verdict on the Pltf. Motion is recorded and it is considered that the sd. Pltf. recover the sd. £3.2.8 ½, the damages afsd. by the jury assessed and costs with one attorney's fee.

In the suit betw. James Ball, Gent., Pltf., and Benjamin Neale, Deft., by attachment against the Estate of the sd. Deft., on the Motion of the sd. Pltf., the sd. attachment is continued till next Court.

The trespass betw. James Ball, Gent., Pltf., and Thomas Mason, Deft., is continued till next Court.

The ejection betw. John Tarr, Pltf., and William Brent, Deft., is continued till next Court at the Deft's Motion & costs.

The suit in Chancery betw. William Everate and Margaret, his wife, Complts., and William Bertrand, Exec. of the Will of Ruth Fouchee, dec'd, Deft., is continued till next Court at the Deft's Motion & costs.

The action of debt betw. Henry Fleet, Wm. Ball, Thomas Carter George Heale, Edwin Conway, Charles Burges, Charles Carter, John Selden, Henry Fleet, Junr., Henry Carter, Hugh Brent and Nicholas Martin, Gent., Co. Justices, Pltfs., and Robert Gibson, Deft., is continued till next Court at the Deft's Motion & costs.

The case betw. Michael Ryan, Pltf., and Edward Sanders, Deft., is continued till next Court at the Plft.'s Motion & costs.

In the action on the case betw. John Mitchell, Doctor of Physick, Pltf., and Thomas Wharton, planter, Deft., Judgment is granted to the sd. Pltf. against the sd. Deft. by Nihil Decit[?].

Ordered that the return of the Division of the Estate of John Mott, dec'd, be returned to next Court.

In the action upon the case betw. George Warrick, Pltf., and Tomas Pinckard, Gent., Deft., an imparlance is granted to the sd. Deft., till the next Court.

In the debt betw. William Stepto, assignee of James Mc Cue, Pltf., and Thomas Lee, Gent., Deft., for 1,363 lbs. tobacco, the sd. Deft. being returned non-[?] &

not appearing on the Motion of the sd. Pltf., is awarded him against the sd. Deft. returnable to next Court.

In the debt betw. Henry Fleet, Junr., Pltf., and Thomas Lee, Gent., for 1,009 lbs. tobacco, Deft., being returned non –[?] & not appearing on the Motion of the sd. Pltf., is awarded him against the sd. Deft. returnable to next Court.

In the suit in Chancery, betw. William Ball, an infant, by William Ball, Junr., Gent., his father & next friend Complt., and James Ball & George Ball, Gent., Execs. of the Will of David Ball, dec'd, the Deft. James put in & made oath to his answer in this suit, which the sd. Complt. has time to consider and on the Motion of the sd. Deft., George, time is given till next Court to put in his answer.

In the suit betw. John Cotes, Pltf., and August Alexander, Deft., by petition for the sd. Pltf., part of the Estate of William Cotes, dec'd, in the Deft. hands by consent of the parties, James Bell, Gent., is appointed to settle the account of the Admin. of the sd. Cotes' Estate and to make a report thereof to the next Court.

The difference depending betw. Chattin Chowning and Ann, his wife, one of the daughters of John Taylor, dec'd, Pltf., and William Sydnor & Katherine Cotes, his wife, Execx. of the Will of the sd. Dec'd, Deft., is referred till the next Court.

Pg 90.   The action of Debt betw. Thomas Lee, Gent., Pltf. and Thomas Bridgford, Deft., is continued as it is till the next Court.

The suit betw. Thomas Lee, Pltf., and William Harvey, Deft., by petition is continued till next Court.

The suit betw. Thomas Burnet, Pltf., and Robert Quibey, Deft., by petition for 420 lbs. tobacco due by account on hearing the parties and the oath of the sd. Deft. in this matter. It is considered that this suit be dismissed and that the sd. Plft. pay unto the sd. Deft. his costs in their behalf expended.

A letter of Attorney from Thomas Tarpley, of St. Ann Lymus, Middlesex co., Mariner, to Thomas Barber, of the Co. of Richmond and nigh Rappahannock River in Virginia, planter, was proved by the oath of Thomas Deve, a witness thereto and admitted to record.

In the case betw. Thomas Nelson, Gent., Pltf., and Francis Burges, James Ball & Edwin Conway, Execs., of the Will of Charles Burges, Gent., dec'd, for £336.9.3 & farthing and £11.10.11, due from the Testator in his lifetime by account. The sd. Deft. confessed Judgment wherefore it is considered that the sd. Pltf. recover his afsd. debt of the Estate of the sd. dec'd, in the hands of the sd. Defts., and on the Motion of the sd. Defts., time is given then till next Court to show reasons why Judgment ought not go against them in this cause of r the costs of this suit.

The action upon the case betw. Thomas Pollard, Pltf., and George Warrick, Deft., for 2,600 lbs. tobacco due on balance of an account is dismissed.

Joseph Stephens and Judith, his wife, came into Court and ackn. their deeds of Lease & Release to William Oliver for & concerning 50 a. of land in St. Mary's White Chappel Parish, in this Co., the sd. Judith being privately examined, which are admitted to record.

In the suit betw. Murrough Nicken, Pltf., and Robert Schofield, Deft., by feire facias, for execution for 6 pence and 397 lbs. tobacco or 247 lbs. of tobacco & 15 shilling & six pence, yet unlevied & unpaid on a Judgment obtained by the sd. Pltf. against the sd. Deft. at a Court held for this Co., the 13th October 1731. it is considered that the sd. Pltf. have execution against the sd. Deft. for her afsd. debt and for her costs in this behalf expended.

William Robinson having attended 3 days as a witness for Thomas Bridgford in suit against Thomas Pinckard, Gent. It is Ordered that Bridgford pay the sd. William for his attendance & costs.

William Olliver having attended 2 days as a witness for Thomas Bridgford in suit against Thomas Pinckard, Gent. It is Ordered that Bridgford pay the sd. William for his attendance & costs.

Robert West having attended 2 days as a witness for Thomas Bridgford in suit against Thomas Pinckard, Gent. It is Ordered that Bridgford pay the sd. Robert for his attendance & costs.

The attachment obtained by James Ball, Gent., against the Estate of Philip Fisher is discontinued.

In the suit betw. John Selden, Gent., Pltf., and Robert Jordan, Deft., by attachment for 400 lbs. tobacco, the sd. Pltf. making oath to the truth of his amount, Judgment is granted him against the sd. Deft. for his debt & costs and it is Ordered that the sd. Attachment be continued till next Court.

152

The attachment obtained by Mary Frizell, against the Estate of Robert Jordan for 284 lbs. tobacco is discontinued.

Ordered that Charles Chelton be summoned to next Court to answer the petition of Peter Percifull against him.

Ordered that the Court be adjourned till the 2nd Wednesday in August next.

Pg 91. At a Court for Lancaster Co. continued on Wednesday, in 8th day of August 1733. Present: William Ball, George Heale, Edwin Conway, William Ball, Junr., Henry Carter; Gent., Justices

The Will of Nicholas George, dec'd, was presented in Court by David George, Exec., therein named, who made oath and being proved by the oaths of John George & Elmore Dogget, witnesses, thereto, is admitted to record and on the Motion of the sd. Exec. was granted probate.

Ordered that David George, Exec. of the Will of Nicholas George, dec'd, bring an Inventory of the sd. testators Estate to the next Court.

In the difference betw. Chattin Chowning & Ann, his wife, one of the In the difference betw. Chattin Chowning & Anne, his wife, one of the daughters of John Taylor, dec'd, Pltfs., and Wm. Sydnor & Katherine, his wife, Execx. of the Will of the sd. dec'd, Defts., James Ball, William Ballendine & William Bertrand, Gent. and appointed to settle an amount of the Admin. of the sd. Testator's Estate and to set apart & deliver to the sd. Pltf.'s the sd. Ann's part thereof and to make a report of their proceedings to the next Court.

Tony, a Negro boy, belonging to Thomas Carter is adjudged to be 14 years of age.

Dinah, a Negro girl, belonging to John Pollard is adjudged to be 12 years of age.

Jack, a Negro boy, belonging to Christopher Kirk is adjudged to be 12 years of age.

Jenny, a Negro girl, belonging to William Hutchins is adjudged to be 12 years of age.

Jenny, a Negro girl, belonging to Henry Knight is adjudged to be 13 years of age.

Jeminey[?], a Negro girl, belonging to Henry Knight is adjudged to be 12 years of age.

Dick, a Negro boy, belonging to John Pinckard, Junr., is adjudged to be 12 years of age.

Philip Duffy, a servant man, belonging to William Hutchins, of this Co., came to Court and voluntarily agreed to serve his master 2 years after his time by indenture custom or former order of Court is expired in consideration of the time his master has lost in his running away & his charges in regaining him and the damage done to his master in several goods he took with him.

On the Motion of John Mitchell praying Martha McCarrol might be bound to him. It appearing to this Court that the sd. Martha was a bastard child heretofore to Elinor Beck, dec'd. It is Ordered that Joseph Burne, Admin., of the Estate of the sd. Elinor be summoned to the next Court to answer to the premises [?].

In the suit betw. John Davis, Peter James Bailey, William Mitchell and John Mitchell, Pltfs., and Capt. George Heale, Deft., by petition the Motion of the Deft. for an appeal from the Judgment ....in this cause at last Court is granted him to the 9th day of the next General Court, Thomas Edwards, Gent., becoming his security to prosecute the appeal with effect.

George Heale, of the Parish of St. Mary's White Chappel and Thomas Edwards, of the Parish of Christ Church in this Co., Gent., came into Court and ackn. themselves jointly & severally indebted to John Davis, Peter James Bailey, William Mitchell and John Mitchell, of the sd. Parish of St. Mary's White Chappel, in the sum of £20 to be levied upon their goods & chattels, lands, & tenements under condition that the sd. Heale appear at next General Court on 9th thereof, and prosecute an appeal, this day granted him from a Judgment of the last Court against him at the suit of the sd. John Davis, Peter James Bailey, William Mitchell and John Mitchell, and if cost in the sd. appeal pay & satisfy unto the sd. law.

In the suit betw. James Ball, Gent., Pltf., and Benjamin Heale, Deft., by attachment, Capt. George Heale appearing & confessing he had in his hands of the sd. Deft's Estate 559 lbs. tobacco and a bushel of corn including a share of a crop of tobacco made by one Costele Hill[?], made on his plantation, which is subject to this attachment, Judgment is granted to the sd. Pltf. against the sd. George for the same. And, it is Ordered that this attachment be discontinued.

154

The action of trespass betw. James Ball, Gent., and Thomas Mason, Deft., is continued till next Court.

The Ejection betw. John Tarr, Pltf. and William Brent, Deft., continued on the Pltf.'s Motion and costs.

Pg. 92. In the suit in Chancery betw. William Everate & Margaret, his wife, Complt., and William Bertrand, Exec. of the Will of Ruth Fouchee, dec'd, Deft., is continued till the next Court at the Complts. notion & costs

In the action of Debt betw. Henry Fleet, William Ball, Thomas Carter, George Heale, Edwin Conway, Charles Burges, Charles Carter, Junr., John Selden, Henry Fleet, Junr., Henry Carter, Hugh Brent & Nicholas Martin, Gent., Justice of the Co., Pltfs., and Robert Gibson, Deft., is continued till next Court on the Pltfs. Motion & costs.

The action upon the case betw. Michael Ryan, Pltf., and Edward Sanders, Deft., is continued till next Court on Deft's Motion & costs.

The action upon the case betw. John Mitchell, Doctor of Physick, Pltf., and Thomas Wharton, Planter, Deft., is continued till next Court on Deft's Motion & costs.

Ordered that the return of the division of the Estate of John Mott, dec'd, be made to the next Court.

The action upon the case betw. George Warrick, Pltf., and Thomas Pinckard, Gent., Deft., the sd. Deft. put in a plea & on the Motion of the sd. Pltf. time is given to consider the same till next Court.

The action upon the case of debt betw. William Stepto assignee of James Mc Lae [?], Pltf., and Thomas Lee, Gent., for 1,263 lbs. tobacco due by obligation payable to the sd. James Mc Lae & assigned to Pltf., the sd. Deft. confessed Judgment whereupon it is Ordered that he forthwith pay unto the sd. Pltf. his afsd. debt with costs.

The action upon the case of debt betw. Henry Fleet, Gent., Pltf., and Thomas Lee, Gent., for 1,009 lbs. tobacco due by bill is dismissed.

The suit betw. John Cotes, Pltf., and Anguish Alexander, Deft., by petition [can't read] either party appearing is dismissed.

The action upon the case of debt betw. Thomas Lee, Gent., Pltf. and Tomas Bridgford, Deft., for 1,390 lbs. tobacco due by amount the Deft. confessing Judgment for 1, 000 lbs., and the Pltf. accepting the same it is continued that the sd. Deft. forthwith pay unto the sd. Pltf. 1,000 lbs. tobacco & costs.

The action upon the case of debt betw. Thomas Lee, Gent., Pltf., and William Harvey, Deft., by petition for 999 lbs. tobacco due on balance of an account is dismissed.

The action upon the case betw. Thomas Nelson, Pltf., and Frances Burges, James Ball & Edwin Conway, Execs., of the Will of Charles Burges, Gent., Deft., It is the opinion of this Court that the Pltf. do not recover his costs against the sd. Deft.

The action upon the case betw. John Selden, Gent., Pltf., and Robert Jordan, Deft., by attachment, Mary Frizzel appeared & confessed she had in her hands of the Deft's Estate 730 lbs. tobacco whereupon it is Ordered that she pay unto the sd. Pltf. his Judgment in this cause and cost out of the same and that this attachment be discontinued.

The action upon the case betw. Peter Percifull, Pltf., and Charles Chelton, Deft., by petition for his freedom dues & is dismissed neither party appearing.

The attachment obtained by Thomas Edwards, against the Estate of Robert Jordan is discontinued.

The action upon the case in Chancery betw. Richard Chichester, Esqr., Complt., and Frances Burges, widow, James Ball & Edwin Conway, Execs., of the Will of Charles Burges, Gent., dec'd, Defts., on the Motion of the sd. Defts. time is given them to answer till next Court.

Matthew Zuill [?], Gent., Pltf., and William Shelton, Deft., for 1,168 lbs. tobacco, due by obligation, the sd. Deft. confessed Judgment whereupon it is Ordered that he forthwith pay unto the sd. Plft. his afsd. debt & costs.

The suit betw. Hezekiah Kirk, Pltf., and Thomas Harte, Deft., by petition for 242 lbs. tobacco due by costs & dismissed.

The action upon the case betw. Marmaduke Beckwith, Pltf., and Job Winder, Deft., by petition is continued for the proof of the Pltf. and till the next Court.

156

The action upon the case betw. Patrick Mullin, Pltf., and Thomas Hunton, Deft., by petition for 500 lbs. tobacco due by audit, the parties were hear and the sd. Deft. in Court promising to pay the costs that should appear to be his due after a hd. tobacco relating to the sd. account should be picked over at Indian Warehouse in which the sd. Pltf. being contented, it is considered that the sd. Pltf. recover against the sd. Deft. his costs in his behalf expended.

Pg 93. The action upon the case betw. Matthew Zuill, Gent, Pltf., and Frances Timberlake, Deft. by petition for 777 lbs. tobacco due by obligation, the sd. Deft. confessed Judgment whereupon it is Ordered that he forthwith pay unto the sd. Pltf. his afsd. debt & costs.

The action upon the case betw. Matthew Zuill, Gent, Pltf., and John Galloway, Deft. by petition for 516 lbs. tobacco due by obligation, the sd. Deft. confessed Judgment whereupon it is Ordered that he forthwith pay unto the sd. Pltf. his afsd. debt & costs.

The action upon the case betw. Ezekiel Gilbert, Pltf., & Thomas James, Exec. of the Will of Frances Kelly, dec'd, Deft., by petition continued for a trial at the next Court.

The action upon the case betw. Thomas Edwards, Pltf., & Arthur Mc Neal, Deft., by petition for 250 lbs. tobacco due by obligation the sd. Deft. confessed Judgment whereupon it is Ordered that he forthwith pay unto the sd. Pltf by afsd. debt. with costs.

Ordered that the Court be adjourned till the 2nd Wednesday in September next. At a Court for Lancaster Co. continued on Wednesday, the 10th day of September next 1733. Present: William Ball, Edwin Conway, William Ball, Junr., Nicholas Martin; Gent., Justices.

By virtue of a Commission under the hand & seal of Mr. Secretary Carter, dated 5 Feb last, Thomas Martin took the Oath to the Government & subscribed the test and had the Oath of Co. Deputy Court Clerk administered to him.

The petition if Moses Carter for Robert Galbreath to be his Guardian is continued till next Court.

George Yerby, on of the Constables for Christ Church Parish, in this Co., making return that he counted 8 tobacco seconds on the plantation whereon Alexander Poor is overseer in his Precinct and it appearing to the Court that the sd. seconds were not turned out with any views of profit or in contempt of the Acts for preventing the same and that they were destroyed in the presence of the sd. Constable. It is considered that no prosecution issue against the sd. Alexander for this breach of the Acts.

The appraisement of the Estate of John Mott, dec'd, was returned and Joseph Mott & Randolph Mott, three of the Execs. making oath to their subscription on the Inventory, Ordered recorded.

Ordered that a return of the division of the Estate of John Mott, dec'd, be made at next Court.

On the complaint by Elizabeth Mitchell against Epaphroditus Lawson for wages, Pltf., & it is Ordered that he be summoned to next Court to answer the complaint.

The difference depending betw. Chattin Chowning & Ann, his wife, one of the daus. of John Taylor, dec'd, Pltf., and Wm. Sydnor & Catherine, his wife, Exec. of the Will of the sd. dec'd, Defts., is continued for a return of the auditor's report.

In the difference betw. John Mitchell, Pltf., and Joseph Burne, dec'd, of the Estate of Ellinor Beck, dec'd, Deft., concerning Martha Mc Corroll, a bastard child heretofore bound to the sd. Ellinor. It is the opinion of the Court that the property of the sd. Martha is in the Deft., whereupon this matter is dismissed.

Pg 94. The action of trespass betw. James Ball, Gent., Pltf., and Thomas Mason, Deft., continued to next Court.

In the ejection between John Tarr, Pltf. and William Brent, Deft., is continued.

In the suit in Chancery betw. William Everate & Margaret, his wife, Complt., and William Bertrand, Exec. of the Will of Ruth Fouchee, dec'd, Deft. – one bed sheets, rug & blanket, curtains & Vallens & bed stead given, bequest to the sd. Complt., Margaret by the Will of the sd. Ruth as in the Complt. bill is et forth- the parties were fully heard and the evidence of James Ball, Gent., taken in this matter whereupon it is the opinion of the Court that the property of the sd. bed sheets, rug, blanket & curtain vallens & bedstead legally vested in the afsd. testatrix, by the Will of James Fouchee, dec'd. It is Ordered that the sd. Complts. recover the afsd. bed sheets, rug, blanket, curtains vallens & bedstead of the Estate of the sd. Ruth in the Defts. hands and the Complts. costs in this behalf expended be disputed at next Court.

Ordered that the Court be adjourned till the 2nd Wednesday in October next. At a Court for Lancaster Co. continued on Wednesday, in 10th day of October 1733. Present: William Ball, George Heale, Edwin Conway, William Ball, Junr., Henry Carter, Nicholas Martin; Gent., Justices.

Boatswain, a Negro boy belonging to John Heale, of this Co., is adjudged to be 9 years old.

Order that the Sheriff summon at least 24 Co. Freeholders & inhabitants to appear at next Court for a Gran Jury be impaneled & sworn to enquire into the breach of the penal laws & present the offenders.

The Inventory of the Estate of Nicholas George, dec'd, was returned and David George, Exec, making Oath to his subscription thereon, Ordered to be recorded.

In the suit betw. Joseph Magoone, Pltf., and Col. William Ball, Deft., by petition is continued for the evidence of James Carter at next Court.

Mary Buckley, widow of John Buckley, late of this Co., dec'd, came into Court and made oath that the sd. John departed this life without a Will … & on her Motion, and giving security, for her just Admin. of his Estate, a certificate was granted for her Admin. on the Estate.

Ordered that James Stott, Thomas Stott, Bryan Pullen & John Callahan or any three of them, sworn bef. a Co. Justice, and appraise the Estate in money and they & the sd. Mary, Adminx., appear at next Court, with their report & Inventory.

In the suit in Chancery betw. William Ball, an infant by William Ball, Junr., Gent. his father & next friend, Complts., & James & George Ball, Gents., Execs., of the Will of David Ball, dec'd, Defts.. The sd. Complts. put in exception to the answer of the sd. Deft. James in this suit, which at the Motion of the sd. James time is given to consider & time is also given to the Deft, George for his answer at next Court.

In the action of Debt betw. Henry Fleet, William Ball, Thomas Carter, George Heale, Edwin Conway, Charles Burges, Charles Carter, Junr., John Selden, Henry Fleet, Junr., Henry Carter, Hugh Brent & Nicholas Martin, Gent., Justice of the Co., Pltfs., and Robert Gibson, Deft., for £100, due by bond as in the declaration. The opinion of the Court being that the person performing this should five forthwith for the costs by the sd. Deft. in this behalf expended in case the suit should be adjudged against the Pltfs.. And, no person offering the same, it is considered that this suit be dismissed and that Robert Tonison, the person presenting the same, pay unto the sd. Deft., his costs herein expended with one attorney's fee.

Pg 95. In the action of betw. Michael Ryan, Pltf., and Edward Sanders, Deft., for £20 damages & the parties fully heard of the Deft's demurrer to the Pltf. in his cause, the Court sees the that the law is with the Deft. It is dismissed & the Pltf. pay the Deft.'s costs & one attorney's fee.

On the prayer of Moses Carter and Aaron Carter, orphans of Peter Carter, dec'd, & Robert Gilbreath is appointed Guardian, having given security, it is Ordered the sd. Robert forthwith possess the Estate of the sd. orphans and exhibit an amount thereof on oath at next Court.

Matthias James, one of the Constables, Christ Church Parish in this Co., while making a return, found 20 tobacco seconds on the plantation of John Cox, in his Precinct, and appearing they were not turned out in contempt of the Acts, they were destroyed in the Constable's presence with no prosecution issue.

In the action of Debt betw. John Mitchell, Doctor of Physick, Pltf., & Thomas Wharton, planter, the Deft. pleaded and the Pltf. joined issue whereupon it is Ordered that the trial be referred till next Court.

In the action betw. George Warrick, Pltf., and Thomas Pinckard, Gent., Deft., is continued at the Pltf.'s Motion & costs till next Court.

In the action in Chancery betw. Richard Chichester, Esqr., Complt., and Frances Burges, widow, James Ball, & Edwin Conway, Gent., Execs., of the Will of Charles Burges, Gent., dec'd, Defts. are given time to answer at next Court.

In the action betw. Marmaduke Beckewith, Gent., Pltf., and Job Winder, Deft., by petition for £4.12.0 due on balance by Deft, and his attorney confessed Judgment and it is considered that he forthwith pay unto the Pltf. the afsd. amount & costs.

The suit betw. Ezekiel Gilbert, Pltf. and Thomas Games, Exec. of the Will of Frances Jelly, Deft., by petition for 900 lbs. tobacco due; is dismissed.

160

In the action betw. Robert Mitchell, Gent., Pltf., and John Stepto, Junr., Deft., being called & not appearing , Judgment is granted against the Deft., and Thomas Lawson, his security shall appear to be justly due to the sd. Pltf. at next Court unless the Deft. shall appear & answer the action.

In the action betw. Robert Mitchell, Gent., Pltf., and William Ballendine, Deft., for £3.1.3 & 496 lbs. tobacco due by amount. And hearing the parties, & the oath of the sd. Pltf., Judgment is granted the Pltf. & Deft Ordered to pay costs

In the action betw. Robert Mitchell, Gent., Pltf., and Henry Taylor, Deft., by petition for 686 lbs. tobacco due by account & the sd. Deft. not appearing, the Pltf. making oath, Judgment is to the sd. Pltf. for his debt, and the Deft, is Ordered to pay & the costs forthwith.

In the difference betw. Chattin Chowning & Ann, his wife, one of the daus. of John Taylor, dec'd, Pltf. and Wm. Sydnor & Catherine, his wife, Execx., of the Will of the sd. dec'd, the audit report presented was returned & admitted to record and the Pltf, failing to prosecute further proceedings dismissed.

The division of the Estate of John Mott, dec'd, was returned and Ordered recorded.

The order of the last Court for summoning Epaphroditus Lawson to answer the complaint of Elizabeth Mitchell, not being performed. It is Ordered that the sd. Epaphroditus Lawson be summoned to next Court to answer the complaint.

Pg 96. In the suit in Chancery betw. William Everate & Margaret, his wife, Complt., and William Bertrand, Exec. of the Will of Ruth Fouchee, dec'd, Deft., the sd. Deft. continued till the next Court.

In the ejection between John Tarr, Pltf. and William Brent, Deft., is continued.

The Will of Thomas Carter, Gent., dec'd, was presented in Court by Annabella Carter, Execx., therein named , who made oath and being proved by the oath of John Carter & Harry Carter, witnesses, is admitted to record and on Motion of Execx. certificate of probate was issued.

Ordered that Elias Edmunds, William Tayloe, Thomas Yerby & Benjamin George, or any three, being sworn bef. a Co. Justice, are to appraise the Estate of Thomas Carter, Gent., dec'd, are make a report with Annabelle Carter, Execx., appear at the next Court with the report & inventory.

For settling the difference betw. John Davis, Peter James Bailey, William Mitchell, Pltfs., against Capt. George & Capt. Heale, Defts., consent to give the afsd. William & Jno. Mitchell lease to set a gate near the place where the upper gates flood on the Heale's land and to move the same as they shall occasion any where betw. where the sd. gate formerly stood & the upper end of the Corn field and the sd. Heale doth agree to allow a bridle path to the same. And, the Heale doth also agree to keep a good cart road to the lower gate on his sd. land but he is to have liberty to move this gate & road anywhere bet w. the place where it now stands & where it formerly stood. On the Motion of the sd. parties was admitted to record.

Ordered that the Court be adjourned till the 2nd Wednesday in November next. At a Court for Lancaster Co. continued on Wednesday, in 14th day of November 1733. Present: William Ball, Henry Fleet, William Ball, Junr., Henry Carter, Hugh Brent; Gent., Justices.

Ordered that Thomas Taff & Mary, his wife, and Robert Mc Tyer & Elizabeth, his wife, Execx., of the Will of Francisco Frizzel, dec'd, be summoned to next Court to answer the Petition of Robert Pritchard, against them.

Mary Veldon, widow of Francis Velden, late of the County, dec'd, came into Court and made oath that he died without a Will, and on her Motion & giving security for her full Admin. of the sd. dec'd Estate & certificate for Administration was granted.

Ordered that William Chelton, James Brent, Richard Davis & George Finch[?], of any three being sworn bef. a Co. Justice, are to appraise the Estate of Francis Velden, dec'd, are make a report in money & make return & appear with Mary Velden, Admin., at the next Court with the report & inventory.

Elizabeth Parker, widow, of Joseph Parker, late of this Co., dec'd, came into Court and made Oath that the sd. Joseph died without a Will, and was granted a certificate for the Administration of his Estate.

Pg 97. Ordered that Thomas Lawson, Epaphroditus Lawson, William Martin & Matthias James, or any three of them, being sworn bef. a Co. Justice, are to appraise the Estate of Joseph Parker, dec'd, in money & make a report & inventory with Elizabeth Parker, Admin., at the next Court.

Martha Tomlin, widow & relict of Stephen Tomlin, late of this Co., dec'd, came to Court and stated that she would not attempt, receive or take legacies to her given & bequeathed by the Will of the sd. Stephen Tomlin and renounced all benefit, etc. by the Will, which on her Motion was admitted to record.

The Will of Stephen Tomlin, dec'd was presented in Court by Martha Tomlin, his widow, who made oath thereto and being proved by the oaths of Joseph Robinson & Wm. Roach, witnesses thereto is admitted to record, and on the Motion of the sd. Martha, was granted a certificate for obtaining probate, and the Will was attached.

Ordered that William Sydnor, James Stott, John Stott, & Robert Mitchell, Gent., or any three being sworn bef. a Co. Justice, are to appraise the Estate of Stephen Tomlin, dec'd, in money & make a report & inventory with Martha Tomlin, Admin., at the next Court.

James Ball, Gent., came into Court and made Oath that the balance of £9.10.10 ½ , was justly due him on the balance of his account against Wm. Jarvis (which account he faithfully compared with his store book) and that he had not received any part of satisfaction for the same, which is Ordered to be certified on the sd. account.

Ordered that William Stamps be summoned to the next Court to answer the Petition of Chattin Chowning against him.

John Bailey, one of the Constables of White Chappel Parish, in this Co., making return found tobacco seconds on the plantations of Samuel Brumley, Junr., and Michael Reason in his Precinct, on hearing the sd. John Bailey it is considered that no prosecution issue against the sd. Samuel & Michael for the aforesaid offense.

The Sheriff under Proclamation that the Court was about to lay the County Levy, they proceeded accordingly. Lancaster Co. – **Pounds of Tobacco:**

John Carter, Esqr., for keeping the Public Ferry one year -1,400

John Pyne for cleaning the Court House & other services – 800

John Tarpley, Junr., Attorney for the King in this Co. - 1,000

John Selden, Gent., Sheriff of the Co. for Public Service – 1,00

Thomas Edwards, Court Clerk for public service – 1,000

Capt. Henry Fleet, Co. Sheriff, for two coroner's Inquests & Constable fees – 366

Mr. Secy. Carter for filing & recording the Inquisitions - 100

Matthias James, Constable for viewing tobacco seconds in his precinct – 200

Thomas Fleet, Constable for the same - 311

John Bailey, Constable for the same - 204

Edward Sanders, Constable for the same - 60

Wm. Dogget, Constable for the same - 190

Henry Horne, Constable for the same - 246

George Yerby, Constable for the same – 264

Pg 98. To 14% for Salary & Commissions on 6,982 lbs. tobacco – 976

Total – 8,325 lbs. tobacco

Credit

The last year's portion in the Sheriff's hands – 367

164

1,503 tithables at 5.25 per pol – 7,890

A remainder to be accounted for to the Sheriff next year – 68

Total – 8,325 lbs. tobacco

The County levy for this present year 1733 amounting in the whole to 5.25 lbs. tobacco per pol, it is Ordered that the Co Sheriff collect so much from every tithable person in this Co., discounting 10 % for convenience where it is paid in Inspector's notes and pay the same to the County Creditors, as the law directs.

Ferry - Ordered that Hon. John Carter, Esqr., do keep the Public Ferry over Corotomon River in the Co., the ensuing year and that he be paid for the same as usual.

Court House – Ordered that John Pyne do find this Court with water & Candles & then the Court house for the ensuing year and that he be paid for the same as usual.

In the action of debt betw. John Mitchell, doctor of Physick, Pltf., and Thomas Wharton, planter, Deft. is continued till next Court.

In the action betw. George Warwick, Pltf., and Thomas Pinckard, Deft., the sd. Pltf. put in a demurrer to the sd. Deft.'s plea in this cause, which on the Motion of the Deft., time is given him to consider till next Court.

In the suit in Chancery betw. Richard Chichester, Esqr., Complt., and Frances Burges, widow, James Ball & Edwin Conway, Gent., Exec. of the Will of Charles Burges, dec'd, Deft., further time is given Deft. to answer till next Court.

In the action betw. Robert Mitchell, Deft., and John Stepto, Junr., an imparlance is granted the sd. Deft., till next Court.

The difference depending betw. Elizabeth Mitchell, Pltf., and Epaphroditus Lawson, Deft., is continued till next Court.

The suit in Chancery betw. William Everate & Margaret, his wife, Complts. and William Bertrand, Exec. of the Will of Ruth Fouchee, dec'd, Deft., is continued to next Court.

The ejection betw. John Tarr, Pltf., and William Brent, Deft. is continued till next Court.

The ejection betw. John Tarr, Pltf., and Thomas Garr, Deft., for lands & tenements in Wiccocomoco Parish in this Co., demised to the Pltf. by Richard Hudnall, planter, neither party appearing , is dismissed.

In the debt betw. James Ball, Gent, Pltf., and Wm. Jacobs, Deft., for 1770 lbs. tobacco due by obligation & account, is dismissed.

The suit betw. Margaret Hogan, Pltf., and John Young, Deft., by petition is continued till next Court.

In the action of trespass betw. John Stepto, Junr., Pltf., and William Hattaway, Deft., for £25 damages, the sd. Deft. being called & not appearing on the Motion of the sd. Pltf., a [can't read] is awarded him against the Deft. returnable to the next Court.

In the suit betw. Lawrence Peirot, Pltf., and George Warrick, Deft., by petition for 500 lbs. tobacco due by obligation, and hearing the parties it is considered that the sd. Pltf. recover for 500 lbs. tobacco & costs.

Pg 99. In the action of Assault & Battery betw. Michael Lee, Pltf., and Thomas Hunton, Deft., is dismissed.

Ordered that the Court be adjourned till the 2nd Wednesday in December next. At a Court for Lancaster Co. continued on Wednesday, in 9th day of January 1733[?]. Present: William Ball, Edwin Conway, Henry Fleet, William Ball, Junr., Henry Carter, Hugh Brent, Nicholas Martin; Gent., Justices.

Charles Kelley came to Court and ackn. his deeds of Lease & Release to Henry Fleet for & concerning 60 acres of land in Christ Church Parish, in this Co., witch on Motion of the sd. Henry were admitted to record.

Elizabeth Kelley, wife of the sd. Charles Kelley came also into Court and voluntarily ackn. she relinquished her right of Dower unto the sd. Henry Fleet, which was admitted to record.

The Petition of Judith Payne against John Brewer & Mary, his wife, Admin. of the Estate of Francis Velden, dec'd, for £2.9.0 due to her from the sd. Francis, in his life time by amount the sd. Judith making Oath to her amount. it is considered that she recover her afsd. debt of Francis Venden, dec'd, in the hands of his sd. Admin. & costs.

The appraisement of the Estate of Francis Velden, dec'd was returned and Mary Brewer, Admin., Exec. thereof making oath according to her subscription on the Inventory, Ordered to be recorded.

The appraisement of the Estate of Stephen Tomlin, dec'd, was returned and Martha Tomlin, Admin. Exec. thereof making oath according to her subscription on the Inventory, Ordered to be recorded.

The appraisement of the Estate of Joseph Parker, dec'd, was returned and Elizabeth Parker, Admin,. Exec. thereof making oath according to her subscription on the Inventory, Ordered to be recorded.

Richard Borriskill, a servant belonging to James Ball, Gent., and James Howard came into Court and voluntarily agreed to serve his master one year after his time by indenture or Custom shall be expired in consideration of him keeping to be a Tailor trade and causing him to be well instructed therein, the sd. Richard also agreed to accept sufficient apparel in lieu of the yearly wages mentioned in the sd. Indenture.

Ordered that Elizabeth Smith, widow, be summoned to the next Court to answer the petition of John [?] and Francis Waddy, Execx.,, of the Will of Charles Smith, dec'd, against her.

Thomas White, orphan of William White, dec'd, 7 years old in December last is by the Court bound to Isaac White, until he attains the age of 21 years, his sd. master to teach him to read & write & the trade of Brick Layer and to find sufficient diet, lodging, apparel, and at the expiration of his servitude to pay him as is appointed for servants by Indenture or custom.

The appraisement of John Buckley, dec'd, was returned and Mary Buckley, Adminx., making oath according to her subscription on the Inventory, Ordered to be recorded.

The Will of William Lewis[?] was presented in Court by George Heale, Gent., Exec., therein named, who made oath thereto and being proved by the oaths of Joseph Wharton & Timothy Thornton, witnesses, which is admitted to record and on Motion was granted a certificate for obtaining probate.

Ordered that Thomas Flint, Thomas Wharton & William Miller & William Mitchell, or any three, after first being sworn by a Co. Justice, are to appraise the Estate of William Lewis, dec'd, in money and make a report of the inventory with George Heale, Gent. Exec., in open Court.

Pg 100.   Ordered that Abraham Currell &Elizabeth, his wife, and William Hobson & Judith, his wife, Execs. of the Will of Henry Fleet, Gent., dec'd, be summoned to next Court to answer the petition of Thomas Lovey against them.

In the suit betw. Joseph Magoon, Pltf., and Col. Wm. Ball, Deft., by petition is continued for evidence of James Carter, till next Court.

In the suit in Chancery betw. William Ball, and infant by William Ball, Junr., Gent., his father, and next friend, Complt. and James Ball & George Ball, Gent., Execs. of the Will of David Ball, dec'd, Defts., is continued till next Court.

In the suit betw. Robert Pritchard, Pltf., and Thomas Taff & Mary, his wife, and Robert Mc Tyer & Elizabeth, his wife, Execx., of the Will of Francisco Frizzel, dec'd, by petition for the part of the sd. Testator's Estate, which belongs to Margaret, the wife of the sd. Pltfs., by consent of the parties. It is referred to James Ball, John Selden & George Payne, Gent., to examine Estate & settle the whole difference relating to this suit. And it is Ordered that they set apart & deliver to the sd. Pltf. what of the afsd. Estate they shall find due to him & make a report of their proceedings in the premises to the next Court.

The suit betw. Chattin Chowning, Pltf., and William Stemp, Deft., by petition is continued on the Deft. Motion till next Court.

In the action of debt betw. John Mitchell, Doctor of Physick, Pltf., and Thomas Wharton, planter, Deft., the sd. Deft., is continued on Deft. Motion till next Court.

The case betw. George Warrick, Pltf., and Thomas Pinckard, Gent., Deft., and the sd. Deft. having joined the Pltf. demurrer in this cause. It is Ordered that the arguments thereon be referred till next Court.

The suit in Chancery betw. Richard Chichester, Esqr., Complt., and Frances Burges, widow, James Ball, & Edwin Conway, Gent., Execs., of the Will of Charles Burges, Gent., dec'd, Deft., is continued till next Court on the Motion of the Complt.

In the action betw. Robert Mitchell, Gent., Pltf., and John Stepto, Junr., Deft., for £150 damages, in the Declaration, is set forth. The sd. Deft. confessed Judgment for 17,847 lbs. of tobacco due the Pltf., accepting of his damages declared. It is considered that the sd. Pltf. recover against the sd. Deft., the afsd. 17, 847 lbs. tobacco & coasts.

On the difference betw. Elizabeth Mitchell, Pltf., and Epaphroditus Lawson, Deft., failed to appear, whereupon is continued on the Motion of the Deft., it is Ordered that the sd. Pltf. pay unto the sd. Deft. his costs thereby occasioned.

The suit in Chancery betw. William Everate & Margaret, his wife, Complts. and William Bertrand, Exec. of the Will of Ruth Fouchee, dec'd, Deft., is continued to next Court.

The ejection issue betw. John Tarr, Pltf., and William Brent, Deft., is continued till next Court.

The suit betw. Margaret Hogan, Pltf., and John Young, Deft., by petition for 350 lbs. tobacco due by note is dismissed, neither party appearing.

In the action of trespass betw. John Stepto, Junr., Pltf., and William Hattaway, Deft., the sd. Deft pleaded and the Pltf. joined and it was Ordered that the trial of the sd. issue be referred till next Court.

The suit betw. Charles Cox, Pltf., and Peter Lee, Deft., by petition for £3.18.0 due by obligation is dismissed, neither party appearing.

John Stepto, Junr., Pltf., and Elizabeth Parker, Admin. of the Estate of Joseph Parker, dec'd, Deft., for £ [?].9.10 due by account. The sd. Pltf. having made oath that £5 money was justly due to him on his afsd. account, the sd. Deft. confessed Judgment for the sd. £5, to be paid out of the sd. dec'd Estate, as the same was appraised, which the sd. Pltf. accepting. It is considered that the sd. Pltf. recover the sd. £5 to be paid as afsd. out of the sd. Testator's Estate in the Deft.'s hands & with costs.

Pg 101. The action of trespass & assault & battery betw. Lawrence Blade, Pltf., and Walter Armes, Deft., the sd. Deft. pleaded & the Pltf. joined issue, whereupon it was Ordered that the trial of the sd. issue be referred to next Court.

In the suit betw. Francis Timberlake, Pltf. and John Mc Gregger, Deft., by petition for 300 lbs. tobacco. The sd. Deft. to appear and the sd. Pltf. made oath to the truth of his claim. It is Ordered that the sd. [can't read] pay unto the sd. Pltf. his afsd. debt & costs.

In the suit betw. Stokely Towles, Pltf., and Robert Galbreath, Deft., by petition. The parties heard and also the testimony of the witnesses is this cause whereupon the Court took time to advise in this matter till next Court.

In the suit betw. William Stepto, Pltf., and Charles Angell, Deft., by attachment against the Estate of the sd. Deft., the sd. Pltf. made oath to the truth of his debt and Judgment is granted him against the Deft., for 448 lbs. tobacco & costs. And, the attachment being returned for & in the hands of George Yerby, Thomas Scott, Hugh Kelley, John Angell, William Oliver & James Hains, & William Oliver, they severally on Oath, they were not indebted to the sd. Deft., when this attachment was served upon them, whereupon the sd. attachment is discontinued, so far as it relates to them and James Haines on oath declaring he was indebted to ye sd. Deft. no more than 4 lbs. tobacco and a half at the time afsd. Judgment is granted to the sd. Pltf. for same. And, on the prayer of the sd. George Yerby & Thomas Scott ye arguments relating to them in this affair as referred and it is Ordered this attachment be continued till the next Court.

The attachment obtained by Thomas Edwards against the Estate of Charles Angell is continued till next Court.

Ordered that the Court be adjourned till the 2nd Wednesday in February next. At a Court for Lancaster Co. continued on Tuesday, in 12th day of February 1733[?] for Proof of Public Claims. Present: William Ball, William Ball, Junr., Henry Carter, Nicholas Martin; Gent., Justices.

The act of assembly recovering Public Claims was read in Court.

Thomas Flint making oath to his certification for taking up a servant man named Patrick Burk belonging to Col. John Grymes of Middlesex Co. and that no satisfaction had been received for the same. It is Ordered that the Court Clerk certify the sd. proof to the assembly.

William Bertrand making oath to his certification for taking up a Negro slave belonging to Charles Carter, of Middlesex Co, Esqr., and that no satisfaction had been received for the same. It is Ordered that the Court Clerk certify the sd. proof to the assembly.

An amount subscribed by Dale Carter, Sub-Co. Sheriff against the Colony of Virginia for 200 lbs. tobacco was presented and sworn by the sd. Dale and the sd. proof Ordered to be certified to the assembly.

At a Court for Lancaster Co. continued on Wednesday, in 13th day of March 1733. Present: William Ball, George Heale, Edwin Conway, Henry Fleet, William Ball, Junr., Hugh Brent, Nicholas Martin; Gent., Justices.

Thomas Lawson came into Court & ackn. his deed with receipt endorsed and his bond for same and performance of covenants for & concerning 24 a. of land in Christ Church Parish. in this Co., unto George Turbervile, Gent., which on the Motion of the sd. George are admitted to record.

Pg 102. On the Motion of John Selden, Gent., Co. Sheriff, William George having taken the oath to the Government & subscribed the test, had the oath of Co. Under-Sheriff, administered to him.

Thomas Phillips, orphan of Joseph Phillips, dec'd, 11 years old on the 25th of this instant, on the prayer of Elizabeth Phillips, his mother by the Court bound to John Mitchell, of this Co., till he attains the age of 21 years, the sd. John to teach him to read & write & the trade of weaver and to find sufficient diet, lodging, apparel, and at the expiration of his servitude to pay him as is appointed for servants by Indenture or custom.

James Hamond making oath to his certificate for taking up a Slave belonging to Thomas Lee of this Co., and that no satisfaction had been received for the same and it is Ordered that the Court Clerk certify the sd. prof to the assembly.

The last Will of Frances Hutchins, dec'd, was presented in Court by John Cox, Exec., therein named who made oath thereto and being proved by the oath of John Yerby witness thereto is admitted to record and on the Motion of the Exec., and obtained probate thereof.

Ordered that John Hendley, Christopher Kirk, George Yerby & John Morriday, or any three of them sworn before a Co. Justice, are to appraise the Estate of Francis Hutchins, dec'd, in money and submit the report, with John Cox, Exec., of the Will, at the next Court.

In the suit betw. John Selden, Pltf., and Luke Hanks, Deft., by attachment for 529 lbs. tobacco, the sd. Pltf. making oath to the truth of the claim, Judgment is granted him for the sd. debt & costs and Joseph Heale, on whom the attachment was made & made oath to an account against the sd. Deft. for 223 lbs. of tobacco, which was allowed and it is Ordered that the attachment be continued till next Court.

In the suit betw. Henry Fleet, Gent., Exec. of the Will of William Fleet, late of King & Queen County , Gent., Thomas Lee, Gent., William Mortin, Robert Gibson & Thomas Lawson, or any three of them sworn before a Co. Justice, are to appraise the Estate of William Fleet, dec'd, in money and submit the report, with the Exec., of the Will, at the next Court.

In the suit betw. John Bell, Clerk, and Francis Waddy, Exec., of he Will of Charles Smith, dec'd, Pltf., and Elizabeth Smith, widow, by Petition is continued till next Court.

In the suit betw. Thomas Lovett, Pltf., and Abraham Currell & Elizabeth, his wife, and William Hobson & Judith, his wife, Exec., of the Will of Henry Fleet, Gent., dec'd, by petition for a certain amount of tobacco, which was lodged in the sd. testator's hands & is now become due to the sd. Pltf., is dismissed.

In the action of trespass & assault & battery betw. Lawrence Blade, Pltf., and Walter Armes, Deft., for £20 damages as in the Declaration, Abraham Currell, James Currell, Wm. Sydnor, Benjamin George, William Edwards, William Bertrand, George Payne, William Hutchins, William Stamps, Richard Davis, George Yerby, & Henry Newby were impaneled & sworn to try the issue and binging in the verdict in these words – " We the Jury do find for the Plaintiff damages of one shilling Sterl. Signed: Abraham Currell. The sd. verdict on the Pltf.'s Motion is recorded and as the battery complaint of in this cause was fully proved. It is considered that the sd. Pltf. recover against the sd. Deft., one shilling the damages by the Jury afsd. assessed and costs together with one attorney's fee.

The suit betw. Robert Prichard, Pltf., and Thomas Taff & Mary, his wife, and Robert Mc Tyer & Elizabeth, his wife, Execx., of the Will of Francis Frizzell, dec'd, Deft., by petition for that part of the sd. Testator's Estate which belongs to the sd. Pltf.'s wife, is dismissed.

Pg 103. In the suit betw. Joseph Magson, Pltf., and Col. William Ball, Deft., by petition for 2 month's wages, the parties being fully heard. It is considered that the suit is dismissed and the sd. Pltf. pay unto the sd. Deft. his costs expended.

172

Thomas Chetwood & Elizabeth, his wife, having attended 2 days as witnesses for Lawrence Blade in a suit by the sd. Lawrence against Walter Armes. It is Ordered that the sd. Lawrence pay the sd. Thomas for four days according to Law & costs.

In the suit in Chancery betw. William Ball, and infant by William Ball, Junr., Gent., , his father & next friend Complt., and James Ball & George Ball, Gent., Execs., of the Will of David Ball, dec'd, Defts. The parties were fully heard on the Complaint exception to the Deft. James's answer in this suit whereupon the sd. answer was adjudged insufficient and is Ordered that the sd. Defts., put in a sufficient answer at the next Court.

Robert Galbreath exhibited and made oath to the amount of the Estate of Moses Carter & Aaron Carter, Orphans under the Guardianship which is admitted to record.

In the suit betw. Chattin Chowning, Pltf., and William Stamps, Deft., by petition for the sd. Pltf.'s part of the Estate of George Chowning, dec'd, in the sd. Deft.'s hands by consent of the Parties, Col. Wm. Ball is appointed to settle all differences on this suit and to make a report to the next Court.

In the suit in Chancery betw. Richard Chichester, Esqr., Complt., and Frances Burges, widow, James Ball, & Edwin Conway, Gent., Execs., of the Will of Charles Burges, Gent., Dec'd, on the prayer of the sd. Complt. leave is given him to amend his bill on this suit he paying all costs occasioned by the sd. Amendment and it is Ordered that the suit be continued to next Court.

In the suit betw. John Mitchell, Doctor of Physick, Pltf., and Thomas Wharton, planter, Deft., for 1,290 lbs. tobacco for sundry medicines administered and sundry visits made to the sd. Deft., and his family by the sd. John, as in the Declaration is set forth, the sd. parties agreed to refer the trial of the joined issue in this cause to the Court and the Pltf. having made oath to the truth of the articles in his account mentioned, the arguments on both sides were fully heard whereupon the Court took time to advise till tomorrow morning.

Ordered that the Court be adjourned till tomorrow morning ten a Clock. At a Court for Lancaster Co. continued on Thursday, in 14th day of March 1733. Present: William Ball, George Heale, Henry Fleet, William Ball, Junr., Hugh Brent, Nicholas Martin; Gent., Justices.

In the action of Debt betw. John Mitchell, Doctor of Physick, Pltf., and Thomas Wharton, planter, Deft. The Court according to yesterday's resolution in this cause having fully advised & considered are of the opinion that the Pltf. recover Against the sd. Deft., 830 lbs. tobacco, which the sd. Deft., is forthwith Ordered to pay with costs and one attorney's fee. From which Judgment the sd. Pltf. prayed an appeal to the ninth day of the next general Court, which is granted him Joseph Ball Esqr., becoming security to prosecute the sd. appeal with effect.

John Mitchell, Doctor of Physick, Pltf., Christ Church Parish, in Middlesex Co. VA, and Joseph Ball, Esqr., of St. Mary's, White Chappel Parish, VA, came to Court and ackn. themselves jointly & severally indebted to Thomas Wharton of this Co., Planter, in the sum of £20 to be levied on their goods & chattels, lands & tenements, under condition that the sd. John Mitchell appear at the next General Court on the 9th day thereof and present an appeal this day granted him from a Judgment of this County Court, his action against the sd. Thomas and if cast in the sd. appeal pay & satisfy unto the sd. Thomas what the Laws of this Colony in such cases require.

In the suit in Chancery betw. William Everate and Margaret, his wife, Complt., and William Bertrand, Exec. of the Will of Ruth Fouchee, dec'd, Deft., on hearing the parties, it is considered that the sd. Pltf. recover against the sd. Deft., their costs in this suit expended.

Pg 104. In the suit betw. Stokely Towles, Pltf., and Robert Galbreath, Deft., by the Petition for £1.6.0 due by amount, it is considered that this suit be dismissed and that the sd. Pltf. pay unto the sd. Deft., his costs in this behalf expended, with one attorney's fee.

The action of trespass betw. John Stepto, Junr., Pltf., and William Hattaway, Deft., is continued till next Court at the Pltf.'s Motion & costs

In the suit betw. William Stepto, Pltf., and Charles Angell, Deft., by attachment is continued till next Court on the Motion of Thomas Scott, a Garnishee, in this cause and at his costs.

In the suit betw. Thomas Edwards, Pltf., and Charles Angell, Deft., by attachment is continued till next Court on the Motion of Thomas Scott ,a Garnishee in this cause and at his costs.

The action of debt betw. William Oliver, Pltf., and James Phillips, Deft., for 2,023 lbs. tobacco due by account, is dismissed.

174

In the suit betw. Richard Chichester, Esqr., Pltf., and Robert Biscoe, Deft., by petition for £2.15.3 cue by account, the sd. Pltf. having lately received £2.5.0 of his afsd. debt and making oath to the truth of his account, Judgment is granted him for £0.10.3 the remainder of the sd. Debt and the Deft. is forthwith Ordered to pay with costs.

In the suit betw. Joseph Ball, Esqr., Pltf., and James Kirk, Deft., by petition for 200 lbs. tobacco due by note the sd. Pltf. making oath to the truth of his claim, Judgment is granted him against the Deft. for the 200 lbs. & costs.

In the suit of trespass betw. Joseph Ball, Esqr., Pltf., and John Pollard, Deft., , is dismissed.

In the suit betw. Thomas Edwards, Pltf., and James Kirk, Deft., by petition for 582 lbs. of tobacco due by account on the oath of the sd. Pltf. in this cause Judgment is granted him against the sd. Deft for 575 lbs. tobacco & costs.

In the suit of trespass & assault & battery betw. William Schofield, Pltf. and Thomas Hunton, Deft., is dismissed.

Henry Carter, Hugh Brent, and Nicholas Martin, Gent., are by this Court presented to the Hon. Lt. Governor's Persons fit & able to Execute the office of Sheriff of this Co. for the ensuing year.

John Heale, Joseph Heale, William Tayloe, Joseph Chinn, Joseph Cater, and William Stepto, Gent., are by this Court presented to the Hon. Lt. Governor's Persons fit & able to execute the office of Justices of the Peace for the Co., who are humbly prayed to commission them accordingly.

Ordered that the Court be adjourned till the second Wednesday in April next. At a Court for Lancaster Co. on Wednesday, in 10th day of April 1734. Present: William Ball, George Heale, Henry Carter, William Ball, Junr., Hugh Brent, Nicholas Martin; Gent., Justices.

A writing containing the Deposition of Richard Holland, of [can't read] in Lancaster Co., in Great Britain, Taylor, was granted by the oaths of John Breakhill & Joseph Selden, witness hereto and admitted to Record.

Pg 105. A letter of Attorney from Elizabeth Culshaw, James Frith & Esther, his wife, and William Pryor & Bridget, his wife, to Edwin Conway, Gent., and Capt. Edward Loxam, was proved in Open Court by John Breakhill & Joseph Selden, witnesses thereto and admitted to record.

A letter of Attorney from Wm. Marden & John Goodwin to the acting Exec. or Execs., of the Will of Charles Burges, merchant, dec'd, was proved in open Court by the oaths of Edward Loxam, John Breakhill & Joseph Seddon, witnesses thereto and is admitted to record.

A Letter of Attorney from William Dawkins, of London, merchant, to John Carter, Esqr., and Richard Lee, was proved in open Court by the oath of Thomas Doge, a witness thereto and admitted to record.

On the petition of Christopher Stephens is admitted to keep an Ordinary at his dwelling house in this Co., George Light, Junr., becoming his security.

Christopher Stephens & George Light, Junr., of St. Mary's White Chappel, Pltf., in this Co., came into Court & ackn. themselves jointly and severally indebted of our King for £24, to be levied upon their goods & chattels, lands, & tenements under condition that the sd. Christopher shall constantly find & provide in the Ordinary he is this day admitted to keep good wholesome & cleanly lodging & dyet for travelers and stableage, fodder, & provender & Pasturage as the season shall require for their horses, for & during the term of one year from the date hereof and shall not suffer for or permit any unlawful gaming in this house nor on the Sabbath Day, suffer any person to tipple or drink more than is necessary.

A letter of Attorney from Edmund Hayworth to Edwin Conway, Gent., and Capt. Edward Loxam was proved in open Court by the oath of John Breakhill, a witness thereto, who deposed that Thomas Darlyshire and Richard Slater, the other witness, were with him at the [can't read] & delivery of the sd. letter of attorney & subscribed as witnesses in his presence whereupon it is admitted to record.

The appraisement of the Estate of Frances Hutchins, dec'd, was returned and (John Cox her Exec. making oath according to his subscription on the Inventory) Ordered to be recorded.

In the suit betw. John Bell, Pltf., and Francis Waddy, Exec. of the Will of Charles Smith, Clerk, dec'd, and Elizabeth Smith, widow, Deft., by petition is continued till next Court for the answer of the sd. Deft.

In the suit in Chancery betw. William Ball, and infant by William Ball, Junr., Gent., his father, and next friend, Complt. and James Ball, Gent., Exec. of the Will of David Ball, dec'd, Defts. The sd. Deft. James pout in a second answer in this cause and time is given the sd. Complt. to consider it and for the answer of the sd. Deft. George [?] till next Court.

In the suit betw. Chattin Chowning, Pltf., and William Stamps, Deft., by petition for the sd. Pltfs., part of the Estate of George Chowning, dec'd, in the Defts. hands a report of Col Wm. Ball in this suit was returned and admitted to record and it is Ordered that the sd. Deft. pay unto the sd. Pltf. £33.16.10 out of the sd. testator's Estate in his hands & costs.

In the suit in Chancery betw. Richard Chichester, Esqr., Complt., and Frances Burges, widow, James Ball, & Edwin Conway, Gent., Execs., of the Will of Charles Burges, Gent., dec'd, the sd. Complt. having this day amended his bill in the cause on the Motion of the sd. Deft, time is given them to answer the same till next Court.

In the action of trespass betw. John Stepto, Junr., Pltf., and John Stepto, Deft., for £25 damage William Bertrand, William Brent, Robert Galbreath, John Stott, Junr., Jon Bailey, Walter Armes, William Sydnor, Thomas Taff, Stokely Towles, Francis Timberlake, George Yerby and Joseph Chinn were impaneled and sworn by the issue joined in this cause and bringing a special verdict the same on the Pltf. Motion is admitted to record and the argument s arising thereon are referred for trial till next Court.

Order that Henry Fleet, Gent, Exec. of the Will, of Wm. Fleet, Gent., dec'd, being an [can't read] of the sd. State to the next Court.

In the suit betw. George Warrick, Pltf., and Thomas Pinckard, Gent., Deft., pleaded and the Pltf. joined issue and is Ordered that the trial be referred till next Court.

In the suit betw. William Stepto, Pltf., and Charles Angell, Deft., by attachment continued to next Court.

In the suit betw. Thomas Edwards, Pltf., and Charles Angell, Deft., by attachment continued to next Court.

In the suit betw. Andrew Donalson, Pltf., and James Garton, Deft,, by petition for 500 lbs. tobacco due by account Judgment is granted to the sd. Pltf. against the sd. Deft. for 368 lbs. tobacco & costs.

The suit betw. Charles Jones, Pltf., and Daniel Rich [?] , Deft., by petition for 300 lbs. tobacco due by account is dismissed.

In the suit betw. Thomas Edwards, Pltf., and William Shelton, Junr., Deft., by petition for 341 lbs. tobacco due by amount on the oath of the sd. Pltf., Judgment it granted him against the sd. Deft. for 326 lbs. of tobacco & costs.

Pg 106. The suit betw. Thomas Edwards, Pltf., & Richard Weaver, Deft., by petition for 319 lbs. of tobacco due by account is dismissed.

In the action on the case betw. John Cralle, Gent., Pltf., and George Dogget, Deft., for £6.11.0 due by account for the sd. Deft., by his attorney confessed Judgment. It is therefore considered that the sd. Pltf., recover the absd. amount against the sd. Deft., with costs.

In the suit betw. Thomas Webster, Pltf., and James Barton, Deft., by attachment for 710 lbs. tobacco due by obligations, the sd. Pltf. making oath to the truth of his claim, Judgment is granted him against the sd. Deft, and the Pltf. to recover the absd. amount with costs and one attorney fee, and the sd. attachment being returned [can't read] in the hands of Judith Payne & James Brent, William Sydnor & Eliza Kenton. It is Ordered that the sd. Judith Payne pay unto the sd. Pltf. 147 lbs. tobacco that the sd. James Brent payment to the sd. Pltf. 25 lbs. tobacco, and Wm. Syndor pay unto the sd. Pltf. 327 lbs. tobacco towards satisfaction of this Judgment and the sd. Eliza Kenton not appearing. It is Ordered that this attachment be continued for her to declare what is in her hands of the sd. Deft. at the next Court.

An additional Inventory of the Estate of David Ball, dec'd, was returned and (George Heale, Gent., his Exec. making oath according to his subscription on the Inventory) Ordered to be recorded.

The appraisement of the Estate of William Lewis, dec'd, was returned and (George Heale, Gent., his Exec. making oath according to his subscription on the Inventory) Ordered to be recorded.

The action of trespass betw. Charles Chelton, Gent., and Joseph Rawsin, Deft., for 1,500 lbs. tobacco damages in the declaration is set forth is dismissed.

Ordered that the Co. Sheriff summon at least 24 Freeholders to appear at the next Court that out of them a grand jury may be then impaneled & sworn to make inquiry into the breach of the penal laws & to present the offenders.

In the action of Debt betw. Rawleigh Chinn, Gent., and Thomas Kelley, Cordwainer, Deft., being called & not appearing on the Motion of the sd. Pltf.,

Judgment is granted him against the sd. Deft., and John Selden, Gent., Sheriff of this Co., for what shall appear to be justly due to the Pltf., at the next Court unless the sd. Deft. shall then appear and answer to the sd. action.

A Conditional Judgment being this day granted to Rawleigh Chinn, Gent., against Thomas Kelley, Cordwainer and John Selden, Gent., Co. Sheriff for 1,632 lbs. tobacco and 17 shillings, on the Motion of the sd. John attachment is awarded him against the Estate of the sd. Thomas for the sd. tobacco & money and costs returnable to the next Court for Judgment.

In the suit betw. Thomas Wren, Pltf., and John Johnson, Deft., by petition for 280 lbs. tobacco due by Account, the sd. Deft. confessed Judgment and it is Ordered that the sd. Deft. forthwith pay unto the sd. Pltf. his afsd. debt & costs.

In the suit betw. Thomas Turner, Gent., Pltf., and John Morris, Junr., Deft., by petition for 612 lbs. tobacco due by account, the sd. Pltf. having made oath to his sd. account at a Court held for King George Co, first day of March last, Judgment was granted to the sd. Pltf. against the sd. Deft. for 612 lbs. tobacco & costs together with one attorney fee.

In pursuance to a clause in the Act of Regulating Ordinarys & restraint of Tipling houses, the Court doth set & rate:

Cider at 15 pence or 12 pounds of tobacco the gallon. Rum & Brandy (except French Brandy) at 8 shillings or 76 lbs. of tobacco the gallon. Punch at 15 pence or 12 lbs. tobacco the Quart. Strong beer at 15 pence or 12 lbs. tobacco the bottle. Madera wine at one shilling, 10 pence half penny or 18 lbs. tobacco the quart. Dyet with small beer to drink at 11 pence, farthing or 9 lbs. tobacco the meal. Lodging at 7 pence, half penny or 6 lbs. tobacco the night. Stabloage & fodder for a horse at 6 pence or 5 lbs. of tobacco the night. Oats or Indian Corn at 6 pence or 5 lbs. tobacco the gallon. [?]

Pg 107. Raune Sadler having attended 2 days a witness for John Stepto, Junr., in his suit against William Hattaway. It is Ordered that the sd. John pay unto the sd. Raune for the sd. attendance costs and for travelling 70 miles both ways for his attendance & costs.

Joseph Angell having attended 2 days a witness for John Stepto, Junr., in his suit against William Hattaway. It is Ordered that the sd. John pay unto the sd. Joseph for the sd. attendance costs.

Charles Smith having attended 3 days a witness for John Stepto, Junr., in his suit against William Hattaway. It is Ordered that the sd. John pay unto the sd. Charles for the sd. attendance costs.

John Cox, Junr. having attended 2 days a witness for John Stepto, Junr., in his suit against William Hattaway. It is Ordered that the sd. John pay unto the sd. John for the sd. attendance costs.

In the suit betw. John Selden, Pltf., and Luke Stanks, Deft., by attachment. it is the opinion of the Court that nothing be deducted out of the Deft's Estate in the hands of Joseph Heale on account of the sd. Joseph's promise to Richard Cundiff and it is considered that the sd. Pltf. recover what of the Deft's Estate shall be in the sd. Joseph's hands after the amount proved in this suit at the Last Court is taken out of the same towards satisfaction of the sd. Pltf.'s Judgment in this cause and that this attachment be discontinued.

Ordered that the Court be adjourned till the second Wednesday in May next. At a Court for Lancaster Co. on Wednesday, in 8th day of May 1734. Present: William Ball, Edwin Conway, William Ball, Junr., Hugh Brent; Gent., Justices.

In the suit betw. John Bell, Clerk, and Francis Waddy, Exec., of he Will of Charles Smith, , Clk., dec'd, Pltf., and Elizabeth Smith, widow, by Petition is continued till next Court.

In the action of trespass betw. John Stepto, Junr., Pltf., and William Hattaway, Deft., is continued till next Court on the Deft. Motion & costs.

In the action betw. William Stepto, Pltf., and Charles Angell, Deft., by attachment on the Motion of Thomas Scott, in what hands this attachment was served is continued till next Court.

In the action betw. Thomas Edwards, Pltf., and Charles Angell, Deft., by attachment is continued till next Court.

In the action betw. George Warrick, Pltf., and Thomas Pinckard, Gent., Deft., is continued till the next Court on the Deft's Motion & costs.

In the action betw. Thomas Webster, Pltf., and James Barton, Deft., by attachment. The sd. Pltf. ackn. the receipt of 50 lbs. tobacco in the hand s of Elizabeth Newton on whom this attachment was served.

180

In the action of debt betw. Rawleigh Chinn, Gent., Pltf., and Thomas Kelley, cordwainer, Deft., is continued till the next Court

In the action betw. Robert Biscoe, Pltf., and John Cox, Junr., by petition is continued till next Court.

In the action betw. Robert Biscoe, Pltf. and Thomas Lee, Gent., is continued till next Court.

In the action betw. Michael Ryan, Pltf., and Alexander Campbell, Deft., by petition for 300 lbs. tobacco due by amount the parties were heard and on the oath of the sd. Deft. admitted in this cause it appearing there was less that 200 lbs. tobacco due on the sd. Pltf.'s account in this suit. It is continued that this suit be dismissed and that the sd. Pltf pay unto the sd. Deft. his costs.

In the action betw. Robert Biscoe, Pltf., and Charles Fox, Deft., by petition is continued till next Court.

The attachment obtained by John Selden, Gent., Co. Sheriff, against the Estate of Thomas Kelley, Cordwainer, for the non-appearance of the sd. Thomas at the suit of Rawleigh Chinn, Gent., his dismissed.

Pg 108. In the action of debt betw. James Ball, Gent., one of the Church Wardens, of St. Mary's White Chappel Parish, Pltf., and Jane Aldridge, Deft., for 500 lbs. tobacco or 50 Shillings, as in the sd. Declaration is set forth, is dismissed.

In the action betw. George Curtis, Pltf., and James Barton, Deft., by petition for 370 lbs. tobacco due by account on hearing the parties, it is considered that the sd. Pltf. recover against the sd. Deft., the sd. 370 lbs. of tobacco and costs. But, 70 lbs. of this Judgment is to be discharged in case the sd. Deft. pay unto the sd. Pltf. 6.5 yards of brown linen within 10 days from this time.

In the suit betw. Robert Biscoe, Pltf., and Thomas Kelley, Deft., by petition for 474 lbs. tobacco due by obligation, on hearing the parties, Judgment is granted to the sd. Pltf., for the afsd. amount of tobacco & costs against the sd. Deft.

In the suit betw. Robert Biscoe, Pltf., and Thomas Gaines & Thomas Kelley, Exec. of the Frances Stelley, dec'd, Deft., by petition for 364 lbs. tobacco due by the sd. Frances, her obligation. The parties being heard and it appearing there was less that 200 lbs tobacco due on the afsd. obligation. It is continued that the suit be dismissed and that the sd. Pltf. pay unto the sd. Deft., their costs hereby occasioned.

William Ball, Gent, is appointed to take the list of tithables in the Lower Precinct in St. Mary's White Chappel Parish, in this Co., for this year.

George Heale, Gent, is appointed to take the list of tithables in the Middle Precinct in St. Mary's White Chappel Parish, in this Co., for this year.

William Ball, Junr., Gent, is appointed to take the list of tithables in the Upper Precinct in St. Mary's White Chappel Parish, in this Co., for this year.

Henry Carter, Gent, is appointed to take the list of tithables in the Lower part of Corotomon Precinct in Christ Church Parish, in this Co., for this year.

Edwin Conway, Gent., is appointed to take the list of tithables in the Upper part of Corotomon Precinct in Christ Church Parish, and in Wiccocomoco Parish, in this Co., for this year.

Hugh Brent, Gent, is appointed to take the list of tithables in the Middle Precinct in Christ Church Parish, in this Co., for this year.

Nicholas Martin, Gent, is appointed to take the list of tithables between Corotomon River and the Main Road which leads from the Church to Mr. Secretary Carter's Mill in Christ Church Parish, in this Co., for this year.

Henry Fleet, Gent, is appointed to take the list of tithables in the Lower Precinct in Christ Church Parish, in this Co., for this year.

Mr. George Ball is appointed Surveyor of the highways from this Co. Court house to Mrs. Judith Payne's in St. Mary's White Chappel Parish in this Co. for this year.

James Brent is appointed Surveyor of the highways from Mrs. Judith Payne's to Mr. Burges's Mill in St. Mary's White Chappel Parish in this Co. for this year.

John Bailey is appointed Surveyor of the highways from the Church to Deep Bottom Run and of the rolling road which leads from Mr. Joseph Chinn's to Deep Creek warehouses in St. Mary's White Chappel Parish in this Co. for this year.

William Bertrand is appointed Surveyor of the highways from Deep Bottom Run to Moraticco Mill in in St. Mary's White Chappel Parish in this Co. for this year.

Thomas Wharton is appointed Surveyor of the highways from Mr. Burges's Mill to Mr. Selden's Mill in St. Mary's White Chappel Parish in this Co. for this year.

John Mott is appointed Surveyor of the highways from [erased] to the road that leads from Col. Ball's Mill to Mr. Burges's Mill in St. Mary's White Chappel Parish in this Co. for this year.

Thomas Chattin is appointed Surveyor of the highways from Bartho. Woods to the Cross Roads where Doctr. Thornton's in St. Mary's White Chappel Parish in this Co. for this year.

Thomas Taylor is appointed Surveyor of the highways from the Main Road by Giles Robinson's to the Main Road which leads to Mr. Selden's Mill and from that Main Road to Cundiff's old field and also of the rolling road in the sd. Precinct in St. Mary's White Chappel Parish in this Co. for this year.

Pg 109. William Goodridge is appointed Surveyor of the rolling road from the Church to Carpenter's Landing in St. Mary's White Chappel Parish in this Co. for this year.

Thomas Carter, planter, is appointed Surveyor of the highways from Mr. Selden's Mill to Mr. Secretary Carter's Mill and all of the main & rolling roads betw. these two branches of Corotomon River in Christ Church & Wiccocomoco Parishes in this County this year.

William Stepto is appointed Surveyor of the highways from Mr. Secretary Carter's Mill to the Cross Roads in Christ Church Parish for this Co. for this year and it is Ordered that he take to his assistance a male laboring tithables belonging to the Plantations before Ordered to assist him besides those belonging to his sd. Precinct.

George Flower is appointed Surveyor of the highways from the Cross Roads to the Clerk's Office of the Court in Christ Church Parish in this Co. for this year.

Thomas Falknor, is appointed Surveyor of the highways from Mr. Charles Carter's Mill to the Main Road, which leads from the Co. Clerk's office in Christ Church Parish, in this Co., for this year, and he is to keep the road in repair with the male laboring tithables belonging to the sd. Carter in the sd. Precinct.

Charles Jones is appointed Surveyor of the highways from the Church to the Cross Roads in Christ Church Parish in this Co. for this year and he is keep the road in repair to the male laboring tithables belonging to Mr. Secretary Carter in the Precinct.

William Martin, is appointed Surveyor of the highways from Mr. Charles Carter's Mill to the white stone and of all the Main Roads near Nantepoizon [?] Rock in Christ Church Parish in this Co. for this year.

Henry Fleet, Gent., is appointed Surveyor of the highways from the Church to Fleet's in Christ Church Parish in this Co. for this year.

John Yerby, is appointed Surveyor of the highways from Mr. Secretary Carter's Quarter on the mouth of the Eastern Branch of Corotomon River to the mill road and from the sd. road to the Church in Christ Church Parish in this Co., for this year.

A lease from Richard Mullis & Elizabeth, his wife, and John Mullis to Dale Carter concerning 40 a. of land in Christ Church Parish, in this Co. was proved by the oath of William George, a witness and ackn. by the sd. Elizabeth & John to be their act & deed and admitted to record.

Order that the Court be adjourned till the 2nd Wednesday in June next.

Memorandum that this 12th of June 1734, by the virtue of a Commission of the Peace relating thereto both dated 23rd April last past, and directed to William, Ball, Richard Chichester, George Heale, Edwin Conway, James Ball, John Selden, Henry Fleet, William Ball, Junr., Robert Mitchell, Henry Carter, Hugh Brent, Nicholas Martin, Henry Lawson, John Heale, Joseph Heale, William Tayloe, Joseph Chinn, Joseph Carter, & William Stepto, Hugh Brent, & Henry Carter, administered the oaths to the Government to William, Ball, Henry Fleet, and William Ball, Junr., who subscribed the test and too the oaths appointed by the Late Act of Assembly of the Colony to be taken by Justices of the Peace & Administered the sd. Oaths& Test to the sd. Henry Carter and also to Joseph Heale and William Tayloe, Gent., James Ball, Robert Mitchell, Hugh Brent, Nicholas Martin, Joseph Carter and William Stepto, Gent, refused to accept of the sd. Commission of the Peace this time.

184

At a Court for Lancaster Co. on Wednesday, in 12th day of June 1734. Present:
William Ball, Henry Fleet, William Ball, Junr., Henry Carter, Joseph Heale,
William Tayloe; Gent., Justices.

Ordered that the Co. Sheriff acquaint George Heale, Edwin Conway Henry
Lawson, John Heale & Joseph Chinn, Gent., that they be at next Court to be
sworn-in to the Commission of the Peace for this Co.

Joseph Ball, Esqr., is appointed Surveyor of the rolling road from Deep Bottom
to the said Ball's pay [can't read] in St. Mary's White Chappel Parish in this
Co., for this year and it is Ordered that the Inhabitants in the sd. Precinct assist
him clearing the same as the Law directs.

On the Motion of David Smith, he has liberty to set gates and bars on the road
which leads through his pasture from Deep Bottom to the dwelling house of
Joseph Ball, Esqr.

John Gibson came into Court and Ackn. his deed of lease & release, and also a
Bond to John Carter, Esqr., for & concerning 130 a. of land lying in Christ
Church Parish, in this Co., was admitted to record. And, Elizabeth Gibson, his
wife, came into Court and ackn. she relinquished her Dower unto the sd. John
Carter, which was also admitted.

Pg 110. John Read came into Court and ackn. his deeds of Lease & release and
also a Bond to John Carter, Esqr., for & concerning 130 a. of land lying in Christ
Church Parish, in this Co., was admitted to record. And, Mary Read, his wife,
came into Court and ackn. she relinquished her Dower unto the sd. John Carter,
which was also admitted.

An additional Inventory of the Estate of Stephen Tomlin, dec'd was returned by
Martha Tomlin, Adminx., thereof with Will annexed and Ordered recorded.

Stokely Towles is appointed Surveyor of the highways from Chetwood's Ferry
to the Main Road near Mrs. Payne's in St. Mary's White Chappel Parish in this
Co. for this year.

A Third Bill of Exchange from John Tarpley to Thomas Dove drawn on William
Dawkins, Merchant, in London for £6.19.9 on the Prayer of the sd. Thomas
Dove is admitted to record.

A Third Bill of Exchange from John Sturman to Robt. Jones drawn on Mess. John Hyde & Company for £9.0.1 & half penny on the Prayer of the sd. Capt. Thomas Dove is admitted to record.

The appraisement of the Estate of Thomas Carter, Gent., dec'd, was returned & Arabella Carter, his Executrix making Oath to her subscription on the Inventory; recorded.

John Dabs, Orphan of John Dabs, dec'd, 4 yrs. old on 1st. March last on the prayer of Mary Dabs, his mother, is by the Court bound to Richard Boatman, of this Co., till he attains the age of 21 years, his sd. master to teach him to read & write & the trade of Shoemaker and to find sufficient diet, lodging, apparel, and at the expiration of his servitude to pay him as is appointed for servants by Indenture or custom.

A deed of gift from Margaret Hineage to her dau., Ann Emberson, was in open Court by the Oaths of Thomas Edwards and Thomas Machen, witnesses, thereto and admitted to record.

A deed of gift from Margaret Hineage to her dau., Elizabeth Hineage, was in open Court by the Oaths of Thomas Edwards and Thomas Machen, witnesses, thereto and admitted to record.

Patrick Mullin of Christ Church Parish, in this Co., set forth that he was very ancient and past his labor, it is Ordered that he be escape from paying any Country or County levies for the future.

George Light of St. Mary's White Chappel Parish in the sd. Co., set forth that he was very ancient and past his labor, it is Ordered that he be escape from paying any Country or County levies for the future.

John Mitchell, Gent., came into Court & made oath that £1.10.6 or 500 lbs. tobacco was justly due his account against Francis Velden and that he had not received anything in satisfaction; Ordered he be certified on the amount.

The Will of Richard Chichester, Esqr., Esqr., dec'd, was presented to Court by Richard Chichester, Gent., Exec., made oath & proved by oaths of Catherine Horne, Joseph Carter & Henry Horne, witnesses, it was admitted to record and on the Motion of the Exec. probate was obtained.

Ordered that Richard Chichester, Esqr., Complt., and Frances Burges, widow, James Ball and Edwin Conway, Gent., Execs., of the Will of Charles Burges,

186

Gent., dec'd, Defts., for £40 and otherwise sums of money & tobacco of he Estate of Wm. [can't read], Gent., dec'd, in the testator's hand, & Complt. being dead; dismissed.

In the suit betw. Hugh Brent, Gent., Church Warden of Christ Church Parish, Pltf., and Elias Edmonds, Junr., Deft., by petition praying that the Deft. may be compelled to bear the Parish harmless from the maintenance of a bastard child sworn to him bef. Capt. Edwin Conway, born of the body of Catherine Harvey, the sd. Catherine came into Court and confessed that the sd. Deft., was never concerned with her but about 6 months bef. the birth of the sd. child, and that the child came to it's full and time. Whereupon it is the opinion of this Court that the sd. Deft. is not the father of the sd. Bastard child; that this prosecution be dismissed.

In addition of Debt betw. Hugh Brent, Gent., Church Warden of Christ Church Parish, in this Co., Pltf., and Catherine Harvey, Deft., for 500 lbs. tobacco or 50 shillings by means of the sd. Deft., having committed fornication and had a bastard child, as in the Declaration is set forth, the sd. Deft. appeared and confessed the fact but failed to pay or give sufficient caution for the payment of the afsd. fine. Whereupon, it is Ordered that she receive on her bare back at the public whipping post, 25 lashes well laid on and be thence discharged.

Pg 111. Ordered that Henry Fleet, Gent., Exec., of the Will of William Fleet, Gent., dec'd, to bring an Inventory of the Estate to the next Court.

The suit of Trespass betw. John Stepto, Junr., Pltf., and William Hattaway, Deft., in continued till next Court.

The action on the case betw. George Warrick, Pltf., and Thomas Pinckard, Gent., Deft., is continued till the next Court.

The suit betw. William Stepto, Pltf. and Charles Nagel, Deft., by attachment is continued till next Court at Thomas Scott, a garnishee, in this cause at his costs.

The suit betw. Thomas Edwards, Pltf., and Charles Angell, Deft., by attachment in continued till next Court.

The suit betw. John Bell, Clerk, and Francis Waddy, Exec. of the Will of Charles Smith, Clerk, dec'd, Pltf., and Elizabeth Smith, widow, Deft., by petition is dismissed. And, on the Motion of the sd. Pltf., it is Ordered that the sd., Deft's. account & sworn to bef. a Co. Justice, this cause be recorded.

The suit betw. Robert Biscoe, Pltf., and Charles Cox, Deft., by petition for 425 lbs. tobacco due by obligation, Judgment is granted to the sd. Pltf., against the sd. Deft., for his afsd. debt. And, it is Ordered that the sd. Deft. forthwith pay the same unto the sd. Pltf., with costs.

In the action of debt betw. Robert Biscoe, Pltf., and Thomas Lee, Gent., Deft., for 2,466 lbs. tobacco due by obligation under the Deft.'s hand & seal, the sd. Deft. confessed Judgment. It is therefore Ordered that the sd. Deft. forthwith pay unto the sd. Pltf. his afsd. debt & costs.

In the action of debt betw. Robert Biscoe, Pltf., and John Cox, Junr., Deft., by petition for 481 lbs. tobacco due by obligation. The sd. Deft. confessed Judgment. It is therefore Ordered that the sd. Deft. forthwith pay unto the sd. Pltf. his afsd. debt & costs.

The suit betw. Frances Brooks, Pltf., and William Scofield, Deft., by petition for 327 lbs. of tobacco sue by obligation is dismissed.

In the suit betw. George Fishpool, Pltf., and Job Winder, Deft., by petition for £4.9.0 by account the sd. Pltf. having made oath to the truth of the sd. account Judgment is granted to the sd. Pltf. for his debt & costs.

On the Prayer of Stokely Towles, only son of Henry Towles, late of this Co., dec'd, for Admin, of the Estate of sd. dec'd. Robert Newsom, Junr., who married one of the daughters of the sd. dec'd., acquainted the Court, the sd. Henry left a Will, and produced William Stamps, an evidence in this matter, who made oath that the sd. Henry in his last sickness abt. 2 days before his death, told him that he had a Will in the house but that it wanted three or four lines to write & the preambles, but if that Will stood, it would be the worse for his son. Whereupon, a Will was confessed to be written by the sd. Henry but not concluded nor dated was produced, and the opinion of the Court being that the same should be recorded as the last Will of the sd. Henry. The sd. Stokely, one of the Exec. of the Will named, made oath thereto and on his performing what is usual in such cases was granted Probate.

In the suit in Chancery betw. William Ball, an infant by William Ball, Junr., Gent. his father & next friend, Complts., & James & George Ball, Gents., Execs., of the Will of David Ball, dec'd, Defts. for one full third part of the residue of the sd. Testator's personal Estate in the Complts. Bill is set forth, the parties agreed to a hearing on the sd. Complts. Bill and the Answer of the Deft., James, in this cause and being deliberately understood on the whole premises it is the bequest made to the Complt. in the Will of the sd. dec'd. And, it is decreed and Ordered that the sd. Complt. recover one-third part of the Personal Estate of the sd. dec'd mentioned inventory there annexed to the afsd. Answer in the hands of the Deft., James, and that the sd. James pay unto the sd. Complts. , his cost in this behalf expended. And, the sd. Complts. failing in his further prosecution against the Deft, George in this in this Cause, it is considered that the James relates to him, be dismissed.

From which since the sd. James Ball prayed an Appeal to the 9th day, of the next General Court, which is granted him, Thomas Edwards becoming his Security, to prosecute the same with Eject[?] and to perform the Judgment of the General Court and to pay damages if the Judgment of the Co. Court shall be confirmed as the law directs.

James Ball, Gent., of St. Mary's White Chappel Parish & Thomas Edwards, of Christ Church Parish, of this Co., came into Court and ackn. themselves jointly and severally indebted to William Ball, Junr., Exec., and Gent., in the sum of £20 to be levied on their goods and chattels, land & tenements, under condition that the sd. James Ball appear at the next General Court on the 9th day then cast & prosecution appeal this day granted him from a degree of this Co., Court against him at the suit of William Ball, an infant of the sd. Wm. Ball, Junr., for one third part of the moveable Estate of David Ball, Gent., dec'd, and if cast in the sd. Appeal shall pay & satisfy unto the sd. William Ball, Junr., as the Law in such cases directs.

Pg 112. Ordered that the Court be adjourned till the 2nd Wednesday in July next. At a Court for Lancaster Co. on Wednesday, in 10th day of July 1734. Present: William Ball, Henry Fleet, William Ball, Junr., Henry Carter, Joseph Heale, William Tayloe; Gent., Justices.

The appraisement of the Estate of William Fleet, Gent., dec'd, was returned and Henry Fleet, Gent., his Exec., making oath according to his subscription, Ordered recorded.

By the Virtue of the Commission of the Peace & Dedimus relating thereto Hugh Brent, Henry Lawson, Joseph Chinn, and Joseph Carter, Gent., having taken the oaths to the government subscribed the tests and the oaths appointed by the late act of Assembly to be taken by Justices of the Peace administered to them. Present: Henry Lawson & Joseph Chinn & Joseph Carter, Gent. Justices.

Hugh Brent, Gent. producing the Governor's Commission appointing him Co. Sheriff, and Dale Carter, as Under Sheriff, took the oaths to the government subscribed the test and had the oath of Co. Sheriff administered to them both.

A bond from Hugh Brent, Henry Fleet, & Henry Carter, Gents. to the King for £1,000 in Open Court ackn. by the sd. Hugh Brent, Henry Fleet, & Henry Carter, Ordered recorded.

John Selden, Gent., refused to accept the Commission of Peace being about to remove out of the Co.

A deed of John Pinckard to Henry Boatman for & concerning a parcel of land upon the eastern branch of Corotomon River, thereon endorsed was in open Court & proved to be the Act and Deed of the sd. John Pinckard by the Oath of William Pinckard & William Pinckard and James Pinckard, witness thereto, recorded.

A deed from Henry Boatman to John Pinckard, for & concerning a parcel of land upon the eastern branch of Corotomon River, & endorsed in open Court by Henry Boatman.

The last Will of Luke Stott, was presented in Court by John Callahan, Exec., therein named, who made oath, and being proved by oaths of John Rogers, & Isaac White, witnesses, was admitted to record and on the Motion of the Exec., was granted probate.

Ordered that Edward Blackmore, John Rogers, Martin Shearman and William Bertrand, or any three of them, going bef. Co Justice, are to appraise the Estate of Luke Stott, dec'd, in money and present their report & Inventory with John Callahan, Exec. of the Will, at next Co. Court.

On the prayer of Margaret Carter & Catherine Carter, Orphans of Peter Carter, dec'd, Robert Galbreath is appointed Guardian, having given security, it is Ordered that the sd. Galbreath forthwith possess himself with the Estate of the sd. Orphans & exhibit an account thereof under oath at next Court.

In the action of trespass betw. John Stepto, Junr., Pltf. and William Hattaway, Deft., for £25, as in the Declaration, the parties were heard on the Special Verdict in this cause which in these words – We the Jury impaneled and sworn to by the issue joined betw. Jno. Stepto, Junr., Pltf. and William Hattaway Deft., do find as follows: We find the Pltf.'s horse mentioned in the Declaration was

190

found dead in the Deft.'s pasture. We find that the sd. horse was shot and that be reason of the shot and wadding which was taken out of him, which wading was believed by one of the evidences to be the same which he put in the gun or some of the same piece as he had given the Deft. some shot in sometime before. We find that the horse together with a certain mare of the afsd. Stepto's were troublesome to one Charles Smith and also to this sd. Deft., and that the sd. Deft. asked the sd. Smith why he did not make away with the sd. mare and that if he did not, he the sd. Deft would with one of them very soon. We, find by the evidence of Joseph Angell there was a fresh track of a horse out of the cornfield, which seemed not to be older, than the morning the sd. horse was found dead in the pasture or the night before and that the sd. track continued from the place 15 steps where he saw blood, and from thence to where the horse lay dead, the blood continued in the sd. track in all 52 steps from the fence. WE find by the evidence of Charles Smith that the same day the horse was found dead, he went to the Deft. house and that the sd. Deft. then told him that he and the sd. Smith was both to go to Prison for killing Mr. Stepto's horse, and that the sd. horse's head lay from the fence towards Smith's gate. WE, find by the evidence of Rand Sadler that upon the Deft's wife being asked where the Rag was which he gave her husband the Shott in. She replied it was made away with and that the sd. Sadler had advised her so to do because if it came to be compared with the wading, it would be Evidence against her husband and that the Deft., when he was asked about the death of the sd. horse, said he was [can't read]. WE, find by the evidence of Rand Sadler that the same morning, the horse was found dead that by the blew that was on the gun lock. She appeared to have been lately discharged but that he did not then handle the sd. gun to be any other wise certain beat it so upon the whole, if the Law be with the Pltf., then we find for the Pltf. £8. current money, if not we find the Deft. Signed: William Bertrand, Foreman.

Whereupon the Opinion of the Court being that the Law is with the Deft., it is considered that this action be dismissed & the sd Pltf. pay unto the sd. Deft. his costs in this behalf expended together with one attorney's fee.

Pg 113. The appraisement of the Estate of Henry Towle's, dec'd, were returned and Stokley Towles, his Exec., making oath cording to his subscription on the Inventory, Ordered to be recorded.

The action upon the case betw. George Warrick, Pltf., and Thomas Pinckard, Gent., Deft., is continued till next Court.

In the suit betw. Edny Tapscott, Pltf., and Benjamin George, Junr., and Ann, his wife, Admin. of the Estate of Henry Tapscott, dec'd, Deft., by petition setting forth that the sd. Deft. had made choice their thirds of the Negroe's belonging to the sd. Estate as appears by the Inventory there by them returned into the Court and praying an Order against the sd. Deft., for one-fifth part of the remainder of the sd. Negroe's on hearing the parties & in the evidence in this matter. It is the opinion of the Court that the sd. Defts., are bound by their afsd. Choice, and it is considered that after the sum & [can't read] pounds which appear due the sd. Defts. as short paid their afsd. thirds by their Choice, is set apart out of the remaining Negroes belonging to the sd. Estate that the sd. Pltf., recover one-fifth part of the residue the sd. Negroes in the sd. Deft.'s hands and that the sd. Parties bare the charges of this prosecution equally.

In the suit betw. William Stepto, Pltf., and Charles Angell, Deft., by attachment against the sd. Deft.'s Estate on hearing the arguments of Thomas Scott, a garnishee in this cause and also the witnesses produced by the sd. Thomas and [can't read] Pltf. in this matter. It is the opinion of the Court that the sd. Thomas was indebted to the sd. Deft., for 1,880 lbs. tobacco at the time when the attachment was served upon him and it is Ordered that out of the same he is to satisfy and pay unto the sd. Pltf. his Judgment against the sd. Deft., in this cause and that this attachment be discontinued.

In the suit betw. Thomas Edwards, Pltf., and Charles Angell, Deft., by attachment against the Deft's Estate. It is Ordered that Thomas Scott, a Garnishee in this cause pay unto the sd. Pltf., his Judgment against the Deft. in this cause out of the sd. Deft's Estate in his hands, if so much remain after a Judgment this day granted to William Stepto against him is satisfied and that this attachment be dis-continued.

In the suit betw. John Cox, Junr., Pltf. and Abraham Currell & William Hobson & Judith, his wife, Execs. of the Will of Henry Fleet, Gent., dec'd, Defts., by petition for 359 lbs. tobacco due by account is dismissed, but by consent of the sd. Deft.'s, it is Ordered that they forthwith pay unto the sd. Pltf. his costs.

In the suit betw. Charles Kelley, Pltf., and John Cox, Junr., Deft. for 325 lbs. tobacco due by account, dismissed.. But, by consent of the Deft., it is Ordered that he pay to the sd. Pltf. his costs.

Ordered that William Ball, first Justice in the Commission of the Peace, for the Co., forthwith take into his possession for ye sd. Co., the standard & weights

Scales and Measures with their appurtenances, now in the hands of Mrs. Elizabeth Fleet, widow, of Majr. Henry Fleet, late dec'd.

Pg 114. Hugh Brent, a Church Warden, of Christ Church Parish, of the Co., stated that Moses Galloway, servant, belonging to Thomas Hubbard, of the afsd. Parish, is so barbarisly used by his master, and is in such a miserable state of health, that the sd. servant being near the end of his servitude, has come away from his master, and is like to become charges to the sd. Parish. It is Ordered that the sd. Thomas be summoned to the next Court to answer the sd. Complaint.

Ordered that the Court be adjourned till the 2nd Wednesday in August next. At a Court for Lancaster Co., on Wednesday, in 14th day of August 1734. Present: William Ball, William Ball, Junr., Henry Carter, William Tayloe, Joseph Chinn, & Joseph Carter; Gent., Justices.

Daniel, a Negro boy, belonging to William Edmonds, is by the Court adjudged to be 11 years old.

Jenny, a Negro girl, belonging to John Boatman, is by the Court adjudged to be 12 years old.

Hannah, a Negro girl, belonging to Robert Edmonds, is by the Court adjudged to be 12 years old.

On the prayer of Thomas Cox, of Christ Church Parish, in this Co., setting forth that he was very ancient and passed his labor. It is Ordered that he be excused from paying any Country or County levy for the future.

The Court be acquainted that the money due to this Co., for rent of Deep Creek Warehouses remains in the hands of William Glascock, of Richmond Co, Gent. It is Ordered that Capt. William Ball forthwith receive the same for the use of this County and render an account thereof at the laying of the next County levy.

Joseph Carter is appointed to clear a road 10 feet wide from the Main Road which leads from this Co. Court House to William Chilton's gate. It is Ordered that William Chilton, William Chilton, Junr., Robert Galbreath, Wm. Fort., James Reves, Thomas Lee and the sd. Carter assist in clearing the same.

Thomas Wale, Orphan of George Wale, aged 15 years, the sixteenth day of this Instant. On the prayer of his mother, is bound unto James Davis till the age of 21 years of age, his sd. Master is to keep him to his learning and to teach him the trade of Carpenter and Joyner and to find sufficient diet, lodging, apparel, and not to carry him out of the Colony, and at the expiration of his servitude to pay him £3.10.0 in lieu of his freedom dues, as is appointed for servants by Indenture or custom.

The Inventory of the Estate of Richard Chichester, Esqr., dec'd, was returned and Richard Chichester, Gent., his Exec., making oath according to his subscription on the Inventory, Ordered recorded.

Hugh Brent, Church Warden, of Christ Church Parish, setting forth that Thomas Hubbard so inhumanly used his servant, Moses Galloway, that the sd. Moses us under grievous indisposition and was removed from his Master's service is likely to become a charge to the afsd. Parish, and the sd. Thomas Hubbard being summoned & appearing and the parties being heard on the premises, it is opinion of the Court that the sd. Deft. take the sd. Galloway, till his time is expired and use his endeavor to get him cured and pay the costs hereby occasioned.

Edwin Conway, Gent. refused to swear to the late Commission of the Peace for this County.

The action of Debt betw. John Stepto, Junr., Pltf., and Henry Lawson, Gent., Deft., for 1,164 lbs. tobacco in the declaration is set forth, neither party appearing, is dismissed.

The suit of Trespass, Assault & Battery, betw. Thomas Mc Cason[?], Pltf., and Robert Scofield, Deft., is dismissed; neither party appearing.

The suit betw. Thomas Scott, Pltf., and Francis Timberlake, Deft., by petition is dismissed.

The suit betw. John Callehan, Exec., of Luke Stott, dec'd., Pltf., Brian Phillips, Deft., by Petition for one cow and calf, on sow & 5 pigs, 2 barrow hogs, of 20 months old each; which was due to the sd. testator on his lifetime of the value of 650 lbs. tobacco, is dismissed.

The suit betw. John Callehan, Exec. of Luke Scott, dec'd, Pltf. and Bryan Phillips, Deft., by petition for £2.12.6 by account & 2 bushels and half of Indian corn & half bushel of wheat and one barrow hog of 2 years old, which was due the Testator in his lifetime, is dismissed.

The suit betw. Christopher Kirk, Pltf. and John Mott, Deft., by petition is continued till next Court at the Deft's. Motion & costs.

194

George Yerby, one of he Constables for Christ Church Parish, in this Co., making return that he found 5 tobacco shorts upon the Plantation of the John Wale, in his Precinct, and it appearing to this Court that the sd. Seconds were not tended in contempt of the Acts for preventing same, and that they were destroyed in the presence of the sd. Constable. It is considered that no prosecution issue against the sd. John for this breach of their sd. Acts but that he pay the costs hereby occasioned.

Pg 115. On the Motion of Hugh Brent, Gent., Co. Sheriff, William Brent having taken the oath of the government and subscribed the test, had the oath of Co. Under Sheriff administered.

In the case betw. George Warrick, Pltf., and Thomas Pinckard, Gent, Deft., is continued at the Deft's Motion and costs, and by consent of both parties, this cause is set for trial at next Court.

Ordered that the Court be adjourned till the 2nd Wednesday in September next. At a Court for Lancaster Co., on Thursday, in 15th day of August 1734. Present: William Ball, William Ball, Junr., Henry Carter, Joseph Chinn, & Joseph Carter; Gent., Justices.

The Act of Assembly concerning Public Claims was read in Court.

The proportion directed to the General Assembly for a law concerning Crows & Squirrels was presented and signed in Court by William Ball, Gent. It is Ordered that the Clerk of the Court certify the same to the sd. Assembly.

A proposition directed [?] to the General Assembly for a law concerning the keeping of all sheep in enclosure from the 15th of May to the 15th of September was presented and signed in Court, by William Bertrand, and Ordered that the Clerk of the Court certify the same to the sd. Assembly.

At a Court for Lancaster Co., on Wednesday, in 11th day of September 1734. Present: William Ball, Henry Fleet, William Ball, Junr., Henry Carter, Henry Lawson, William Tayloe, Joseph Chinn, & Joseph Carter; Gent., Justices.

Sue, a Negro girl, belonging to William Martin, is by the Court adjudged to be 14 years old.

Obasset, a Negro boy, belonging to Mr. Rawleigh Chinn, is by the Court adjudged to be 12 years old.

Jack, a Negro boy, belonging to Thomas Pollard, is by the Court adjudged to be 13 years old.

Present – Joseph Heale, Gent.

Harry, a Negro boy, belonging to John Carter, Esqr., is by the Court adjudged to be 13 years old.

Jo, a Negro boy, belonging to John Carter, Esqr., is by the Court adjudged to be 12 years old.

Sam, a Negro boy, belonging to John Carter, Esqr., is by the Court adjudged to be 11 years old.

Duke, a Negro boy, belonging to John Carter, Esqr., is by the Court adjudged to be 11 years old.

Sarah, a Negro girl, belonging to Thomas Hunton, is by the Court adjudged to be 5 years old.

On the Motion of Thomas Flint, Admin. of Tellie[?] Bell, dec'd, desiring to know what he should be allowed for what tobacco he had paid in discharge of the debts due to the creditors of the sd. dec'd. it is the opinion of the Court that he be allowed for the same after the rate of 15 shillings per hundred.

Gabriel Moor, a servant, belonging to Thomas Chattin came into Court and voluntarily agreed to serve his sd. master one year after his Indenture time is expired, in consideration his sd. master is to keep him constant at the shoemaker's trade that he now follows and not to compel him to work tending tobacco.

The suit betw. Christopher Kirk, Pltf. , and John Mott, Deft., by petition for £1.10.0 due by account, the parties and the evidences on both sides being heard on the whole premises, it is the Court's opinion that the sd. Pltf. recover against the sd. Deft., of his debt with costs.

The suit betw. Phillip Smith, Gent., Pltf., and William Ballendine, Deft., by petition is continued till next Court.

The suit of trespass & assault & battery, betw. George Jackson, Pltf., and Charles Cox, Deft., is dismissed.

196

The suit betw. George Warrick, Pltf., and Thomas Pinckard, Gent., Deft., for 2,700 lbs. of tobacco damages in the Declaration sets forth, Thomas Hunton, Robert Edmonds, William Ballendine, William Hutchins, Isaac Currell, Thomas Wharton, Christopher Kirk, Thomas Flint, John Mott, George Light, Junr., William Edwards & Thomas Chattin were impaneled and sworn to try the issue joined in this cause & gave a verdict in these words – "We, of the Jury find the Pltf. 511 lbs. of tobacco damage." Signed: Thomas Hunton, Foreman. This verdict on the Motion of the sd. Pltf. is recorded and it is considered that the sd. Pltf. recover against the sd. Deft., 511 lbs. tobacco, damages afsd. by the Jury afsd. assessed and costs together with one attorney's fee.

Pg 116. Ordered that the Court be adjourned till the 2nd Wednesday in October next. At a Court for Lancaster Co., on Wednesday, in 9th day of October 1734. Present: William Ball, Henry Fleet, William Ball, Junr., Henry Carter, Henry Lawson, & Joseph Carter; Gent., Justices.

The appraisement of the Estate of Luke Stott, dec'd, was returned and John Callahan, his Exec., making oath and Inventory was recorded.

Ordered that the Co. Sheriff summon 24 freeholders & inhabitants to appear at next Court for a Grand jury to be impanelled & sworn making inquiry to the breach of the Penal Laws and present the offenders.

Thomas Lawson, Gent., came into Court & ackn. his deed endorsed and concerning 100 a. of land in Christ Church Parish, in this Co., unto John Stepto, Junr., & was admitted to record.

Ordered the Court Clerk give notice by causing notes to be setup at the Parish Churches in this Co., that this Court will make sale of the money due for the rent of the warehouses in the sd. Co, to the 10th November last for tobacco to discharge the Co. Levy to the highest bidder at the next Court by twelve o'clock in the forenoon, if a fair day, if not, at the same time in December Court.

Jemima, a Negro girl, belonging to Rawleigh Chinn, is by the Court adjudged to be 13 years old.

Phillis, a Negro girl, belonging to Robert Mitchell, Junr., is by the Court adjudged to be 13 years old.

Mary Doggett and William Threlkeld came into Court & ackn. their deed of Lease & Release to Alexr. Harrower, for & concerning 60 a. lying in this Co., was recorded.

Ruth Threlkeld, wife of William Threlkeld, came into Court and voluntarily ackn, she relinquished her Right of Dower to the land in the deed conveyed to Alexander Harrower, and was recorded.

In the suit betw. Phillip Smith, Gent., Pltf., and William Ballendine, Deft., by petition for £1.10.11 due by account the sd. Deft. did not appear, but hearing Capt. William Eustace, an evidence in this cause, and the Pltf. oath , Judgment is granted the sd. Pltf., for £1.10, the balance due on the account & costs.

The action of trespass and assault & battery betw. Elizabeth Samson, Pltf. and Nicholas Collings, Deft., is dismissed.

The suit betw. George Brent, Pltf., and Thomas Cox, Junr., Deft., by petition for 250 lbs. tobacco due by obligation, is dismissed.

Ordered that the Court be adjourned till the 2nd Wednesday in November next. At a Court for Lancaster Co., on Wednesday, in 13th day of November 1734. Present: William Ball, Henry Fleet, William Ball, Junr., Henry Carter, Henry Lawson, William Tayloe, Joseph Heale, Joseph Chinn, & Joseph Carter; Gent., Justices.

James Camell came into Court and ackn. his deed & bond to Joseph Carter, Gent., for 40 a., in St. Mary's White Chappel Parish, in this Co., was recorded.

Jane Cammell, wife of sd. James Cammell, came into Court and voluntarily ackn., she relinquished her Right of Dower to the land in the deed conveyed in the sd. deed, and was recorded.

The Will of John Pinckard, dec'd, was presented in Court by Mary Pinckard, Execx., and it was proved by the oaths if Edward Railey & Richard Boatman, witnesses, and the Execx. obtained Probate, and was recorded.

Henry Fleet, Gent., producing the Gov's. Commission. dated 2 Nov last appointing him Co. Coroner.

York, a Negro boy, belonging to the Reverend John Bell, is by the Court adjudged to be 13 years old.

198

Dick, a Negro boy, belonging to the Robert Mitchell, is by the Court adjudged to be 15 years old.

Comania [?], a Negro girl, belonging to the Rawleigh Chinn, is by the Court adjudged to be 13 years old.

Plesenta [?], a Negro girl, belonging to the Mr. Bryan Pullen, is by the Court adjudged to be 14 years old.

Pg 117. The Sheriff having made Proclamation that the Court was about to lay the County Levy, they proceeded accordingly. Lancaster Co. – **Pounds of Tobacco:**

John Carter, Esqr., for keeping the Public Ferry one year -1,400

Thomas Edwards, Court Clerk, for public service – 1,000

John Tarpley, Junr., Attorney for the King in this Co. - 1,000

John Pyne for cleaning the Court House & other services – 800

Hugh Brent, Gent., Sheriff of the Co. for Public Service – 1,000

Mr. Secretary Carter for filing & recording two coroner's Inquests & Constable fees – 100

Mr. Secretary Carter for a Commission of the Peace to Administer Oaths - 160

Mr. Secretary Carter for issuing a writ for Election of a Burges - 350

Mr. Edwin Conway for his attendance as a Burges at the last Session of Assembly & for coming & going – 6,700

Mr. Edwin Conway for Ferrages - £1.3.6

Capt. James Ball for his attendance as a Burges at the last Session of the Assembly & for coming & going – 5,273

Capt. James Ball for Ferrages - £1.3.6

Mr. Nicholas Martin for one Coroner's Inquest – 133

Matthias James for summoning the Jury for the same - 50

Dale Carter, Sub. Sheriff on his Account – 158

William George, late Sub. Sheriff on his Account - 60

George Brent for bringing 6 books of the Laws for the Clerk & Justices from Williamsburgh - 150

Edward Sanders, Constable for viewing tobacco seconds in his precinct – 79

Thomas Flint, Constable for the same – 299

George Yerby, Constable for the same – 258

Henry Horne, Constable for the same - 228

John Bailey, Constable for the same - 194

Matthias James, Constable for the same - 199

William Dogget, Constable for the same – 199 – sub total – 20,018 lbs.

Capt. William Ball on his Inspector's Account - £2.3.0

Mr. Joseph Carter on his Inspector's Account – £3.17.6

The fraction in the Sheriff's hands ---------------------------------520 lbs.

4 % for Collecting 15,303 – 595 lbs.

Total – 20,538 plus 595= 21,133 lbs.   Annual Levy

Credit – By Capt. Conway for £38.12.0, the money balance due to this Co. for the rent of Deep Creek Warehouses and for the rents of Davis's Warehouses for the years 1732 &1733 – 5,150 lbs. tobacco. By 1,454,Tithables at 11 tobacco per Pol.

The Country & County Levy for this present year 1734, amounting the whole to eleven lbs of tobacco per pol. It is Ordered that the Co. Sheriff collect so much of every tithable person in the sd. Co. discounting 10 % for convening in the County Levy, where it is paid in Inspector's notes and pay, the same to the Country & County Creditors, as the law directs.

On the Prayer of William Hay [?] setting forth that he is blind and not able to get his living. It is Ordered that he be excused from paying any Country and Country levies for the future.

On the Prayer of William Denny setting forth that he is afflicted with sickness that he is not able to get his living. It is Ordered that he be excused from paying any Country and Country levies for the future.

Ordered that John Carter, Esqr., do keep the Public Ferry over Corotomon River the ensuing year that he be paid the same as usual.

Ordered that John Payne do find this Court with water & candles and cleaning the Court House the ensuing year and that he be paid the same as usual.

Ordered that William Ballendine and Mary Ann, his wife, Bryan Pullen and William Bertrand, Execs., of Charles Ewell, dec'd, be summoned to the next Court to answer the petition of Darby Gallahew and Sharlott, his wife.

Pg 118. Ordered that the Court be adjourned till the 2nd Wednesday in December next. At a Court for Lancaster Co., on Wednesday, in 12th day of February 1734. Present: William Ball, William Ball, Junr., Henry Carter, Henry Lawson, William Tayloe, Joseph Chinn, & Joseph Carter; Gent., Justices.

John Brewer and Mary, his wife, cane to Court & ackn. there deed to James Cammell, for & concerning 100 a. of land in St. Mary's, White Chappel Parish, in this Co., the sd. Mary being privately examined, which on the Motion of the sd. Camell is admitted to record.

The Will of John Fendla, dec'd, was presented in Court by George Flower, one of the Execs., therein, who made oath and being proved by the oaths of James Donnellane & John Mason, witnesses, was admitted to record and was granted Probate.

Ordered that William Hutchhins, John Yerby, John Merriday and Thomas Yerby, or any three of them being first sworn before a Co. Judge, are to appraise the Estate in money and make a report of same along with George Flower, Exec., at the next Court.

Robert Galbreath exhibited and made oath to his account of the Estate of Margaret & Catherine Carter, Orphans under his Guardianship, which is admitted to record.

In the suit betw. Darby Gallahew and Sharlott, his wife, Pltfs., and William Ballendine & Mary Ann, his wife, William Bertrand & Bryan Pullen, Execs. of Charles Ewell, Deft., by Petition for the Legacy given & bequeathed to the sd. Sharlott, in the Will of the sd. Charles Ewell, dec'd, by consent of the Parties, Joseph Ball, Esqr., Edwin Conway and Robert Mitchell, Gent., or any two of them are to settle all differences betw. the parties in this suit & make a report of their proceedings to next Court.

On the prayer of John Miller, orphan of William Miller, dec'd, Dale Carter is appointed as Guardian, William George becoming his security for his sd. Guardianship, who enter into recognizance in the sum of £100 to the Court's Justices that the sd. Orphan shall be fully & justly paid what the Estate shall become to him when he comes of age. And, it is Ordered that the sd. Dale Carter, be forthwith possessed with the Estate and Exhibit an account thereon Oath to the next Court.

The action of debt betw. Frances Burges, widow, & Edwin Conway & James Ball, Gent., Exec. of Charles Burges, Gent., Pltf., and James Garton, Deft., is dismissed.

The action of debt betw. Francis Burges, widow, & Edwin Conway & James Ball, Gent., Exec. of Charles Burges, Gent., Pltf., and Arthur Mc Neale, Deft., for 2,107 lbs. tobacco due by obligation & account, the parties being heard Judgment was granted to the sd. Pltfs. against the sd. Deft. for 1,906 lbs. tobacco & costs.

In the suit betw. Thomas Draper, Pltf., and George Gibson, Deft., by petition for 600 lbs. tobacco by obligation under the sd. Deft.'s hand. The Deft. confessed Judgment and whereupon, it is Ordered that he forthwith pay to the sd. Pltf. his afsd. debt with costs.

In the suit betw. Richard Davis, Junr., and Joseph Marshall, Deft., by attachment against the Estate of the sd. Deft., the Pltf. making oath to the of his debt. Judgment is granted to him against the sd. Deft. for 120 lbs. tobacco, ten bushels of Indian Corn & costs. And, the sd. Attachment being returned & served upon a horse & saddle & 100 lbs. tobacco, which is in the hands of Chattin Chowning. It appearing to the Court that the sd. Chattin was indebted to the sd. Deft. no more than 50 lbs. tobacco at the time Judgment is ranted to the sd. Pltf., for the same. And, it is Ordered that is case the goods afsd. shall be replivied, as the law directs, that they be sold and disposed of for and towards

202

the Judgment in the same manner as goods taken in Execution upon a writ of feire facias and that this attachment be continued till next Court.

In the action of debt betw. William Oliver, Pltf., and Thomas Bridgford, Deft., the sd. Deft. pleaded and the Pltf. joined issue whereupon it is Ordered that the trial on the issue be referred till next Court.

In the suit betw. William Shelton, Pltf., and James Shelton, Deft., by petition for 500 lbs. tobacco is dismissed.

In the suit betw. Annabelle Carter, Execx., of the Will of Capt. Thomas Carter, dec'd, Pltf., and Richard Carter, Deft., by petition for 30 [can't read] of tobacco made in the year1733 and the [can't read] slave belonging to the sd. dec'd on hearing the Parties. It is Ordered that the sd. Deft. forthwith pay unto the sd. Pltf. 45lbs. of tobacco and costs.

Pg. 119. In the suit betw. James Ball, Gent., Pltf., and Joseph Burne, Deft., by petition for 419 lbs. tobacco & 9 shillings cash by Account, the sd. Deft., not appearing and the Pltf. making oath to the truth of debt. Judgment is granted to the Pltf.

On petition of John Brewer & Mary, his wife, late widow of John Vangover, dec'd, against Frances Burges & James Ball, & Edwin Conway, Gent., Exec. of Charles Burges, Gent., dec'd, setting forth that the sd. Vangover in his Will gave diverse legacies to the sd. Mary and appointed Charles Burges, Gent., his Exec., who took it upon himself, but did never deliver any part of the sd. Legacy to the sd. Petitioners. Joseph Ball, Esqr. is appointed to settle the accounts indifference betw. the sd. parties on this suit and to make a report of his proceedings to the next Court.

Margaret Denny made oath that William Denny, late of this Co., dec'd, departed this life without a Will, and on her petition & giving security for her administering the sd. Estate & she obtained the Letters of Administration.

Ordered that Christopher Kirk, William Hutchings, Charles Hammond & George Brent, or any three of them, first sworn before a Co. Justice, are to appraise the Estate of William Denny, dec'd, and make a report with Margaret Denny, Adminx., at the next Court.

On the petition of Henry Horne against John Brewer, and Mary, his wife, for admin. of the sd. Velden Estate and that sd. Brewer is removing out of this Co., by consent of the parties, Joseph Carter, Gent., is appointed to settle the account of the Admin. of the sd. Francis Velden Estate and to deliver the petition or such to the Orphan of the sd. Velden, dec'd., & make report to the next Court.

Ordered that the Court be adjourned till the 2nd Wednesday in March next. At a Court for Lancaster Co., on Wednesday, in 12th day of March 1734. Present: William Ball, William Ball, Junr., Henry Carter, Joseph Chinn, & Joseph Carter; Gent., Justices.

The Will of Matthew Machan, dec'd, was presented in Court, by John Mott, Exec., made Oath, and being proved by Sebra Rutherford, a witness, the Will was admitted to record & the Exec. obtained Probate of the Will.

Ordered that Thomas Chattin, Giles Robinson, Thomas Taff, Thomas Flint or any three being first sworn, are to appraise Estate of Matthew Machan, dec'd, in money and make a report, and present same along with John Mott, Exec. of the Will, at the next Court.

John Mott, Exec. of Matthew Machan, dec'd, made Oath that the sd. Machan desired at his death that Thomas Pullen should have his servant man, John Floyd, which he had lately agreed with the sd. Pullen for which Servant, the sd. Pullen agreeing to take & discharge the Estate from the Consideration he was to have for him, and the agreement was recorded.

The Will of John Nash, dec'd, was presented in Court by John Kent, Junr., Exec., named in the sd. Will, who make oath thereto & proved by the oath of Edwin Conway, Gent., & William Bowman, witnesses, and it was admitted to record, and the Exec. obtained probate.

Ordered that George Brent, Thomas Hubbard, Clement Lattimore and John Hubbard, or any three first sworn bef. a Co. Justice, are to appraise the Estate of John Nash, dec'd, in money and make a report of same with John Kent, Exec. of Will, at the next Court.

The Will of John Buckles, dec'd, was presented in Court by James Rob, one of the Execs. of the Will, which was proved by oaths by Henry Carter, Gent., & John Merredith, witnesses, was admitted to the record, and the Exec. obtained Probate.

Ordered that James Rob, Exec. of the Will of John Buckles, dec'd, to bring the Inventory of the sd. Estate to the next Court and make oath thereto.

The Will of William Bailey, dec'd, was presented in Court by Joseph Stephens and John Mitchell, Execs. of the Will, who made oath and was proved by the oath of Sabra Robinson, one of the Witnesses, was admitted on a Motion and Probate was obtained.

Ordered that Thomas Wharten, Thomas Flint, Thomas Chattin & Robert Mc Tire, and any three are to appraise the Estate in money and make a report and appear in Court with Joseph Stephens & John Mitchell, Execs., at the next Court.

Pg 120. The Will od Francis Wallis, dec'd, was presented in Court by Alexander Poor, Exec., made Oath, and being proved by the Oaths of John Kent & John Kent, Junr., witnesses, admitted to record and the Exec. obtained probate.

Ordered the William Hutchins, Clement Lattimore, Benjamin George, Junr. and William Pasquet, or any three, being first sworn bef. a Justice, are to appraise the Estate of Francis Wallis, in money and make a report with Alexander Poor, Exec. of the Will at the next Court.

The appraisal of the Estate of John Pinckard, dec'd, was returned and Mary Pinckard, Execx., made oath to her subscription of the Inventory was recorded.

The appraisal of the Estate of John Fendla, dec'd, was returned & George Flower, Exec. made oath to his subscription of the Inventory was recorded.

In the suit betw. Darby Gallahew, and Sharlott, his wife, Pltf., and William Ballendine and Mary, his wife, William Bertrand, and Bryan Pullen, Execs., of Charles Ewell, dec'd, Deft., by Petition, a report of the auditors appointed in this case was returned and admitted to record and Judgment is granted to the Pltfs. for £7.3.0, the sum the auditors found & costs of the Estate of he dec'd, that was in the hands of the Defts., but execution of same is stayed till the sd. Pltfs. shall give security to the sd. Defts. to contribute a one-sixth part towards such part of the charges of he suit in General Court against Gusavina[?] Bowden, which was dismissed and also their due proportion to any debts or necessary charges that may have after be recovered against the sd. Defts.

In the debt betw. William Oliver, Pltf., and Thomas Bridgford, Deft., is continued to next Court at the Pltf.'s Motion & costs.

In the suit betw. Jno. Brewer, and Mary, his wife, Pltfs., and Frances Burges and James Ball & Edwin Conway, Gent., Execs., of Charles Burges, Gent., is continued for the report of Joseph Ball, Esqr., the auditor appointed in this cause till the next Court.

In the debt betw. Richard Davis, Junr., Pltf., and Joseph Marshall, Deft., by attachment, the Sheriff returning that he had made 240 lbs. tobacco by the sale of the horse and saddle attached in this cause and the sd. Pltf. failing to prosecute any further, the attachment is discontinued.

In the debt betw. Henry Horn, Pltf., and John Brewer & Mary, his wife, late widow of Francis Velden, dec'd, Deft., by petition. The opinion of the Court being that what tobacco is chargeable against the sd. Estate shall be discounted and it is Ordered that the report of Joseph Carter, Gent., the auditor appointed in this cause be made & to the next Court.

In the suit betw. Thomas Edwards, Pltf., and Michall Ryan, Deft., by petition for 204 lbs. tobacco and £1.9.2 due by account, is dismissed.

In the action of debt betw. Frances Burges, widow, and Edwin Conway & James Ball, Gent., Execs. of Charles Burges, Gent., dec'd, Pltf. and John Brewer, Deft., by consent of the parties, is continued till next Court.

In the suit betw. James Ball & George Ball, Gents., Execs. of the Will of David Ball, Gent., dec'd, Pltfs., and William Ball, Junr., Gent., Deft., the sd, Deft. put in pleas and on the Motion of the Pltf., time is given him to consider the same. till next Court.

In the suit betw. John Stepto, Junr., Pltf., and James Shelton, Deft., by attachment & the sd. Petition making oath to the truth of the debt, Judgment is granted him against the sd. Deft. for 1,268 lbs. of tobacco & costs, and the as attachment being returned served upon one feather bed, one rug, two blankets, a bed stead, hide & cord, a chest, a curved hat, one large history book, and blades and tacks, 3 small balls of shoe thread, gimlet, 6 gunflints, one fence, a fiddle & 6 balls of cotton, one [?], box, hat, 2 jackets, old pr. breeches with some cotton in them, two old common prayer books, an old Bible, bog iron, and heater, one pewter tankard, 5 qrt. bottles, old pair yarn stockings, old wallet, white case, 2 porringers, iron pot, hook, old shirt, old pair shoes, broad hoe, narrow hoe, frying pan, chamber pot, 4 new plates, old plate, basin, dish, meal sifter, bag of wool, corn in ears, 5 pieces bacon, broad ax. It is Ordered in case the goods afsd. shall not be replevied, as the suit directs, that they be sold and disposed of, for and towards satisfaction of this Judgment the same manner of goods taken in execution upon a writ , and that this attachment be continued till next Court.

The suit of attachment betw. William Gardner, Pltf., and James Shelton, Deft., for 400 lbs. of tobacco, neither party appearing, is dismissed.

In the suit betw. Thomas Gaskins, Pltf. and John Stacy, Deft., by attachment for 500 lbs. tobacco, which attachment was returned served in the hands of Robert Edwards, on hearing the sd. Pltf., and the sd. Robert. It is the opinion of the Court that the sd. Edwards was not indebted to the sd. Stacy at the time the sd. attachment was served upon him whereupon it is Ordered that this attachment be discontinued.

Pg 121. Michael Ryan producing and making oath to his amount against the sd. Estate of John Buckley, dec'd, for 250 lbs. tobacco, James Rob, Exec. of the sd. dec'd, confessed Judgment for the sd. debt whereupon it is Ordered that the sd. James pay the same to the sd. Michael, out of the Estate of the sd. dec'd, in his hands with costs.

William Ball, Henry Carter & William Tayloe, Gent., are appointed to agree with some person for the complete covering and substantial repairing Davis Warehouses between this next Court.

The appraisement of the Estate of William Denny, dec'd was returned and Margaret Denny, his Admin., making oath to the Inventory, Ordered to be recorded.

Ordered that the Court be adjourned till the 2nd Wednesday in April next. At a Court for Lancaster Co., on Wednesday, in 14th day of May 1735. Present: William Ball, Henry Fleet, William Ball, Junr., Henry Carter, Henry Lawson, Joseph Heale, William Tayloe, & Joseph Carter; Gent., Justices.

William Ball, Gent., is appointed to take the list of Tithables in the Lower Precinct in St. Mary's, White Chappel Parish in the Co., for this year.

Joseph Chinn, is appointed to take the list of Tithables in the Middle Precinct in St. Mary's, White Chappel Parish in the Co., for this year.

William Ball, Junr., Gent., is appointed to take the list of Tithables in the Upper Precinct in St. Mary's, White Chappel Parish in the Co., for this year.

Henry Carter, Gent., is appointed to take the list of Tithables in the Lower part, of Corotomon Precinct in Christ Church Parish in the Co., for this year.

Henry Lawson, Gent., is appointed to take the list of Tithables in the Middle Precinct in Christ Church Parish in the Co., for this year.

William Tayloe, Gent., is appointed to take the list of Tithables in the Upper part, of Corotomon Precinct in Christ Church Parish in Wiccocomoco Parish, in this Co., for this year.

Henry Fleet, Gent., is appointed to take the list of Tithables between Corotomon River & the main road which leads from the Church to Mr. Secretary Carter's Mill and in the Lower Precinct in Christ Church Parish, in the Co., for this year.

Mr. George Ball is appointed Surveyor of the highways from this Co. Court House to Mrs. Judith Payne's, in St Mary's, White Chappel Parish, in this Co., for this year.

James Brent is appointed Surveyor of the highways from this Co. Court House to Mrs. Judith Payne's to Mrs. Burges's Mill, in St Mary's, White Chappel Parish, in this Co., for this year.

John Bailey is appointed Surveyor of the highways from the Church to Deep Bottom Run and of the Rolling Road, which leads from Mr. Joseph Chinn's to Deep Creek warehouses in St Mary's, White Chappel Parish, in this Co., for this year.

John Rogers is appointed Surveyor of the highways from Deep Bottom run to Morattico Mill in St Mary's, White Chappel Parish, in this Co., for this year.

John Mitchell, is appointed Surveyor of the highways from Mrs. Burges's Mill to Mr. Selden's Mill in St Mary's, White Chappel Parish, in this Co., for this year.

John Mott is appointed Surveyor of the highways from Bryan Stott's to the road that leads from Col. Ball's Mill to Mrs. Burges's Mill in St Mary's, White Chappel Parish, in this Co., for this year.

Thomas Chattin is appointed Surveyor of the highways from Bartholomew Woods to the cross roads near Doctr. Thornton in St Mary's, White Chappel Parish, in this Co., for this year.

Thomas Taylor is appointed Surveyor of the highways from the Main Road to Cundiff's old field and also of the rolling road in the sd. Precinct in St Mary's, White Chappel Parish, in this Co., for this year.

William Goodridge is appointed Surveyor of the rolling road, which leads from the Church road to Carpenter's landing in St Mary's, White Chappel Parish, in this Co., for this year.

Thomas Carter, planter, is appointed Surveyor of the highways from Mr. Selden's Mill and of all of main and rolling roads between these two branches of Corotomon River in Christ Church and Wicocomoco Parishes in this C., for this year.

Pg 122. William Stepto, Gent, is appointed Surveyor of the highways from Mr. Secretary Carter's Mill, to the cross roads in Christ Church Parish, in this Co., for the year. And, it is Ordered that he take to his assistance the male laboring Tithables belonging to his plantation to the plantation, before Ordered to assist him thereof belonging to this Precinct.

George Flower is appointed Surveyor of the highways from the Cross Roads to the [can't read] in Christ Church Parish in this Co., for the year.

Thomas Faulkner is appointed is appointed Surveyor of the highways from Mr. Charles Carter's Mill to the main road which leads from the Clerk's office in Christ Church Parish, in this Co., for this year, and he is to keep the sd. road in repair with the male laboring Tithables belonging to the sd. Carter in the sd. Precinct,

Charles Jones is appointed is appointed Surveyor of the highways from the Church to the cross roads in Christ Church Parish in this Co., for this year and he is to keep the sd. road in repair with the male laboring Tithables belonging to Mr. Secretary Carter, in the sd. Precinct.

William Martin is appointed is appointed Surveyor of the highways from Mr. Charles Carter's Mill to the white stone and of all the main roads in Nantepeizen Neck in Christ Church Parish, in this Co., for this year.

Henry Fleet, Gent., is appointed is appointed Surveyor of the highways from the Church to Mr. Stepto's, in Christ Church Parish, in this Co., for this year.

John Yerby is appointed is appointed Surveyor of the highways from Mr.

Secretary Carter's Quarter, on the mouth of the Eastern branch of Corotomon River to the Mill Road and from the road to the Church, in Christ Church Parish in this Co., for this year.

The Will of William Carter, dec'd, was presented in Court by Daniel Carter & Isaac Currell, Execs., who made oath& being proved by the oath of Solomon Horn, witness thereto, it is admitted on a Motion and probate was granted.

Ordered that William Martin, Abraham Currell, Thomas Lawson & John Cox, Execs., or any three of them, being proved by the oath of Solomon Horn, a witness, are to appraise the Estate of William Carter, dec'd, in money and make a report, and present it along with the Execs. of Will at the next Court.

Samuel Brumley came into Court and made oath that Michael Reaser, late of this Co., dec'd, died without a Will, and giving security for his Admin. of the Estate of the deceased, was granted Admin. of the Estate.

Ordered that John Rogers, Thomas Stott, William Bertrand & James Stott, or any three of them are to appraise the Estate of Michael Reason, dec'd, in money and make a report, and present it along with Samuel Brumley, Admin. of the Estate at the next Court.

The appraisement of the Estate of Matthew Machen, dec'd, was returned and John Mott, Exec., making oath to his subscription on the Inventory, Ordered to be recorded.

The appraisement of the Estate of John Nash, dec'd, was returned and John Kent, Junr., Exec., making oath to his subscription on the Inventory, Ordered to be recorded.

The appraisement of the Estate of Francis Wallis, dec'd, was returned and Alexander Poor, Exec., making oath to his subscription on the Inventory, Ordered to be recorded.

The Inventory of the Estate of John Buckles, dec'd, was taken and James Rob, Exec., making oath & his subscription on the Inventory, Ordered to be recorded.

The appraisement of the Estate of William Bailey, dec'd, was returned and John Mitchell and Joseph Stephens, Execs., making oath to his subscription on the Inventory, Ordered to be recorded.

In the suit betw. John Brown and Mary, his wife, late widow of John Vangover, dec'd, Pltf., and Frances Burges & James Ball & Edwin Conway, Gent., Execs., of the Will of Charles Burges, Gent., Defts., by petition for the sd. Mary, her part of the sd. John Vangover Estate, in the hands of the sd. Defts., as is set forth in the Petition & report of Joseph Ball, Esqr., was this day returned and on the Motion of the sd. Defts., admitted to record where upon it is considered that this suit be dismissed, and the Pltfs., pay unto the sd. Defts., their costs hereby occasioned.

The Will of Elizabeth Smith, dec'd, was presented in Court by Edny Tapscott, Exec. of the Will, who made oath and proved by Henry Tapscott, a witness, was admitted to record, & on Motion of the Exec. was granted probate.

Pg 123. Ordered that Clement Lattimore, William Hayden, Richard Lewis & Edward Sanders, or any three of them are to appraise the Estate of Elizabeth Smith, dec'd, in money & make & present a report, along with Edny Tapscott, Exec., at the next Co. Court.

The suit betw. Henry Horn, Pltf., and John Brewer, & Mary, his wife, late widow of John Vangover, dec'd, Defts., by petition neither party appearing, is dismissed.

In the action upon the case between James Ball & George Ball, Gent., Execs., of the Will of David Ball, Gent., dec'd, Pltfs., & William Ball, Junr., Gent., Deft., the sd. Pltf. this day put in demurrer to the sd. Deft.'s plea in this cause & time is given to the sd. Deft., till next Court to be considered.

In the attachment obtained by John Stepto against the Estate of James Shelton, the Sheriff having made a return of what is in the hands towards Satisfaction of the sd. John's Judgment in their Cause, the same was admitted to record being [can't read]. Followeth Lancaster by virtue of the within orders & he within goods were disposed of by Public outcry for tobacco, the whole amounting to 1,156 lbs. tobacco. Dale Carter, Sub- Sheriff. Whereupon, it is Ordered that the sd. attachment be discontinued.

In the suit betw. Thomas Gaskins, Pltf., and Thomas Davis, Deft., by petition for 311 lbs. tobacco due by the Deft., not appearing and the Pltf. making oath to the truth of his debt, Judgment is granted to the Pltf. against the sd. Deft., for his sd. debt & costs.

In the action of Debt betw. Robert Mitchell, Gent, Pltf., and John Mott, Exec. of Will of Matthew Machan, dec'd, Deft., for 1,112 lbs. tobacco due by bill in the declaration, the sd. Pltf. making oath to the truth of his claim, Judgment is granted to the sd. Pltf. against the sd. Deft., for the sd. debt & it is Ordered that he pay the same out of the Estate of the dec'd, which is in his hands, with costs.

In the suit betw. Thomas Flint, Pltf., and John Mott, Exec. of the Will of Matthew Machan, dec'd, Deft., by petition for 800 lbs. tobacco due by note under the hand of the dec'd, the parties were heard and on the oath of the Pltf., in this cause, Judgment is granted him for 568 lbs. tobacco out of the dec'd Estate in his hands, with costs. But, execution on the Judgment is to be delayed till Christmas next.

In the suit betw. Frances Burges, widow, and Edwin Conway and James Ball, Gent., Execs. of the Will of Charles Burges, Pltfs., and William Watts, Deft., by attachment against the estate of the sd. Deft, for 972 lbs. of tobacco due by bill, the sd. Pltf. making oath to their claim, Judgment is granted them against the sd. Deft., for the sd. tobacco, costs and the attachment being returned served in the hands of George Dogget, & the sd. Dogget appeared & on his oath declared that the sd. Deft. Ordered him to pay 600 lbs. tobacco before in his hands before this attachment was served to Capt. William Eustace, which he promised accordingly by whereupon, it is considered that he pay unto the sd. Pltfs. the over plus of the sd. Deft.'s tobacco remaining in his hands. In discharge of the Judgment and the attachment be discontinued.

In the action of debt betw. Frances Burges, widow and James Ball and Edwin Conway, Gent., Exec. of Charles Burges, Gent, dec'd, Pltf., and John Brewer, Deft., in continued till next Court.

In the action of debt betw. Frances Burges, widow and James Ball and Edwin Conway, Gent., Execs. of Charles Burges, Gent, dec'd, Pltf., and John Mott, Exec. of the Will of Matthew Machan, dec'd, Deft., is continued till next Court.

In the suit of John Grahame, Merchant, Pltf., and Darby Gallahew, Deft., by petition for £3 due by note and Pltf. not appearing, is dismissed.

The action of trespass & assault & battery betw. Christopher Collins, Pltf., and Charles Cox, Deft., for £10 as in the declaration is set forth, is dismissed.

The action upon the case betw. John Selden, Gent., Pltf., and John Mott, Exec. of the Will of Matthew Machan, dec'd, is continued till next Court.

The suit betw. Judith Jones, Pltf., and Thomas Davis, Deft., by petition is continued till next Court.

In the action of Debt betw. John Carter, Esqr., and Hugh Brent, Gent., Church Wardens, of Christ Church Parish, in this Co., Pltfs., and Mary Humphris, Deft., for 500 lbs., tobacco & cask or 50 shillings by mean of the Deft. having committed fornication had a bastard child, as in the Declaration sets forth, the sd. Deft. appeared & confessed but failed to pay or to give sufficient caution for the payment of the fine. Whereupon, it is Ordered she receive on her bare back at the public whipping post 25 lashes, well laid on, and be then discharged.

The Noncupative Will of Andrew Donaldson, dec'd, was exhibited in Court by Mary Donaldson, his widow, but Christopher Collings, who married one of the daughters of the sd. dec'd, objected against the proof thereof. Ordered that the matter of this proof be referred to next Court.

Pg 124. In the action of John Mott, Exec. of the Will of Matthew Machan, dec'd, Pltf., and Thomas Dallis, Deft., the sd. Deft. appeared and in custody of the Sheriff, pleaded and the Pltf. joined issue whereupon it is Ordered that the trial of the sd. issue be referred till next Court.

A deed from Alexander Poor to William Stepto, Gent., for and concerning 50 a. of land lying in Christ Church Parish, thereon endorsed was in open Court ackn. by the sd. Poor to which act & deed, was admitted to record.

Catherine, wife of Alexander Poor, also came to Court and relinquished her Right to Dower and the premises in the sd. deed conveyed to the sd. Stepto, was admitted to record.

In action betw. William Oliver, brick layer, Pltf., and Thomas Bridgford, Deft., for £15 as in the Declaration, William Bertrand, William Hutchings, Abraham Currell, John Bailey, George Dogget, George Kirk, James Rob, John Mott, Robert Galbreath, John Mitchell, George Yerby, and Thomas Flint, were impaneled and sworn to try the issue and bringing in their verdict in these words – "We, the Jury do find for the Pltf. £2.2.7 in current money damages." Signed: William Bertrand, Foreman. The sd. verdict on the Motion of the sd. Pltf. is recorded and it is considered that the sd. Pltf. recover against the sd. Deft. £2.2.7 the damages afsd. by the Jury afsd. assessed and costs together with one attorney's fee.

James Clark having attended 2 days as witness for William Oliver, brick layer, in his suit against Thomas Bridgford. It is Ordered that the sd. William pay to the sd. James for his attendance & for travelling 80 miles each way from the place of the sd. attendance according to law & costs.

Ordered that the Court be adjourned till the 2nd Wednesday in June next. At a Court for Lancaster Co., on Wednesday, in 11th day of June 1735. Present: William Ball, Henry Fleet, William Ball, Junr., Henry Carter, Joseph Heale, Joseph Chinn & Joseph Carter; Gent., Justices.

On the petition of Christopher Stephens, he is admitted to keep Ordinary at is dwelling house in this County as use.

Pursuant to a late Act of Assembly, Ordered that the brass weights of half hundred, quarter half, quarter seven pound, four pounds, two pounds, & one pounds weight according to the Standard of the Exchange in England. Also, proper scales for the sd. weights be by Co. Justices purchased at the sd. County's Charge for the use of the sd. Co.

Ordered that the Vestry of Christ Church Parish in the Co, divide their Parish into so many Precincts as to them shall seem on out convenient for processioning every particular person's land in their sd. Parish and appoint particular[?] times betw. the last day of September and the last day of March next when such processioning shall be made in every Precinct. And, also appoint two intelligent, honest freeholders in every Precinct to do such processioning performed and to take and return to the sd. Vestry an account of every person on land they shall procession and of the persons absent at the time and of what lands in their Precinct they shall fail to procession and of the particular reasons of such failure.

Ordered that the Vestry of St. Mary's, White Chappel Parish in the Co, divide their Parish into so many Precincts as to them shall seem on out convenient for processioning every particular person's land in their sd. Parish and appoint particular[?] times betw. the last day of September and the last day of March next when such processioning shall be made in every Precinct. And, also appoint two intelligent, honest freeholders in every Precinct to do such processioning performed and to take and return to the sd. Vestry an account of every person on land they shall procession and of the persons absent at the time and of what lands in their Precinct they shall fail to procession and of the particular reasons of such failure.

214

The Will of Thomas Lee, Gent., dec'd, was presented in Court by Elizabeth Lee, one of the Exec. of the Will, who made oath thereto & being proved by the oaths of Ezekiel Gilbert & Isaac Currell, witnesses, it was admitted to record, and on Motion was granted Probate.

Pg 125. Ordered that Abraham Currell, William Martin, Thomas Lawrence & Isaac Currell, or any three of them, going bef. Co. Justice, are to appraise the Estate of Thomas Lee, Gent., in money and present their report & Inventory with Elizabeth Lee, Execx. of the Will, at next Co. Court.

The appraisement of the Estate of William Carter, dec'd, was returned & Daniel Carter and James Currell, his Execs., making oath according to his subscription of the Inventory, Ordered recorded.

Hannah, a Negro girl belonging to Robert Galbreath is by the Court adjudged to be 14 years of age.

In the action on the case betw. James Ball & George Ball, Gent., Execs. of the Will of David Ball, Gent., dec'd. Pltfs., and William Ball, Junr., Gent., Deft., the sd. Deft. put in a second plea and on the Motion of the sd. Pltfs., time is given them to consider the same at next Court.

The action of the debt betw. Frances Burges, widow, and Edwin Conway and James Ball, Gent., Execs. of the Will of Charles Burges, Gent. dec'd, Pltfs., and John Brewer, Deft., is dismissed.

Dale Carter exhibited and made oath to his amount of the Estate of John Miller, Orphan, under his Guardianship, which is admitted to record.

In the action upon the case betw. Frances Burges, widow, and Edwin Conway, James Ball, Gent., Execs. of the Will of Charles Burges, Gent., dec'd, Pltf., and John Mott, Exec. of the Will of Matthew Machan, dec'd, Deft., for 3,039 lbs. tobacco and £0.1.2 due by bill and account within the Declaration is set forth the sd. Pltf., making oath to the truth of their claim. Judgment is granted to the sd. Pltf. against the sd. Deft., for the sd. debt and is Ordered that he pay the same out of the Estate of the sd. dec'd, in his hands and costs.

The case betw. John Selden, Gent., Pltf., & John Mott, Execs. of the Will of Matthew Machan, dec'd, Deft., for 1,600 lbs. tobacco due by account, as in the declaration, and on the oath of the Pltf., in Court and full hearing, Judgment is to the Pltf., and the Deft. is to pay 1,383 lbs. tobacco to the Pltf. with costs from the Estate of the dec'd, which is in his hands.

In the suit betw. Judith Jones, Pltf., and Thomas David, Deft., by Petition for £2.5.0 due by account, Judgment is granted to the sd. Pltf. against the sd. Deft. for her costs expended.

In the suit betw. Thomas Everet, Pltf., and John Mott, Exec. of the Will of William Machan, dec'd, Deft., for 880 lbs. of tobacco on the oath of the Pltf., and Judgment is granted to the Pltf., for 840 lbs. tobacco and to pay same from the Estate is the Deft's hands with costs.

The suit by petition betw. John Mitchell, Pltf., and John Brewer & Mary, his wife, Admins., of Francis Velden, dec'd, Deft., for £1.10.6 or 305 lbs. tobacco, due by account is dismissed, neither party appearing.

In the suit betw. Frances Burges, widow, and Edwin Conway and James Ball, Gent., Execs. of the Will of Charles Burges, Pltfs., and William Hobson and Abraham Currell, Execs. of the Will of Major Henry Fleet, dec'd, Defts., for 1,500 lbs. tobacco as in the Declaration, of the Pltfs., Judgment is granted them 1,010 lbs. of tobacco, and it is Ordered the sd. Deft. pay the same from the Estate of the Pltfs. in their hand and the costs.

In the case betw. John Mott, Exec. of the Will of Matthew Mahan, Pltf., and Thomas Dallis, Deft., for 1,100 lbs. tobacco in the Declaration, by consent of the parties, the trial on the issue joined, was referred to the Court. Whereupon, the parties and their evidences were heard. It is considered that this suit be dismissed and that the sd. Pltf. pay unto the sd. Deft. his costs & one attorney's fee.

In the suit betw. Edmond Forrest, Pltf., and Thomas Dallis, Deft., by petition for 324 lbs. of tobacco & £1.15.0 due by account the sd. Deft. came into Court and confessed Judgment for the whole debt; Ordered he pay the same to the Pltf, & costs.

A report of the settlement of John Brewer & Mary, his wife, their account of their Admin., of the of the Estate of Francis Velden, dec'd, and was exhibited in Court by Joseph Carter, Gent., who was appointed to settle it. It is Ordered that the report be recorded.

216

Pg 126.   Ordered that the Court be adjourned till the 2nd Wednesday in July next. At a Court for Lancaster Co., on Wednesday, in 9th day of July 1735. Present: William Ball, William Ball, Junr., Henry Lawson, William Tayloe, Joseph Chinn & Joseph Carter; Gent., Justices.

The appraisement of Thomas Lee, Gent., dec'd, was returned and Elizabeth Lee, his Execx., making oath to her subscription on the Inventory was recorded.

George Yerby was appointed Surveyor of the highways fro Mr. Secretary Carter's Mill, to the cross roads in Christ Church Parish , in this Co, for this year. And, it is Ordered that he take to his assistance the male laboring Tithables belonging to the plantations before Ordered to assist in clearing the sd. road besides these belonging to his sd. Precinct.

Edwin Conway, Gent., came into Court and made oath that John Robinson, late of this Co., dec'd, departed life without making a Will, and on hi Motion and giving security for his faithful Admin. of the Estate of the sd. dec'd, it was granted.

Ordered that Thomas Hubbard, John Hubbard, and Henry Boatman & George Brent, or any three of them after being first sworn before a Co. Judge, are to appraise the Estate of John Robinson, dec'd, in money, and to make a report of same in Court with Edwin Conway, Admin., of the Estate.

The Will of Thomas Carter, dec'd, was presented in Court by Joan Carter, his Execx., who made oath and being proved was admitted to record and obtained Probate.

Ordered that Joan Carter, Execx., of the Will of Thomas Carter, dec'd, Ordered to bring the Inventory of the Estate to the next Court.

The appraisement of the Estate of Elizabeth Smith, dec'd, was returned and Edny Tapscott, her Exec., making oath to his subscription on the Inventory was recorded.

Kate, a Negro girl belonging to William Brent is by the Court adjudged 14 years old.

Arabella, a Negro girl belonging to William Brent is by the Court adjudged 13 years old.

Tom, a Negro boy belonging to William Brent is by the Court adjudged 14 years old.

Keila, a Negro boy belonging to William Brent is by the Court adjudged 12 years old.

Celia, a Negro girl belonging to Nicholas Martin is by the Court adjudged 12 years old.

Sophia Patterson, a servant woman, belonging to Richard Davis, Junr., came to Court and voluntarily agreed to serve her master one year after her time by Indenture custom or former order of Court, is expired in consideration of his having purchased her from her former master.

Sophia Patterson, a servant woman, belonging to Richard Davis, Junr., came to Court and confessed that she ran away from John Mitchell, her former master twice & was absent the first time 10 days and 2 days the second time, and that the sd. Mitchell was out 200 lbs. tobacco regaining her. Ordered that she serve her present Master for the same as the Mitchell was out 200 lbs. tobacco in regaining her. Ordered that she serve her present Master for the [can't read].

A deed from William Taite and Ann, his wife, to William Wey and Margaret, his wife, for 100 a., in St. Mary's, White Chappel Parish, in this Co., was proved by the oaths of John Watts and Richard Vanlandingham and Alex. Anderson, witnesses thereto; recorded.

Pg 127. Maurice Harrington, a servant man belonging to Catherine Delany complaining against as he said the Mistress for beating and abusing him. It is Ordered that the sd. Catherine be summoned to answer the sd. Complaint at next Court.

Mary Dabbs, Orphan, of John Dabbs, dec'd, 12 years in April next is by the Court bound to Charles Hamond, of this Co., till he attains the age of 18 years, the sd. Charles to teach her to read sew, knit, and spin, & also find sufficient diet, lodging, apparel, and at the expiration of his servitude to pay him as is appointed for servants by Indenture or custom.

The suit betw. Epaphroditus Lawson. Pltf., and Francis Timberlake, Deft., is continued till next Court for the Deft's. witnesses.

Hanah, a Negro girl belonging to Joseph Carter, Gent., is by the Court adjudged to be 14 years of age.

On the petition of Moses Robinson against Wm. Robinson, it was Ordered that the sd. William be summoned to answer the sd. Petition at the next Court.

Ordered that the Court be adjourned till the 2nd Wednesday in August next. At a Court for Lancaster Co., on Wednesday, in 13th day of August 1735. Present: William Ball, Henry Fleet, William Ball, Junr., Henry Carter, Henry Lawson, William Tayloe, Joseph Chinn & Joseph Carter; Gent., Justices.

Judy, a Negro girl belonging to Charles Kelley is by the Court adjudged to be 12 years of age.

Glasgow, a Negro boy belonging to Charles Kelley is by the Court adjudged to be 11 years of age.

Sary, a Negro girl belonging to Mr. William Stepto is by the Court adjudged to be 14 years of age.

Winney, a Negro girl belonging to Mr. William Stepto is by the Court adjudged to be 14 years of age.

Bob, a Negro boy belonging to John Seaton[?] is by the Court adjudged to be 11 years of age.

Toby, a Negro boy belonging to Thomas Hunton is by the Court adjudged to be 9 years of age.

Moll, a Negro girl belonging to Mrs. Sarah Ball is by the Court adjudged to be 13 years of age.

In the action in the case betw. James Ball and George Ball, Gent., Execs. of the Will of David Ball, Gent., dec'd, Pltfs., and William Ball, Junr., Gent., Deft., the sd. Pltf. having heretofore filed their Replication in this Cause, it is continued till next Court at the Defts. Motion & costs.

Charles Ewell made oath to an account due to the Estate of Charles Burges, dec'd, from John Robinson, dec'd, that the same is a true copy from the sd. Burges's books & on oath of James Ball & Edwin Conway, Gent., Execs. of the sd. Burges that no satisfaction has been rec'd for the balance of the sd. account since Burges's death, and the account was admitted to record.

Tom, a Negro boy, belonging to John Stott, Junr., is by the Court adjudged to be 15 years of age.

The appraisement of the Estate of John Robinson, dec'd, was returned and Edwin Conway, Gent., his Admin., on making oath of his subscription on the Inventory, and also to his account of the Admin. of the sd. Estate annexed and the sd. Inventory and Account were recorded.

The appraisement of the Estate of Michael Reason, dec'd, was returned and Samuel Brumley, his Admin., making oath to his subscription of the Inventory; Ordered recorded.

The Will of Andrew Donaldson, dec'd, was presented in Court, by Mary Donaldson, his Execx., made oath, and was proved by oaths of Matthias James and Thos. Battany, witnesses, it was admitted probate in due form. And, a Motion by Christopher Collins made against the proof of the Will, was discontinued.

Ordered that Mary Donaldson, Execx. of the Will of Andrew Donaldson, dec'd, bring an Inventory of the Testator's Estate to the next Court and then appear and make oath thereto.

Pg 128. The suit betw. William Ball, Gent., Pltf., and William Shelton, Deft., by petition is continued till next Court for the Deft's witnesses.

On the complaint of Maurice Harrington against his Mistress Catherine Delany for beating and abusing him, both parties were heard. And, the opinion of the Court is that the sd. Catherine use the sd. Maurice better for the future and pay the costs hereby occasioned.

In the suit betw. Epaphroditus Lawson, Pltf., and Francis Timberlake, Deft., for £3.17 and 1.5 pennies due by account. On hearing the parties and the evidences in this cause, it is opinion of the Court that the sd. Pltf. recover against the sd. Deft., the sd. £3.17 and 1.5 pennies and costs.

In the suit betw. Moses Robinson, Pltf., and William Robinson, Deft., by petition for one-fourth part of the Estate of Moses Robinson, dec'd, James Ball, Gent. and Thomas Chattin are appointed to settle the matter in dispute betw. the sd. parties on this suit. And, by consent there report to be the evidence in this suit and it is Ordered that the sd. report be made to the next Court.

In the action upon the case betw. William Brent, Pltf., and John Galloway, Deft., Thomas Bridgford became Special Bail for the sd. Deft. in this suit.

Whereupon, the sd. Deft. pleaded and the Pltf. joined issue, whereupon it is Ordered that the trial of the sd. issue be referred till next Court.

The action of debt betw. John Irons, Pltf. and Robert Biscoe & Charles Mearnes, Defts., by consent doe the parties is continued till next Court.

In the action betw. Robert Mitchell, Gent., Pltf. and Nicholas Cary, Deft., for 1,303 lbs. tobacco due by account, as in the declaration as set forth. James Ball, Gent., becoming Special Bail for the Deft., in this suit, the parties were fully heard, and Judgment is granted to the sd. Pltf. for the sd. amount and costs. And, it is Ordered that the sd. Pltf. be allowed 2% for what of the tobacco is not paid in a crop note.

Robert Reach came in to Court and agreed to voluntarily serve Thomas Murphy 2 years after the 2nd December next. In consideration that the sd. Thomas is to teach him the trade of a weaver and t o find and provide for him sufficient diet, lodging, apparel, and at the expiration of his servitude to give him a suit of Drugget clothes, a hat, a pair of shoes and stockings and 2shirts, which is Ordered to be recorded.

Ordered that the Court be adjourned till the 2nd Wednesday in September next. At a Court for Lancaster Co., on Wednesday, in 10th day of September 1735. Present: William Ball, William Ball, Junr., Henry Lawson, William Tayloe, Joseph Chinn & Joseph Carter; Gent., Justices.

Winny, a Negro girl, belonging to the Rev. John Bell, is by the Court adjudged to be 14 years of age.

Jenney, a Negro girl, belonging to Patrick Connelly, is by the Court adjudged to be 11 years of age.

Ordered that the Sheriff provide a substantial stock lock and pad locks for the prison door of this Co., and get the door mended and the locks set on and the bar fixed with substantial staples and that it be forthwith done at the charge of the Co.

William Galloway and Martha, his wife, and Henrietta Everitt came into court & acknowledged their deed to John Webb for and concerning land. The sd. Martha being privately examined; which was recorded.

The Inventory of the Estate of Thomas Carter, dec'd, was returned and Joan Carter, his Execx., making oath & her subscription thereon; Ordered to be recorded.

Pg 129. The Inventory of the Estate of Andrew Donaldson, dec'd, was returned and Mary Donaldson, his Execx., making oath and her subscription on same, was recorded.

The suit betw. Moses Robinson, Pltf., and William Robinson, Deft., by petition, neither party appearing; is dismissed.

In the action of debt betw. John Irons& John Jenns, Pltf., & Robert Biscoe & Charles Mearns, Defts., for £5.17.0 due by obligation under the Defts. hands as in the declaration, the Defts. pleaded and the Pltfs. joined issue, whereupon the trial being referred to the court, it is considered that the sd. Pltf. recover against the sd. Defts., the said amount of £5.17.0, and costs and one attorney's fee.

Joseph Ball, Esqr., having misbehaved himself towards this Court and in a particular manner towards Col. William Ball and William Ball, Junr., members now sitting on this bench. It is Ordered that for his obscene he forthwith give security for his good behavior. Whereupon, the sd. Joseph Ball, and Thomas Edwards, of St. Mary's White Chappel Parish in open Court ackn. themselves jointly and severally indebted to the King, in the sum of £50 to be levied on their goods & chattels, lands & tenements to the use of the King under Condition for the good behavior of the sd. Joseph for one year from the date thereof.

In the case of William Brent, Pltf., and John Galloway, Deft., for 1,100 lbs. tobacco in the declaration for John Mott, George Kirk, William Oliver, John Yerby, Martin Shearman, Robert Biscoe, Henry Newby, Thomas Carter, James Cammell, David Flint, William Shelton and George Yerby were impaneled and sworn to try the issue joined in the cause & bringing in their verdict in these words – "We, the Jury do find for the Pltf. 1,089 lbs. tobacco. Signed: Martin Shearman, Forman. The sd. verdict on the Motion of the sd. Pltf. is recorded and it is considered that the Pltf. recover against the sd. Deft., the sd. amount of tobacco and the damage afsd. by the Jury afsd. assessed and costs together with an attorney's fee.

Thomas George having attended one day as witness for John Galloway in the suit by William Brent, Ordered he pay the sd. George for his attendance.

James Curtis having attended one day as witness for John Galloway in the suit by William Brent, Ordered he pay the sd. Curtis for his attendance.

In the action of Trespass & Assault & Battery betw. Ann Hines, Pltf., and John Mott, Deft., an Imparlance is granted him till next Court.

In the suit betw. Thomas Bridgford, Pltf., and Henry Lawson, Gent., Deft., by petition Thomas Lawson & Thomas Hunton are appointed to value the horse mentioned in the Pltf.'s account in this case and Thomas George, William Oliver, and George Warrick were appointed to value the work mentioned in the sd. Account. And, it is Ordered that a report of the proceedings herein be made to the next Court.

Ordered that the Court be adjourned till the 2nd Wednesday in October next. At a Court for Lancaster Co., on Wednesday, in 29th day of September 1735, for the examination of Robert Dickson on suspicion of Felony. Present: William Ball, William Ball, Junr., Joseph Chinn & Joseph Carter; Gent., Justices.

Robert Dickson charged with the Felonious taking of a silver watch from Capt. George Heale, being brought to the Bar. He confessed that he had the watch but that he took the same not with an intent to steal it, that only [can't read] of a Drunken Frollick and that he designed to carry it home that night he was taken with it. Whereupon, Charles Brady and Nicholas C[can't read], the witnesses against the sd. Prisoner were sworn and examined and Mature Deliberation being had on the whole Premises, it is the opinion of the Court that the sd. Robert Dickson ought not to be tried for his afsd. fait at the General Court but that he receive at the Public Whipping post of this Co., five lashes on hi s bare back, well laid on for his afsd. offense and pay all the costs hereby occasioned and then discharged.

Pg 130. At a Court for Lancaster Co., on Wednesday, in 8th day of October 1735. Present: William Ball, Henry Fleet, William Ball, Junr., Henry Lawson, Joseph Heale, William Tayloe, & Joseph Carter; Gent., Justices.

William Sanders, a servant, belonging to David Alexander Flint, confessing he had run away from his sd. Master's service 29 days. Ordered that he serve his sd. Master for the same 58 days after his time by Indenture Custom or former order of Court is expired as the law directs.

William Sanders, a servant, belonging to David Alexander Flint, came into Court and voluntarily agreed to serve his Master six months after his time by

Indenture Custom or firmer order of Court is expired in consideration of the great loss his sd. Master has sustained by his running away.

Benjamin Brown came into Court and ackn. his deed to George Payne for concerning 175 a. of land in this Co, which on the Motion of the sd. George is admitted to record.

Ann Brown, wife of Benjamin Brown came into Court and relinquished her Right of Dower to the lands and premises in the sd. deed conveyed and also admitted to record.

The Will of Giles Robinson, dec'd, was presented in Court by Agnes Robinson, his Execx., who made oath thereto and proved by the oath of Robert Mitchell, Gent., a witness thereto, is admitted to the record and obtaining probate.

Ordered that George Payne, Thomas Flint, Thomas Chattin and James Straton, or any three of them to appraise the Estate of Giles Robinson, dec'd, in money and submit a report at next Court and Agnes Robinson, Execx., of the Estate to appear with the Inventory.

John Kirk, Orphan of Thomas Kirk, dec'd, 11 years old the 26th of September last, on the prayer of Sarah Reeves, his mother, is by the Court bound to John Wale, of this Co., till he attains the age of 21 years, his sd. master to teach him to read & write & the trade of Weaver and to find sufficient diet, lodging, apparel, and at the expiration of his servitude to pay him as is appointed for servants by Indenture or custom.

In the case betw. James Ball and George Ball, Gent., Execs. of David Ball, Gent., dec'd, Pltfs., and Wm. Ball, Junr., Gent., Deft., for £12 as in the Declaration is set forth & the Pltfs. not appearing, is dismissed.

In the case betw. William Ball, Gent., Pltf., and William Shelton, Deft., by petition for 248 lbs. tobacco on balance of account at the parties by their attorneys, Mr. Tarpley for the Pltf., and Edwin Conway, Gent., for the Deft., were fully heard. Were upon, it is considered that this suit be dismissed and that the sd. Pltf. pay to the Deft. his costs.

George Brent, having attended 2 days as a witness for William Shelton in the suit brought against him by Wm. Ball, Gent., it is Ordered that the sd. Shelton pay the sd. George for his attendance & costs.

Pg 131. John Yerby, having attended 2 days as a witness for William Shelton in the suit brought against him by Wm. Ball, Gent., it is Ordered that the sd. Shelton pay the sd. John for his attendance & costs.

John King, having attended 2 days as a witness for William Shelton in the suit brought against him by Wm. Ball, Gent., it is Ordered that the sd. Shelton pay the sd. John for his attendance & costs.

Benjamin Shelton, having attended 2 days as a witness for William Shelton in the suit brought against him by Wm. Ball, Gent., it is Ordered that the sd. Shelton pay the sd. Benjamin for his attendance & costs.

The action of Trespass & Assault & Battery betw. Ann Hynes, Pltf., and John Mott, Deft., for £50 damages as in the declaration is set forth; is dismissed.

In the suit betw. Thomas Bridgford, Pltf., & Henry Lawson, Gent., Deft., by petition. The order of the last Court appointing Thomas Lawson & Thomas Hunton to value the horse mentioned in the Pltf.'s account in this cause. And, Thomas George, William Oliver and George Warrick to value the work mentioned in the sd. account not being performed is renewed. And, it is Ordered that the same be performed and a report thereof made to the next Court.

Ordered that the Co. Sheriff summon 24 Co. Freeholders, inhabitants, to appear at the next Court, that out of them a Grand Jury may be impaneled and sworn to make inquiry into the breach of the Penal Laws and to present the offenders.

Ordered that the Court be adjourned till the Second Wednesday in November next. At a Court for Lancaster Co., on Wednesday, in 12th day of November 1735. Present: William Ball, Henry Fleet, William Ball, Junr., Henry Lawson, Joseph Heale, William Tayloe, & Joseph Carter; Gent., Justices.

John Hart came into Court and acknowledged his Deed of Lease and Release to John Tully for and concerning 100 a. of land lying in Christ Church Parish in the Co., which were admitted to record.

The Will of Charles Hamond [Hamon?], dec'd, was presented in Court by Darcus Hamond, his Execx., being proved by the oaths of William Thomas, John Hart, & Clement Lattimer, witnesses thereto is admitted to record and probate was obtained.

Ordered that William Hayden, Thomas Hayden, John Simons and Benjamin George, Junr., or any three of them, being first sworn to appraise the Estate of

Charles Hamond, dec'd, in money and submit a report at next Court with Darcus Hamond, Execx., of the Estate to appear with the Inventory.

The Will of Edward Nicken, dec'd, was presented in Court by Mary Nicken, his wife, who made path thereto and proved by the oaths of Richard Weaver and Elizabeth Weaver, witnesses thereto admitted to record and probate was obtained.

Ordered that William Hutchings, John Meridith, Thomas Taff, and Gabriel Thatcher, or any three of them, being first sworn to appraise the Estate of Edward Nicken, dec'd, in money and submit a report at next Court with Mary Nicken, Execx., of the Estate to appear with the Inventory.

John Floyd, a servant man belonging to William Tiler[?] came into Court and freely & voluntarily ackn. to serve his sd. Master, 3 years, after his time by Indenture custom or former order of Court is expired in consideration that his sd. Master keep him to the Tailor's trade and instruct him therein during his servitude.

Pg 132. The appraisement of the Estate of Giles Robinson, dec'd, was returned and Agnes Robinson, his Execx. making oath according to her subscription on the Inventory; Ordered recorded.

Hannah Denny came into Court and made oath that Edmond Denny, late of this County, dec'd, departed this life without making a Will, and on his Motion & giving security, he was granted Letters of Admin., of the Estate.

Ordered that Benjamin George, Junr., William Hayden, Thomas Hayden, & Clement Lattimer, or any three of them, and going before a Co. Justice, to appraise the Estate of Edmond Denny, dec'd, in money and submit a report at next Court with Hannah Denny, Admin., of the Estate to appear with the Inventory.

In the suit betw. Joseph Heale, Gent., Pltf., and Agnes Robinson, Exec. of Giles Robinson, dec'd, Deft., by Petition for 488 lbs. of tobacco, due by bill under the hand and the sd. Pltf. making oath that he had never received any part of the sd. debt, Judgment granted him for the same, and it is Ordered that the sd. Deft. pay the same to the sd. Pltf. out of the Estate of the sd. dec'd, with costs.

The action of Detinue betw. Lawrence Blade, Pltf., and Christopher Collins, Deft., neither party appearing; dismissed.

The action of debt betw. John Carter, Esqr., one of the Church Wardens of Christ Church Parish, in this Co., Pltf., and Elizabeth Branson, Deft., for 500 lbs. tobacco & cask or 50 Shillings, as on the Declaration; dismissed.

The action of debt betw. John Carter, Esqr., one of the Church Wardens of Christ Church Parish, in this Co., Pltf., and Ann Powell, Deft., for 500 lbs. tobacco & cask or 50 Shillings, as on the Declaration; dismissed.

In the suit betw. Thomas Bridgford, Pltf., and Henry Lawson, Gent., Deft., by petition for 770 lbs. tobacco, due by account, Judgment is granted to sd. Pltf., for 633 lbs. tobacco & costs.

A Grand Jury for the Co., being impaneled, and the Court having appointed Bryan Pullen, Foreman, and sworn, and then the others, to wit. James Cammell, William Reves, William Pinckard, Thomas Pinckard, William Sydnor, Wm. Dogget, John Stott, Junr., Henry Newby, William Mitchell, John King, George Lighte, Junr., Thomas Taff, William Miller, Peter Revere, William Edwards, Thomas Taylor, Thomas Young and Peter Miller, who were sworn, then withdrew and after time returned to Court and gave their Presentments, and were then discharged.

The Sheriff made proclamation that the Court was about to Lay the County Levy, they proceeded accordingly. Lancaster Co. Levy - 1735

Lancaster Co. – **<u>Pounds of Tobacco:</u>**

John Carter, Esqr., for keeping the Public Ferry one year -1,260

Thomas Edwards, Court Clerk, for public service – 900

John Tarpley, Junr., Attorney for the King in this Co. - 900

John Pines [Pynes?] for cleaning the Court House & other services – 720

Hugh Brent, Gent., Sheriff of the Co. for Public Service – 900

Mr. Secretary Carter for filing & recording two coroner's Inquests & Constable fees – 100

Mr. Secretary Carter for a Commission of the Peace to Administer Oaths - 160

Mr. Secretary Carter for issuing a writ for Election of a Burges - 350

Mr. Edwin Conway for his attendance as a Burges at the last Session of Assembly & for coming & going – 6,700

Mr. Edwin Conway for Ferrages - £1.3.6

Capt. James Ball for his attendance as a Burges at the last Session of the Assembly & for coming & going – 5,273

Capt. James Ball for Ferrages - £1.3.6

Mr. Nicholas Martin for one Coroner's Inquest – 133

Matthias James for summoning the Jury for the same - 50

Dale Carter, Sub. Sheriff on his Account – 158

William George, late Sub. Sheriff on his Account - 60

George Brent for bringing 6 books of the Laws for the Clerk & Justices from Williamsburgh - 150

Edward Sanders, Constable for viewing tobacco scuccors in his precinct – 72

Thomas Flint, Constable for the same – 302

George Yerby, Constable for the same & for one levy over charged last year – 243

Henry Horne, Constable for viewing tobacco succors – 146

John Bailey, Constable for the same - 176

Matthias James, Constable for the same - 192

William Dogget, Constable for the same – 202

Dale Carter, Sub. Sheriff on his account - 492

William Ballendine for two levies over charged last year - 35

The Salary for receiving 6,420 lbs. tobacco at 4 percent - 250 lbs.

Total – Salaries 6,891

228

Income

By Squirrels and Crow's heads wanting 300 – 600

The last years fraction in the Sheriff's hands – 468

1,410 Tithables at 4 % Pol – 5,640 Fraction to be allowed the Sheriff next year – 183.

Total Income – 6,891

The present Levy this year 1735 amounting in the whole to 400 lbs. tobacco per Pol. It is Ordered that the Sheriff collect so much from every tithable person in this Co. and pay same to the County Creditors, as the law directs.

Ordered that John Carter, Esqr., do keep the Public Ferry over Corotomon River the ensuing year and that he be paid for the same as usual.

Ordered that John Pyne do find this Court with water and candles and clean the Court house the ensuing year and that he be paid for the same as usual.

Pg 133. Thomas Hunton having attended 2 days as a witness for Thomas Bridgford in his suit by petition against Henry Lawson, Gent. Ordered that the sd. Bridgford pay the sd. Thomas Hunton for his attendance according to Law & costs.

Ordered that the Court be adjourned till the 2nd Wednesday in December next.

Memorandum, that this 10th day December, 1735, by virtue of the Commission of the Peace and a Dedimus relating thereto both dated 1 Nov last past, directed to William Ball, George Heale, Edwin Conway, James Ball, Henry Fleet, Joseph Heale, William Tayloe, Joseph Chinn, Joseph Carter and William Stepto, Gent. William Tayloe and Joseph Chinn, administered the Oaths to the Government to Edwin Conway & James Ball, who subscribed the test and took the oaths appointed by a late Act of Assembly, of this Colony, to be taken by Justices of the Peace. And, Administered the sd. Oaths & Test to Henry Carter, Joseph Heale, Joseph Carter, and William Tayloe and Joseph Chinn.

At a Court for Lancaster Co., on Wednesday, in 10th day of December 1735. Present: Edwin Conway, James Ball, Henry Carter, Joseph Heale, William Tayloe, Joseph Chinn, Joseph Carter; Gent., Justices.

Ordered that the Co. Sheriff acquaint William Ball, George Heale, Robert Mitchell, Nicholas Martin, Henry Lawson, John Heale, and William Stepto, Gent., that they be at the next Court to be sworn to the Commission of Peace for this Co.

Ordered that Thos. Lawson, Epaphroditus Lawson and John Stepto for the processioning for Fleet's Bay Precinct in Christ Church Parish be summoned to the next Court to answer the Complaint of Thomas Hunton concerning the processioning of the Bounds of his land in the sd. Precinct.

Pg 134. Ordered that Richard Wooding be summoned to answer the petition of John Samon against him at next Court.

Ordered that Joseph Burr be summoned to answer the petition of John Samon against him at next Court.

The Will of Denis Conree, dec'd, was presented to Court by John Conree, his Exec., who made oath, and being proved by the oaths of the sd. Exec., and Probate was Ordered.

Ordered that Moses Taylor, James Taylor, Benjamin Taylor, and John Everit, or any three of them, and going before a Co. Justice, to appraise the Estate of Dennis Conree, dec'd, in money and submit a report at next Court with John Conree, Admin., of the Estate to appear with the Inventory.

The action of Debt betw. Robert Gibson, Pltf., and John Griggs, Deft., for 500 lbs. tobacco damages in the declaration is set forth, neither party appearing; dismissed.

In the suit betw. James Ball & Edwin Conway, Gent., Execs., of the Will of Charles Burges, Gent. dec'd, , Pltf., and John Woodson, Deft., for £4.0.4 & half penny; is dismissed.

The action upon the case betw. Robert Mitchell, Junr., Pltf., and James Stott, Deft., for dealing with his Negro, contrary to Laws of this Colony, in such cases made and provided, as is set forth & neither party appearing; dismissed.

The action on the case betw. Presley Neale, Exec., of the Will of John Cooper, dec'd, Pltf., and John Heale, Gent., Deft., for 1,140 lbs. tobacco & Pltf. not appearing; dismissed.

230

The suit betw. Mary Donaldson, Exec. of the Will of Andrew Donaldson, dec'd, Pltf., and James Garton, Deft., by petition is continued at the Pltf.'s costs till next Court.

James Ball and Joseph Chinn, Gent., are appointed to try the weights at Deep Creek Warehouses as the Law directs, betw. this and the next Court.

Ordered that the Court be adjourned till the 2nd Wednesday in January Next. At a Court for Lancaster Co., on Wednesday, in 11th day of February 1735. Present: Edwin Conway, James Ball, Henry Carter, William Tayloe, Joseph Chinn, Joseph Carter; Gent., Justices.

Samuel Hinton is appointed Surveyor of the highway from the Church to Maj. Fleet's in Christ Church Parish in this Co. for this year.

By virtue of the Commission and a Dedimus relating thereto William Ball & Nicholas Martin, Gent., having taken oaths to the government and subscribed the test and had the oaths appointed by the late Act of Assembly, to be taken by Justices of the Peace, administered to them. Present – William Ball & Nicholas Martin, Gent., Justices.

John Pollard is appointed Constable in St. Mary's White Chappel Parish in his Co., in the room of the sd. John Bailey, dec'd[?]. It is Ordered that he be summoned to the next Court to be Sworn.

Pg 135. The Will of Henry Fleet, Gent., dec'd, was presented in Court, by Samuel Hinton, one of his Execs., who made oath thereto & being proved by oath of David Pugh, one of the witnesses, was thereto admitted to record, and on Motion the Exec. obtained Probate.

Ordered that John Stepto, Junr., Thomas Lawson, Epaphroditus Lawson, and William Martin, or any three of them are to appraise the Estate of Henry Fleet, Gent, dec'd, in money & make & present a report, along with Samuel Hinton, Exec., at the next Co. Court.

James Machan, orphan of Mathias Machan, dec'd, by the consent of John Mott, is by the Court bound to James Stewart till he attains 19 years of age, the sd. Stewart to teach him to what learning he has and to teach him the trade of Taylor and to find sufficient diet, lodging, apparel, and at the expiration of his servitude to pay him as is appointed for servants by Indenture or custom, & if the afsd.

James Stevens died before his servitude is ended, the sd. Apprentice is to be free.

William Potter, orphan of John Potter, dec'd, is by the Court bound to William Stott, his Exec., & Admin., till he attains the age of 21 years, he or they are to learn him to read & write and the trade of Weaver, and to find sufficient diet, lodging, apparel, and at the expiration of his servitude to pay him as is appointed for servants by Indenture or custom.

On the prayer of Nicholas Lawson, orphan of Epaphroditus Lawson, dec'd, Nicholas Martin, Gent. is appointed his Guardian. Ordered that the sd. Martin forthwith possess himself with the Estate of the sd. Orphan and exhibit an account of the same at next Court.

It appearing to this Court that Joseph Coats is incapable of supporting and bringing up his children. Order that the Church Wardens of St. Mary's White Chappel Parish bind out the sd. children as the law directs.

James Brent having taken the oaths to the Governor, and subscribed the test, had the oath of the Co. Under Sheriff administered to him.

Ellison Davis, orphan of Henry Davis, dec'd, is by the Court bound to John Gollover & Ann, his wife, till she attains the age of 18 years & they are to teach her to read, sew, knit & spin, and to find sufficient diet, lodging, apparel, and at the expiration of her servitude to pay her as is appointed for servants by Indenture or custom.

The appraisement of the Estate of Denis Conree, dec'd, was returned and John Conree, Exec., making oath to his subscription; Ordered recorded.

The appraisement of the Estate of Edward Nicken, dec'd, was returned and Mary Nicken, Execx., making oath to his subscription; Ordered recorded.

The appraisement of the Estate of Edmond Denny, dec'd, was returned and Hannah Denny, Admin., making oath to his subscription; Ordered recorded.

The complaint by Thomas Hunton against Thomas Lawson, Epaphroditus Lawson, John Stepto, Junr., processioners, for Fleet's Bay Precinct in Christ Church Parish in this Co., is dismissed.

On the petition of William Ballendine against Joseph Burne, for the Estate of Ellinor Beck, dec'd, for Administration whereof he was security with the sd.

Joseph Burne, the sd. Joseph being summoned and not appearing, it is Ordered that the sd. Joseph forthwith deliver the sd. Estate to the sd. petitioner for his indemnification and pay the costs hereby occasioned.

The petition of John Samon[?] against Richard Wooding, for his wife's part of her father Thomas Pierce's Estate, is dismissed.

In the suit betw. Mary Donaldson, Execx., of the Will of Andrew Donaldson, dec'd, Pltf., and James Garton, Deft., for 449 lbs. of tobacco, which was due to the sd. dec'd, in his lifetime, by Judgment of this Court. Judgment is granted to the sd. Pltf. against the sd. Deft., for the afsd. debt. It is Ordered that the sd. Deft. forthwith pay the same to the sd. Pltf, with costs.

The suit betw. Richard Chapman, Pltf., and Abraham Currell and Elizabeth, his wife, and William Hebron, and his wife, Judith, Execs., of the Will of Henry Fleet, Gent., dec'd, Deft., by petition for 554 lbs. tobacco due by account, is dismissed.

Pg 136. The action of debt betw. Tobias Horton, Pltf., and Alexander Campbell, Deft., for 1,800 lbs. tobacco, per Declaration as set forth, neither party appearing, is dismissed.

The suit betw. Tobias Horton, Junr., Pltf., and William Brent, Deft., by petition for £4.6.6, by amount neither party appearing, is dismissed.

The suit betw. Alexander Campbell, Pltf. and Tobias Horton, Deft., for £10 damages, is set forth and neither party appearing, is dismissed.

The suit betw. John Carter, Charles Carter & Landon Carter, Esqrs., Execs. of the Honorable Robert Carter, Esqr., dec'd, Pltfs., and Abraham Currell and Elizabeth, his wife, and William Hobson & Judith, his wife, Execs. of Henry Fleet, Gent., dec'd, Defts., for 1,025 lbs. tobacco, or £6.8.1 and half-penny, & neither party appearing, is dismissed.

In the suit of Debt betw. Frances Burges, widow, & Edwin Conway & James Ball, & Gent, Execs., of the Will of Charles Burges, Gent, dec'd, Pltfs., a Richard Wooding, Deft., for 2,190 lbs. tobacco due by note, on hearing the parties, Judgment was granted to the sd. Pltf., against the Deft, for 1,780 lbs. tobacco & costs.

In the suit of Debt betw. Frances Burges, widow, & James Ball, & Edwin Conway, Gent, Execs., of the Will of Charles Burges, Gent, dec'd, Pltfs., a

Richard Haines, Deft., being called and not appearing on the Motion of the Pltfs., a conditional Judgment is granted them against the sd. Deft. and Christopher Stephens, his security, for what shall appear to be justly due to ye sd. Pltfs., at the next Court unless the sd. Deft., shall then appear & answer the sd. action.

In the suit betw. Edwin Conway and James Ball, Gents, Execs. of the Will of Charles Burges, Gent, dec'd, Pltfs., and George Finch, Deft., by petition for 808 lbs. tobacco due by Bond under the Deft's hand, dated 12 May 1732. Judgment is granted to the sd. Pltf., against the Deft, for the sd. same to be discharged upon paying 404 lbs. tobacco, the principal debt together with interest on the same till the sd. 404 lbs. tobacco shall be fully satisfied & costs.

In the debt betw. John Carter, Charles Carter, and Landon Carter, Esqr., Execs. of the Will of Robert Carter, Esqr., dec'd, Pltfs., and Elizabeth Lee, Execx. of the Will of Thomas Lee, Gent., dec'd, Deft., for £5.7.1 & half-penny, due by account, neither party appearing; dismissed.

In the debt betw. John Carter, Esqr., Church Wardens of Christ Church Parish, in this Co., Pltf., and Elizabeth White, Deft., for 500 lbs. tobacco & cask or 50 shillings, per the Declaration; neither party appearing; dismissed.

In the suit betw. Thomas Edwards, Pltf. and Thomas Davis, Deft., for £1.11.3 money & 836 lbs. tobacco; dismissed.

In the suit betw. James Ball, Gent., Pltf, and George Finch, Deft., by petition for £2.11.6 due by balance of an account. Judgment is granted to the Pltf. for the Deft. to pay the afsd. debt & costs.

In the suit betw. James Hubbard, merchant, Pltf., and Eaton Reeves, Deft. by petition for £2.8.2, due by account. Judgment is granted to the Pltf. for the Deft. to forthwith pay the afsd. debt & costs.

In the Debt betw. Frances Burges, widow, to James Ball and Edwin Conway, Gent., Execs. of the Will of Charles Burges, Gent. dec'd, Pltf., and John Brown, Deft., for 1,049 lbs. tobacco due by Bond; dismissed.

Nicholas Martin, Joseph Heale, & William Tayloe, Gent., are by the Court presented to the Hon. Lt. Governor, as persons fit & able to execute the Office of Co. Sheriff for the ensuing year.

Ordered that the Court be adjourned till the 2nd Wednesday in March Next. At a Court for Lancaster Co., on Wednesday, in 10th day of March 1735. Present: William Ball, Edwin Conway, James Ball, Nicholas Martin, Joseph Carter; Gent., Justices.

Pg 137. By virtue of the Commission of he Peace & a Dedimus relating thereto Henry Lawson, John Heale & William Stepto, Gent., having taken the Oaths to the Government subscribed the Test and had the oaths appointed by a late Act of Assembly of this Colony to be taken by Justices of the Peace administered to them. Present – Henry Lawson, John Heale, & William Stepto, Gent. Justices.

John Pollard & Thomas Flint took the oaths to the Government and subscribed the test and had the oath of Constable for St. Mary's White Chappel Parish, administered to them.

On the petition of Robert Biscoe leave is given him to set gates and draw barrs cross the main road which leads through his plantation from Christ Church to Majr. Fleet's,

This Court is satisfied by three of the bench that the new main road that Mr. Henry Lawson cleared through his plantation from Christ Church to Major Fleets is a better way and nearer the old road. Ordered that the sd. Lawson have liberty to shut up his gates, that is a cross the sd. old road and open his ditch.

Agnes Grier came into Court and voluntarily ackn. to serve Capt. William Ball, 3 years from the 25th of December next, in consideration the sd. Ball pay David Blair, Mariner, what was due to him for her passage into this Colony and to allow her at the expiration of her servitude what is appointed for servants by Indenture or Custom.

On the petition of John Miller against Henry Taylor. Ordered that the sd. Henry be summoned to answer the sd. petition at next Court.

John Rogers and Elizabeth Rogers, Orphans of William Rogers, dec'd, and Thomas Flint is appointed Guardian, with Capt. William Ball, as his Security fir the sd, Guardianship, who entered recognizance in the sum of £200 to the Justices of the Court, that the sd. Orphans shall be fully and justly paid what Estate shall become due to them when they come of age, and it is Ordered that the sd. Thomas Flint be forthwith possessed with the Estate of the sd. Orphans and be exhibited thereof on oath to the Court.

On petition of Potsifull [Persifull?]Pierce against Thomas Pullen Ordered the sd. Thomas be summoned to answer the sd. Petition; next Court.

The appraisement of the Estate of Charles Hamond, dec'd, was returned and Darius Thomas, as his Exec., making oath according to subscription on the Inventory; Ordered recorded.

On the Motion of Daniel Stephens, Exec. of John Ferman, dec'd, praying to be advised what he should be allowed for the tobacco he had paid in discharging of the debt due to the Creditors of the sd. dec'd. It was the opinion of the Court that he be allowed for the same after the rate of 12 shillings, 6 pence per hundred.

On the Motion of Samuel Brumley setting forth that he was security with Hannah Bush, for her Admin. on the Estate of Isaac Bush, dec'd., & that the sd. Hannah is now dead. It is therefore Ordered that the sd. Samuel forthwith take into his possession the Estate of the sd. Isaac for his Indemnification.

In the Debt betw. Frances Burges, widow, to James Ball and Edwin Conway, Gent., Execs. of the Will of Charles Burges, Gent., Pltf., and Richard Harnes[?], Deft., for £7.6.0 due by bond, dated 23 Oct 1732, the Deft. came into Court and contest Judgment for the sd. same and consent of the sd. Deft., it was Ordered that Col. Ball deliver up so much of the sd. Deft.'s Estate that is now on the sd. Ball's plantation, as will be of value sufficient to be satisfy the sum of £3.13.0 shall be fully satisfied and Costs.

The suit betw. Thomas Edwards, Pltf., and Henry Duke, Deft., by attachment; dismissed.

Pg 138. In pursuance to a clause in the Act of Regulating Ordinarys & restraint of Tipling houses, the Court doth set & rate: Rum at 8 shillings the gallon. Punch with loaf sugar at 12 the Quart. Cider at 12 pence the gallon. Madera wine at two shillings the quart. Strong beer at 15 pence the Quart. Claret at 4 shillings the Quart. Red port at 4 shillings the Quart. White wine at 4 shillings the Quart. Dyet with small beer to drink at 10 shillings the meal. Lodging at 6 pence the night. Corn at 6 pence the gallon. Stabloage & fodder for a horse at 6 pence the night.

Ordered that the Court be adjourned till the 2nd Wednesday in April Next. At a Court for Lancaster Co., on Wednesday, in 14th day of March 1736. Present:

Edwin Conway, James Ball, Henry Carter, Henry Lawson, Nicholas Martin, Joseph Chinn, William Stepto; Gent., Justices.

James Ball, Gent., came into Court and ackn. his deed of Indenture of bargain & sale to Joseph Chinn, Gent., for & concerning 340 a. of land lying on Morrattico Creek, in St, Mary's White Chappel Parish, in this Co.; admitted to record.

On the petition of Robert Embry against the Estate of Charles Hamond, dec'd, for 752 lbs. tobacco, due by account, the sd. Petitioner & making oath to his claim, Judgment is granted him against Wm. Thomas and Darcus, his wife, Execs., of the sd. dec'd for the sd. debt. It is Ordered that he pay same to the sd. Robert out of the Estate of the dec'd in their hands & costs.

On the petition of Peter Cox against John Porter, Ordered the sd. Porter be summoned to next Court to answer the petition.

The appraisal of the Estate of Henry Fleet, Gent., dec'd, was returned and Samuel Hinson, one of the Execs. making oath & his subscription on the Inventory; Ordered recorded.

On the information of Samuel Hinton, Surveyor, of the highways from Christ Church to Major. Fleet's against Robert Biscoe, Thomas Hunton, and Mary Harwood for running their fences too near the main road. Ordered that John Stepto, William Martin and Abraham Currell view the sd. road and make their report to the next Court.

Ordered that the Co. Sheriff summons at least 24 freeholders & inhabitants of this Co., to appear at next Court for a Grand Jury to make inquiry as to the breach of the penal laws and to present the offenders.

On petition of Potsifull [Persifull?]Pierce against Thomas Pullen, Admin. of Thomas Pierce, dec'd, for 50 shillings due to time for his part of the sd. dec'd father's Estate. Ordered that the sd. Thos. Pullen pay the same to Wm. Samon for the use of the sd. Potsifull Pierce with costs.

On the petition of John Miller against Henry Taylor, for one suit of clothes, which he, the sd. Henry was to pay him at the expiration of his servitude, as by an Order of this Court, dated 12 January1725, will appear. It is therefore Ordered that the sd. Henry pay the sd. John Miller, one suit of good Drugget Clothes lined & thoroughly trimmed and pay the costs hereby occasioned.

The suit betw. Thomas Edwards, Pltf., and Thomas Davis, Deft., by attachment is continued till next Court, at Pltf.'s costs.

Pg 139. In the action of debt betw. Hon. Thomas Lee, Esqr., Pltf. and Charles Cox, Deft., the sd. Deft being called and not appearing on the Motion of the Pltf., Judgment is granted him against Deft., and Hugh Brent, Co. Sheriff, for what shall appear to be justly to the sd. Pltf. at the next Court unless, the sd. Deft. shall then appear and answer the sd. action.

The action of debt betw. Thomas Edwards, Pltf., and Charles Cox, Deft., is discontinued.

The action of Trespass & Assault & Battery betw. Thomas English, Pltf., and Francis Scott, Deft., for £20, as in the Declaration; is dismissed.

The action of debt betw. James Ball, Gent., Pltf., and John Parish, Deft., for 3,276 lbs. tobacco, due by Bond and account, as in the Declaration. The sd. Deft. confessed Judgment for 440 lbs., tobacco due by account & 2,807 lbs. tobacco due by his bond, dated 12 Aug 1734, wherefore, it is considered that he forthwith pay the sd. 3,247 lbs. tobacco to the sd. Pltf., with interest on the tobacco mentioned in the bond, till the same be fully satisfied & costs.

The action of the case betw. James Ball, Gent., Pltf., and William Sydnor, Deft., for 1,000 lbs. tobacco damage, as in the Declaration is set forth; dismissed.

In the action of debt, betw. John Hart, Pltf., and William Thomas, and Darcus, his wife, Execs. of Charles Hammond, dec'd, Deft., for 1,096 lbs. if tobacco due by account, per the Declaration, the sd. Pltf making oath to the truth of his account, Judgment granted him for his sd. debt and it is Ordered that the sd. William Thomas & Darcus, his wife, Execs., pay the same to the sd. Pltf. out of the Estate of the sd. dec'd, in their hands, with costs.

Ordered that Samuel Hinton, one of the Execs. of Henry Fleet, Gent., dec'd, deliver to Henry Lawson, Gent., the books of the VA Laws in his possession.

Ordered that the Court be adjourned till the 2nd Wednesday in May Next. At a Court for Lancaster Co., on Wednesday, in 12th day of May 1736. Present: William Ball, Edwin Conway, James Ball, Henry Carter, Henry Lawson, Wm. Tayloe, Joseph Chinn, Joseph Heale, Joseph Carter, William Stepto; Gent., Justices.

238

A deed from Rawleigh Chinn to Rawleigh Chinn, Junr., for & concerning 30 a. of land in St. Mary's White Chappel Parish, in this Co., was proved in open Court by the oaths of Joseph Ball, Esqr., Joseph Chinn and John Chinn, witnesses and on Motion of Rawleigh Chinn, Junr.; admitted to record.

The last Will of Christopher Kirk, dec'd, was presented in Court by John Stepto, his Exec, who made oath thereto and was proved by oaths of William Hutchings, and William Stepto, Gent., witnesses & it was admitted to record, and on Motion by the Exec., Probate was granted.

Ordered that William Hutchings, John Yerby, George Brent, and John Merideth, or any three of them being first sworn before a Co. Judge, are to appraise the Estate of Christopher Kirk in money and make a report of same along with John Stepto, Exec., with the Inventory at the next Court.

The Will of William Wren, dec'd, was presented in Court by Elizabeth Wren, his Execx., who made oath & proved by the oath of Charles Jones, a witness, thererto, was admitted to record, and by Motion by Execx., obtained probate.

Ordered that Epaphroditus Lawson, John Stepto, Junr,., and Robert Biscoe and Thomas Lawson, or any three of them, being first sworn before a Co. Judge, are to appraise the Estate of William Wren, in money and make a report of same along with Elizabeth Wren, Execx., with the Inventory at the next Court.

Pg. 140. The last Will of John Cox, dec'd, was presented in Court by Ann Cox, Execx., who made oath and being proved by the oaths of Robert Biscoe & James Fleming, witnesses, and on Motion probate was obtained.

Ordered that William Martin, Isaac Currell, Abraham Currell and Robert Biscoe. or any three of them being first sworn before a Co. Judge, are to appraise the Estate of John Cox, dec'd, in money and make a report of same along with Ann Cox, Execx., with the Inventory at the next Court.

The probate of the Will of Henry Fleet, Gent., dec'd, heretofore proved in Court, was granted to Thos. Edwards, one of the Execs., named in the Will.

The Will of Thomas Chattin, dec'd, was presented to Court by George Doggett & Joseph Chattin, Execs., who made oath & being proved by the oath of Thos. Dallis, a witness, it was admitted to record and Probate was obtained.

Ordered that Bryan Pullen, John Rogers, John Callahan and Nathaniel Carpenter, or any three of them being first sworn before a Co. Judge, are to appraise the Estate of Thomas Chattin, dec'd, in money and make a report of same along with George Dogget and Joseph Chattin, Execs., with the Inventory at the next Court.

A writing under the hand of Margaret Chattin, widow of Thomas Chattin, dec'd, renouncing any benefit of the Will of the dec'd, was presented in Court by her and was admitted to record.

A deposition of Thomas Dallis relating to the Will of Thomas Chattin, dec'd, was proved and Ordered recorded with the Will.

Thomas Edwards made path to his account against Philemon Gregory for 278 lbs. of tobacco and £21.10.2, which was Ordered to be certified.

Ordered that the Co. Sheriff to contrive the scales & weights this day delivered up by Thomas Edwards, and also the scales and weights & measures, in the hands of the Execs. of the last Major Henry Fleet, dec'd, into the possession of Col. William Ball, President of this Court at the charge of this Co.

The Will of John Pyne, dec'd, was presented in Court by Christopher Stephens, his Exec., who made oath thereto and was proved by the oaths of Laurance Blade and John Stephens, witnesses, was admitted to record and Probate was obtained.

Ordered that Daniel Stephens, Joseph Stephens, John Pinckard and William Chilton, or any three of them being first sworn before a Co. Judge, are to appraise the Estate of John Pyne, dec'd, in money and make a report of same along with Christopher Stephens, Exec., with the Inventory at the next Court.

On the Petition of Christopher Stevens, he is appointed to clean the Court House and to provide candles and water in the place of John Pyne, dec'd, and to be paid for the same as usual.

William Tayloe, Gent., producing the Governor's Commission appointing him Co, Sheriff took the oath to the Government and subscribed the test and had the oath of Co Sheriff administered to him.

Pg 141. A bond from William Tayloe, William Ball and James Ball, Gent., to the King, for £1,000, was in Court ackn. by the above three persons, to be their act and Ordered to be recorded.

Dale Carter & Wm. Dogget having taken the oaths to the Government, subscribed the test and the oath of Co. Under-Sheriff, administered to them.

Stephen Mullis being appointed Constable in Christ Church Parish, in this Co., in the room of William Dogget, the sd. Stephen Took the oath to the Government, subscribed the test and took the oath of Co. Constable administered to him.

Ordered that Christopher Stevens be summoned to next Court to answer the petition of Frances Gorden against him.

William Ball, Gent, is appointed to take the list of Tithables in the Lower Precinct of St Mary's White Chappel Parish, in this Co. for this year.

James Ball, Gent, is appointed to take the list of Tithables in Morattico Precinct of St Mary's White Chappel Parish, in this Co. for this year.

Joseph Heale, Gent., is appointed to take the list of Tithables in the Middle Precinct of St Mary's White Chappel Parish, in this Co. for this year.

Henry Carter, Gent., is appointed to take the list of Tithables in the Lower part of Corotomon Precinct, in Christ Church Parish in this Co. for this year.

William Stepto, Gent., is appointed to take the list of Tithables in the betw. Corotomon River and the main road, which leads from the Church to Col. Carter's Great Mill in Christ Church Parish in this Co., for this year.

Edwin Conway, Gent., is appointed to take the list of Tithables in the Upper Part of Corotomon Precinct in Christ Church Parish and in Wiccocomoco Parish in this Co, for this year.

Nicholas Martin, Gent., in the Middle & Lower Precincts in Christ Church Parish in this Co., for this year.

James Wayton, & Rebecca, his wife, came into Court and ackn. their deed endorsed to John Everit, for and concerning 36 a. of land in this County, and the sd. Rebecca being first privately examined, and was recorded.

William Chilton is appointed Surveyor of the Highways from this Co. Court House to Mrs. Judith Paynes and the rolling road from the sd. Chelton's to the main road in St. Mary's White Chappel Parish in this Co. for this year.

James Brent is appointed Surveyor of the Highways from Mrs. Judith Paynes to Mrs. Burges's Mill in St. Mary's White Chappel Parish in this Co. for this year.

John Pollard is appointed Surveyor of the Highways from Deep Bottom Run to the Church and from the cross roads that leads from Mr. Joseph Chinn's down to the wharf of the Deep Bottom Creek Warehouses in St. Mary's White Chappel Parish in this Co. for this year.

John Mott is appointed Surveyor of the Highways from the road that leads by John Stott's to Moraticco main road in St. Mary's White Chappel Parish in this Co. for this year.

John Rogers is appointed Surveyor of the Highways from the road Deep Bottom Run to Moraticco Mill in in St. Mary's White Chappel Parish in this Co. for this year.

John Mitchell is appointed Surveyor of the Highways from Mrs. Burges's Mill to Mr. Selden's Mill in St. Mary's White Chappel Parish in this Co. for this year.

George Payne is appointed Surveyor of the Highways from Bartholomew Woods to the cross roads near Doctor Thornton's in St. Mary's White Chappel Parish in this Co. for this year.

Thomas Taylor is appointed Surveyor of the Highways from the main road to Cardiff's old field and also of the rolling road in the precinct in St. Mary's White Chappel Parish in this Co. for this year.

William Goodridge is appointed Surveyor of the Highways and the rolling road, which leads from the Church to Carpenter's Landing in the precinct in St. Mary's White Chappel Parish in this Co. for this year.

Pg 142. John Porter is appointed Surveyor of the Highways from Mr. Selden's Mill to Mr. Secretary Carter's Mill and the main road in Wiccocomoco Parish in this Co. and that he take to his assistance, the male laboring Tithables belonging to Capt. Edwin Conway, Mr. William Tayloe, Richard Boatman and John King and the male laboring Tithables on the north side the sd. road in Christ Church Parish and in Wicocomoco Parish in this Co. for this year.

Thomas Yerby is appointed is appointed Surveyor of the Highways of all the road betw. the two branches of Corrotomon River in Christ Church Parish in this Co. for this year.

242

George Yerby is appointed Surveyor of the highways from Mr. Secretary Carter's Mill to the Cross Roads in Christ Church Parish in this Co., for the year. And, it is Ordered that he take to his assistance the male laboring Tithables belonging to the Plantation before Ordered to assist him, besides those belonging to the sd. Precinct.

George Flower is appointed Surveyor of the highways from the Cross Roads to the Clerk's Office in Christ Church Parish in this Co. for this year.

Anthony Sedner [?] is appointed Surveyor of the highways from Mr. Charles Carter's Mill to the main road, which leads from the Clerk's Office in Christ Church Parish in this Co. for this year and he is to keep the sd. road in good repair with the male laboring Tithables belonging to the sd. Carter in the sd. Precinct.

Hezekiah Kirk is appointed Surveyor of the highways from the Church to the Cross Roads in Christ Church Parish in this Co. for this year, and he is to keep the sd. road in good repair with the male Laboring Tithables belonging to Mr. Secretary Carter in the sd. Precinct.

William Martin is appointed Surveyor of the highways from Mr. Charles Carter's Mill to the white stone and of all the main roads in Nantepoizen Neck in Christ Church Parish in this Co. for this year.

John Yerby is appointed Surveyor of the highways from Mr. Secretary's Carter's Quarter on the mouth of the eastern branch of Corotomon River to the sd. Mill Road and from the road to the Church in Christ Church Parish in this Co. for this year.

On the prayer of Matthias Rofe, of St. Mary's White Chappel Parish in this Co. setting forth that he is very ancient and past his Labor, it is Ordered that he be excised from paying any Country or County Levy for the future.

In the suit betw. Thomas Edwards, Pltf., and Thomas Davis, Deft. by attachment against the Estate of the sd. Deft., the sd. Pltf. made oath to the truth of his debt and Judgment is granted him against the sd. Deft., for £1.11.3 & 836 lbs. tobacco in the hands of Thomas George. It is Ordered that the sd. Thomas George pay the same to the sd. Pltf. and that this attachment be dismissed.

The action of debt betw. Thos. Lee, Gent, Pltf. and Charles Cox, Deft., for £12.9.4 & half-penny, as is set forth the Conditional Ordered of the Court on 14

April last against the sd. Deft., and Thomas Edwards, his security, was confirmed and Judgment to the sd. Pltf., against the sd. Deft. and his security for the debt with interest from the time of payment, with attorney's fee and costs. But, execution is to be stayed till Christmas next.

The suit by Petition betw. Peter Cox, Pltf., and John Porter, Deft., for freedom dues is dismissed.

In the suit betw. James Ball, Gent., Pltf., and Thomas English, Deft., by petition for £4.10.5 due by account, the Deft came to Court and confessed Judgment for the debt, & Ordered that he pay the same to the Pltf., with costs.

The suit betw. Thos. Edwards, Pltf., and Robert Hughs [Hughes?], deft. by petition in continued till next Court.

Pg 143. In the suit of Alexander Harrower, Pltf., and Wm. Lewis, Deft., by Petition for 205 lbs. tobacco due by account, the sd. Pltf., making oath to his claim, Judgment is granted to him for the debt and it is Ordered the Deft. pay same with costs.

The suit betw. Thomas Edwards, Pltf., and John Griggs, Deft., by petition for £2.5.5 due by account, and Deft. called and not appearing, and the Pltf. making oath of his account, Judgment is granted him for sd. debt and is Ordered that the Deft. pay the debt & costs.

The suit betw. Alexander Harrower, Pltf., and George Light, Deft., for 302 lbs. of tobacco due by note and account is dismissed.

The suit betw. Judith Payne, Pltf., and Arthur Neale, Deft., by for 400 lbs. of tobacco due by the balance of an account; dismissed.

The action of Detinue betw. John Ball, Pltf., and Thomas Pinckard, Gent, Deft., is continued to next Court at Pltf.'s Motion & costs.

The action of debt betw. William Eustace, Gent., Pltf., and William Thomas and Darcus Thomas, Execs., of Charles Hamond, dec'd, Deft. The sd. Deft being called and not appearing nor any security returned, Judgment is granted to the sd. Pltf. against the sd. Deft., and Hugh Brent, Gent, & Co. Sheriff, for what shall appear to be justly due to the Pltf. at the next Court, unless the sd. Deft. do then appear & answer the sd. action.

The suit of debt betw. Matthew Zuill, Gent., Pltf., and Richard Curtis, Deft., for 4,200 lbs. tobacco due by obligation is set forth, the Deft came into Court confessed Judgment for 675 lbs. of tobacco to the sd. Pltf. and costs.

A Grand Jury for the Co. was impaneled by Court order, having appointed George Payne, foreman, who was sworn, and called Epaphroditus Lawson, Thomas Yerby, John Stepto, John Yerby, Thomas Hubbard, Thomas Hunton, George Flower, George Dogget, William Edwards, Benjamin George, Junr., John Simmons, Richard Lewis, John Mott, Robert Biscoe, James Cammell, William Goodridge, William Chilton, Henry Horne, Isaac White, Robert Mc Tire, Nathaniel Carpenter, and George Young, who having received their charge withdrew and after some time returned to Court and gave their Presentments and were discharged, which Presentments were by the Court Ordered to be recorded and are as follows – "We of the Grand Jury do make the following Presentments." Signed: George Payne, Foreman.

Elizabeth Nash, of Christ Church Parish for being delivered of a child 11 months after her husband's death within 7 days.

James Barton of St. Mary's White Chappel Parish for absenting from Church for one whole month last past.

John Stewart of St. Mary's White Chappel Parish for absenting from Church for one whole month last past.

Charles Cox, of Christ Church Parish for absenting from Church for one whole month last past.

John Coates of St. Mary's White Chappel Parish for being a common swearer.

Thomas Stott, of St. Mary's White Chappel Parish for being a common swearer.

John Mc Math, and his wife, Jane, of Christ Church Parish for absenting from Church for one whole month last past.

Thomas Scott of Christ Church Parish for being a common swearer.

William Nelms of Christ Church Parish for being a common swearer.

Ordered that James Barton, John Stewart, John Coates and Thomas Stott of St. Mary's White Chappel Parish., of this Co., were summoned to the next Court to answer the Grand Jury Presentment against them.

Ordered that Elizabeth Nash, Charles Cox, John Mack Math and, Jane, his wife, Thomas Scott & William Nelms, of Christ Church Parish, in this Co., be summoned to the Court to answer the Presentments against them.

Pg 144. The suit betw. Alexander Harrower, Pltf., and Wm. Chilton, Deft. by petition for 1 shilling and 325 lbs. tobacco due by account. Judgment is granted to the sd. Pltf. against the sd. Deft., for 1 shilling and 373 lbs. of tobacco, being the balance of the account, to pay forthwith with costs.

The suit betw. Peter Harley and Helen[Hannah?], his wife, Pltf., and Henry Horne and Catherine, his wife, Execx. of Wm. Dare, dec'd, Defts., no appearance; dismissed.

The report of John Stepto, Junr., and William Martin, and Abraham Currell, persons appointed by Court to view the main road which leads by Mary Harwood's, Robert Bisco's and Thomas Hunton's plantations by the Information of James Hinton, Surveyor, thereof is returned & Ordered to be recorded, and the information of the said surveys against the sd. Mary Harwood, Robert Bisco and Thomas Hunton, discontinued.

Ordered that the Court be adjourned till the 2nd Wednesday in June Next. At a Court for Lancaster Co., on Wednesday, in 14th day of July 1736. Present: William Ball, Edwin Conway, James Ball, Henry Lawson, Joseph Chinn, John Heale, Joseph Heale, William Stepto; Gent., Justices.

The Act of Assembly concerning Public Claims was read in Court.

Robert Hughs making oath that he had not received and satisfaction for taking up a servant man belonging to Richard Langson, of Northumberland Co. It is Ordered that the Clerk of this Court certify the same to the General Assembly.

Bryan Pullen making oath that he had not received and satisfaction for taking up a servant man belonging to Charles Stagg, of York Co. It is Ordered that the Clerk of this Court certify the same to the General Assembly.

Ezekiel Gilbert that he had not received and satisfaction for taking up a servant man belonging to Robert Key, of Caroline Co. It is Ordered that the Clerk of this Court certify the same to the General Assembly.

At a Court for Lancaster Co., on Wednesday, in 14th day of July 1736. Present: William Ball, Edwin Conway, James Ball, Henry Lawson, Joseph Chinn, John

246

Heale, Joseph Heale, Henry Carter, Nicholas Martin, Joseph Carter, William Stepto; Gent., Justices.

The Will of Robert Wells, dec'd, was presented in Court by Hannah Wells, Execx., who made oath & being proved by the oath of Wm. Abby, a witness, it was admitted to record and probate was obtained.

Ordered that John Pollard, William Sydnor, John Parish and Henry Newby, or any three of them being first sworn before a Co. Judge, are to appraise the Estate of Robert Wells in money and make a report of same along with Hannah Wells, Execx, with the Inventory at the next Court.

The appraisement of the Estate of John Pynes, dec'd, was returned and Christopher Stephens, his Exec., making oath to his subscription on the Inventory; Ordered recorded.

Pg 145. The appraisement of John Cox, dec'd, was returned and Ann Cox, his Execx., made oath to her subscription on the Inventory; Ordered recorded.

The appraisement of the Estate of Christopher Kirk, dec'd was returned and John Stepto, his Exec., making oath to his subscription on the Inventory; Ordered recorded.

The appraisement of the Estate of William Wren, dec'd was returned and Elizabeth Wren, his Execx., making oath to his subscription on the Inventory; Ordered recorded.

The appraisement of the Estate of Thomas Chattin, dec'd was returned and George Dogget. Joseph Chattin, his Execs., making oath to his subscription on the Inventory; Ordered recorded.

On the prayer of Joseph Chattin, orphan of Thomas Chattin, dec'd, & Margaret Chattin is appointed his Guardian, with John Mott, her security, for her Guardianship, and was Ordered that sd. Margaret be possessed with the Estate of the sd. Orphan and exhibit an account thereof at next Court.

On the petition of Christopher Stephens, he was admitted to keep an Ordinary at his dwelling house in this Co., with Walter Arms, his security.

Christopher Stevens, Exec., of the Will of John Pynes, dec'd, exhibited and made oath to his account against the sd. Estate, for £3.12.0, which being examined in Court, was allowed.

Grippa, a Negro boy belonging to Joseph Carter, Gent., was adjudged to be 12 years of age.

Rose, a Negro girl belonging to Joseph Carter, Gent., was adjudged to be 11 years of age.

Margaret Reason, Orphan of Michael Reason, aged 8 years the 7th of Sept. next, is by the Court bound to John Stott, till she attains the age of 18 years & her sd. Master to teach her to sew, knit & spin, and to find her sufficient diet, lodging, apparel, and at the expiration of her servitude to pay her as is appointed for servants by Indenture or custom.

The suit betw. Thomas Edwards, Pltf., and Robt. Hughs, Deft., by petition for 309 lbs. tobacco, due by account, the Deft. came into Court and confessed, Judgment for the afsd. debt Ordered to be paid to Pltf. with costs.

The action of Detinue betw. John Ball, Pltf., and Thomas Pinckard, Deft.; continued to next Court at Pltf.'s Motion and costs.

In the action of debt betw. William Eustace, Gent., Pltf., and William Thomas and Darcus, his wife, Execx., of Charles Hamond, dec'd. for 3,000 lbs. tobacco due by account, as set forth, the Deft., being called & not appearing, the Pltf. made oath that 242 lbs. tobacco was justly due to him on the account. Judgment granted him for same & Ordered the Deft. pay same out of the Estate of the dec'd that is in their hands, with costs.

The suit betw. Frances Gorden, Pltf., and Christopher Stephens, Execs., of the Will of John Pyne, dec'd, Deft., £6 for two years wages, the Pltf. not appearing, is dismissed.

In the suit betw. Thos. Edwards, Pltf., and William Thomas, Deft., by petition for 354 lbs. tobacco due by account, the Deft, not appearing and Pltf. making oath that 336 lbs. tobacco, the balance of the account was justly due; Ordered Pltf. pay same with costs.

In the suit betw. Robert Hughs, Pltf., and Thos. Williams, Deft., by petition for £2 due on account, the parties being heard, Judgment granted to Pltf., for £1.5.0 and Deft. to pay same with costs.

The suit betw. Peter Cox, Pltf., and Jno. Webb[?], Deft., by petition for 300 lbs. tobacco; dismissed.

Pg 146. In the suit betw. Robert Biscoe, Pltf, and Christopher Stephens, Exec., of John Pynes dec'd, Deft., by petition for 340 lbs. tobacco, and Pltf. granted the sd. debt and costs. Ordered the sd. Deft. pay same from the Estate.

In the suit betw. John Woodbridge, Gent., Pltf., and George Gibson , Deft. by petition for 483 lbs. tobacco due by a Judgment of this Court dated 12 Feb 1734, the Deft. being called and not appearing, the Pltf. made oath that 397 lbs. of tobacco was justly due. Judgment granted Pltf. 97 lbs. of tobacco & costs.

The action of debt betw. Robert Mitchell, Gent. Pltf., and Thomas Taff, Deft., for 1,600 lbs. tobacco due by account; Pltf. not appearing; is dismissed.

On Presentment of the Grand Jury against Charles Cox, of Christ Church Parish, for being absent a month from Church and also swearing. He was called and not appearing, Judgment is granted to the Church Wardens against him for 10 shillings or 100 lbs. tobacco, and it is Ordered he pay the same to the Church Wardens for the use of the poor of the sd. Parish, with costs.

On Presentment of the Grand Jury against John Mc Math, and Jane, his wife, of Christ Church Parish, for being absent a month from Church and being summoned and not appearing; Judgment is granted to the Church Wardens for £5 or 50 lbs. tobacco for the use of the poor of the sd. Parish, with costs.

On Presentment of the Grand Jury against Thomas Scott of Christ Church Parish, for being a common swearer and he being summoned and not appearing; Judgment is granted to the Church Wardens for £5 or 50 lbs. tobacco for the use of the poor of the sd. Parish, with costs.

On Presentment of the Grand Jury against Wm. Nelmes of Christ Church Parish, for being a common swearer and he being summoned and not appearing; Judgment is granted to the Church Wardens for £5 or 50 lbs. tobacco for the use of the poor of the sd. Parish, with costs.

On Presentment of the Grand Jury against James Barton of St. Mary's White Chappel Parish, for being absent for one month Judgment is granted to the Church Wardens for £5 or 50 lbs. tobacco for the use of the poor of the sd. Parish, with costs.

On Presentment of the Grand Jury against John Steward of St. Mary's White Chappel Parish, for being absent for one month, and being summoned and not appearing; Judgment is granted to the Church Wardens for £5 or 50 lbs. tobacco for the use of the poor of the sd. Parish, with costs.

Pg 147. On Presentment of the Grand Jury against John Coates, of St. Mary's White Chappel Parish, for being a common swearer, and being summoned and not appearing; Judgment is granted to the Church Wardens for £5 or 50 lbs. tobacco for the use of the poor of the sd. Parish, with costs.

On Presentment of the Grand Jury against Thos. Stott, of St. Mary's White Chappel Parish, for being a common swearer, and being summoned and not appearing; Judgment is granted to the Church Wardens for £5 or 50 lbs. tobacco for the use of the poor of the sd. Parish, with costs.

The action of debt betw. Thos. Edwards and Saml. Hinton, Execs., of the Will of Henry Fleet, Gent., dec'd, Pltfs., and Richard Haines and John Davis, Defts., for £7.10.0 on the Motion of sd. Pltfs., awarded to them, returnable at next Court.

In the suit betw. Daniel Hornby, Gent., Pltf., and Richard Van Landigan, Gent. Deft., by petition for 418 lbs. tobacco by account. Deft. being called and not appearing & Pltf. making oath to the truth of his account Judgment is made against Deft. for the debt & costs

On the Petition of John Bell, Clerk, exec. of Charles Smith, Clerk, dec'd against George Brent, Exec., of Thos. Purcel, dec'd, for 2,328 lbs. tobacco due by account. Ordered the sd. Brent be summoned to answer the petition at next Court.

John Merryman, Pltf., and Alexander Matson, Deft., by petition for 830 lbs. tobacco due by obligation under the Deft. hands, dated 3 Jan 1734/5, the parties fully heard, Judgment granted to Pltf. for 690 lbs. tobacco.

The suit betw. Thos. Edwards, Pltf., and Thos. Burnet, Deft. by petition for £2.11.3 & 87 lbs. tobacco due by account, the Deft. called and not appearing, and Pltf. making oath to his account for 251 lbs. justly due to him on account; Ordered the Deft. pay 250 lbs. tobacco with costs.

Pg 148. Ordered that the Court be adjourned till the 2nd Wednesday in July Next. At a Court for Lancaster Co., on Wednesday, in 11th day of August 1736. Present: William Ball, Henry Carter, Henry Lawson, Joseph Chinn, John Heale, Joseph Heale, Joseph Carter, William Stepto; Gent., Justices.

On the petition of Thos. William against Hannah Wells, Execx., of Robt. Wells, dec'd, Ordered she be summoned to answer the sd. petition at next Court.

By virtue of the Commission of Peace & dedimus relating thereto George Heale, Gent., having taken the oaths of the Government, the test and had oaths appointed by late Assembly of the Colony to be taken by justices of the peace administered to him.   Present – George Heale, Gent.

David Flint making oath that he had never rec'd any satisfaction for taking up a servant belonging to Mosely Battley of Spotsilvania Co., it is Ordered that the Court Clerk certify the same to the General Assembly.

Cavan Dulany, Gent., producing his Commission empowering him to plead as an attorney in the Co. Court took the oaths to the Gov. subscribed the test and oath appointed to be taken by attorney practicing in the Co. Courts administered to him.

Sary, a Negro girl, belonging to Eliz. Wren is by the Court adjudged to be 12 years of age.

The Will of Robt. Wells, dec'd, proved by the oath of William Abby, a witness thereto, is admitted to record.

Timothy Collins, a servant man, belonging to James Rob confessing he had run away from his Master's service 5 days and his sd. Master making appear that he had expended 200 lbs. tobacco in regaining hi. It is Ordered that the sd. Timothy serve his Master 3 calendar months & 10 days for the same after his time by Indenture Custom or former order of Court is expired.

A deed from Peter James Bailey to James Ball, Gent., for & concerning 50 a. of land in St. Mary's White Chappel Parish, in this Co., was ackn. by the sd. Peter James Bailey to sd. Ball; recorded.

On the Petition of Feilding Nash & Hannah, his wife, against John Bailey & Mary, his wife, Admins. of Wm. Pitman, dec'd, for the petitioners part of sd. William Pitman's Estate in the hand of the sd. John & Mary by consent of the parties, Robert Mitchell, John Heale & Jos. Chinn, Gent., or any three of them are appointed to examine, state and settle the accounts relating to this Cause and to make their report at next Court.

Pg 149. The Presentment of the Grand Jury against Elizabeth Nash of Christ Church Parish, in this Co., for being delivered of a child 11 months after her husband's death within 7 days; is dismissed.

The suit by Petition betw. the Rev. John Bell, Exec., of Charles Smith, Clerk, dec'd, Pltf., & George Brent, exec., of Thomas Purcel, dec'd, is continued till next Court.

The action of Detinue betw. John Ball, Pltf., and Thomas Pinckard, Gent., Deft., the Deft. pleaded and the Pltf. joined, whereupon it is Ordered that the trial of the issue be referred till next Court.

The last Will of Wm. Ballendine, dec'd, was presented in Court by Charles Ewell, of the Execs., who made oath thereto and proved by the oath of William Bertrand, a Witness thereto is admitted to record and the Motion the Exec. obtained Probate.

Ordered that Charles Ewell, Exec., of the Will of Wm. Ballendine, dec'd, bring an Inventory of the sd. Estate to the next Court.

Ordered that the Court be adjourned till the 2nd Wednesday in September Next. At a Court for Lancaster Co., on Wednesday, in 8th day of September 1736. Present: Henry Carter, Henry Lawson, Joseph Chinn, John Heale, Joseph Carter, William Stepto; Gent., Justices.

William Chelton is appointed to clear a rolling road from his gate to the main road that leads to the Court House in his precinct.

The appraisement of the estate of Robt. Wells, dec'd, was returned and Hannah Wells, his Admin., making oath according to her subscription on the Inventory.

On the petition of James Doggett, it is Ordered that the Surveyor of this Co. set apart the Dower of sd. Mary Dogget in certain lands & premises belonging to the petitioner in Christ Church Parish, in this Co., & possess the sd. Mary therewith and make a report of his proceedings therein to the next Court.

Phillis, a Negro girl, belonging to George Payne is by the Court adjudged to be 10 years of age.

Ordered that Margaret Chattin, Guardian of Joseph Chattin be summoned to the next Court to exhibit & make oath to an account of the sd. Orphan's Estate.

252

Ordered that Nicholas Martin, Gent., Guardian of Nicholas Lawson be summoned to the next Court & make Oath to an account of the sd. Orphan's Estate.

On the prayer of John Heale, Gent., Peter James Bailey's deed to John Bailey with the Clerk's Certificate of the acknowledgment of them on the order book be now recorded, it being omitted heretofore.

The action upon the case betw. James Ball, Gent., Pltf., and Hannah Wells, Execs., of the Will of Robt. Wells, dec'd. Deft. for 1,450 lbs. of tobacco due by account, the Pltf., making oath that 1,300 lbs. of tobacco, the balance of his sd. Account was justly due him. Judgment is granted him for the same and it is Ordered that the sd. Deft. pay the same plus costs to the Pltf. out of the Estate in her hands of the sd. dec'd.

Pg 150. Hannah Wells produced her account of the Admin. of her husband's Estate [Robt. Wells], which was allowed & admitted to record. Also, Ordered that the tobacco now due from the sd. Estate be allowed against the appraisement after the rate of 12 shillings & 6 pence percent.

In the suit betw. Thomas Williams, Pltf., and Hannah Wells, Execx., of the Will of Robert Wells, dec'd, by petition for 3 head of cattle. Judgment is granted to the sd. Pltf. against the sd. Deft. for a cow, a heifer going of 3 year old and a yearling, or £2.14.3, and it is Ordered that the sd. Deft. forthwith pay the cattle or money out of the Estate, which is in her hands, and Judgment is granted to the sd. Pltf. for cost, when assets shall come to the Deft's hands.

Sharper, a Negro boy, belonging to Wm. Miller is by the Court adjudged to be 12 years of age.

Nan, a Negro girl, belonging to Margt. Chatten is by the Court adjudged to be 10 years of age.

Duke, a Negro boy, belonging to Robt. Mitchell, Gent., is by the Court adjudged to be 13 years of age.

On the prayer of James Haines Ordered that his number of **Scalps** be added to the list of tithables returned by Mr. Martin to the last Court.

In the suit, betw. Fielding Nash & Hannah, his wife, Pltf., & John Bailey, and Mary, his wife, Admin. of Wm. Pitman, dec'd, Deft. It is the opinion of the Court that the tobacco mentioned in the auditors account be deducted out of the appraisement at 2 pence per pound and that the sd. account be again referred to the sd. auditors to settle and make a report of their proceedings to the next Court.

In the suit betw. John Bell, Clerk, Exec. of the Will of Charles Smith, Clerk, dec'd, Pltf., and George Brent, exec. of the Will of Thos. Purcell, dec'd, by petition for 3,588 lbs. tobacco due by account both parties agreed to be tried by the Court on the consent of the Pltf., it is the opinion of the Court that the balance of the above account amounting to 3,328 lbs. tobacco satisfy the Legacy's, Purcel's Children are entitled to from the sd. Smith's Will provided there be sufficient to pay the sd. Smith's debts without it and that this petition be discontinued.

The action of Detinue betw. John Ball, Pltf., and Thomas Pinckard, Gent., Deft., in continued till next Court at the Pltf.'s Motion & costs.

The suit betw. John Woodbridge, Gent., Pltf., and Arthur Neale, Deft., by Petition for 770 lbs., tobacco due by bill, the Deft., being called & not appearing, Judgment is granted to sd. Pltf. for his debt and it is Ordered that the sd. Deft. pay the same to the sd. Pltf. with costs.

The suit betw. Phillip Smith, Gent., Pltf. and Robt. West, Deft. by petition for £1.10.2 by account; is dismissed.

Pg 151. The action of Debt betw. Alexander Campbell, Pltf., and Robert West. Deft., for £5.0.5 due by account, and the Deft confessed; Judgment for the debt Ordered that he pay the same to Pltf. with costs.

Stephen Mullis, a Constable for Christ Church Parish: In this Co., making return that he found two tobacco seconds upon the plantation of Wm. Pinckard in this Precinct and it appearing to the Court that the sd. seconds were not turned out in contempt of the Acts for preventing the same and that they were destroyed in the presence of the sd. Constable . It is considered that the sd. Wm. be excused from any prosecution for this breach of the sd. act, on paying the costs hereby occasioned.

Ordered that the Court be adjourned till the 2nd Wednesday in October Next. At a Court for Lancaster Co., on Wednesday, the 13th day of October 1736. Present: William Ball, Edwin Conway, Henry Carter, John Heale, Nicholas Martin, Joseph Chinn, Joseph Carter, William Stepto; Gent., Justices.

254

Nicholas Martin, Gent, exhibited and made oath to his account of the Estate of Nicholas Lawson, an Orphan under his Guardianship, which is Ordered to be recorded.

Ordered that the Sheriff summon 24 Co. inhabitants, freeholders, to appear at the next Court, and that out of them a grand jury my be impaneled & sworn to make inquiry in the breach of the penal laws & to present the offenders.

A Letter of Attorney from Isaac Cundiff to Isaac Basey, was this day proved in Open Court by the oaths of John Webb and Jonathan Cundiff, witnesses thereto and by the Court, admitted to record.

A Letter of Attorney from Mary Cundiff to Isaac Basey, was this day proved in Open Court by the oaths of John Webb and Jonathan Cundiff, witnesses thereto and by the Court, admitted to record.

Daffney, a Negro girl, belonging to Richard Edwards, son of Thomas Edwards, Gent., is adjudged by the Court to be 10 years of age.

Dick, a Negro boy, belonging to Barnabus Birch, is adjudged by the Court to be 14 years of age.

In the suit betw. Fielding Nash and Hannah, his wife, Pltfs., and John Bailey, and Mary, his wife, Adminx., of the Estate of Wm. Pitman, dec'd, Defts., by petition the report of Robert Mitchell, John Heale and Joseph Heale, Gent., auditors appointed to settle the Account in this cause, was returned and it is Ordered that the sd. report be recorded and that the suit be dismissed.

Pg 152. In the suit betw. James Doggett, Pltf., and Mary Doggett, Deft., by petition, by consent of both parties, Henry Carter & William Tayloe, Gent., and George Brent are appointed to set apart the Dower of the sd, Mary Doggett in certain lands and premises belonging to the sd, petitioner in Christ Church Parish, in this Co., and possess the sd. Mary, therewith and make report of their proceedings to the next Court.

The action of Detinue betw. John Ball, Pltf., and Thomas Pinckard, Gent., Deft., is continued till next Court at the Deft. Motion and costs.

 The suit betw. Thomas Thornton, Pltf., and Hannah Wells, Execx. of Robert Wells, dec'd, by petition for 350 lbs. tobacco due by bill; dismissed.

Wm. Ball, Junr., Gent., came into Court and made oath that his account against the Estate of Eliza. Keene, dec'd, was justly due to him. Ordered that the Clerk of this Court certify the same on the sd. account.

William Ball & Joseph Carter, Gent., are appointed to try the Seals & Weights at the Warehouses at Davis's and Queens Town by the Standard Weights of this Co., according to Law.

Ordered that the Co. Sheriff give notice by setting up Notes at the Church Doors of this Co., that if no person appears to Admin. on the Estate of Elizabeth Keene, dec'd, at the next Court, an order will be then made for the Sheriff to sell the sd. Estate at Public Outcry.

William Ball & Joseph Chinn, Gent., are appointed to try the Scales & Weights at the Warehouses at Deep Creek by the Standard Weights of this Co. according to Law.

Ordered that the Court be adjourned till the 2nd Friday in November Next. At a Court for Lancaster Co., on Friday, the 12th day of November 1736. Present: William Ball, Edwin Conway, James Ball, Nicholas Martin, John Heale, Joseph Heale, Joseph Chinn, Joseph Carter, William Stepto; Gent., Justices.

Ordered that Benjamin Neale and Thomas Taylor be summoned to the next Court to answer the Presentment of the Grand Jury against them.

In the suit betw. James Dogget, Pltf., and Mary Dogget, Deft., by petition on the prayer of both parties Edwin Conway, Gent., is appointed to set apart the Dower of the sd, Mary in certain lands and premises belonging to the Pltf. in Christ Church Parish, in this Co., as also to determine the whole difference betw. them on this suit and fir him to make a report at next Court and by consent of the sd. parties, the sd. determination is to conclude them in this matter.

Pg 153. Ordered that Henry Horne & Catherine, his wife, of the Execs. of Wm. Dare, dec'd, be summoned to the next Court to answer the petition of Peter Harley & Elinor, his wife, against them.

On the prayer of Charles Hamond, by Wm. Eustace, Gent., his Guardian, & William Thomas and Darius, his wife, Execx., of Charles Hammond, dec'd, Clement Lattimer, Benja. George, Junr., and Wm. Pasquet are appointed to examine, rate and settle the sd. Execx., her account of the Administration of the sd. deceased Estate, and it is Ordered that they deliver to the sd. William

Eustace, the sd. Orphan's part of the same and make a report of their proceedings at next Court.

On the prayer of George Turbervile, Gent., a deed from Charles Kelly[?] & Jane, his wife, to William Simmons for and concerning 62 a. of land in this Co. together with a certificate of acknowledgment of the sd. deed by the sd. Charles & Jane by the Court, admitted to record.

A bond from George Heale, Gent., to Judith Heale, widow for £500, being proved by the Oath of Thomas Edwards, a witness thereto, was by the Court admitted to record.

A Grand Jury for the body of this Co., being this Impaneled, according to the Order of the last Court and the Court having appointed William Stephens, foreman, who was sworn & then the rest who having received their charge withdrew & after sometime returned into Court and gave in their Presentments and were discharged, which Presentments were by the Court Ordered to be recorded and are as follows: At a Court held in Lancaster Co., on Friday the 12th of Nov. 1736, we of the Grand Jury make a Presentment, as follows: Against Benjamin Neale for swearing of Five Oaths this day against Thomas Taylor for not keeping a lawful Bridge at Matthew Machan's Swamp. Signed: Wm. Stephens, Foreman.

The Will of George Heale, Gent, dec'd, was presented to Court by John Heale & Joseph Heale, Gent., Execs., herein named whereupon William Davenport & Elizabeth, his wife, one of the daughters of the sd. dec'd. entered a Caveat against the proving thereof and time is given the sd. Parties till the next Court, for a hearing on the premises.

On the attachment granted to Richd. Jackson, merchant, against the Estate of Edward Anderson for 2,918 lbs. of tobacco by account, the sd. Richard making oath to the truth of his account. Judgment is granted him against the sd. Edward for his sd. debt with an Attorney for and costs & Judith Payne on whom this attachment was served appearing, made oath that she had in her hands, of the Estate of the sd. Edward £45 as a security, for her answering so munch money to a certain John Sears in case a bill of Exchange drawn by Saml. Gwyn for that sum to the sd. Edward & by the sd. Edward endorsed to the sd. John should be returned protested. Order that in case the afsd. Bill of Exchange should not be returned protested & recovery of the sd. money made against the sd. Judith Payne that she pay unto the sd. Richard the contents of this Judgment out of the sd. £45.

Pg 154. John Wanghop, Gent. came into Court and made oath that Eliza. Keene, late of this Co., dec'd, died without a Will, and on his Motion and giving security for his just and faithful Admin. of the sd. Estate of the deceased, and Administration of the Estate was granted.

Ordered that Joseph Stephens, Daniel Stephens, Walter Armes, and George Light, Junr., any three of them being first sworn before a Co. Judge, are to appraise the Estate of Elizabeth Keene in money and make a report of same along with John Wanghop, Gent., Admin., with the Inventory at the next Court.

William Samon came into Court and made oath that Hannah Bush, late of this Co., dec'd, departed this life without a Will, and on his Motion, and giving security for his just and faithful Admin. of the sd. Estate of the deceased, and Administration of the Estate was granted.

Ordered that John Stott, Junr., William Sydnor, Henry Newby, & Edward Blackmore, any three of them being first sworn before a Co. Judge, are to appraise the Estate of Hannah Bush in money and make a report of same along with William Samon, Admin., with the Inventory at the next Court.

An Indenture betw. William Thomas and Darcus, his wife, & Elias Lowry, for and concerning the sd. Darcus, her title of Dower in 130 a. of land lying in Wicocomoco Parish, in this Co., was ackn. in open Court by the sd. William and Darcus, examined privately, and was admitted to record.

A bond for Elias Lowry to William Thomas & Darcus, his wife, for £60, was in Open Court ackn. by the sd. Ellis and admitted to record.

Ordered that the Court be adjourned till tomorrow morning. At a Court for Lancaster Co., on Saturday, the 13th day of November 1736. Present: William Ball, Edwin Conway, James Ball, Nicholas Martin, Joseph Heale, Joseph Chinn, Joseph Carter, William Stepto; Gent., Justices.

Pg 155. On the prayer of Margaret Chattin and George Dogget and Joseph Chattin, Execs. of Thomas Chattin, dec'd, Edwin Conway and James Ball, Gent., were appointed to set apart and deliver to the sd. Margaret, her Dower of the Estate of the sd. dec'd, and to make a report of their proceedings to the Court

Ordered that Margaret Chattin, Guardian of Joseph Chattin, exhibit & make Oath to an Account of the sd. Orphan's Estate to the next Court.

The Sheriff having made proclamation that the Court was about to Lay the County Levy, they proceeded accordingly. Lancaster Co. Levy

Lancaster Co. – **Pounds of Tobacco:**

John Carter, Esqr., for keeping the Public Ferry one year -1,260

Thomas Edwards, Court Clerk, for public service – 900

William Tayloe, Gent., Sheriff of this Co. for public service - 900

John Tarpley, Junr., Attorney for the King in this Co. - 900

Christopher Stephens for John Pynes for cleaning the Court House for 6 months & for the sd. Stephens performing the same the remaining part of the year - 720

Edward Saunders, Constable for viewing tobacco succors - 77

Thomas Flint, Constable for the same - 273

George Yerby, Constable for the same – 236

Henry Horne, Constable for a mistake last year - 253

John Pollard, Constable for viewing tobacco succors - 180

Matthias James, Constable for viewing tobacco succors – 182

Stephen Mullis, Constable, for the same – 208

John Carter, Esqr., on Account of Secretary fees – 449

Mrs. Frances Burges on her Acc't - £1.4.2

Jos. Chinn, Gent., on his Acc't – 6 shillings

Mr. Thomas Edwards on his Acc't - £22.16.9

Total - £24.6.11

Col. Conway for £8.19.0 money to be paid to Thos. Edwards for the Balance of the Account – 1,790 lbs. tobacco

Salary for Receiving – 9,020 lbs. at 6 per centum – 941 lbs. tobacco

The Public Levy – 10, 575

Total lbs. tobacco paid – 20,136

Contra - Credit

By Squirrels and Crow's heads wanting 387 - 774 lbs. tobacco

1,434 @ 13.5 tobacco per pol – 19,359 lbs. tobacco

A fraction to be allowed the Sheriff next Levy – 3 lbs. tobacco

Total – 20,136 lbs. tobacco

By Col. Conway for 1,790 lbs. tobacco = £8.19.0

Capt. Wm. Ball balance in his hands for the rent of Davis's for 1733 - £1.11.7

Mr. Joseph Carter for balance in his hands per centum of sd. Warehouses for 1734 & 1735 - £14

Total in Cash - £24.6.11

The Country & County Levy for this present year 1736 amounting in the whole to thirteen pounds & an half of tobacco per pol. It is Ordered that the Co, Sheriff collect so much of every Tithable person in this Co. and pay the same to the Country & County Creditors, as the Law directs.

Pg 156. Ordered that John Carter, Esqr., do keep the public ferry over Corotomon River, the ensuing year and that he be paid the same as usual.

Ordered that Christopher Stephens do find this Court with water & candles and clean the Court House the ensuing year and that he be paid for the same as usual.

On the action of Detinue betw. John Ball, Pltf., and Thomas Pinckard, Gent., Deft., the sd. Deft. having heretofore pleaded & the Pltf. joined the issue in this cause, William Stephens, George Dogget, Stephen Mullis, Henry Newby, William George, Junr., William Stamps, Henry Horn, William Hutchings, Alexander Matson, Benjamin George, Junr., Thomas George, and Joseph Stephens were impaneled and sworn to try the sd. issue, who bringing in a Special Verdict on the Motion of the sd. Pltf., it is admitted to record and it is Ordered that the argument thereon be referred till next Court.

William Pasquet having attended 2 days as a witness for John Ball in the suit against Thomas Pinckard, Gent., Ordered that he pay the sd. George Ball, Junr., for his attendance.

George Ball, Junr., having attended 3 days as a witness for John Ball in the suit against Thomas Pinckard, Gent., Ordered that he pay the sd. George Ball, Junr., for his attendance.

In the suit betw. Joseph George, Pltf., and Thomas George, Deft., by petition for 400 lbs. tobacco due for 40 days work; no appearance; dismissed.

In the suit betw. James Ball, Gent., Pltf., and Charles Hamilton, Deft., by petition for 653 lbs. tobacco due by balance of account, the sd. Pltf., making oath to the truth of his claim and the Deft. not appearing, Judgment granted him for his afsd. debt and costs.

Pg 157. The suit betw. James Patton, Pltf. and Edward Anderson, Deft., by attachment is continued till next Court at the Pltf.'s costs.

Ordered that the Court be adjourned the 2nd Friday on December. At a Court for Lancaster Co., on Saturday, the 10th day of December 1736. Present: William Ball, Edwin Conway, James Ball, Joseph Heale, Joseph Carter, William Stepto; Gent., Justices.

By virtue of the Commission of Peace & dedimus relating thereto Hugh Brent, Gent., having taken the oaths of the Government, the test and had oaths appointed by late Assembly of the Colony to be taken by justices of the peace administered to him.   Present – Hugh Brent, Gent.

Ordered that John Heale, Joseph Heale, Gent., Execs. of George Heale, Gent., dec'd, be summoned to the next Court to deliver up the books of the Laws, which have been delivered to the sd. dec'd, in his lifetime, as a Co. Justice, as the law directs.

In the suit betw. James Patton, Pltf., against Edward Anderson, Deft., by attachment of the sd. Deft's Estate for £2.10.7, due by account, the sd. Pltf. making oath to the sd. account, Judgment is granted him against the sd. Deft., for his sd. debt & costs, and the sd. attachment being served on one boat and the Estate of the sd. Deft., in the hands of Judith Payne. It id Ordered that in case the boat afsd. shall not be replevied, as the Law directs, the same be sold and disposed of for & towards a satisfaction of this Judgment in the same manner as goods taken in Execution by a Writ and that this attachment be continued till next Court.

Thomas Hubbard came into Court and made oath that Jane Robinson, late of this Co., dec'd, departed this life without making a Will, and on Motion and giving security for his just and faithful Admin. of the sd. Estate of the dec'd, the Letters of Admin. were granted.

Ordered that George Brent, John Hubbard, Peter Rivere, Junr., and John King, or any three of them being first sworn before a Co. Judge, are to appraise the Estate of Jane Robinson, dec'd, in money and make a report of same, along with Thomas Hubbard, Admin. of the Estate , and appear with the Inventory at the next Court.

The appraisal of the Estate of Elizabeth Keene, dec'd, was returned and John Waughop[?], Gent., Admin., thereof making oath according to his subscription on the Inventory; Ordered recorded.

Pg 158. On the petition of Chattin Chowning, he is appointed to keep the ferry, from his house to Urbanna cross Rappahanock River. Ordered that he give Bond for the same at the next Court.

Ordered that John Heale & Joseph Heale, Gent., Execs. of George Heale, dec'd, be summoned to next Court to deliver up the Books of Law, which have been delivered to the sd. dec'd, in his life time as a Co. Justice.

The suit betw. William Davenport & Elizabeth, his wife, Pltfs., against John Heale & Joseph Heale, Gent., Deft., on the caveat preferred by the sd. Pltf. against the proof of the Will of George Heale, Gent., dec'd, is continued till next Court.

On the Presentment of the Grand Jury against Benjamin Neale, of St. Mary's White Chappel Parish, in this Co., for swearing five oaths. Judgment is granted to the Church Wardens, of the afsd. Parish, against him for 25 shillings or 250 lbs. tobacco, and it is Ordered that the sd. Benjamin pay the same to the sd. Church Wardens, for the use of the poor of the sd. Parish, with costs.

On the Presentment of the Grand Jury against Thos. Taylor, of St. Mary's White Chappel Parish, in this Co., for not keeping a lawful bridge at Matthew Machan's Swamp, is dismissed.

In the suit betw. James Dogget, Pltf., & Mary Dogget, Deft., by petition the report of Edwin Conway, Gent., in this cause was returned. Ordered that the sd. report be recorded and that this suit be dismissed.

The suit betw. Peter Harley & Elliner, his wife, Pltfs., against Henry Horner & Catherine, his wife, one of the Execs. of William Dare, dec'd, by petition is dismissed.

The suit betw. Charles Hammond by William Eustace, Gent., his Guardian, Pltf., & WilliamThomas & Darcus, his wife, Execx. of Charles Hammond, dec'd, is continued till next Court.

Edwin Conway & James Ball, Gent., having returned their Report concerning the dower of Margaret Chattin, in the slave belonging to the Estate of Thomas Chattin, dec'd, the same is Ordered recorded and the further proceedings herein discontinued.

Margaret Chattin, Guardian of Joseph Chattin, this day returned an account of the sd. Orphan's Estate on Oath, which is Ordered to be recorded.

The action of Detinue betw. John Ball, Pltf., and Thos. Pinckard, Gent., Deft., is continued till next Court at the Pltfs. Motion & costs.

In the suit in Chancery betw. Francis Timberlake, and Judith, his wife, Complts., and Hugh Brent, Gent., and William Martin, Deft., time is given to the sd. Deft. to answer till the next Court.

In the action of trespass betw. Henry Newby, Pltf., and John Pollard, Deft., is continued till next Court at the Pltfs. Motion and costs.

The Inventory of the Estate of William Ballendine, dec'd, was returned by Charles Ewell, one of his Execs., who made Oath to his subscription thereon, whereupon it is Ordered that the sd. Inventory be recorded.

Pg 159. Ordered the Court be adjourned till the 2nd Friday in January next.

Memorandum this 9th of Nov. 1736, by virtue of a Commission of Oyer & Terminer and a Dedimus relating thereto, dated the second day of this Instant, directed to William Ball, Edwin Conway, James Ball, Robert Mitchell, Henry Carter, Hugh Brent, Nicholas Martin, Henry Lawson, John Heale, Joseph Heale, Joseph Chinn, Joseph Carter, & William Stepto, Gents, Nicholas Martin & Henry Lawson, Gent., Administered the Oaths to the Government to the sd.

William Ball, Edwin Conway, James Ball, Robert Mitchell, Henry Carter, & Joseph Chinn, who subscribed the Test and took the oaths of Justices, Oyer & Terminer & Administered the sd. Oaths & Test to the sd. Nicholas Martin & Henry Lawson.

At a Court of Oyer & Terminer held at Lancaster Co. Court house, the 8th day of February 1736, for the trial of Dick, a Negro man, Slave, belonging to John Stepto, Gent. Present: William Ball, Edwin Conway, James Ball, Robert Mitchell, Henry Carter, Nicholas Martin, Henry Lawson & Joseph Chinn – Gent. Justices.

The prisoner being set to the barr, according to the Courts direction, the usual proclamations were made and the Indictment read in these words – "Lanc. – Dick you stand indicted by the name of Dick, a Negro man Slave belonging to John Stepto of Northumberland County, Gent., for that you in the night of the 27th day of January in the tenth year of the Reign of our Sovereign Lord George, the Second, of Great Britain, King, not having the fear of God before your eyes, but being moved and seduced by the instigations of the Devil with malice prepensed in your mind on the body of Ben, a Negro man Slave, belonging to the Hon. John Carter, of this Co., Esqr., at the Parish of Christ Church in this County, an assault did make and him, the sd. Ben, then & there being with axes, clubs, swords & knives didst Feloniously murder and kill against the peace of our sd. Sovereign Lord his Crown and Dignity, etc." to which Indictment, the sd. Dock upon his arraignment pleaded not guilty, whereupon the Witnesses against him to wit: William Stepto, Gent., and Thomas Hunton were examined as also the testimony of Dick, Nan & Isaac, Negroes, belonging to the sd. William Stepto, and Bess, a Negro, belonging to the afsd. John Stepto. It appearing to this Court, that the prisoner is guilty of the murder whereof he stands indicted. It is considered that he be hanged by the neck till he be dead, and it is Ordered that he be executed on Friday, the 11th instant between the hours of ten & twelve in the Forenoon of the sd. day.

Dick, a Negro man, Slave, lately belonging to John Stepto of Northumberland County, Gent., this day condemned for Murder is by this Court valued at £35 current money, which is Ordered to be certified to the next Assembly.

Pg 160. At a Court for Lancaster Co., on Saturday, the 11th day of February 1736. Present: William Ball, Edwin Conway, James Ball, Henry Carter, Hugh Brent, Nicholas Martin, Joseph Heale, Joseph Chinn, Joseph Carter, William Stepto; Gent., Justices.

Tom, a Negro boy, belonging to Robert Gibson is by the Court adjudged to be 13 years of age.

William Ball, Junr., Gent., came into Court and ackn. his deed of gift to his son, Richard Ball, for & concerning 400 a. of land in St. Mary's White Chappel Parish, in this Co., which was admitted to record.

Charles, a Negro boy, belonging to Thomas Greswit is by the Court adjudged to be 14 years of age.

Sue, a Negro girl, belonging to Anthony Sidnor is by the Court adjudged to be 14 years of age.

Mercury, a Negro boy, belonging to Doct. Rich Chapman is by the Court adjudged to be 8 years of age.

Ordered that Richard Davis be summoned to the next Court to answer the petition of Eliza. Davis against him.

On the petition of Thomas Yerby, he is appointed Guardian of John Edwards, Orphan of William Edwards, dec'd. George Yerby becoming security and is Ordered the sd. Thomas possess himself of the Estate of the sd. Orphan and exhibit an account of same at Court.

The Will of Ann Towles, dec'd was presented in Court, by Stokely Towles and Robert Newsom, Junr., her Execs., who made oath, proved by Alexander Matson & Robert Newson[m], witnesses, and was admitted to record and Probate was granted.

Ordered that William Stamps, Daniel Stephens, Walter Arcues and Joseph Stephens, or any three of them being first sworn before a Co. Judge, are to appraise the Estate of Ann Towles, dec'd, in money and make a report of same along with Stokely Towles & Robert Newson[m], Junr., her Execs., with the Inventory at the next Court.

Margaret Pritchard, relict of Robert Pritchard, dec'd, came into Court and made oath that the sd. Robert died without making a Will, and on her Motion giving security, and she obtained the Letters of Administration for the Estate.

Pg 161. Ordered that James Straton, Thomas Flint, John Mott, and Giles Robinson, or any three of them being first sworn before a Co. Judge, are to appraise the Estate of Robert Pritchard in money and make a report of same along with Margaret Pritchard, Admin., with the Inventory at the next Court.

Elizabeth Ben, daughter of Richard Ben, aged 8 years old the 13th of March next, is by her sd. father bound to Thomas Charles and [blank], his wife are to teach him to read, sew, knit, & spin to find and allow her sufficient and cleanly diet, lodging, and apparel, and at the end of her servitude to give her a complete suit of cloths.

The petition of Thomas Marshall against Joseph Carter, Gent., and Daniel Stephens is continued against the sd. Joseph & it is Ordered that the sd. Daniel be summoned to the next Court the answer the same.

Ordered that William Sydnor be summoned to the next Court to answer the petition of Chattin[g?] Chowning against him.

On the attachment obtained by William Eustace, Gent., against the Estate of Edward Savage for 40 lbs. of tobacco, which attachment was served in the hands of Thomas Yerby & upon one pr. of men's shoes, one pr. of women's shoes, one calico gown and some other trifles. Judgment is granted to the sd. Pltf. against the sd. Deft. for the sd. 740 lbs. tobacco and costs & on hearing the afsd. Thos. Yerby, it is Ordered that he pay unto the sd. Plaintiff £0.6.6 towards his afsd. Judgment, and that in case the goods afsd. shall not be replevied, as the Law directs, they be sold & disposed for and towards the sd. Pltf.'s further satisfaction of this Judgment in the same manner as goods taken in Execution by a writ of Fieri Facias, and it is Ordered that this attachment be continued till the next Court.

An attachment obtained by Richard Flint against the Estate of Peter Harley, for £2.10.0, which attachment was served in the hands of Henry Horne. Judgment is granted to the sd. Pltf. against the sd. Deft. for the sd. £2.10.0 & costs. And, on hearing the sd. Henry Horne, it is the opinion of the Court that the sd. Henry hath not any of the Estate of the sd. Deft. in his hands whereupon the sd. attachment is discontinued.

The sale of the Estate of Eliza. Keene, dec'd, by way of Outcry was this day returned by John Waughop, Gent., Admin., thereof, and on his Motion admitted to record.

James Nicken, Orphan of Edward Nicken, dec'd, is by the Court bound unto John Hubbard till he attains the age of 21 years. The sd. John to teach him to read & write & the trade of a shoemaker and to find sufficient diet, lodging, apparel, and at the expiration of his servitude to pay him as is appointed for servants by Indenture or custom.

The suit betw. William Davenport & Elizabeth, his wife, and John Heale and Joseph Heale, Gent., by Caveat is continued till the next Court, and on the Motion of the sd. Deft., James Ball & Thomas Edwards, Gent., are appointed to take the evidence of William Mitchell in this matter betw. this and the next Court. They, the sd. Defts., giving the sd. Pltf. 10 days notice of the time of taking the sd. Evidence, and it is Ordered that the Court Clerk attend at the sd. Examination with the original Will against the proof of which the sd. Caveat is preferred.

In the suit betw. Charles Hammond by William Eustace, Gent., his Guardian, and William Thomas & Darcus, his wife, Execx. of Charles Hammond, dec'd, a Report of the auditors in this cause was returned & admitted to record and it is Ordered that the suit be dismissed.

Pg 162. The suit betw. James Patton, Pltf., and Edwd. Anderson, Deft., by attachment against the Estate of the sd. Deft. is continued till next Court.

The action of Detinue betw. John Ball, Pltf., and Thos. Pinchard, Deft., for £30 damage as in the Declaration is et forth & neither party appearing; dismissed.

A deed of Gift from Thomas Pinckard, Gent., to John Ball & Margaret, his wife, for 6 Negroes, was proved in open Court to be the act & deed of the sd. Thomas Pinckard by the oaths of Thomas Edwards, Hugh Brent, and William Stepto, witnesses thereto and is admitted to record.

In the suit in Chancery, betw. Francis Timberlake and Judith, his wife, Complts., and Hugh Brent, Gent., and William Martin, Defts., further time is given the sd. Defts. to answer.

In the action of Trespass betw. Henry Newby, Pltf., and John Pollard, Deft, for £20 damages as is set forth; dismissed.

An additional Inventory of the Estate of John Robinson, dec'd, was returned by Edwin Conway, Gent., Admin., thereof, and Ordered to be recorded.

In the suit betw. James Ball, Gent., Pltf., and Joseph George, Deft., by petition for 578 lbs. tobacco by account. Judgment granted to the sd. Pltf. for the sd. debt and costs.

In the action of debt betw. James Ball, Gent. , Pltf., and Benjamin Neale, Deft., for 2,963 lbs. tobacco, due by obligation, as was set forth; dismissed.

In the action of debt betw. James Ball, Gent. , Pltf., and Nicholas Cary, Deft., for 1,766 lbs. tobacco due by account, the sd. Deft. confessing Judgment, it is considered that he forthwith pay unto the sd. Pltf. his afsd. debt, with costs.

The suit betw. William Eustace, Gent., Pltf., and Edward Savage, Deft., by petition for 750 lbs. tobacco by account; is dismissed.

The suit betw. Thomas Eustace, Gent., Pltf., and Simon Shewcraft, Deft., by petition for one fowling piece handsomely mounted having a brass plate to it's Cock of the value of £3; is dismissed.

The suit betw. John Webb, Pltf., and Joseph Bottom, Deft., by petition for 500 lbs. by Bill; dismissed.

Pg 163. A bond from George Heale, Gent., to Judith Heale, widow, for £500, was this day further proved in Court to be the act & deed of the afsd. George by the oath of Aaron Carter, one of the witnesses thereto.

At a Court for Lancaster Co., on Friday, the 8th day of April 1737. Present: Edwin Conway, James Ball, Henry Carter, Hugh Brent, Nicholas Martin, Henry Lawson, Joseph Chinn, Joseph Carter, William Stepto; Gent., Justices.

Ordered that the Co. Sheriff summon at least 24 freeholders to appear at the next Court for a Grand Jury may be impanelled & sworn and make inquiry into the breach of Penal Laws & to present the offenders.

On the petition of Thomas James, it is Ordered that William Hutchins, John Meredith, George Yerby and Anthony Sydnor, or any three of them meet and settle the accounts of the estate of Thomas Carter, Junr., dec'd, and set apart the portions belonging to the children of the sd. dec'd, out of the same according to the Will of the sd. dec'd and make a report of their proceedings to the next Court.

On the attachment obtained by William Kelmes [Helms?] against the Estate of John Lake, for 1.8.0, which attachment was served on one horse on hearing the evidence produced in this matter & the oath of the sd. Pltf., to the truth of this claim. It is the opinion of the Court that the sd. Pltf. is entitled to the afsd. Horse till the afsd. debt and the costs occasioned are fully paid him and that the attachment be discontinued.

268

In the suit betw. Sarah Biddlecome, Pltf., and Richard Boatman, Deft., Judgment is granted the sd. Pltf. against the sd. Deft., for 278 lbs. tobacco & costs.

In the petition of Henry Tapscot against Benja. George, Junr., for the petitioner's proportion of the Estate of Henry Tapscott, his dec'd father, that is in the sd. Benjamin's hands. It is the opinion of the Court that the sd. petitioner is entitled to the Negro given him by his sd. father's deed of gift at the price the sd. Negro was appraised to in the Appraisement of the sd. deeds, Estate, and it is Ordered that William Pasquet, Thomas Hayden, William Hayden & John Porter, or any three of them settle the accounts in Difference in this cause & set apart to the sd. Pltf.'s proportion of the afsd. Estate, and make a report of their proceedings to the next Court.

The Will of William Edwards, dec'd, was presented to Court by Eliza. Edwards, Execx. named in the Will, who made oath thereto & being proved by the oaths of Henry Carter, Thomas Pinckard and Mary Humphries, witnesses thereto, it is admitted to record and she was granted Probate.

Pg 164. Ordered that Benjamin George, Richard Boatman, William Stephens & Henry Boatman, or any three of them, being first sworn before a Co. Judge, are to appraise the Estate of William Edwards, dec'd, in money and make a report of same along with Elizabeth Edwards, his Execx., with the Inventory at the next Court.

The appraisement of the Estate of Robert Pritchard, dec'd, was returned and Margaret Pritchard, Admin., thereof making Oath according to her subscription on the Inventory, Ordered to be recorded.

The appraisement of the Estate of Hannah Bush, dec'd, was returned, and William Samon, Admin. thereof making oath according to his subscription on the inventory; Ordered recorded.

On the attachment by William Eustace, Gent., against the Estate of John Lake for £0.31.5, which attachment was served in the hands of William Martin & Matthias James, Constable, on oath of the sd. Pltf. to the truth of his claim. Judgment is granted him against the sd. Deft. for his afsd. debt & costs and the Court being of the opinion that the Horse in the hands of the sd. Matthias James was not liable to this attachment.

John Porter and Sarah, his wife, came into Court and ackn. their deeds of Lease & Release to Thomas Edwards, Gent., for and concerning 62 a. of land in

Wicocomoco Parish in this Co., the sd. Sarah having been first examined privately; the deed were admitted to record.

John Frame & Joshen, his wife, came into Court and ackn. their deeds of Lease & Release to William Eustace, Gent., for and concerning 62 a. and 52 perches of land in Wicocomoco Parish in this Co., the sd. Joshen having been first examined privately; the deed were admitted to record.

In the suit betw. Eliza. Davis, Pltf. and John Davis, Deft., by petition, the parties were heard and it is considered that the sd. Pltf. recover against the sd. Deft., 250 lbs. tobacco & coats.

William Morris having attended 2 days as a witness for John Davis at the suit of Eliza. Davis, it is Ordered that the sd. John pay the sd. William for the same according to law & costs.

The nuncupative Will of John Yerby, dec'd, was presented in Court by Catherine Yerby, Thomas Yerby and George Yerby, who made oath thereto and being proved by the Oaths of George Yerby & John Merredith, witnesses, thereto is admitted to record and on the notion of the sd. Catherine Yerby, Thomas Yerby & George Yerby and their having given security of their just and faithful Admin. of the sd. decedent's Estate, with his Will annexed, and they were granted Letters of Admin., in due form.

Ordered that Elias Edmunds, James Haines, John Merredith & William Hutchins, or any three of them are to appraise the Estate of John Yerby, dec'd in money and make a report of same along with Catherine Yerby, Thomas Yerby, & George Yerby, Administrators, with the Inventory at the next Court.

Pg 165. On the prayer of John Edwards by Tho. Yerby, his Guardian, it is Ordered that Benjamin George, Richard Boatman, William Stephens, and Henry Boatman, or any three of them, set apart the sd. Orphan's proportion of the Estate of the dec'd father, William Edwards, when they re-appraise the sd. Estate and make a report of their proceedings and bring at next Court.

The suit betw. Thomas Marshall, Pltf., and Joseph Carter & Daniel Stephens, Defts., by petition for the sd. Pltf.'s Estate in the Defts. hands; is dismissed.

The suit betw. Chattin Chowning, Pltf., and William Sydnor, Deft., by petition is continued till next Court.

In the suit betw. William Devanporte & Eliza., his wife, Pltf., and John Heale and Joseph Heale, Defts., by caveat is continued till next Court at the Deft.'s Motion & costs.

The suit between James Patton, Pltf., and Edwd. Anderson, Deft., by attachment is continued till next Court.

In the suit in Chancery betw. Francis Timberlake & Judith, his wife, Complts., and Hugh Brent, Gent., & William Martin, Defts., an answer was this day returned sworn to which on the Motion of the sd. Complts., they have time to consider till next Court

The action of trespass betw. William Samon, Pltf., and Samuel Brumley, Deft., for £10 damages is set forth; dismissed.

The suit betw. William Gardiner, Pltf., and William Thomas, Deft., by petition for 680 lbs. tobacco by account; dismissed.

In the action of debt betw. Frances Burges, widow, and Edwin Conway & James Ball, Gent., Execs., of the Will of Charles Burges, Gent., dec'd and David Alexander Flint, Deft., for 3,660 lbs. tobacco due from the Deft. to the testator in his lifetime by obligation and account, Judgment is granted to the Pltf., for their afsd debt. and it is Ordered that the sd. Deft., forthwith pay the same with costs.

On the attachment obtained by James Fleming against the Estate of Thomas Scott for 470 lbs. tobacco, which attachment was served upon a mare in the hands of David Pugh, on the oath of the sd. Pltf., Judgment is granted him against the sd. Deft. for his afsd. debt & costs, and it is Ordered that in case the mare afsd. shall not be replevied, she be sold & disposed for an towards satisfaction of this Judgment in the same manner as goods taken in Execution by a Writ of fieri facias, and that this attachment be continued till next Court.

Pg 166. Ordered that the Court be adjourned till the Second Friday in May Next.   At a Court for Lancaster Co., on Wednesday, the 13th day of May 1737. Present: William Ball, Edwin Conway, James Ball, Henry Carter, Hugh Brent, Henry Lawson, Joseph Heale, Joseph Carter, William Stepto; Gent., Justices.

On the prayer of Nicholas Tarkilson of Christ Church Parish, in this Co., setting forth that he is very ancient and past his labor. It is Ordered that he be excused from paying and Country or County levy for the future.

A deed of gift from James Scrosby, Leanna Lee, Eliz. Lee, Lucia Lee and Anna Lee, daughters, of Thos. Lee, dec'd, for an concerning Negro Slaves was proved in Open Court by the Oath of Nicholas Martin, Gent., one of the witnesses thereto and admitted to record.

Present: Mr. John Heale, Joseph Chinn, Gent., Justices.

On the motion of Christopher Stephens, he is admitted to keep an Ordinary at this County Court House for one year next ensuing Stokely Towles becoming his security.

Christopher Stephens and Stokely Towles, of St. Mary's White Chappel Parish, in this Co., came into Court and ackn. themselves jointly and severally indebted to our King for £50, to be levied upon their goods and Chattels, lands and tenements, under condition that the sd. Christopher shall constantly find & provide in the Ordinary, he is this day admitted to keep, good wholesome and cleanly diet & lodging for travelers and stableage, fodder and provender and pasturage as the Season shall require for their horses for and during the term of one year from the date hereof and shall not suffer or permit any unlawful gaming in his House, nor on the Sabbath day to suffer and person to Tipple & drink more than necessary.

In pursuance to a clause in the act of Regulating Ordinaries & restraint of Tipling houses, the Court doth set & rate. Rum at 8 shillings the gallon. Punch with loaf sugar at 12 pence the Quart. Cider at 12 pence the gallon. Madeira Wine at 2 shillings the quart. Strong Beer at 15 pence the quart. Claret at 4 shillings the Quart. Red port at4 shillings the Quart. White wine at 5 shillings the Quart. Stableage & fodder for a horse at 6 pence the night. Lodging at 6 pence the night. Corn at 6 pence the Gall. Diet with small beer to drink at 6 pence the meal.

The End of Volume 1

G

S